Feminist D
on Internati

successes, tensions, futures

GINA HEATHCOTE

OXFORD
UNIVERSITY PRESS

OXFORD

UNIVERSITY PRESS

Great Clarendon Street, Oxford, OX2 6DP,
United Kingdom

Oxford University Press is a department of the University of Oxford.
It furthers the University's objective of excellence in research, scholarship,
and education by publishing worldwide. Oxford is a registered trade mark of
Oxford University Press in the UK and in certain other countries

Published in the United States of America by Oxford University Press
198 Madison Avenue, New York, NY 10016, United States of America

British Library Cataloguing in Publication Data
Data available

Library of Congress Control Number: 2018957183

ISBN 978–0–19–968510–3

Printed and bound by
CPI Group (UK) Ltd, Croydon, CR0 4YY

FEMINIST DIALOGUES ON INTERNATIONAL LAW

Acknowledgements

I acknowledge the Boonwurrung people of the Kulin nation as the traditional owners of the land on which I was born and on which I grew into adulthood. I acknowledge that their land was stolen, and that sovereignty was never ceded. I pay my respects to their elders past and present.

Thanks to colleagues at SOAS University of London, supportive and inspiring in the diverse work they undertake. Thanks to the Feminist Review Collective past and present. Thanks to my doctoral students—I hope you will see the traces of our dialogues in these pages—and thanks to the many MA and LLM students I have worked with at SOAS. Kate and Irene thank you for helping me find the end and the kindness of your readings and advice, as well as Rose. Thanks to Paola Zichi for research assistance. Thanks to my family. Inspiration abounds.

Table of Contents

List of Abbreviations

AU	African Union
CEDAW	Convention on the Elimination of all Forms of Discrimination Against Women
CERD	Convention on the Elimination of all Forms of Racial Discrimination
CTC	Counter Terrorism Committee
DAW	Division for the Advancement of Women
DBP	Democratic Party of the Regions
DEVAW	Declaration on the Elimination of Violence Against Women
DRC	Democratic Republic of the Congo
ECOSOC	Economic and Social Council
ECOWAS	Economic Community of West African States
GF/GFeminism	Governance Feminism
HIC	High Income Countries
HRC	Human Rights Council
ICAN	International Campaign to Abolish Nuclear Weapons
ICC	International Criminal Court
ICISS	International Commission on Intervention and State Sovereignty
ICJ	International Court of Justice
ILC	International Law Commission
LMIC	Low and Middle-Income Countries
MDG	Millennium Development Goals
NATO	North Atlantic Treaty Organisation
NGO	Non-Government Organisation
OSAGI	Office of the Special Adviser to the Secretary-General on Gender Issues and Advancement of Women
PBC	Peace Building Commission
SADC	Southern African Development Community
SDG	Sustainable Development Goals
TWAIL	Third World Approaches to International Law
UN	United Nations
UN-INSTRAW	United Nations International Research and Training Institute for the Advancement of Women
UNGA	United Nations General Assembly
UNIFEM	United Nations Development Fund for Women
UNSC	United Nations Security Council
UPR	Universal Periodic Review
UK	United Kingdom of Great Britain and Northern Ireland
US	United States of America
USSR	United Socialist Soviet Republic
WASH	Water, Sanitation and Hygiene
WHO	World Health Organisation
WILPF	Women's International League for Peace and Freedom
WPS	Women, Peace and Security
YFAS	Youth Feminist Action School

Prologue

Two factors delayed the publication of this book and are worth mentioning to the reader. The first involved the unexpected arrival of additional caring responsibilities just as I had hoped to conclude the preparation of the manuscript in 2014. The second factor has been the changing face of higher education, in the UK and beyond, towards a distinctly neoliberal model of university governance.

As the carer of somebody with a mental health diagnosis, the production of the manuscript was delayed from September 2014 until early in 2018. I was fortunate enough to encounter a sympathetic and supportive publishing team over this period—thank you Emma, Merel, Kimberley, and Jack I am very grateful for your patience. From 2014 to 2018, I also noticed a drastic change in the way academic life was experienced: students became 'clients' and 'customers' in the UK as increased undergraduate fees, to be repaid via a deferred taxation model, made excessive student debt the new reality in the higher education landscape. The commodification of knowledge meant that university outputs (both teaching and research) increasingly needed to be quantified and economic factors (costs and profits) became the easiest measure as the marketisation of higher education became the new reality. This significantly changed perceptions about what to teach and what is valued in the university, at least at the level of senior management and decision-making in UK universities.

Both mental health and neoliberal governance techniques, in the university and beyond, seem intertwined: and not just because both seemed to usurp my time and leave little space for writing. Both mental health and neoliberal governance have important gender dimensions and produce a useful way to introduce the central themes of the book.

First, like feminist knowledge, both mental health and neoliberal governance structures have simultaneously become objects of public consumption while also suffering from the thin accounts dominating the popular discourse. For feminist knowledge prevalent in global media spaces this can be characterised by the attention to gender with very little engagement with feminist histories, feminist diversity, and feminist methodologies, or where feminist knowledge production occurs. In a similar fashion, mental health awareness has become a prolific site of public debate in Western states—online and within institutional structures. In the UK, universities have been drawing attention to the worsening mental health crisis on campus and the incapacity of existing support structures to manage the impact on university students and staff. As the carer of someone suffering the effects and aftermath of a serious mental health diagnosis, what strikes me is the space between the reality of living with a mental health diagnosis and popular accounts of the need to acknowledge and speak about mental health—in all its messy, challenging, and non-confirming behaviours and the many campaigns for #mentalhealth, #endthestigma, #notalone, #headstogether that at once communicate an effective message yet erase the reality of living with a mental illness. These campaigns seem to contribute to the very odd period of history we find ourselves within; clicking a petition or posting a meme as evidence of connection and concern, as a representation of activism, while those suffering the physical and mental anguish remain isolated and unsupported, misunderstood, and often chastised, dismissed, or ignored.

The politics of austerity, which have been very much at the centre of the UK political landscape since 2009, continue to alienate and punish those who are unwell, poor, or poor and unwell: stigmatising them for not contributing to society rather than in need of society's compassion and in need of the support of their community. This is the neoliberal state at its heartless best. As I write the book which you now hold in your hands (or on your screen), the nexus between neoliberalism and the prevalence of messages that inundate the everyday via social media (whether on gender #metoo, on mental health #endthestigma, or on other key preoccupations #occupy, #endneoliberalism, #nomorewar) seems to exist in the (necessarily?) thin—or perhaps cartoon-like—perception of complex issues that become reduced to a hashtag or a slogan.[1] Similarly, this book is interested in how, when feminist scholars and activists turn to international law to produce change, gender law reforms and change produced by gender law reforms are often a thin facsimile of the original feminist intervention. Media attention and #hashtags are not inherently good or bad; but there needs to be more discussion and analysis of the work they do in minimising the history, effects, and complexity of knowledge while, paradoxically, giving issues greater audience and engagement. Similarly, in this book, I examine how the structures of the global order—relying on technologies of expertise and measurement—take up the messages but not the methodologies of feminist approaches. I argue for renewed dialogues on feminism that engage feminist methodologies with the foundations of global governance.

To make this argument it is necessary to accept gender as an embedded power structure in global governance—such that gender perspectives are not something to be added but rather to be understood as already configuring the global order. That is, the recognition that gender does not happen in isolation is vital. Gender is a component of power relations and constructs privilege and disadvantages. My journey into navigating the world of mental health care has taught me something similar. By this I mean that mental health has clear gender dimensions.[2] It also has class, race, and ableist dimensions, likewise sexuality matters and configures access to resources and health care, just as religion does. A key battle in surviving mental health care in the UK is challenging the intersectional assumptions about how you have arrived at a clinic. Accessing health care therefore requires overcoming different kinds of stigmas depending on who you are—and the intersection of these markers makes this a considerably more complex barrier for some. This illuminates how the structures around us also contain, and operate through, assumptions with regard to

---

[1] However, also see alternative approaches to digital activism discussed in chapter 6. Gail Lewis, 'Questions of Presence' (2017) 117 Feminist Review 1; Jia Tan, 'Digital Masquerading: Feminist Media Activism in China' (2017) 13(2) Crime, Media, Culture 171.

[2] Gina Heathcote, 'Eating Us out of House and Home' (2016) 112 Feminist Review 8.

gender, class, race, able-bodiedness, sexuality, and religion that are usually invisible to those who identify with mainstream categorisations and thus acquire privilege that is essentially the invisibility of dominant identities. Not discussed in this book but of equal relevance, is the intersection of these privileges with age. For example, mental health care for the elderly recedes into social care. Consequently, insufficient attention to the mental health dimensions of increasingly prevalent conditions, such as the various forms of dementia, with racialised and gendered factors impacting on who provides and who navigates social care.[3] The production of the invisibility of privilege as a cornerstone of neoliberalism is then compounded: the need for comprehensive welfare provisions or investment in community structures or comprehensive strategies to address exclusion is displaced by narratives prioritising choice and agency. The intersectional production and maintenance of power is a preoccupation of this book. In particular, I focus on analysing how gender law reforms often function to legitimate global governance and international legal structures, especially if gender is conceived, analysed, and understood as a single power structure rather than an embedded one.

To live with and care for someone with a mental health diagnosis has taught me to accept restraints on my time in new ways. The hardest thing for me has been to learn to shift from providing solutions—or even to analyse—to listening as an aspect of the care required. The role of listening also forms one of the conclusions of the book. That is, I argue that feminist scholars writing on and researching global governance, in order to participate in disruptive dialogues that are also transformative, rather than replicating the existing global order, are required to embark on intense and careful listening. I argue that this has a temporal and geographic dimension. The temporal attends to the imperial history of international law and the need to recognise the stake all international lawyers—including feminist ones—have in the continuity of that history. The geographical attends to the recognition of the structures that alienate some voices from the core concerns of international law, pushing key actors and knowledge to the peripheries of the discipline. Disruption (or what I argue is a politics of interruption)[4] requires listening to indigenous voices, feminists in the global south and feminists from outside of academia—but not to save and not to appropriate their texts. Rather, to ask, and then to listen, to what matters and how things must change for their lives to matter. Throughout the text I engage different methods for doing this listening—sometimes within the structures of international law and sometimes outside of them.[5] This, I argue, is the first step to understanding how my privilege creates the conditions for my writing and thus should silence me in favour of listening; to work in concert and re-imagine the international as a space for feminist change. To reach such a conclusion, this book provides an analysis of some of the

[3] Yasmin Gunaratnam, *Death and the Migrant: Borders, Bodies, and Care* (Bloomsbury, 2013).

[4] Irene Gedalof, 'Interruptions, Reproduction and the Genealogies of Staying Put in Diaspora Space' (2012) 100 Feminist Review 72.

[5] Dianne Otto, 'Beyond Legal Justice: Some Personal Reflections on People's Tribunals, Listening and Responsibility' (2017) 5 London Review of International Law 225.

key structural and foundational aspects of international law: expertise, fragmentation, sovereignty, institutions, and authority. I do not mention mental health or the neoliberal university and yet both remain threaded into the production of the text, as does my privilege as a white, Western subject living and working in Europe in 2018.

GH

April 2018

1

Feminist Dialogues

1. Introduction

In the first two decades of the new millennium, international institutions have increased the attention given to women's rights and gender perspectives. This transformation of, predominantly Western second wave, feminism into an accepted and mainstream component of international law forms the springboard for the concerns of this book; at the same time I am interested in why non-Western and critical feminist engagements with global governance are undervalued, under-discussed, and pushed to the peripheries of strategies for change.[1] I argue that feminist 'success' stories within international law require dialogue on how this success has come about, whose interests are served, which tensions are ignored, and what the contours of these successes actually are. This book presents an analysis of feminist methodologies within international law and reflects on which gender law reforms have been achieved. At the centre of the book is the view that feminist dialogues on international law ought to shift towards an understanding of feminist tensions, as an integral and necessary part of feminist methodologies, and in distinction from the narrow feminist approaches encapsulated in gender law reform in global governance. This, I argue, requires attention to dialogues and the politics of listening as feminist methodologies.

To undertake this inquiry, the book examines which feminist projects have been hoisted into spaces of global governance and which spaces of feminist knowledge have been left as outliers to global governance. I argue that a series of tensions within feminist approaches—on the relationship between race and gender, sexuality and gender, on colonial histories, on the subject of feminism, on able-bodiedness, the political economy of gender, and the intersection of these dialogues—need to be understood and confronted for there to be feminist 'success' stories worth telling. In imagining new feminist strategies for international law, the book draws on a number of contradictory and complex dialogues drawn from feminist and gender theories within, and outside of, feminist legal scholarship. As such, the term *dialogue* is used with mindfulness of the open-ended and dynamic quality of the knowledge drawn upon and to prompt a series of conversations (as opposed to prescriptions) for future

---

[1] Myra Marx Ferree and Aili Mari Tripp (eds), *Global Feminism: Transnational Women's Activism, Organizing, and Human Rights* (New York University Press 2006); Rawwida Baksh and Wendy Harcourt (eds), *The Oxford Handbook of Transnational Feminist Movements* (Oxford University Press 2015).

Feminist Dialogues on International Law. Gina Heathcote. © Gina Heathcote 2019. Published 2019 by Oxford University Press.

,gagements within international law. Attentiveness to the listening aspect ,ie, I argue, is particularly important for feminists with access to elite spaces. ,nore, as a white Western feminist, who benefits from the privileges linked to ,n colour and geographical location, I articulate a feminist politics defined by dialogue as a mechanism to dislodge the privileging of my own perspective. I pursue a feminist politics that actively and consciously (and always with more to discover) attempts to make political space for those who do not have the privilege to speak in the same forums as I have. My political and ethical commitments are best expressed by Baars, when they express their desire to 'lose the whitesupremacistableistspeciei stimperialistcapitalistcisheteropatriarchy': in this book I am primarily interested in the feminist methodologies that extend from this political positioning.[2]

Alongside the rapid incorporation of gender as a tool into specific international institutional structures since the 1990s and into the new millennium, there has been a visible surfacing of grassroots mobilisation of women via global, regional, national, transnational, and local NGOs that seek to instrumentalise feminist thinking through engagement with international structures. The sentiment behind these moves is encapsulated in the words of Nobel Peace Laureate, Leymah Gbowee, who states: 'It's time for women to stop being politely angry'.[3] Gbowee characterises a mood that compels action and change on issues of discrimination and harm that curtail the lives of women across communities and lobbies for voice within global governance. Despite the richness of this transnational feminist activism, gender law reform is not always described as responding to and emerging from transnational feminisms within international legal scholarships. Moreover, the effectiveness of transnational feminist activism as a mechanism for understanding the production of feminist knowledge has not attracted significant attention from critical feminist academic accounts within international law. A shift to examine how transnational feminisms critically challenge the status quo of mainstream, Western, feminist approaches to law and global governance is necessary. This represents one of the tensions, or dialogues, that I am interested in across the various chapters of the book. In chapters 2 and 3 I examine gender law reform through the critical legal lens of expertise and fragmentation to study how feminist knowledge, including transnational feminist knowledge, is transferred into gender law reform.

Encapsulated within the tension between activist and critical academic approaches is the role of the legal subject and the subject of feminism. Despite feminist theorising interrogating the notion of a unitary feminist subject, the political and legal imperatives for a clear focus within legal reform strategies present a background tension in feminist accounts.[4] That is, the need for law reform to revolve around a

---

[2] Grietje Baars, '#LesbiansAreHot: On Oil, Imperialism, and What it Means to Queer International Law' 7(1) feminists@law <http://journals.kent.ac.uk/index.php/feministsatlaw/article/view/398> last accessed 31 May 2018.

[3] Abigail Pesta, 'Leymah Gbowee: Nobel Winner Gbowee: Where are Angry American Women?' (*Daily Beast*, 3 September 2009) <https://www.thedailybeast.com/nobel-winner-gbowee-where-are-the-angry-american-women> last accessed 31 May 2018.

[4] Hilary Charlesworth and Christine Chinkin, *The Boundaries of International Law: A Feminist Analysis* (Manchester 2000) 54.

female subject can disrupt specific feminist knowledge that attends to the fluidity and instability of gender. Sometimes this is regarded as a tension between academia/critique and activism, sometimes as a tension between different strands of activism. As Drakopoulou notes, feminist legal theories are:

confronted with having to fit the diversity of women's experience into the straitjacket of a unitary legal subject which still appears indispensable for the articulation of feminist critiques of law and the formulation of proposals for its development.[5]

One of my goals in writing this book is to think through this tension from the perspective of non-legal feminist critiques; these can often be dismissive of feminist projects that mobilise around women and can be critical of feminist gains within law due to the loss of the complexity of the theorisation of gender resulting from the centring of women as the subject of gender law reform. Given law, too, builds around a unitary subject and requires categories of inclusion and exclusion, by definition, the amenability of specific feminist approaches to international law that adhere to a unitary account of subjectivity should not be surprising. Transnational feminisms further complicate this knowledge, however, mobilising around women and yet developing distinct knowledge practices that have not always been acknowledged within feminist legal theories. I argue that there is a necessity for feminist legal academics and activists to think differently about subjectivity, within law and within feminist projects, to mobilise a critique of law that need not collapse back into accounts of women as victims and marked as eternally vulnerable, uniform in her experiences, or absent of the effect of additional power differentials. Dialogues within this approach would benefit from drawing in the creative feminist methodologies of transnational feminisms.

I analyse diverse—and divergent—voices that build transnational feminism and how the reproduction of these voices within international law is too often reduced to a thin description which ignores this complexity. The diversity of transnational feminisms, and their histories, is continually pushed to the peripheries in exchange for projects of gender law reform that assert a narrow gender agenda. As such, throughout the book I explore feminist dialogues that challenge a monolithic representation of women in gender law reform and, in the words of Mohanty, explore how:

[t]he assumption of women as an already constituted and coherent group with identical interests and desires, regardless of class, ethnic or racial location, implies a notion of gender or sexual difference or even patriarchy which can be applied universally and cross-culturally.[6]

I draw on Mohanty's shift, from the articulation of difference to challenging the assertion of Western feminist experiences as universal, while noting the silencing of non-Western feminist worldviews, to inform the underlying approach of the book.

---

[5] Maria Drakopoulou, 'The Ethic of Care, Feminist Subjectivity and Feminist Legal Scholarship' (2000) 8 Feminist Legal Studies 199, 200; see also Robyn Wiegman, *Object Lessons* (Duke University Press 2012).

[6] Chandra Talpade Mohanty, 'Under Western Eyes: Feminist Scholarship and Colonial Discourse' (1988) 30 Feminist Review 61, 64.

To develop my approach, feminist legal and non-legal scholarship that is mindful of intersectionality, mindful of the production of sexuality and able-bodiedness in accounts of gender, and mindful of the embedded colonial histories of international law are given prominence throughout the text. Consequently, I argue that feminist futures within international law and global governance must draw knowledge from transnational, postcolonial, and indigenous feminisms to analyse the co-optation of gender law reform into new civilising narratives; while drawing this into further dialogues with queer and crip theories. At the same time, and mindful of prevailing advances on gender law reform within international law, I argue that feminist dialogues must be undertaken in conversation with the contours of existing feminist approaches to international law to avoid the replication of the current thin accounts of feminist knowledge that masquerade as gender law reforms within global governance.

I contend that stories of feminist 'success' in international law are pre-emptory; consequently, instead of feminist 'successes' I use the terminology of gender law reform to acknowledge the developments within international law that have been in response to feminist interventions.[7] I analyse what conditions are imposed on feminist interventions for the production of gender law reform and, in the process, reflect on which feminist knowledge is drawn on to construct international legal developments and which feminist knowledge remains on the peripheries of global governance. Through analysing gender law reforms within global governance, I call for a revival of feminist attention to methodologies rather than feminist messages as the coordinating aspect of future dialogues.[8] The notion of a split between feminist message and method is drawn from Charlesworth's description of the tensions between feminist knowledge on law, on the one hand, and gender projects within international law, on the other. For Charlesworth, there is 'a distinction between feminist messages and methods in international law. The former has been influential in rhetorical terms, while the latter have been ignored.'[9] This book analyses how the message/method distinction embeds specific knowledge projects within international law, in particular with regard to civilising impulses, the reproduction of a racialised, able-bodied, and heteronormative status quo, as well economic hierarchies within international law through gender law reforms.

Following Mohanty, I argue the production of a feminist legal subject both in international law and in feminism would benefit from feminist methodologies that disrupt the stability of any assumed feminist (or female) legal subject. I use the book to shift critical feminist dialogues from challenging gender law reform as insufficient in delivering on this aspect of feminist thinking. In doing so I make a case for building new conversations about the feminist methodologies that might be deployed to situate women's difference. This approach conceptualises women's

---

[7] Janet Halley, Prabha Kotiswaran, Rachel Rebouché, and Hila Shamir (eds), *Governance Feminism: Notes from the Field* (University of Minnesota Press 2018) 25.

[8] Hilary Charlesworth, 'Talking to Ourselves? Feminist Scholarship in International Law' in Sari Kouvo and Zoe Pearson (eds), *Feminist Perspectives on Contemporary International Law: Between Resistance and Compliance?* (Hart 2011) 17.

[9] ibid 32.

difference not as a story of the 'Other' (to save or rescue or even to invite to participate) but to be listened to as feminist voices that have been moved to the peripheries
of feminist legal work outside of dominant liberal, radical, and cultural feminisms.
Consequently, I enlarge international feminist epistemologies on gender law reform
through attention to scholarship that theorises gender and race, and the politics of
location, to actively write the international legal history and legacies of colonialism
as a necessary element of feminist methodologies that are also inclusive of challenges
to heteronormativity and ableism.

Through drawing on accounts of diaspora, peripheral, and nomadic subjects
I work to move beyond critical feminist accounts of gender law reform towards
thinking through the types of dialogues necessary to build transformative spaces of
feminist knowledge. This approach leads to an argument, in chapter 3, for a feminist
epistemology drawn from plural subjectivities.[10] Similarly, in chapter 4 I analyse the
relational dimensions of feminist theorising to centre the idea of split subjectivity
as a corrective to the traditional mode of state sovereignty that is built on subjects
assumed autonomous and acting as an isolated entity. I use the split subject to explore alternative accounts of how legal subjects exist in both connection and separateness from others that have temporal and geographical dimensions. In chapter 5
I explore alternative feminist epistemologies—on the maternal, on the politics of
location, on the political economy of gender, as well as crip and queer approaches
to law—to return to the underlying theme of dialogues and to allow different voices
and approaches to be heard through the text. The general cohesion and focus on
international law as a space for feminist theorising and action in the future is then
disrupted in the final chapter. I question whose authority informs feminist texts,
how authority is both enacted and legitimated within international law by gender
law reforms, and the conditions of privilege that produce this. In chapter 6 I think
through the conditions for further evolution of gender law reform within international law and the spaces of feminist transformation that strategise outside of the
constraints of traditional legal structures.

For Otomo, the tension between evolution (within the law) and revolution (outside of law) within feminist writing and action on international law ought also to inform future dialogues.[11] As such, both Charlesworth and Otomo recognise the role
institutional and legal structures play in reducing the underlying feminist knowledge adopted within law (or methods) and an overplaying of feminist messages. For
example, feminist legal theorising on legal responses to sexual violence is rich and
varied, developing in response to procedural, structural, and legal limitations, while
using varied methods as a means to explore the types of legal, and non-legal, solutions that might prevent sexual violence. Within international law the recognition

---

[10] Ratna Kapur, *Erotic Justice: Law and the New Politics of Postcolonialism* (Routledge 2005); Avtar
Brah, 'Diaspora, Border and Transnational Identities' in *Cartographies of Diaspora: Contesting Identities
(Gender, Racism, Ethnicity)* (Routledge 1996) 178; Rosi Braidotti, *Nomadic Subjects: Embodiment and
Sexual Difference in Contemporary Feminist Theory* (2nd edn, Columbia 2011).

[11] Yoriko Otomo, 'Searching for Virtue in International Law' in Sari Kouvo and Zoe Pearson
(eds), *Feminist Perspectives on Contemporary International Law: Between Resistance and Compliance?*
(Hart 2011).

that sexual violence occurs within armed conflict and post-conflict communities is well established (hence the 'feminist' messages appears to have been appropriated within international law).[12] However, the techniques and methods for responding to this 'message' have largely resulted in the establishment of criminal justice techniques and models that reproduce the structures and limitations of dominant and existing criminal justice models. As such, the shift to develop an international criminal justice response to conflict-related sexual violence has reproduced a singular feminist message—about the prevalence of sexual violence as a form of gendered harm and violence that renders women vulnerable in conflict spaces and about the criminal justice system's ability to remedy this. This message, in the absence of feminist methods, has not shifted the status quo of conflict-related sexual violence or challenged the underlying structural, procedural, and legal limitations of the criminal justice model.[13] This book looks beyond the turn to law as a mechanism for reproducing the messages of feminist and gender work, to explore the potentialities of future feminist dialogues on international law that are attentive to feminist methodologies, including those that might involve turning away from legal reform as a feminist project.

In previous texts, I have indicated a desire for a return to structural bias feminism, where the pillars of international law and global governance are critiqued through feminist approaches.[14] This book also takes a structural bias feminism approach as the starting point for the series of conversations developed. I define structural bias feminism as the use of diverse feminist methodologies to interrogate and expose the role gendered assumptions play in the construction of the foundations of law. To structural bias feminisms I bring a conversation drawn from postcolonial and transnational feminisms, non-Western feminist methodologies, and feminist theories on knowledge production, acknowledging these as components of Charlesworth and Chinkin's structural bias feminism that has often been overlooked in the attempt to achieve legal outcomes.[15] In inserting alternative, often non-legal, feminist and gender approaches into feminist dialogues on international law, a series of interlocking claims about the nature of which feminist messages are 'received' within global governance are developed. This includes claims about the relationship between the production of raced, gendered, able-bodied, and heteronormative actors within the global order and the manner that feminist methodologies, even

---

[12] Security Council Resolution 1820 (19 June 2008) UN Doc S/RES/1820; Security Council Resolution 1888 (30 September 2009) UN Doc S/RES/1888; Security Council Resolution 1960 (16 December 2010) UN Doc S/RES/1960; Security Council Resolution 2106 (24 June 2013) UN Doc S/RES/2106; Security Council Resolution 2272 (11 March 2016) UN Doc S/RES/2272.

[13] Clare McGlynn and Vanessa Munro (eds), *Rethinking Rape Law: International and Comparative Perspectives* (Routledge 2010).

[14] Gina Heathcote, *The Law on the Use of Force: A Feminist Analysis* (Routledge 2012) 6–7; Gina Heathcote, 'Naming and Shaming: Human Rights Accountability in Security Council Resolution 1960 (2010) on Women, Peace and Security' (2012) 4(1) Journal of Human Rights Practice 82; see also Hilary Charlesworth, Gina Heathcote, and Emily Jones, 'Feminist Scholarship on International Law in the 1990s and Today' (2018) Feminist Legal Studies, (forthcoming) available online: https://doi.org/10.1007/s10691-018-9384-1 (last accessed December 2018).

[15] Charlesworth and Chinkin (n 4) ch 2.

when in tension across strands of feminist theories, are incorporated. My approach is in contrast to the plethora of post-millennium feminist works that engage and analyse specific elements of international law while centring women as the subject of feminism, and that have developed primarily in response to conflict and post-conflict violations of women's rights. The book's preoccupation for the most part is with rethinking feminist methodologies that articulate plural subjectivities rather than reproducing a static legal subject, while asking what that means for gender law reform.[16] In addition, I am concerned to work against locating conflict and post-conflict as the primary spaces for gender law reform within international law: to this end I examine areas of international law as diverse as the UN climate change framework, the World Health Organisation, state sovereignty, gender expertise, and the Human Rights Council, while also acknowledging and engaging the gender law reforms within international criminal law, within collective security, as jurisprudence on the Convention for the Elimination of Discrimination Against Women (CEDAW), and as gender mainstreaming.

To articulate the future spaces for feminist dialogues in international law the book provides a feminist analysis of some of the pillars of international law: sovereignty, the nature of legal authority, and the role of international organisations, while also examining the impact of contemporary developments on the structures of global governance, in particular fragmentation and the rise of international legal experts. While each of these topics are of central importance to contemporary international lawyers they have not benefited from sustained feminist analysis, although this was likely within the type of project Charlesworth and Chinkin conceived when they argued 'feminists should tackle international law on a number of levels at the same time'.[17] In addition to developing dialogues across different strands and different disciplinary feminist works I also engage critical legal work on global governance in conversation with the feminist voices drawn on throughout the book.

The baseline feminist knowledge that I rely on to build a dialogue on feminist methodologies is to regard gender as a methodology rather than an identity informing feminist scholarship.[18] Women's lived experiences form part of my work in the sense of informing how knowledge is gendered. However, my approach to gender is drawn from the diversity of feminist approaches: it recognises gender as socially constructed, as performative, as invested in institutions and social organising, as pervasive, invisible, ever present, consistent and yet diverse in its forms and representations, temporally and geographically. I understand gender as a power relation that intersects with other power relations to mask inequalities and violence and to prop up the status quo of unequal political arrangements. I approach gender as something that is easily understood via the representation/s of maleness and femaleness, seemingly easy to 'read' in social interactions, and yet diversely practised and performed across geographies, communities, and generations, within groups and within structures. I regard gender approached in isolation to other power relations

---

[16] Nicola Lacey, *Unspeakable Subjects: Feminist Essays in Legal and Social Theory* (Hart 1998).
[17] Charlesworth and Chinkin (n 4) 336.
[18] Joan W Scott, *The Fantasy of Feminist History* (Duke University Press 2011).

as likely to reify power rather than dismantle power. I understand women as human, humans the subject/s of feminism, and gender as an analytical tool useful for identifying and dismantling the excesses of violence, harm, and discrimination across human lives, while positing feminist approaches as useful for imagining diverse and different political and legal arrangements.[19]

In this chapter I introduce gender law reform and structural bias feminisms in the following section. In section 3 I introduce my understanding of successes, tensions, and futures within feminist approaches to international law. The final section of the chapter introduces the structure of the book.

2. Gender Law Reform

Throughout the text I distinguish between gender law reform and feminist approaches to international law. I make this distinction to underscore the transformation of feminist thinking into international legal provisions, signalling the loss of the complexity of feminist methodologies along the way. I argue that a thin version of feminist theories emerges in gender law reform, that those reforms are closest to radical, liberal, and cultural feminist approaches, and that significant feminist approaches that have not filtered into (or have been filtered out of) gender law reform require attention. This is a response to articulations of gender law reform in international law described as governance feminism and equally a recognition of the thoughtful feminist work behind the emergence of gender law reform.

Halley identifies the role of specific US feminist legal scholarship within international gender law reforms describing 'Unitedstatesean feminism' as an approach that centres 'the idea that sexuality is a distinct domain of women's subordination'.[20] In addition to her critiques of the hyper-focus on the gendered sexual vulnerability produced through these Unitedstatesean approaches, Halley draws out the importance of the history of queer, anti-racist, and postcolonial dimensions that engage with, and break from, the hyper-focus on gender and sex difference.[21] Halley argues that the Unitedstatesean approach functions as a radical feminist account that is structuralist; while queer, anti-racist, and postcolonial dialogues continually bring tensions into feminist spaces as they challenge the centring of gender, and sex difference, in feminist legal accounts. Halley's recognition of the contributions of anti-racist, queer, and postcolonial feminisms in the US context is valuable. Furthermore, Halley's later work that renames US radical feminism as 'governance feminism' has had significant impact on feminist approaches within international law.[22] However, this scholarship fixates on the development

---

[19] Carol Cohn, 'Women and Wars: Towards a Conceptual Framework' in Carol Cohn (ed), *Women and Wars: Contested Histories, Uncertain Futures* (Polity Press 2013).

[20] Janet Halley, 'Take a Break from Feminism?' in Karen Knop (ed), *Gender and Human Rights* (Oxford University Press 2004) 78.

[21] ibid 64.

[22] Janet Halley, 'Rape at Rome: Feminist Inventions in the Criminalization of Sex-Related Violence in Positive International Criminal Law' (2009) 30 Michigan Journal of International Law 1, 6; Sari

of prosecution strategies around conflict-related sexual violence and (by definition) tracks the influence of a specifically US feminist account of developments within global governance. As such, Halley's work is referenced throughout the text but, in looking beyond international criminal law, I identify the additional liberal feminist and cultural feminist features within gender law reforms, as found in the women, peace, and security framework and CEDAW.[23] In addition, while I use US critical race feminist Crenshaw's work to explore the potential value of intersectionality as a feminist methodology, I work throughout the book to incorporate feminist and gender theories outside of the dominant US accounts.[24]

Engle's account of governance feminism identifies an additional split amongst feminist approaches to international law that centres on the extent that international institutions are seen to reshape feminist messages to legitimate and expand the agendas of powerful actors within the institution. For Engle:

feminists were not simply co-opted. The successful structural bias feminists had already elevated the harm of sexual violence as the principal harm to women in general and especially in war. When they were debating other feminists, sexual violence was gender violence (and vice versa). When they went out into the world, their language of sexual violence resonated with political and institutional actors across political, national, cultural and religious lines.[25]

Engle notes that her view differs from other critical feminist accounts. Otto, for example, focuses on the co-optation of feminist ideas by the structures of global governance while Chappell inquires to how the 'nestedness' of institutions in existing structures and forms shapes feminist gains.[26] Closer to Engle's approach, Powell describes how the anti-subordination approach that centres sex difference, incorporated into international law via the development of women, peace, and security resolutions and via the agitation of US feminist actors, drew towards a securitisation model that is instrumentalist.[27] For Engle the intentionality of feminist actors pursuing conflict-related sexual violence requires greater interrogation; for others the interplay between institutions and feminist interventions is less straightforward. However, for the most part these accounts overlook the non-US feminist actors working in transnational contexts and through transnational feminist networks. Tracing where gender law reform derives from transnational feminist agitating, the

Kouvo and Zoe Pearson (eds), *Feminist Perspectives on Contemporary International Law: Between Resistance and Compliance?* (Hart 2011).

[23] Catherine Powell, 'Gender Indicators as Global Governance: Not Your Father's World Bank' (2016) 17 Georgetown Journal of Gender and Law 777.

[24] Kimberlé Crenshaw, 'Mapping the Margins: Intersectionality, Identity Politics and Violence against Women of Colour' (1991) 43(6) Stanford Law Review 1241.

[25] Karen Engle, 'Feminist Governance and International Law: From Liberal to Carceral Feminism' in Janet Halley, Prabha Kotiswaran, Rachel Rebouché, and Hila Shamir (eds), *Governance Feminism: Notes from the Field* (University of Minnesota Press 2018).

[26] Dianne Otto, 'The Exile of Inclusion: Reflections on Gender Issues in International Law over the Last Decade' (2009) 10 Melbourne Journal of International Law 11; Louise Chappell, *The Politics of Gender Justice at the International Criminal Court: Legacies and Legitimacies* (Oxford University Press 2016).

[27] Catherine Powell, 'How Women Could Save the World if Only We Would Let Them: Gender Essentialism and Inclusive Security' (2017) 28 Yale Journal of Law and Feminism 271, 301.

ıability of specific US feminisms, or the role of international institutional struc-
ᵼes is likely impossible: my approach is to move beyond critique and description of
ᵼnder law reform towards thinking: what next?

Halley identifies how the pursuit of consensus by feminist actors undoes important feminist debates and removes them from global governance.[28] Halley argues
that consensus therefore obscures tensions that emerge from the placement of sex
difference as the key organising model for feminist approaches. Within gender and
conflict scholarship, different feminist accounts on anti-militarisation are also ob-
scured in the Security Council resolutions on women, peace, and security.[29] Otto
describes one of the costs of this agenda as the 'softening of the feminist opposition
to war' and instead advocates for methodologies that engage the history of feminist peace activism as a guide that prioritises equal participation, disarmament, and
attention to the adverse effects of war on women.[30] Otto also speaks to the need
for feminist methodologies to be informed by 'queer, indigenous and postcolonial'
politics.[31] In drawing these arguments together, I argue that the dominance of sex
difference as the feminist epistemology that is drawn into gender law reform within
international law reproduces a gender binary that is heteronormative and that ignores the role of gender as a civilising mechanism in international legal histories. For
feminist dialogues on international law to develop beyond contemporary gender
law reforms these tensions must be surfaced and the focus on feminist dialogues approached as integral to feminist epistemologies. Throughout the book I argue that
resurfacing the tensions within feminist dialogues is a method towards undoing the
co-optation that results from the suppression of difference and aids the development
of transformative feminist methodologies.

I also examine how the US-centric focus of the debates on gender law reform
in international law leaves off the transnational feminist histories that have agi-
tated for change to global governance. Tripp defines transnational feminism as
recognising that

[f]eminism today, with all its local variation, is best understood to be a truly global phenomenon: a product of transnational dialogues, coalitions and networks. In spite of the common
perception that feminism originated in the West and diffused to the rest of the world ... the
influences have been historically multidirectional and a product of transnational mutual
learning and sharing.[32]

The histories of transnational feminist organising have not translated well into international legal accounts of gender law reform and are often absent from accounts
of how gender law reform within international law happens.[33] The debates on

---

[28] Halley, 'Rape at Rome' (n 22) 122.
[29] Felicity Ruby, 'Security Council 1325: A Tool for Conflict Resolution?' in Gina Heathcote and
Dianne Otto (eds), *Rethinking Peacekeeping, Gender Equality and Collective Security* (Palgrave 2014);
Karen Engle, 'International Human Rights and Feminism: When Discourses Meet' (1992) 13 Michigan
Journal of International Law 317.
[30] Dianne Otto, 'Women, Peace and Security: A Critical Analysis of the Security Council's Vision' in
Fionnuala Ní Aolaín, Naomi Cahn, Dina Francesca Haynes, and Nahla Valji, *The Oxford Handbook on
Gender and Conflict* (Oxford University Press 2018) 106.
[31] ibid.   [32] Ferree and Tripp (n 1) viii.   [33] Engle, 'Feminist Governance' (n 25).

governance feminism, co-optation, and sex difference have elided the horizontal knowledge processes, the acts of translation and communication, the movements between local, regional, and international spaces of organising, and the diverse feminist forms that constitute transnational feminist spaces. Seeing this work is often difficult, as the priorities of transnational feminist actors are often focused on local injustices that both benefit and suffer from the attention of gender law reforms within global governance. To incorporate this knowledge into the text I theorise plural subjectivities as a mechanism that draws out transnational legal feminisms. Within this approach, I argue for attention to legal pluralism as a mechanism to shift from acknowledging women's difference within feminist legal theories as descriptive; difference is thus the normative platform for feminist engagement. This draws towards a theorisation of difference as that which constitutes the human condition while also functioning as a normative claim that feminist legal approaches bring to international law.

When I articulate a desire for structural bias feminisms I am thinking about the deep structures of law as designed through a series of biases that require rethinking in terms of knowledge production. The feminist knowledge I analyse as a means to think differently about law always regards gender as co-opted into power relations and thus cannot be examined in isolation from other powerful social markers—or histories. Charlesworth and Chinkin recognise throughout their analysis of international law the uneasy tension between gender law reform and the difficulty of acknowledging that 'the international legal system is gendered at a deep level and its mantle of rationality and objectivity is a chimera'.[34] Charlesworth and Chinkin provide a study of international law that includes law-making, treaty law, statehood, institutions, human rights, the use of force, and the settlement of disputes.[35] Subsequent scholarship that engages and critiques the 'deep level' of this gendering has proved to be less popular than the study of gender law reform; in this book I hope to move closer to finding dialogues for feminist legal theorists to continue to analyse the foundational structures of international law.

Charlesworth and Chinkin acknowledge the conditions that facilitate their access to scholarship: 'we are able to write about the boundaries of international law because our own lives are made comfortable and secure by other types of boundaries'.[36] The recognition of the privilege that constructs the conditions for the production of feminist approaches to international law informs a considerable segment of the book. In recognising dialogues as a feminist methodology, I draw on Otto's account of the political responsibility of listening.[37] Otto argues for the 'setting aside of sympathies' so that listening is required for 'reflecting, instead, on the ways that we may be implicated in the violence and benefit from the underlying structural conditions of inequality'.[38] This is the political responsibility of listening that I draw from Otto and I argue is central to future feminist dialogues on international law. I develop this

[34] Charlesworth and Chinkin (n 4) 95.   [35] ibid.   [36] ibid 22.
[37] Dianne Otto, 'Beyond Legal Justice: Some Personal Reflections on People's Tribunals, Listening and Responsibility' (2017) 5(2) London Review of International Law 225.
[38] ibid 248.

as a methodology to question the silences and suppressions in feminist legal projects that are unable to articulate the conditions of their own scripting: in particular, imperial histories, legacies, and continuities. The amenability of gender law reform to the embedded structures of international law seems inevitable in the absence of feminist work on listening to how Western and elite women and feminist actors are seen from the peripheries.[39] This includes critical race projects in the United States where Gunning writes of world travelling premised on seeing oneself through the eyes of others, Black British feminisms that render the invisibility of continued violence enacted on black bodies as a feature of white feminist privilege, indigenous feminisms and indigenous women's writing that challenge the structures of nation and belonging that they carry, and the diverse non-Western feminist knowledges that comprise transnational feminisms.[40] The importance of listening as an epistemological shift in feminist dialogues on international law preoccupies my final chapter and displaces the possibility of conclusions with the possibility of learning to hear and read the conditions of difference that make the page, this page, possible.

Lewis writes:

But what would the possibility of growth in the presence of 'black woman' require? One thing would be to acknowledge what becomes absent in us when we absent or disappear her particularity from our collective histories, current realities, future potentialities. Another requirement would involve development of our courage to acknowledge the harm done her, historically and in the here and now, by utilising the resources we have in the archive in the interests of practising presencing.[41]

Moreton-Robinson writes:

... the real challenge for white feminists is to theorise the relinquishment of power so that feminist practice can contribute to changing the racial order. Until this challenge is addressed, the subject position middle-class white woman will remain the central site of dominance.[42]

Inspired by Charlesworth and Chinkin's earlier recognition of non-legal feminist and gender theories informing the design of their epistemology, I endeavour to write these voices into my thinking as a strategy of political listening, opening up dialogues for plurality as a cornerstone of feminist accounts. I pay particular attention to Black British feminisms and indigenous Australian feminisms as forming disruptive dialogues that interrupt the possibility of gender law reform within international law and the fantasy of feminist futures. Black British feminisms and indigenous Australian voices speak specifically to the conditions of my own privilege and thus are given specific prominence; however, they are also representative of the ushering in of difference theorised in the text via plural subjectivities as methodology. In

---

[39] Kapur (n 10).

[40] Isabelle Gunning, 'Arrogant Perceptions, World-Travelling and Multicultural Feminism: The Case of Female Genital Surgeries' (1992) 23 Columbia Human Rights Law Review 189; Gail Lewis, 'Questions of Presence' (2017) 117 Feminist Review 1; Aileen Moreton-Robinson, *Talkin' Up to the White Woman: Indigenous Women and Feminism* (University of Queensland Press 2000); Ferree and Tripp (n 1).

[41] Lewis (n 40) 8.   [42] Moreton-Robinson (n 40) 186.

chapter 2 I theorise plural subjectivities as a necessary foundational legal device to usher space for political listening which I then develop across the remaining chapters of the text.

Likewise, I acknowledge queer approaches to international law and crip theories as important interruptions to existing gender law reform dialogues with a specific attention to this knowledge in chapter 5. I regard these as not dialogues for Western feminist appropriation but as interwoven into understanding gender and thus needing to be listened to, learnt from, and articulated as central to a feminist account of gender. In chapter 5 I use queer and crip interruptions as mechanisms to think about how feminist dialogues might approach gender law reform differently. For Otto such a methodology stems from queer curiosity:

Queer curiosity brings to the mix of emancipatory (improper) curiosities, and the critical analysis they foster, a particular concern with conventions of sexuality and the part they play in signifying hierarchical relations of power—not only in their attachment to material bodies, but to structures of understanding that constitute the norms and practices of international law.[43]

Otto recognises the feminist nexus to queer projects alongside the unease between some modes of feminist theorising and queer projects.[44] Otto's conclusion that 'queer theory expands the feminist project' has yet to transform gender law reform within international law; in fact, following Hamzić, there needs to be recognition that the take-up of LGBT agendas by specific international institutions replicates many of the troubles with gender law reform I analyse across the book.[45]

Long develops the conversation on queer approaches further, arguing, '[t]hinking through non-normative crip and queer bodies, and the ways in which they are repressed, contained, and managed, in collaborations between feminist theory and disability studies can be complementary'.[46] Focusing her critique on neoliberal governance structures rather than international law, Long identifies convergences such that:

Neoliberalism requires the regulation of sexuality to ensure a healthy and (re)productive workforce, built on the foundation of the stable, nuclear family. There are close connections between the workings of heteronormativity and able-bodied hegemony under neoliberalism, where the body becomes a site for self-regulation and self-correction to align with these neoliberal imperatives.[47]

---

[43] Dianne Otto, 'Introduction: Embracing Queer Curiosity' in Dianne Otto (ed), *Queering International Law: Possibilities, Alliances, Complicities, Risks* (Routledge 2018) 6.

[44] ibid.

[45] Vanja Hamzić, 'International Law as Violence: Competing Absences of the Other' in Dianne Otto (ed), *Queering International Law: Possibilities, Alliances, Complicities, Risks* (Routledge 2018) 77; Vanja Hamzić, 'Unlearning Human Rights and False Grand Dichotomies: Indonesian Archipelagic Selves beyond Sexual/Gender Universality' (2014) 4 (1) Jindal Global Law Review 157.

[46] Robyn Long, 'Sexual Subjectivities within Neoliberalism: Can Queer and Crip Engagements Offer an Alternative Praxis?' (2018) 19(1) Journal of International Women's Studies 78, 82.

[47] ibid 84.

Drawing this knowledge into a feminist dialogue on international law has thus far seen insufficient legal change; a first step, I argue, is a recognition of the capacity of intersectionality to reframe epistemologies rather than to articulate an additive approach that rests on identity politics.[48] The turn to plural subjectivities is therefore a mechanism to open up the foundational knowledge and assumptions of feminist approaches rather than being limited to participation or quotas for inclusion that are not necessarily transformative in terms of knowledge production.

Holding a range of different disciplinary approaches in mind, while centring international legal possibilities, has been the challenge of the book. In addition, writing a theory of listening demands a different type of analysis than the forms and conventions which academic writing dictates. Hemmings' dialogue on the role of feminist citations and the shaping of narratives of progress, loss, and reform, draw me to question my voice and its position as authority throughout the text, with the most significant impact of this effect drawn out in chapter 6.[49] The consequence is a kaleidoscope of feminist knowledge, that tilts and shifts—as dialogues do—throughout the different chapters. This is an attempt to resist settling at the moment of critique to consciously propose alternative ways of imagining gender law reform; while also avoiding closure on the tilting and the shifting, on the changing light and colours. I hope that the book opens up dialogues and possibilities to disrupt a sense of satisfaction with gender law reform as it is, while still acknowledging the varied feminist spaces that created those reforms.

3. Feminist Successes, Tensions, Futures

Feminist Dialogues recognises the immense shift in international law that had seen a general silence on women's issues outside of the CEDAW process and only minimal feminist scholarship on international law (but not human rights) prior to 1991. Recognition of how gender law reform has been incorporated into institutional developments is an important aspect of the argument presented in this book, examined in chapters 2 and 3. It is possible, however, to both celebrate these achievements, in international criminal law, in collective security, in the work of UN Women, and on women's human rights while writing to demonstrate how the 'accepted' story of feminist approaches plays a role in diminishing the visibility of 'troublesome' feminist histories that continually disrupt the category of women,[50] that seek out non-Western knowledge to frame and reframe knowledge,[51] and that often work happily within tensions and paradoxes in a manner that fits less well with legal reforms. This is the conversation, with all the implicit tensions, that I explore throughout the book. There has been a shift towards gender law reform within international law.

---

[48] ibid 81.

[49] Clare Hemmings, *Why Stories Matter: The Political Grammar of Feminist Theory* (Duke 2011).

[50] Denise Riley, *'Am I that Name?': Feminism and the Category of Women in History* (Palgrave 1988).

[51] Vasuki Nesiah, 'The Ground Beneath Her Feet: "Third World" Feminisms' (2003) 4(3) Journal of International Women's Studies 30; Kapur (n 10); Prabha Kotiswaran, *Dangerous Sex, Invisible Labour: Sex Work and the Law in India* (Princeton 2011).

This is the product of multiple feminist actors, often from transnational feminist networks across states and regions. The institutional outcomes of this action, however, are often best described as reflecting a narrow range of feminist approaches.

Both Knop and Otto have demonstrated how these silences are misrepresented with respect to women's participation in both the League of Nations and the United Nations.[52] Outside of international law scholarship, contemporary gender theorists are alert to a similar fashioning of feminist histories to write out women's anger and feminist histories,[53] reducing crucial intersections with race, sexuality, and ableist politics to footnotes rather than substantive engagements,[54] and a feminist history narrative that is more often presented as static rather than varied, contradictory, and evolving.[55] Implicit in the myopic views developed within gender law reform, then, is a form of erasure of feminism dialogues that are not accommodated by institutional agendas. Nesiah argues that this requires 'a re-orientating of our critical energies from merely taking sides in a debate, to a questioning of the material and ideological lens that interpolates the debate'; a project barely begun within feminist analysis of international law.[56] The manner in which international institutions have incorporated specific feminist agendas and reshaped these into 'gender perspectives',[57] 'gender balancing',[58] and 'gender equality'[59] remain an important component and aspect of any future feminist dialogues but, I argue, only as a starting point for searching what is left out, what is consolidated, and what is silenced by gender law reform. In the following subsections I briefly introduce feminist successes within international institutions, the resistant feminist tensions, and begin to elaborate the threads and stories that future feminist dialogues might listen to.

3.1 Successes

The accommodation of specific feminist dialogues on international law into the mainstream of international law has produced, and continues to produce, important outcomes, for the United Nations, for women across communities, and for feminist and women's rights advocates. International criminal law and the Security Council women, peace, and security agenda are two key sites where feminist interventions have had legal implications. In addition, the longer history of women's human rights initiatives and the incorporation of these, via CEDAW and various

---

[52] Dianne Otto, 'A Sign of "Weakness"? Disrupting Gender Certainties in the Implementation of Security Council Resolution 1325' (2006–2007) 13 Michigan Journal of Gender and the Law 113; Karen Knop, 'Re/Statements: Feminism and State Sovereignty in International Law' (1993) 3 Transnational Law and Contemporary Problems 293.

[53] Angela McRobbie, *The Aftermath of Feminism: Gender, Culture and Social Change* (Sage 2009) 13–23.

[54] Hemmings (n 49).   [55] Scott (n 18).   [56] Nesiah (n 51).

[57] This is the term preferred by the Security Council in resolutions on women, peace, and security, although this seems to be a reference to 'women's perspectives'.

[58] Gender balancing is the process of increasing women's representation within institutional structures.

[59] The term gender equality is used regularly in mainstream literature and institutional documents for any work that focuses on women's needs or rights.

World Conferences (on human rights and on women), into international legal dialogues, are important histories of diverse sites of feminist action within international spaces, including the development of institutional models on intersectionality. One specific outcome of these dialogues has been the appointment of gender experts as a form of gender law reform. I analyse how a significant amount of gender law reform within global governance appears to rely on gender expertise as a mechanism to circumvent attention to feminist method and/or interrogation of the structures of international law, in chapter 2.

Tripp and Badri note how African transnational feminists and women's rights activists have 'been influential, particularly in areas such as the political representation of women, in advancing women as economic actors, in adopting strategies to promote peace, and in tackling cultural restraints on women'.[60] At the same time, accounts of African feminist approaches, the interventions of Middle Eastern feminist actors, the voices of South and Central American feminists, and the work of feminists from South Asia to the Pacific, remain fairly muted within feminist accounts of international law. The imagined construction of this transnational feminist work as outside of the discipline of international law contributes to the construction of feminist 'Others' pushed to the peripheries of feminist dialogues on international law. The presence and influence of transnational feminist voices in the history of international law challenges dominant scholarship on global governance to listen to alternative accounts and to theorise both the silences and the actions. For example, one of the important advances that emerged from the Beijing Fourth UN Conference on Women in 1995 was the creation of gender-sensitive budget initiatives by women's organisations in over forty states by 2002. These initiatives commenced in the global south and were later taken up as feminist projects in the global north.[61] This example highlights three important features of transnational feminist practice: First, that transnational feminist knowledge travels horizontally—it need not wait for an international law to produce transformative change. Second, the flow of knowledge across transnational feminist networks is multi-directional, reacting to the international, enacted at the local, yet travelling across regions. Third, unlike gender law reform within international law, which seems to reproduce specific sexed and gendered tropes, transnational feminist knowledge adapts as it travels via the process of translation to local contexts. I am interested in how these features might form the epistemology for future feminist engagements with international law, as a template for re-imagining knowledge and law. Furthermore, I argue that to embark on dialogues prompted by transnational feminist histories incorporates a response to legal pluralism that is relevant to future international legal strategies. This understanding influences my conclusions in chapter 3, in the analysis of fragmentation, where I argue for an epistemological shift towards feminist knowledge of plural subjectivities.

In terms of specific legal outcomes, gender law reform within international law emerges primarily in human rights, international criminal law, and collective

---

[60] Aili Mari Tripp and Balghis Badri (eds), *Women's Activism in Africa* (Zed Books 2017) 29.
[61] ibid 17.

security. I come back to each of these areas of gender law reform within international law across the book, attending to the types of law produced. In inquiring into the transnational movement of gender law reforms, I hope to disrupt the assumptions about gender law reform as derived only from 'Unitedstatesaen' feminisms.[62] While many of the outputs from international institutions do appear to align and reproduce US feminist approaches, the application in local spaces embraces transnational feminist methodologies, reshaping the potentials of these laws at the same time.[63] I argue that future feminist scholarship on international law would benefit from studying transnational feminist methodologies to commence different dialogues, beyond the dominant gender law reforms evidenced in international criminal law, collective security, and international human rights law.

Feminist engagement with international law emerged in the early twentieth century, a form of transnational feminism that attracted the existing suffrage networks to work towards articulating feminist peace projects.[64] The Hague Peace Conference held in 1915 produced an outcome document on securing peace and constituted the early network that would later become the Women's International League for Peace and Freedom (WILPF).[65] The participants at the Peace Conference were largely from states in Europe and North America, although some states refused to give permission for delegates to attend.[66] Although the Peace Resolutions incorporate specifically women-centred agendas, for example with respect to women's political participation, the document articulates a vision for peace rather than a vision for women's lives.[67]

Women's networks also petitioned the League of Nations and worked to influence the League processes throughout its existence. Pederson notes during this period women's presence was 'politically and ideologically significant in that it helped to legitimate a particular understanding of European imperialism between the wars'.[68] That understanding was one where women's rights and women's voices were mobilised as a tool that ultimately 'could justify the perpetuation of nonconsensual alien rule' in mandate territories.[69] The nexus between the support for women's inclusion in international law and international law's imperial dimensions is a feature I return to throughout the book. In chapter 4, I enlarge the analysis of gender and imperialism through the study of sovereignty. I argue that a rethinking of state sovereignty through attention to the gender of colonial histories and the relational

[62] Halley, 'Take a Break' (n 20) 64.

[63] Karen Knop, 'Here and There: International Law in Domestic Courts' (2000) 32 New York University Journal of International Law and Politics 501; Ferree and Tripp (n 1).

[64] Otto, 'A Sign of "Weakness"?' (n 52).

[65] Christine Chinkin, Gina Heathcote, Emily Jones, and Henry Jones, 'Bozkurt Case (aka the Lotus Case) France v Turkey: Two Ships that Go Bump in the Night' in Loveday Hodson and Troy J Lavers (eds), *Feminist International Judgement Project* (Hart 2018).

[66] Freya Baetens, 'The Forgotten Peace Conference: The 1915 Congress of Women' in Rüdiger Wolfrum (ed), *Max Planck Encyclopedia of Public International Law* (Oxford University Press 2010).

[67] Otto, 'Women, Peace and Security' (n 30).

[68] Susan Pederson, 'Metaphors of the Schoolroom: Women Working the Mandate System of the League of Nations' (2008) 66 History Workshop Journal 188.

[69] ibid 192.

nature of inter-state interactions is an important feminist methodology drawn from dialogues currently peripheral to dominant gender law reforms. In this I draw on Nesiah's recognition that 'the making and unmaking of the ground beneath one's feet powerfully resonates with both the impetus and the impact of many third world feminist interventions'.[70] Following Nesiah, I seek out the discomfort and tensions that become apparent when feminist 'successes' within international law are placed in dialogue with feminist accounts that start with recognition of the plural and split subjectivities of feminist approaches.

By the time the CEDAW was ratified in 1979 the machinery for women's human rights had a significant history—across World Conferences and human rights initiatives. The work of the CEDAW Committee, in the articulation of General Recommendations, has considerably enlarged the purpose and object of the CEDAW process. Likewise, attention to regional human rights processes demonstrates the transnational developments in the field of women's human rights. O'Rourke and Swaine argue that the CEDAW Committee has used the General Recommendations process to construct a series of checks and balances across gender law reform, such that the re-iteration of similar agendas across different spaces within the United Nations facilitates a sophisticated and evolving space for gender law reform.[71] Despite the impact of the General Recommendations as tools for expanding the remit of CEDAW and country-specific reports incorporating an intersectional understanding of gender, the human rights structures work from a model of liberal inclusion—adding in women's rights to the largely liberal model of human rights. The general failure to engage the limitations of rights as a tool for change is returned to in chapter 4 when I examine the Human Rights Council through the lens of feminist dialogues on international law.

Within international criminal law the impact of gender law reforms is well documented, influencing the categories of crimes in the Rome Statute, the jurisprudence of the ad hoc tribunals, and the selection processes for those who people the International Criminal Court. Chappell identifies how the emergence of gender law reform within the International Criminal Court falls victim to the 'nestedness' of the institution, which produces less ambitious feminist outcomes than some of the proponents of these gender laws might have hoped for. The carceral model developed within international criminal law has also attracted significant criticism from feminist scholars.[72] The racial dynamics of international criminal law, the limited preventative model, and the hyper-attention to women's sexual vulnerability reproduce a series of gendered tropes that do little to dislodge the claims about sex and gender from which these reforms ostensibly spring.[73]

---

[70] Nesiah (n 51).

[71] Catherine O'Rourke and Aisling Swaine, 'CEDAW and the Security Council: Enhancing Women's Rights in Conflict' (2018) 67 International and Comparative Law Quarterly 167.

[72] Engle (n 25).

[73] Doris Buss, 'The Curious Visibility of Wartime Rape: Gender and Ethnicity in International Criminal Law' (2007) 25(1) Windsor Journal of Access to Justice 3; Doris Buss, 'Performing Legal Order: Some Feminist Thoughts on International Criminal Law' (2011) 11 International Criminal Law Review: Special Issue on Women & International Criminal Law 409.

Beyond human rights approaches and developments within international criminal law, the attention of scholars to collective security after the issuing of Security Council resolution 1325 in 2000 has been significant.[74] The Security Council has gone on to issue seven additional resolutions on women, peace, and security; the Secretary-General has produced annual reports on women, peace, and security since 2003, and in 2015 a High-Level Panel was convened to review the first fifteen years of institutional engagement.[75] As noted above, this institutional development was preceded by feminist peace activism through the work of WILPF that can be traced back to The Hague Peace Conferences in 1915 and 1919. The women, peace, and security resolutions work through four pillars—participation, prevention, protection, and relief and recovery—with each resolution often emphasising different aspects of the agenda, while consolidating and repeating some aspects and incorporating an interesting corpus of gender law reform within the work of the Security Council. Unlike the creation of the International Criminal Court and CEDAW, which were both established through treaty law, the women, peace, and security resolutions are soft laws that are issued under the Security Council's chapter VI powers established in the United Nations Charter as a source of non-binding obligations for states. Despite their status as non-binding law, the women, peace, and security resolutions have had a substantial impact on gender law reform within global governance, influencing institutional and state approaches to gender.

Throughout the book I raise discussion on these three areas of law, international criminal law, international human rights law and collective security, via the gender law reform that has occurred within these spaces. My primary agenda is not only to present a critique of existing gender law reforms within global governance but to engage the knowledge that they build on, so as to commence a dialogue about the knowledge produced via these reforms. To think about feminist knowledge projects, I argue there is a need to surface the tensions that are often ignored in the turn to institutions. In examining feminist tensions, I seek to move beyond a feminist commitment to gender law reform as it is currently articulated and to build on dialogues that ask about the foundational structures of law. In doing so I call for dialogue on structural bias feminisms that consciously shift away from the organisation around sex difference to ask about feminist methodologies as structural tools geared towards using the insight of intersectionality approaches to rethink strategies for gender law reform. This is informed by an understanding of sex, gender, and sexuality as fluid: across lifetimes, within communities, and across communities. In contrast, gender law reform, as it currently exists whether in international criminal law, collective security, or human rights laws has drawn on a notion of gender that is binary

---

[74] Security Council Resolution 1325 (31 October 2000) UN Doc S/RES/1325; Gina Heathcote and Dianne Otto (eds), *Rethinking Peacekeeping, Gender Equality and Collective Security* (Palgrave 2014).

[75] Security Council Resolution 1820 (19 June 2008) UN Doc S/RES/1820; Security Council Resolution 1888 (30 September 2009) UN Doc S/RES/1888; Security Council Resolution 1889 (5 October 2009) UN Doc S/RES/1889; Security Council Resolution 1960 (16 December 2010) UN Doc S/RES/1960; Security Council Resolution 2106 (24 June 2013) UN Doc S/RES/2106; Security Council Resolution 2122 (18 October 2013) UN Doc S/RES/2122; Security Council Resolution 2242 (13 October 2015) UN Doc S/RES/2242.

and does not attend to internal assumptions with regard to gender. Holding sexuality, gender, race, histories of colonialism, economic harms, and ableism present in the configurations of feminist methodologies is a fairly difficult task; as such, rather than pursuing answers this book examines where dialogues might evolve.

In articulating intersectionality as a process for building structural bias epistemologies it is *hoped* that plural subjectivities articulate means for additional voices to continue to shape feminist accounts of law. Hope, however, can be a weak tool. It is important to also account for the normalising of bodies in some gender spaces, constructing the conditions for how bodies are read and understood. Crip theories draw in the embodied nature of sexuality and gender as well as the silent performance of each in lives rendered and produced as 'normal':

> the disabled body is not merely 'out of place', it is a threat to the Western ideal of an enlightened, stable self; seeing 'the self gone out of control' reminds us that the cultural 'Other' is buried within this self, and may at any time appear to destabilise it.[76]

By way of example, despite the disabling and maiming of bodies as a significant outcome of armed conflict, alongside the large corpus of feminist scholarship on international law attending to issues related to conflict and post-conflict, the silence on the production of able-bodiedness within feminist dialogues is quite powerful and once registered, the rethinking of feminist legal knowledge is inevitable.[77] I theorise plural and split subjectivities as a methodology to approach the dialogues produced as always attentive to these intersections.

3.2 Tensions

In this section I further elaborate the approach to tensions that I argue need to surface in feminist dialogues on international law. I develop an account of three specific tensions that appear to have been glossed over in international legal scholarship: essentialism, imperialism, and materiality. With a commitment to feminist dialogues, I hope that through articulating these tensions apertures for further conversations are opened—as these are hardly the only tensions within feminist approaches and gender law reform.

The first tension, essentialism, is insufficiently recognised in approaches to gender law reform and risks the reproduction of gendered tropes, rather than their disruption. Charlesworth and Chinkin define essentialism as a focus on sex difference as the site of women's oppression 'without regard to other influences such as race, class or sexuality'.[78] Following Mohanty, Charlesworth and Chinkin recognise the need for horizontal structures of feminist organising that actively work to render visible difference and disagreement, despite the value of universal categories as a strategic methodology in legal projects.[79] This tension—between the law's construction of

---

[76] Long (n 46) 80.
[77] Gina Heathcote, 'War's Perpetuity: Disabled Bodies of War and the Exoskeleton of Equality' (2018) 44(1) Australian Feminist Law Journal 71.
[78] Charlesworth and Chinkin (n 4) 43.   [79] Mohanty (n 6).

categories of inclusion and exclusion and a feminist methodology that starts with difference—has received insufficient attention in subsequent feminist scholarship on international law. Charlesworth and Chinkin acknowledge that the 'international legal system has been slow to recognise the diversity of women', however they counsel that '[f]eminist analysis must negotiate a strategic path between theoretical purity and political principle'.[80] Feminist dialogues on international law after Charlesworth and Chinkin have not, for the most part, furthered understanding of this tension.

A significant consequence is the underlying heteronormativity of the gender binary and the universalising of elite women's experiences in international legal reforms which have been insufficiently challenged in feminist writing on international law. This leaves unchallenged the assertion of a gender binary which is explicitly relied on by some scholars as a mechanism to silence trans women.[81] Thus far, mainstream feminist approaches to international law are yet to incorporate queer and trans scholarship into feminist accounts; consequently heteronormativity and cisgenderism is 'carried' in the gender binary that is reasserted via gender law reform.[82] Following Paige, this approach reasserts the heteronormative and cisgendered violence of international law, violence that results in 'the invisibility of individuals who do not neatly fit into the normalised gender binary' and reproduction of the 'fear of undermining heteronormative social structures'.[83] Queer approaches to international law already commence a dialogue with feminist approaches to international law: I argue that this dialogue must cease to be ignored by feminist accounts. Feminist scholarship on international law must be engaged in conversation with critical race, postcolonial, crip, and queer epistemologies to disrupt the production of gender law reform that essentialises a female subject as the subject of feminism.[84] As such, I regard attention and dialogue on intersectionality, in particular what this means in terms of law reform, as a necessary space of feminist theorising for questioning privilege and for identifying what is shifted to the peripheries of feminist approaches to international law: the complexity of surfacing this dialogue is a key preoccupation of the book.

The second tension I discuss is the legacy of imperialism within international law and the co-optation of gender projects to obscure the imperial tendencies of international law. Drawing this into present discussions on gender law reform produces important spaces for listening and I draw on the writing of postcolonial and indigenous scholars to challenge the authority with which I come to write this text. Again, surfacing this tension—acknowledging the history of imperialist international law as always pursuing gender as a civilising force—is disruptive and uncomfortable for actors focused on gender law reform. Strategies for law reform become less clear and questions about assumptions within feminist theories with regard to who is

---

[80] Charlesworth and Chinkin (n 4) 54–55.

[81] Sheila Jeffreys, *Gender Hurts: A Feminist Analysis of the Politics of Transgenderism* (Routledge 2014).

[82] Tasmin Phillipa Paige, 'The Maintenance of International Peace and Security Heteronormativity' in Dianne Otto (ed), *Queering International Law: Possibilities, Alliances, Complicities, Risks* (Routledge 2018) 91.

[83] ibid 107.   [84] Otto, 'Introduction' (n 43) 6.

positioned to speak on gender law reform and who is to be imagined as the recipient of law reform challenges the neatness of the page. A commitment to holding this uncomfortable knowledge informs the ways in which I wrote the text and my hope is that this permits spaces for listening rather than for a continued dominance of elite women's dialogues on international law. Following Otto, I acknowledge '[w]e need to recognise our collective responsibilities by acknowledging the benefits we may enjoy as a result of the present system'.[85] Chapter 6, on authority, thus maps how this tension shapes the contours of gender law reform and articulates the conditions of my own capacity to write.

The third tension, materiality, is highlighted to engage dialogue on the production of gendered and sexed bodies by gender law reform. These dialogues require recognition of gender as fluid and changeable alongside the need for attention to lived, embodied experience of gender. A key suppression within work on international law has been the sustained dialogue found in feminist theories (beyond legal feminisms) with the meaning and diversity of accounts of gender, this includes the tension between postmodernist and political economy approaches, the need to theorise the embodied effects of gender, and approaches to gender as affect. For example, Andrijesivic writes of the 'multiple subjects positions' that migrant subjects take up as transnational workers and citizens. Consequently, theorisations of sovereignty are significantly disrupted and the gendered understanding of sexuality that states cling to are demonstrated as reproducing nationalist notions of belonging that also dictate access to resources, including citizenship.[86] Dialogues on feminist approaches to international law that acknowledge how labour conditions and the material are implicated within gender law reform tend to lie at the peripheries of the international feminist knowledge and would benefit from continued articulation. I draw on this in chapter 4 to consider the political economy of gender—placing political economy accounts in dialogue with feminist legal approaches, and queer and crip approaches, to aid the development of a theory of interruptions.

These three tensions, I argue, significantly reduce the capacity for gender law reform that is responsive to feminist methodologies. The gaps in feminist dialogues on international law consequently reproduce the space for international actors to articulate gendered meanings within law that reflect dominant power arrangements rather than unsettling those arrangements and attending to feminist tensions. The failure of attention to tensions, a casualty of the pursuit of consensus, effects the futurity of feminist projects, dismantling the capacity of feminist approaches to ask questions of themselves. In contrast, I argue for a resurfacing of these tensions within feminist dialogues as tools for opening up critical questions on international law, gender law reform, and feminist methodologies. To commence a reflection on these tensions I regard dialogues on intersectionality as vital to international legal projects. This is not to imagine a feminist future

---

[85] Otto, 'Beyond Legal Justice' (n 37) 248.
[86] Rutvica Andrijasevic, 'Sex on the Move: Gender, Subjectivity and Differential Inclusion' (2009) 29 Subjectivity 389, 403.

that designs feminist law via a reductionist version of intersectionality but to use intersectionality to understand how feminist legal knowledge is often implicated in the perpetuation of privilege.

I have previously considered the role of utopias in feminist thinking as an element of the process of critique—utopia—reform.[87] Lacey's articulation of the unrealised nature of feminist utopias, at once a horizon and never the present, and the loop this creates into critique, continues to influence my approach. I regard the idea of feminist utopias as the fantasy of feminism that feminism both assumes and avoids discussing in its international manifestations of gender law reform. For Lacey, 'the sort of rhetorical politics which is imagined in utopian thought may, if directly institutionalized have effects different from those ideally envisioned'.[88] Acknowledging this within international law requires feminist scholars to address their different expectations and different starting points: this is a dialogue insufficiently embarked on in current iterations of feminist approaches to international law. Addressing embedded feminist judgements or acknowledging the limits of feminist utopias, following Scott, is not to end the feminist project; rather it is to see the methodologies of feminism, the thinking of gender theory, the desire for critique anew, as the process that sex/gender as analytics makes possible.[89] These are the tensions embedded within critiques of essentialism and which produce a commitment to intersectionality that informs my choice of methodology throughout the project.

Furthermore, the exposure of sex and gender as co-opted into the vectors of power within international law and legal scholarship is central. I define sex and gender as always in dialogue with sexuality, race, ethnicity, stories of colonialism and ableism, such that to speak of sex and/or gender without these conversations is to reproduce the status quo of gender law reform. Scott thus defines a feminist methodology as requiring recognition that:

... there is neither a self nor a collective identity without an Other; there is no inclusiveness without exclusion, no universal without a rejected particular, no neutrality that doesn't privilege an interested point of view; and power is always an issue in the articulation of these relationships.[90]

Throughout the book these dialogues are returned to, to develop understanding of how these tensions both propel and restrain feminist thinking, with the goal of moving towards acceptance of these tensions (or dialogues) as vital to the continued development of feminist approaches within international law. The consequent complexity requires feminist dialogues on international law that are attentive to epistemologies and assumptions rather than signalling a desire for spaces of inclusion.

---

[87] Nicola Lacey, 'Feminist Legal Theory and the Rights of Women' in Karen Knop (ed), *Gender and Human Rights* (Oxford University Press 2004) 13; Heathcote, *The Law on the Use of Force* (n 14) 8.
[88] Lacey, 'Feminist Legal Theory' (n 87) 46. [89] Scott (n 18) 73. [90] ibid.

3.3 Futures

feminist history as the story of a circulating critical passion, slipping metonymically along a chain of contiguous objects, alighting for a while in an unexpected place, accomplishing a task, and then moving on . . .[91]

Contemporary feminist scholarship looks beyond the categories of 'women/woman' to develop understandings of feminism as a process[92] or a story/narrative[93] that unfolds and retells itself and that need not collapse under the weight of its own critiques or its arrival within the institution/academy. Throughout this book, contemporary gender theorists and feminist scholars working outside the space of legal discourse are drawn on to reconsider and disrupt feminist approaches to international law. In this section I review how some of these approaches influence my approach to feminist dialogues.

Scott characterises gender as the

history of articulations of the masculine/feminine, male/female distinction . . . It does not assume the prior existence of the masculine/feminine, male/female distinction, but rather examines the complicated, contradictory, and ambivalent way it has emerged in different social and political discourses.[94]

Developing this further Scott defines her project as one where 'critical reading replaces the operations of classification'.[95] This understanding of gender is distinct from the one emergent within international law, where gender perspectives/balancing/mainstream/equality all embed rather than disrupt gendered approaches. As such, I argue for recognition of the manner in which institutional gender projects produce a reliance on the gender binary and reduce the possibilities for understanding of gender as a mechanism for moving beyond the heteronormative production of female and maleness within international approaches to gender law reform.

I had originally imagined this chapter as a telling of the arrival, the loss, and resurgence of feminist approaches on international law. However, Hemmings' *Why Stories Matter* challenged this reading as I recognised the 'progress/loss/return' narrative that she writes of and I have consequently found the expected narrative a difficult one to write in this chapter.[96] Hemmings's call for feminist projects to 'pay attention to how feminist progress narratives operate' so as to see how 'erasure of a complex past is a necessary condition of their positivity' resonates with contemporary feminist dialogues on international law and disrupted the story or narrative I was about to tell.[97] In the place of a narrative on the progress, loss, and return within feminist approaches to international law, I have offered varied ideas and reflections on how feminist approaches have represented themselves within international law. The remainder of this book works to simultaneously accept and reject this narrative. The goal is to ultimately define feminist approaches as a process and a series of ongoing, mutating, critical interventions that may or may not have been

---

[91] ibid 33.   [92] ibid.   [93] Hemmings (n 49).   [94] Scott (n 18) ch 1.
[95] ibid.   [96] Hemmings (n 49).   [97] ibid 57.

disrupted by the early twenty-first-century uptake of gender law reform by and through international institutions. I regard the pursuit of a definitive answer to the impact of gender law reform as less important than interrogation of the knowledge projects both inside and outside of these agendas.

Hemmings is also attentive to the way established narratives push certain intersections to the footnotes/history of feminist thinking. Feminist approaches to international law might take heed of Hemmings's identification of the substitution of substantive engagement with strategic footnotes to tell the 'story' of feminist thinking in academic terms: the challenge of this book is to both represent a series of feminist interventions and outcomes while attending to the ruptures and silences these narratives contain. In international law the 'loss' narrative when feminist 'successes' arrive within international institutions is countered by the gains in legitimacy to the institutions themselves and the increased currency of feminist terms, methods, and thinking. Accepting the 'letting go' of feminist understandings once they are no longer only 'feminist' but also institutional components is a difficult narrative for feminist approaches to comprehend because it pushes a social movement that defined itself through its outsider status into the mainstream. How both feminist legal approaches and critical legal scholarship on international law encounter this ushering into mainstream dialogues is a background concern of the text, and I am particularly attentive to how further dialogues between critical legal scholars and feminist legal engagements are necessary to enhance both accounts.

Throughout the book my argument is not that feminist futures lie in the mythical place of 'non-Western feminism' or the 'true' intersection of vectors of difference. This is an unrealisable strategy that ignores the manner in which some non-Western feminist approaches might draw on the same methodological apparatus as Western feminist approaches or may choose to speak alongside or through Western platforms. Difference is not 'out there'; it is within the prejudices and failures of dominant knowledge frames. To see the Other is to see the difference located in the self, through assumptions of inclusion and exclusion. I argue that self-reflection on the production of difference is necessary in feminist thinking, just as intersectionality projects that only see race and gender are themselves exclusionary projects. Within this approach, I take it for granted that the internalisation of difference produces material, lived effects that perpetuate harm and discrimination across communities. Consequently, the purpose of this book is to unlock future feminist approaches to international law where questions contribute to further questions, further projects, new mappings, new understandings of power, discourse, and law, mechanisms for listening with responsibility, while re-representing sex/gender as temporally and geographically fluid. I am reminded of Lucy Parsons's words: 'a reinvention of everyday involves walking off the edges of our maps'.[98] While this book, throughout, reads international law and its mainstream, highlighting the intersection of critical and feminist projects, the answers the book offers are partial, fluid, processes,

---

[98] Elizabeth Kerri Mahon, 'Lucy Parsons—An American Revolutionary' (*Scandalous Women*, 5 February 2008) <http://scandalouswoman.blogspot.co.uk/2008/02/lucy-parsons-american-revolutionary.html> last accessed 31 May 2018.

less answers more disruptive questions walking 'off the edges' than new maps for international law.

Returning again to Scott's work:

> The elusiveness of sexual difference is both unrealizable and for that very reason, historical. It is a quest that never ends. As such, it interrupts the certainty of established categories, thus creating openings to the future.[99]

Scott's feminist engagement with sexual difference informs the project undertaken in this book, where creative openings and interruptions are interjected into the certainty of established categories, in mainstream approaches to international law, in critical legal approaches and feminist approaches to international law. The feminist futures imagined diverge and stray from the expected paths of prior gender law reforms and attend to the knowledge behind foundational legal structures.

4. The Structure of This Book

Drawing on the dialogues above, I argue throughout the book that feminist dialogues on international law must expand in the following ways. First, there must be attention to feminist approaches to international law that are more often shifted to the peripheries and not visible within the contours of gender law reform. This includes transnational and postcolonial feminist writings and activism, as well as queer and crip theories that engage feminist methodologies or dialogues. Second, I argue that feminist dialogues on international law, if engaging the foundations of the discipline, must offer comprehensive dialogue with other critical strands of international legal theory. As a dialogue this would be a multivocal conversation that develops further engagement with feminist theories from these theorists, expanding on the preliminary analysis offered by Chimni and Bianchi and rendering visible the larger *oeuvre* of feminist scholarship beyond Charlesworth and Chinkin's work.[100] Third, in expansion of the methodologies that inspired the original academic feminist writings on international law, there is a necessity for feminist approaches to international law to remain in dialogue and to sustain dialogues with feminist and gender theories, both within legal spaces and outside of legal scholarship. Throughout the text I draw on Black British feminisms, queer feminisms, crip feminisms, and indigenous feminisms as well as critical race feminisms, postcolonial feminisms, and TWAIL feminisms, feminist institutionalism, and contemporary works from gender theory: these are inspiring, attentive to methodologies, and important in bringing tools from which feminist approaches within international law can benefit, through listening to their epistemological contributions.

---

[99] Scott (n 18) 22.
[100] BS Chimni, *International Law and the World Order* (Cambridge University Press 2017); Andrea Bianchi, *International Legal Theories: An Inquiry into Different Ways of Thinking* (Oxford University Press 2016).

To undertake the above project the book arranges itself around key foundational concerns within international law to begin to articulate feminist dialogues on expertise, fragmentation, sovereignty, institutions, and authority. Through these topics I engage a range of feminist methodologies, some well-established within feminist approaches, such as intersectionality, and others, such as plural subjectivities and split subjects, reflecting the preoccupations of the book with the foundations of legal structures. The book closes with an analysis of authority within international law, questioning the feminist desire for gender law reform as the solution to a host of issues as well as questioning the authority of the author and the terms on which I come to write the book. The result is very much a kaleidoscope of ideas and dialogues, none of which are considered as *the* feminist approach to international law; all of which, I hope, inspire further feminist dialogues on the successes, tensions, and futures of gender law reform in the global order.

In chapter 2 I start with an analysis of the rise of expertise in the global order. This chapter is influenced by the work of critical legal scholar Kennedy on the rise of expertise as a technique of global governance.[101] I draw out the importance of expertise, its connection to other technologies of global governance, such as indicators and metrics, and analyse the emergence of gender expertise as a specific technology of the contemporary global order. I find gender expertise becomes the technique of global governance and with insufficient investment from international actors beyond the appointment of gender expertise, the difficult and careful work of UN Women becomes a specialised regime within the global order that frustrates earlier commitments within the UN to gender mainstreaming. The Paris Agreement on climate change, the use of gender expertise during the Ebola crisis in West Africa, and the African Women's decade provide examples of the light touch of expertise. The examples draw out the same conclusions: that the contours of international law shape gender expertise to produce radical, liberal, and cultural feminist outcomes that diminish the capacity for entrenched intersectionality. I conclude the chapter with a discussion of intersectionality, drawing on Otto's description of the politics of listening as an important adjunct to dialogues on developing intersectionality within international law.

Chapter 3 builds the argument in favour of an embedded intersectionality within feminist dialogues on international law through an analysis of fragmentation (or diversification). I argue that engaging with contemporary accounts of fragmentation illuminates the fragmentation of gender law reform across specific spaces of global governance, while also explaining the development of gender expertise as a specialised regime. The additional consequence is a fragmented feminism that sees the rise of some feminist approaches within the global order while other approaches are pushed to the peripheries. Mindful of the risk of replicating difference I use fragmentation, and the developed critical accounts of legal pluralism, to theorise

---

[101] David Kennedy, *A World of Struggle: How Power, Law and Expertise Shape Global Political Economy* (Princeton 2016); Gina Heathcote, 'From "People with Projects" to "Encountering Expertise": A Feminist Reading of Kennedy's A World of Struggle' (2016) 4(3) London Review of International Law 467.

difference as requiring an epistemological shift towards plural subjectivities, thus entrenching difference as a feminist knowledge rather than a description of individuals. Drawing on Brah's writing on diasporic subjectivities, Braidotti's account of the nomad, and Kapur's articulation of peripheral subjects I argue for the arrival of diversity through an account of intersectionality that is attentive to difference at its base.[102]

Chapter 4 analyses state sovereignty. Feminist attention within international law to state sovereignty benefits from some important early studies, from Knop and Charlesworth, but very little analysis of the state as a foundational element of the international law order appears in the new millennium.[103] Chapter 4 attempts to revive feminist dialogues on state sovereignty and builds a case for the redescription of legal subjectivity as split subjects, to better account for the relational nature of all subjects. The chapter responds to Otomo's call for feminist accounts to fill 'the *space* created by failures of masculinist international law' and imagines how legal subjectivity might be rescripted as relational and with a capacity to incorporate historical ties and splits between subjects.[104] I provide an analysis of the responsibility to protect and the law on secession in chapter 4 to demonstrate the usefulness of legal subjectivity understood as built around split subjects. Chapter 4 argues for the split subject as a methodology building an international order centred on the capacity to work in concert rather than through coercion.

Chapter 5 expands the feminist dialogues further through an analysis of international institutions. Rather than focusing on gender law reform I provide an analysis of the structure and design of three different international institutions: the Human Rights Council, the World Health Organisation, and the Peacebuilding Commission. I develop the account of plural and split subjects from previous chapters to further engage feminist epistemologies as a mechanism for structural bias feminisms. To this end I explore theories of the maternal, in particular Gedalof's description of a theory of interruption,[105] the politics of location,[106] and the political economy of gender,[107] not as isolated approaches but as the types of feminist conversations that might be evolved to rethink approaching international institutions. I then expand these conversations further; thinking through strategies for mindfulness of the richness of crip and queer approaches.

The book concludes with an analysis of authority—including, in terms of how the executive authority of the Security Council is enhanced via the advances in gender law reform. I question the feminist proclivity for seeking legal responses and the authority from which feminist scholars, in this case me, write. The chapter seeks to push forward the dialogues engaged throughout the book through appreciating

---

[102] Brah (n 10); Braidotti (n 10); Kapur (n 10).

[103] Knop, 'Re/Statements' (n 52); Hilary Charlesworth, 'The Sex of the State in International Law' in Ngaire Naffine and Rosemary Owens (eds), *Sexing the Subject of Law* (Law Book Company 1997).

[104] Otomo (n 11) 35.

[105] Irene Gedalof, 'Interruptions, Reproduction and the Genealogies of Staying Put in Diaspora Space' (2012) 100 Feminist Review 72.

[106] Sara Ahmed, *Strange Encounters: Embodied Others in Postcoloniality* (Routledge 2000).

[107] Jacqui True, *The Political Economy of Violence against Women* (Oxford University Press 2012).

fully what the call to prioritise a politics of listening means in practice. The chapter examines the Security Council's counterterrorism strategies and how the women, peace, and security framework has been used to develop gender initiatives in some but not all of the Counter Terrorism Committee's work. Drawing on literature and non-legal feminist strategies, I analyse the desire for the law to grant legitimacy to feminist projects. The chapter concludes with the voices of indigenous Australian women, having noted that part of the conditions of my own speaking is the suppression of indigenous voices, histories, and knowledge in Australia.

To return to Gbowee's call to feminist action—'[i]t's time for women to stop being politely angry'[108]—presupposes a female form that women, globally, are imagined to understand and internalise in a universal fashion. This approach sits comfortably within the realm of sex difference and accepts heterosexual privilege and ordering. As noted above, this book calls for a different sort of feminist action: a series of feminist dialogues that are concentrated on knowledge-production and epistemologies for change, thinking through what it means to have a feminist approach to international law that is no longer dependent on the category of 'women', that searches out the nuances, silences, and differences in feminist histories, that embraces, disrupts, and expands feminist methodologies, ponders feminist transnationalism, and centres international law as a part of future dialogues, successes, and tensions.

---

[108] Pesta (n 3).

2

Expertise

1. Introduction

On 1 April 2016, the Institute for Digital Archaeology reconstructed and erected a near-replica of the Palmyra Arch in Trafalgar Square in London, UK using 3-D printer technology.[1] The expertise and technology behind the endeavour is as much a celebration of contemporary know-how as it is celebration of the arch, destroyed by violence unleased by ISIS in the Syrian state.[2] The creative impulse to reconstruct the relic was intended as a symbolic and powerful message to those who continue to use violence to gain political power. And yet. And yet, the building of the £100,000 arch through 3-D printer technology is also, in many ways, a triumph of expertise and technology that masks the inhumanity of the violence in Syria: violence not only eradicating cultural relics, such as the architectural wonder of Palmyra, but also the ongoing violence of multiple actors, including the Syrian state, that has displaced and killed millions of people in Syria. Likewise, the fraught history of looting and loss in relation to cultural property that exists between London and the Middle East is ignored in the erection of the arch in Trafalgar Square, or as Burch writes, 'Trafalgar Square is a haunt replete with monumental ghosts of empire'.[3]

No technology can replicate the lives and meaning lost to displacement and death and geopolitical histories implicated in military violence. In traversing the current era of technology and expertise it is easy to be blind to the persistent relic and cultural legacy of humanity: destruction, killing, cruelty, and inhumane acts that emerge in all decades, all centuries, and all millennia.[4] This chapter considers

---

[1] Mark Brown, 'Palmyra's Arch of Triumph recreated in Trafalgar Square' *The Guardian* (London, 19 April 2016) <http://www.theguardian.com/culture/2016/apr/19/palmyras-triumphal-arch-recreated-in-trafalgar-square> last accessed 31 May 2018; Stuart Burch, 'A Virtual Oasis: Trafalgar Square's Arch of Palmyra' (2017) 11(3) International Journal of Architectural Research 58, 67, indicating 'What was eventually built, however, was a two-thirds scale model of the curved Arch of Triumph that formed one end of Palmyra's colonnade. As well as being reduced in size, it is also shorn of the two lesser arches by which it was flanked.'

[2] Opinions differ on what the Arch celebrates and records: see Burch (n 1) 72, stating: 'It is a crowning irony that a movement seeking to deprive other groups of their monuments should be gifted a memorial to their destructiveness'; also see Sam Kriss, 'Views My Own: Why Recreating the Palmyra Arch in London was Smug, Hypocritical and Tacky' (*Vice*, 25 April 2016) <http://www.vice.com/en_uk/read/palmyras-arch-trafalgar-square-dubai-new-york> last accessed 31 May 2018.

[3] Burch (n 1) 63.

[4] A quite different reconstruction has been undertaken by Amnesty International to create a virtual model of the Saydnaya prison, and the violence associated with it: Eyal Weizman, 'Saydnaya: Inside a Syrian Torture Prison' (*Amnesty International*, 2016) <https://saydnaya.amnesty.org/> last accessed 31

Feminist Dialogues on International Law. Gina Heathcote. © Gina Heathcote 2019. Published 2019 by Oxford University Press.

expertise and technology as well as the latent political and ethical meanings within technology that can obscure the space of political action and reduce it to, what Arendt describes as, know-how.[5] There is a gap between a 3-D printed arch, which provides a snapshot or facsimile of the relic at a single moment in time, and the arch destroyed that had persisted/transformed over generations.[6] Likewise, there is a gap between gender expertise, as a technique of global governance, and the transnational feminisms that, I argue, gender law reform becomes a near-replica of. Consequently, this chapter examines the rise of gender expertise within global governance to pay attention to what is lost, subsumed and forgotten in the techniques of global governance; just as attention to what is lost in the technologically clever 3-D replica of the arch of Palmyra is useful for understanding the interplay of history, technology, violence, and political progress.

My argument extends from the role of expertise within international institutions, as examined by scholars across various critical spaces of inquiry, to the specifics of gender expertise. The chapter examines how transnational feminist histories and actions become subsumed within and yet expunged from gender law reform within international law.[7] In particular, I pay attention to the violent, raced, colonial histories of gender—at once more complex than global governance can represent and embroiled in the history of global governance itself. Just as the imperial signifiers of the arch-in-London cannot be ignored, the imperial dimensions of gender law reform cannot be overlooked. Furthermore, I consider that a great deal of gender law reform functions as a plastic, near-replica of the complex feminist transnational knowledge and histories that the reforms are expected to incorporate and replicate within global governance; ultimately erasing more feminist knowledge than they integrate.

While I focus on expertise in this chapter, the argument interlocks with studies of other technologies of contemporary global governance such as indicators, metrics, and measures. In Powell's study of World Bank gender indicators, she describes the development of gender technologies within international institutions as having:

May 2018; similarly the #newpalmyra project, founded by Bassel Khartabil—who was unlawfully executed by the Syrian regime in 2017—works to construct a detailed and accurate virtual version of the arch: see <http://www.newpalmyra.org/> last accessed 31 May 2018.

[5] Hannah Arendt, *The Human Condition* (2nd edn, Chicago 1998); Gina Heathcote, 'LAWs, UFOs and UAVs: Feminist Encounters with the Law of Armed Conflict' in Dale Stephens and Paul Barbie (eds), *Imagining Law: Essays in Conversation with Judith Gardam* (University of Adelaide Press 2017) 253.

[6] Burch (n 1) 72: 'Copious archives of artistic depictions and historical photographs capture it in various states of preservation. Consequently, the object has existed in multiple guises through recorded history. An asynchronous composite reconstruction would retain memories of the life of the monument as opposed to simply how it just happened to have been constituted before its evisceration'; Mohamed Abdulmonem, 'Architectural and Urban Heritage in the Digital Age: Dilemmas of Authenticity, Originality and Reproduction' (2017) 11 International Journal of Architectural Research 5.

[7] Hilary Charlesworth, 'Talking to Ourselves? Feminist Scholarship in International Law' in Sari Kouvo and Zoe Pearson (eds), *Feminist Perspectives on Contemporary International Law: Between Resistance and Compliance* (Hart 2011) 17.

limited capacity either to deconstruct structures of dominance and subordination or to pave the way to new structures that move societies toward substantive equality. Instead, these gender indicators are geared toward measuring and coaxing inclusion of women in existing structures, which are largely defined by traditional 'male-oriented' models of success.[8]

I focus on expertise, rather than indicators, metrics, or technology, to address the proclivity of global institutions to insert a 'gender expert' as a mechanism of gender law reform. At the same time I trace the relationship between the turn to expertise as a component of the turn to indicators, metrics, and technology and the techniques of neoliberal modes of global governance.[9]

In addressing the deployment of gender expertise as a technology of global governance, the chapter follows Arendt's study of knowledge as know-how, absent of (political) thought and action.[10] In terms of gender law reform, I align Arendt's ideas on know-how with Charlesworth's recognition of feminist messages, absent feminist methods, as a feature of gender law reform.[11] I argue for the necessity of listening to the political and ethical histories that are stripped from visibility in the application of measurement tools and via the curating of gender expertise within the global order. This gives insight into how transnational feminist histories are subsumed and expunged, such that gender becomes segregated from other sites of power and privilege and co-opted into civilising and/or neoliberal governance models. For example, and as a consequence, the importance of intersectionality within transnational feminist frameworks does not 'travel' into gender law reform within global governance. This perpetuates the imperial and legitimating dimensions of gender law reform, that then attract labels of 'neoliberal feminism',[12] 'governance feminism',[13] and 'faux feminism',[14] amongst others.[15] I analyse a range of examples of gender law reform and the incorporated notions of gender expertise in this chapter: the Paris Agreement on Climate Change, the deployment of gender expertise to West Africa in 2014 to respond to the spread of Ebola, the incorporation of gender into NATO training initiatives, and the configuration of the African Women's Decade. I demonstrate the fraught positioning of the gender expert as representative of a host of feminist strategies, and ideas, and yet constrained by the existing institutional and legal structures. In the discussion of the Paris Agreement I demonstrate the gap between the agenda of UN Women and the realisation of its various projects within the specific sub-regimes of the United Nations, highlighting

---

[8] Catherine Powell, 'Gender Indicators as Global Governance: Not Your Father's World Bank' (2016) 17 Georgetown Journal of Gender and Law 777, 806.

[9] UNSC Resolution 1889 (5 October 2009) UN Doc S/RES/1889 para 7 'requests the Secretary-General to continue, as appropriate, to appoint gender advisors and/or women-protection advisors to United Nations missions'.

[10] Arendt (n 5).   [11] Charlesworth (n 7).

[12] Catherine Rottenberg, 'The Rise of Neoliberal Feminism' (2014) 28 Cultural Studies 418.

[13] Janet Halley, Prabha Kotiswaran, Hila Shamir, and Chantal Thomas, 'From the International to the Local in Feminist Legal Responses to Rape, Prostitution/ Sex Work and Sex Trafficking: Four Cases Studies in Contemporary Governance Feminism' (2006) 29 Harvard Journal of Law and Governance 335.

[14] Angela McRobbie, *The Aftermath of Feminism: Gender, Culture and Social Change* (Sage 2009) 24.

[15] Elisabeth Prügl, 'Neoliberalising Feminism' (2015) 20 New Political Economy 614, 615.

the uneven development of gender expertise within global governance, as well as the very narrow message of gender law reform contained (or rather the message that the expert is the gender law reform).[16] As a consequence, important legal tools, such as the Paris Agreement, remain resistant to the complexity of messages and methods within feminist scholarship, despite the productive history of feminist engagement with, in this example, environmental issues and understandings of the gender implications of climate change.[17]

Beyond expertise, the range of emergent technologies and international legal responses to technology (including automated weapons systems, unmanned ground and/or aerial vehicles, and human enhancement systems, such as exoskeletons) and the very limited analysis of the regimes of technology transfer and the role of scientific expertise within global governance,[18] raise complex ethical and legal questions. Additional concerns with respect to global inequalities, which are often masked by the focus on the technology or scientific knowledge, are also overlooked.[19] I speak of both technologies, in the sense of methods of ordering and disciplining individuals through tools of governmentality that encourage subjects to internalise interdictions, and technology, in the sense of devices developed through the application of science and innovation.[20] These discussions haunt the focus of this chapter which examines expertise in the international realm as a technology of global governance and examines how this has shifted political spaces drawn from thought, in the sense of political action grounded through a connection to ideologies and communities. I examine how this facilitates a shift towards the international political domain as a space increasingly directed via know-how that is understood through the rise of expertise as a central component of the global order.[21] Technology also frames the

---

[16] UN Doc FCCC/CP/2015/L9/Rev (12 December 2015).

[17] Ruth Meinzen-Dick, Chiara Kovarik, and Agnes B Quisumbing, 'Gender and Sustainability' (2014) 39 Annual Review of Environmental Resources 29; Sherilyn MacGregor, *Routledge Handbook of Gender and Environment* (Routledge 2017); Farah Kabir, 'Toward a More Gender-Inclusive Climate Change Policy' in Nazmunnessa Mahtab, Tania Hague, Ishrat Khan, M Mynul Islam, and Ishret B Wahid (eds), *Handbook of Research on Women's Issues and Rights in the Developing World* (IGI Global 2018); Amber J Fletcher, 'More Than Women and Men: A Framework for Intersectionality Research on Environmental Crisis' in Christianne Frölich, Giovanna Gioli, Roger Cremades, and Henri Myrttinen (eds), *Water Security Across the Gender Divide* (Springer 2018); Farhana Sultana, 'Gender and Water in a Changing Climate: Challenges and Opportunities' in Christianne Frölich, Giovanna Gioli, Roger Cremades, and Henri Myrttinen (eds), *Water Security Across the Gender Divide* (Springer 2018).

[18] Gina Heathcote, 'War's Perpetuity: Disabled Bodies of War and the Exoskeleton of Equality' (2018) 44(1) Australian Feminist Law Journal 71.

[19] Elisa Morgera and Mara Ntona, 'Linking Small-scale Fisheries to International Obligations on Marine Technology Transfer' (2017) 93 Marine Policy <https://doi.org/10.1016/j.marpol.2017.07.021> last accessed 31 May 2018; Arianna Broggiato, 'Marine Genetic Resources Beyond National Jurisdiction: Coordination and Harmonisation of Governance Regimes' (2011) 41(1) Environmental Law and Policy 35; Arianna Broggiato, Sophie Arnaud-Haond, Claudio Chiarolla, and Thomas Greiber, 'Fair and Equitable Sharing of Benefits from the Utilization of Marine Genetic Resources in Areas Beyond National Jurisdiction: Bridging the Gaps between Science and Policy' (2014) 49(c) Marine Policy 176; Philippe Cullet, *Differential Treatment in Environmental Law* (Routledge 2032).

[20] Michel Foucault, 'Technologies of the Self' in Luther Martin (ed), *Technologies of the Self: A Seminar with Michel Foucault* (Tavistock 1988).

[21] Sally Engle Merry, 'Measuring the World: Indicators, Human Rights and Global Governance' (2011) 52(S3) Current Anthropology S83; David Kennedy, 'Challenging Expert Rule: The Politics

discussion as holding the potential for the expansion of the rise of expertise into new technological forms in the near future of international law.[22] Expertise raises the spectre of both technologies and technology as integral to the future of global governance, and with specific gendered meanings embedded in both process and products.[23] In this sense, the chapter is an adjunct to contemporary analysis of the use of indicators and metrics within global governance, and to work on present and future technology, as an integral component of neoliberal law and governance techniques.[24]

The ethical and political dimensions of non-human intelligence and human enhancement systems link concretely with the deployment of metrics and measures via institutional apparatus and the use of algorithms as both measurement tool and predecessor to new technological forms and, potentially, new subjects.[25] A persistent set of claims with respect to new forms of technology is that they are not inherently good or bad, that they eliminate human bias, and that they eradicate human errors.[26] This chapter considers how these understandings of technology are already configured in the work of international institutions through the work of expertise—which is rendered scientific, objective, and measurable such that human error, human choice, and ethical/political concerns are assumed to be stripped from their application. In the words of Kennedy, experts are framed as 'background' actors who provide common sense tools for foreground (politically motivated) actors.[27] I argue that contrary to the view of technology and expertise as neutral, technologies of early twenty-first-century governance entrench specific world views that can be demonstrated via an analysis of gender expertise similar to how measures and indicators have been analysed.[28] Consequently, beyond measurements and indicators and prior to engagement with new technology, attention needs to be paid to expertise to account for the entrenched bias and assumptions reproduced in the deployment of

---

of Global Governance' (2005) 27 Sydney Law Review, 5; Martti Koskenniemi, 'The Fate of Public International Law: Between Techniques and Politics' (2007) 70 Modern Law Review 1.

[22] Yoriko Otomo, *Unconditional Life: The Postwar International Law Settlement* (Oxford University Press 2016) 49–63.

[23] Doris Buss, 'Measurement Imperatives and Gender Politics: An Introduction' (2015) 22 Social Policy: International Studies in Gender, State and Society 381.

[24] Amanda Perry-Kessaris, 'The Re-co-construction of Legitimacy of/through the Doing Business Indicators' (2018) 13 International Journal of Law in Context 498; Tor Krever, 'Quantifying Law: Legal Indicator Projects and the Reproduction of Neoliberal Commonsense' (2013) 34 Third World Quarterly 131.

[25] Fleur Johns, 'Global Governance through the Pairing of List and Algorithm' (2016) 34 Environment and Planning D: Society and Space 126.

[26] Linell Letendre, 'Women Warriors: Why the Robotics Revolution Changes the Combat Equation' (2016) 6 PRISM 91, 95–98.

[27] David Kennedy, *A World of Struggle: How Power, Law and Expertise Shape Global Political Economy* (Princeton 2016) 7; Gina Heathcote, 'From "People with Projects" to "Encountering Expertise": A Feminist Reading of Kennedy's A World of Struggle' (2016) 4(3) London Review of International Law 467.

[28] Amanda Perry-Kessaris, 'Prepare Your Indicators: Economic Imperialism on the Shores of Law and Development' (2011) 7 International Journal of Law in Context 401; Kevin E Davis, Angelina Fisher, Benedict Kingsbury, and Sally Engle Merry, *Governance by Indicators: Global Power through Quantification and Rankings* (Oxford University Press 2012); Buss (n 23).

expertise, or to use Kennedy's terminology, to bring the background actors into the foreground. Unlike Kennedy I do not refer here to the actual actors, rather I wish to centre on how the idea of gender expertise is a governance technique. As such, gender expertise often functions to frame and entrench the position of the institution deploying it rather than opening up avenues for feminist law reform.

In the next section, after a review of Arendt's distinction between know-how and political action, I introduce gender expertise and key critical scholarship on the technologies of neoliberalism understood via study of indicators and expertise. I add to this a review of existing feminist analysis of gender expertise found in the work of feminist international relations and development scholars. In section 3 I look with greater detail at the affects and effects of gender expertise as a form of gender law reform. I examine the specific manifestations of gender expertise within the Paris Agreement on climate change, during the Ebola crisis in West Africa, in the work of NATO, and through the lens of the African Women's Decade. I conclude the chapter with an analysis of transnational feminist histories and intersectionality, as feminist methods, as tools (or methods) for understanding gender expertise, and gender law reform, in global governance differently.

Throughout this chapter I am mindful that academic critiques of gender law reform within international law and institutions are often precariously poised as potential criticisms of the work of individual gender experts and actors. It is important to explicitly state that this chapter is not a criticism, or even critique, of the work of the individuals who inhabit the role of gender expert in the global order. Rather, this chapter seeks to explore the limitations of academic feminist accounts that at once demand more from gender experts and yet imagine the gender expert as a feminist actor with almost magical power to transform international legal structures from the inside. Through connecting the account to the critical legal study of the role of expertise within the global order, the chapter demonstrates, like the study of fragmentation in the following chapter, the continuities between developments with respect to gender and those within the discipline of international law. However, the chapter works to look beyond the critique offered, to work to construct multiple alternatives to a model of gender cast as a series of technical interventions and as a space of know-how. In doing so, I hope to render visible how gender expertise in the international realm is often dislodged from the thinking that characterises the political and ethical origins of gender analysis and techniques (feminism). I argue that this is due to the demands of the institutional arena that are ultimately inimical to multiple feminisms and feminist methods.

2. Approaching Expertise

In this section I briefly introduce Arendt's distinction between know-how and political action and then provide a general map of the role gender expertise has come to play within international institutional structures. This is followed by a review of the key critical legal scholarship on the technologies of neoliberalism understood via study of indicators and expertise. As the notion of the gender expert as a technique of global governance has received only limited attention from feminist legal scholars, I turn to the existing feminist analysis of gender expertise found in the work of feminist international relations and development scholars to conclude this section. Through examining both the spaces and the potential of gender experts in global governance this chapter illuminates the fraught role of the gender expert within these international institutional structures and advances.

My approach in this chapter is influenced by the work of Arendt that posits a distinction between knowledge/know-how and thought.[29] For Arendt, knowledge is characterised as technical and scientific know-how, while thought is derived through engagements, reflections, and encounters within the political domain (characterised as action by Arendt). For Arendt, the late-twentieth-century shift towards knowledge, rendered possible through developments in technology (and perhaps further enumerated in the post-millennium era), leaves humanity 'at the mercy of every gadget which is technically possible no matter how murderous it is'.[30] The move away from the political sphere of action, where thought is valued and characterised, towards a space of doing, characterised by technical know-how, seems to epitomise the shift from feminist politics and ethics, as theorised, reflected, and debated in transnational and transversal spaces,[31] towards the spectre of gender as technical, measurable, and understood via indicators and expertise in the international institutional space. A desire to understand this shift from feminist thinking (encompassing message and methods, as well as the multiplicities of feminist approaches) towards a constant need for know-how in the international order produced via expertise, and the consequent implications for feminist approaches to international law, propels this chapter. I make the argument that gender expertise within international law functions as both technology, in the sense of being deployed as devoid of political or ethical commitments and thus a space for perceived technical competencies, and as a technology of global governance, in the sense of disciplining some subjects and imposing a form of gender law reform that never refracts back onto the institution deploying expertise.

To explore how gender expertise operates in these ways within the global order I will begin by mapping the locations where gender expertise has emerged as a component of institutional workings on the international plane. This is no easy task, as there are multiple sites where gender expertise functions as a site of knowledge (or know-how) within international institutions and is an ever-increasing arena of global governance. I will divide the description into the international, regional, and national to understand different sites of expertise, although as the description develops it is clear that across these three sites temporal and geographic continuities link these actors and the circles they operate both in and through. In looking at how gender expertise emerges within the global order, I demonstrate how the institutional ordering compounds the failure of gender reflexivity within international

---

[29] Arendt (n 5) 3.   [30] ibid.
[31] Nira Yuval-Davis, 'Human/Women's Rights and Feminist Transversal Politics' in Myra Marx Ferree and Aili Mari Tripp (eds), *Transnational Feminisms: Women's Global Activism and Human Rights* (New York University Press 2006).

institutions through the selective apertures that open to accommodate very specific types of expertise.

Gender expertise at the international level has its UN antecedents in the creation of the Committee for the Status of Women in 1946, International Women's Year in 1975, the UN Decade for Women 1976–1985, the Declaration on the Elimination of Discrimination Against Women, and the drafting of the Convention on the Elimination of Discrimination Against Women (CEDAW) between 1976 and 1979. Prior to this, women's initiatives existed throughout the life of the League of Nations and the life of international relations more generally although the stories and impacts are more often left out of official histories.[32] The Women's Peace Congress at The Hague in 1915 saw 1,200 women from twelve states meet in The Hague and produce a series of resolutions on peace and cooperation in the international order. The resolutions are focused on achieving peace, rather than specifically focusing on women's issues. Furthermore, throughout the twentieth century women lobbied and acted through both the League and the UN, as well as regionally and nationally, nevertheless most accounts focus on post-CEDAW initiatives as the history of international women's movements.[33] Important feminist voices from Jane Addams to Madame Anna Bugge-Wicksell and Valentine Dannevig in Western states are not recorded in international legal histories.[34] Likewise, despite their presence, female and feminist actors are not recognised as contributors to the formation of international legal knowledge and, most certainly, women beyond Western states are even harder to trace although their presence and views contributed to the development of international law and its institutions.

The Beijing Conference on Women in 1995 was the fourth World Conference on Women and saw the emergence of the language of gender mainstreaming within the UN, and more broadly in global initiatives, as well as stronger transnational links between women's groups, globally, that were also strengthened by the changing technologies developed during this period.[35] By the time the Beijing plus Five Report was issued in 2000,[36] these networks had orchestrated a space for concerted women's advocacy within the new International Criminal Court, at the Security Council,

[32] Dianne Otto, 'Sign of "Weakness"? Disrupting Gender Certainties in Security Council Resolution 1325' (2006) 13 Michigan Journal of Gender and Law 113; Jane Rendall, *The Origins of Modern Feminism: Women in Britain, France and the United States 1780–1860* (Palgrave 1985); Andrea Bianchi, *International Law Theories: An Inquiry into Different Ways of Thinking* (Oxford University Press 2016) ch 9; Arvonne Fraser, 'Becoming Human: The Origins and Development of Women's Human Rights' (1999) 21 Human Rights Quarterly 853.

[33] Aili Mari Tripp, 'The Evolution of Transnational Feminisms: Consensus, Conflict and New Dynamics' in Myra Marx Ferree and Aili Mari Tripp (eds), *Global Feminism: Transnational Women's Activism, Organizing, and Human Rights* (New York University Press 2006).

[34] Christine Chinkin, Gina Heathcote, Emily Jones, and Henry Jones, 'Bozkurt Case (aka the Lotus Case) France v Turkey: Two Ships that Go Bump in the Night' in Loveday Hodson and J Troy Lavers, *Feminist International Judgement Project* (Hart 2019); Susan Pederson, 'Metaphors of the Schoolroom: Women Working the Mandate System of the League of Nations' (2008) 66 History Workshop Journal 188.

[35] Julie Mertus, 'The Kitchen Table' in Marguerite Waller and Jennifer Rycenga (eds), *Frontline Feminisms: Women, War, and Resistance* (Routledge 2000).

[36] UNGA, 'Implementation of the Outcome of the Fourth World Conference on Women and of the Special Session of the General Assembly entitled "Women 2000: Gender Equality, Development and Peace in the Twenty First Century" ' (30 August 2000) 55th Session (2000) UN Doc A/55/341; Dianne

and within Economic and Social policy at the UN. The UN had, by this stage, developed four primary sites where expertise on women's lives emerged: the UN Development Fund for Women (UNIFEM); the Division for the Advancement of Women (DAW), incorporating the CEDAW and the Commission on the Status of Women (CSW); the Office of the Special Adviser on Gender Issues (OSAGI), and the UN International Research and Training Institute for the Advancement of Women (UN-INSTRAW). After 2010 these institutional bodies became linked via the creation of the overarching structure of UN Women. With the creation of UN Women, the visibility of gender expertise within UN structures mirrors the rise of experts more concretely within international institutions: as potential background actors who are called to give advice and know-how across an increasing range of concerns and actions. Elsewhere, Hodson describes the CEDAW Committee as holding 'positions both at the centre and at the periphery of international law' and a similar claim might be made of UN Women.[37] The creation of UN Women was intended to draw gender law reform into a central coordinated space at the UN; however, its creation also, potentially, pushes gender to the periphery of the concerns of other specialised agencies and international organisations, as is demonstrated in the analysis of the Paris Agreement, below.

The CEDAW monitoring mechanisms have also been influential in giving rise to a space for gender expertise, despite the treaty's anti-discrimination focus.[38] Furthermore, the CEDAW Committee's role in advancing and developing awareness of the interlocking nature of discrimination and violence against women has been instrumental in guiding state level transformation, for individual women and via policy.[39] This has included attention from the CEDAW Committee to the intersectional dimensions in the application of the treaty in specific states, where attention to the different needs of rural, economically disadvantaged, and migrant women has occurred. However, the CEDAW regime, as a space for human rights protections and specifically anti-discrimination review is distinct from the other sites of gender expertise analysed in this section. That is, whereas CEDAW speaks to states and engages states on issues raised through its reporting mechanisms, the bulk of gender expertise functions within and across UN/institutional dialogues rather than as directives with regard to legal change internal to a state. Beyond CEDAW the capacity for international institutions to lead change at the level of state practice, therefore, is less evident in terms of the 'successes' of feminist approaches within international law. However, the capacity of the reporting mechanisms under

Otto, 'Holding Up Half the Sky: A Critical Analysis of the Fourth World Conference on Women' (1996) 6 Australian Feminist Law Journal 7.

[37] Loveday Hodson, 'Women's Rights and the Periphery: CEDAW's Optional Protocol' (2014) 25(2) European Journal of International Law 561.

[38] Hodson (ibid 565) describes CEDAW as 'forged through formal legal processes. Its creators were not terribly ambitious for it and it is clearly a constricted instrument. CEDAW adopts a minimalist liberal agenda, focussing, its name suggests, primarily on the equality of men and women.'

[39] Hodson (n 37); Catherine O'Rourke and Aisling Swaine, 'CEDAW and the Security Council: Enhancing Women's Rights in Conflict' (2018) 67 International and Comparative Law Quarterly 167, 171 describing the CEDAW Committee as 'singularly capable of pursuing meaningful State accountability within a human rights framework'.

CEDAW to change, rather than simply hope to influence, state behaviour is limited. The Security Council's requirement of National Action Plans from states on women, peace, and security creates one space of additional dialogue between international institutions and states. Nevertheless, there remains a structural distinction between states that articulate normative developments and those states that are the perceived recipients of those developments. This distinction remains embedded in the construction of gender law reform, particularly in the context of gender and security, and reasserts the imperial history of international law, where gender law reform has a clear history as a marker of civilised status.[40]

In addition to tensions between who gender law reform addresses and the civilising role it often takes, significant pockets of global governance remain distanced from global gender law reform, in particular international financial institutions,[41] technical and scientific bodies, and those attentive to foundational legal knowledge, for example, the International Law Commission, the International Court of Justice, and the General Assembly (except within its specific gender/women-focused sub-bodies). Furthermore, late-twentieth-century accounts of international legal histories are focused primarily on the production of specific institutional advances with respect to gender law reform, despite important critical projects challenging the distinction between objects, subjects, and standard histories of international law.[42] Interrogation of when and where—and to whom—gender law reform is regarded as important has received insufficient attention. Key early developments on gender, such as the 1915 Peace Resolutions, or more recent regional contributions, such as the Maputo Protocol, that champion and transform institutional responses to both international law and women's lives are often under researched and/or under-represented in both scholarly and institutional accounts. Even the Beijing Platform for Action has rarely been analysed in terms of the substantive contribution it made to international law, as the focus is usually on the gender law reform possibilities.

In a similar vein, Cornwall and Rivas, in analysing gender and development strategies, argue for a need to build feminist institutional transformations that 'can deliver the kinds of deep-rooted structural changes needed to achieve a more just and equal world'.[43] The impact of gender law reform on international law and its institutions is not yet a focus of analysis (as opposed to the impact of gender law reform on women's issues). At the same time the institutional developments 'stand in' as feminist success stories so that it is possible to tell (at least) two tales of gender consciousness within the structures of global governance. The first tale centres on the existing

---

[40] I discuss this further in chapter 5.

[41] The World Bank presents an interesting example where gender is used as a structure to impose targets on receiver states but not a goal or aspiration for donor states or the institution itself: see Lucy Ferguson, ' "This is Our Gender Person": The Messy Business of Working as a Gender Expert in Gender and Development' (2015) 17 International Feminist Journal of Politics 380.

[42] Madeleine Chaim, Luis Eslava, Genevieve R Painter, Sydney R Parfitt, and Charlotte Peevers, 'History, Anthropology and the Archive of International Law' (2017) 5(1) London Review of International Law 3.

[43] Andrea Cornwall and Althea-Maria Rivas, 'From "Gender Equality" to "Women's Empowerment" to Global Justice: Reclaiming a Transformative Agenda for Gender and Development' (2015) 36(2) Third World Quarterly 396, 397.

mechanisms that are attentive to, and have a history of, focus on women's rights and concerns as well as, more recently, gender mainstreaming or gender equality. The second story is one of absence with respect to gender perspectives, mainstreaming, or women's rights and is largely found in structures of global governance that might be deemed functional, technical, or foundational. Even within institutions such as the Security Council which has a gender agenda through the women, peace, and security resolutions, there is a silence on gender in relation to its core work on collective security, in particular the authorisation of force.

Regional governing spaces have less often attracted attention from international legal scholars for how gender expertise has emerged, despite functioning as an important component of institutional structures. In fact, women's NGOs and networks often function parallel to large regional networks; for example, Asian women's networks are an effective site of lobbying, action, and policy.[44] In regional African structures, gender initiatives, such as the African Union's Women, Gender, and Development Unit, alongside the Economic Community of West African States (ECOWAS) Gender Development Centre, and the Southern African Development Community (SADC) Protocol on Gender Development, provide important regional specific regimes and policies on gender and women's rights that have histories that have often gained insufficient attention within global arenas.[45] The AU's decision to make 2010 through to 2020 the African Women's Decade has also helped entrench policies on gender and women's rights within the organisation and within member states. The AU's gender institutions function through coordinating the work of Gender Ministers in member states and providing a forum for Gender Ministers to work together. The consequence is strategies on gender mainstreaming on the African continent that are rarely developed or mirrored in the global order. For example, no international forum for women's ministers exists and many states do not have women's ministers. In terms of regional African law, the Maputo Protocol remains a comprehensive international instrument on women's rights—with a much wider remit than CEDAW.[46] The existence of regional initiatives and law highlights the myopic view of global governance that exists within international legal scholarship which pays little, if any, attention to these sites of knowledge and the application of existing provisions on women's rights and gender reform outside of the Global North and within states that often find themselves on the peripheries of international law-making.

Beyond the regional, domestic reliance on gender expertise emerges through international policies imposing expectations regarding gender indicators, as well as via the development of specific domestic structures with global impact, such as militaries, development organisations, and funding structures. Within domestic

---

[44] The work of the Asia Pacific Forum and Women, Law and Development is an excellent example: see <http://apwld.org/> last accessed 31 May 2018.

[45] Aili Mari Tripp and Balghis Badri, 'African Influences and Global Women's Activism: An Overview' in Aili Mari Tripp and Balghis Badri, *Women's Activism in Africa: Struggles for Rights and Representation* (Zed Books 2017).

[46] Fareda Banda, 'Blazing a Trail: The African Protocol on Women's Rights comes into Force' (2006) 50 Journal of African Law 72.

law, government offices for women and gender are often fragile in the sense of being vulnerable to political change, poorly funded, and insufficiently integrated into the larger work of government. The interlocking of regional and national gender structures—such as has evolved through the work of the AU—assists the entrenching of gender and women structures within domestic governance. The instigation of National Action Plans and Regional Action Plans under the women, peace, and security framework has created a specific space promoting the development of gender expertise on peace and security issues within states,[47] while national and regional military structures have also developed a range of roles for gender expertise to guide pre-deployment training and advice on gender matters.[48] However, these often reflect global inequalities in terms the entrenched distinction between states where these developments are expected to be incorporated and those where the normative structures are imagined to be articulated.

The additional space where gender experts have emerged is within post-conflict initiatives—as components of UN and regional missions, and as actors within newly constituted governing structures for post-conflict states. As a consequence of the women, peace, and security agenda and the Security Council's rule of law resolutions, the role of gender expertise ranges from peacekeeping, peacebuilding, and security sector reforms and, less often, peace enforcement. In 2015, the Security Council indicated Senior Gender Advisors would be placed in the offices of the Special Representatives of the Secretary-General, under UN Security Council Resolution 2242, as well as other senior gender advisors to be budgeted for and recruited to all UN missions.[49] The placing of gender advisors with seniority within UN peacekeeping and building missions was a specific attempt to prioritise women as leaders. The slippage here between the creation of senior gender posts and the prioritising of women in leadership posts is important in underscoring the confusion between women's participation and feminist/gender strategies.[50] This, it can be argued, is a constant tension present in all the initiatives described, whether regional, national, or international. Gender expertise and gender law reform are continually collapsed into responses to women's lives and/or the creation of roles for women. The result is a reification of gender as shorthand for women, and women as thus in need of legal protections or legal tools to assist women's participation, rather than gender as analytical expertise that raises different, important questions about the work of institutions, states, and law. Gender is better understood as 'not a thing: it

---

[47] Laura J Shepherd, 'The Women, Peace and Security Agenda at the United Nations' in Anthony Burke and Rita Parker (eds), *Global Insecurity: Futures of Global Chaos and Governance* (Springer 2017) 139, 147.

[48] Megan Bastick, 'Gender, Militaries and Security Sector Reform' in Rachel Woodward and Claire Duncanson (eds), *The Palgrave Handbook of Gender and the Military* (Palgrave 2017) 387, 393.

[49] UNSC Res 2242 (13 October 2015) UN Doc S/RES/2242.

[50] ibid, para 7 (which speaks of a commitment to developing gender expertise and to creating and enhancing women's leadership); Kenneth McDonagh and Maria-Adriana Deiana, *Add Women and Hope? Assessing the Gender Impact of EU Common Security and Defence Policy Missions: A Policy Report* January 2017 (Dublin City University 2017) <http://doras.dcu.ie/21744/1/Policy_Report_on_Add_Women_and_Hope_Feb_2017.pdf> last accessed 31 May 2018.

is a relation or more accurately a presentation of a relation',[51] and thus requiring gender expertise that engages analysis of the relational and framing power of gender.

Existing work on gender experts within international development discourse acknowledges the restraints on the capacity of gender experts within the developmental institutional agenda,[52] while critical legal studies evidence the masking of political agendas within quantitative measures.[53] Analysis from gender and development contexts also demonstrates how restraints include the existing hierarchies within those institutions and organisations,[54] the tension between the outward focus of gender agendas and gendered structures internalised by the organisation and/or institution, the space between academic reflexivity and institutional demands, and the 'low economic value' of gender expertise.[55] Despite this scholarship from within the discipline of gender and development, as well as critical legal scholarship on expertise in global governance,[56] and international relations scholarship on gender expertise, engagement with the role and expectations placed on gender experts has received little, if any, attention from within international legal accounts. Likewise, very little feminist legal scholarship on the way in which international law engages with the role of gender experts and the deployment of gender expertise currently exists.[57]

In identifying contemporary work on gender expertise that has emerged from feminist scholars and the range of claims made regarding the techniques and modes of expertise within development and international relations contexts, as well as the contribution from scholars writing on techniques of governance, such as indicators and metrics, within international law, I move towards a space for reflecting on what this means for gender law reform within international law and what this means in terms of feminist futures.[58] As such, this chapter extends work on gender expertise and global governance to posit the value of recognising tensions within feminist approaches that disrupt the very possibility of agreed metrics, measures, and indicators for gender work. In doing so, feminist analysis of structures and foundations, as well as feminist transnationalism attentive to historical and geographical diversity, is called into focus. Grewal and Kaplan describe this as a need to:

articulate the relationship of gender to scattered hegemonies, such as global economic structures, patriarchal nationalisms, 'authentic' forms of tradition, local structures of domination, and legal–judicial oppression on multiple levels … to compare multiple, overlapping and discrete oppressions rather than to construe a theory of hegemony under a unified category of gender.[59]

[51] Elspeth Probyn, *Eating the Ocean* (Duke University Press 2016) 108.

[52] Rottenberg (n 12).   [53] Merry (n 21).   [54] Ferguson (n 41).   [55] ibid.

[56] Kennedy, 'Challenging Expert Rule' (n 21).

[57] Charlesworth (n 7); Hilary Charlesworth and Mary Wood, 'Women and Human Rights in the Rebuilding of East Timor' (2002) 71 Nordic Journal of International Law 325.

[58] Prügl (n 15) 625 identifies a range of terms for feminist successes, suggesting 'scholars have coined new names for this type of feminism, one that seems far from generating structural change'. Prügl then lists market feminism, free market feminism, hegemonic feminism, imperial and management feminism, transnational business feminism, governance feminism, post-feminism, and faux feminism as the range of names given to feminist successes by a range of scholars across a range of disciplines.

[59] Inderpal Grewel and Caren Kaplan, 'Introduction: Transnational Feminist Practices and Questions of Postmodernity' in Inderpal Grewal and Caren Kaplan (eds), *Scattered Hegemonies: Postmodernity and Transnational Feminist Practices* (University of Minnesota Press 2006) 17.

I use Arendt's understanding of the know-how/thought distinction here to consider the consequences of feminist interventions into international law that re-emerge institutionally as gender expertise and that 'dismantle' the complexity of contemporary feminist thought.[60] In doing so I question the flattening out of feminist ethical and political tensions, as well as the dialogues produced by the turn to expertise, linking my account with broader critical legal work on indicators and expertise.[61]

Within scholarship on gender and development, key studies connect the rise of neoliberal development agendas with the co-optation of feminist projects into a specific series of methods and techniques of global governance. For Prügl the effect is threefold:

The different meanings of neoliberalism resonate in feminist critiques of contemporary feminism, describing three different facets of its neoliberalism, i.e. (a) the co-optation of feminism within neoliberal projects, (b) the integration of feminism into neoliberal ideology and (c) the interweaving of feminist ideas into rationalities and technologies of neoliberal governmentality.[62]

The concern, for Prügl, is the production of nostalgia for a feminist past or the ongoing production of these 'feminist critiques of feminism' without the production of feminist scholarship that conceives of strategies beyond the linkage between feminism and the contemporary neoliberal amenability.[63] Likewise, this chapter is less about asserting a narrative of feminism lost via the emergence of gender expertise in the global order or producing a story of the need for feminist return to former approaches.[64] I draw on Prügl to at once express my dissatisfaction with contemporary approaches to gender expertise while also regarding this as a building block for whatever might come next.

In examining gender expertise, I am interested in how gender law reform within international institutions reduces the multiplicity and methodologies central to feminist theories, including the tensions and disagreements that create a rich debate within feminist thinking. Questioning the neoliberal amenability of feminist projects, therefore, not only requires raising questions around which feminist messages are taken up and developed in the context of international institutions, but an additional project of identifying and understanding what is left out, how specific feminist projects and histories are silenced within neoliberal agendas and discourse. The amenability of a specific series of feminist ethical claims are not only deployed at a global level and via strategies of global governance, but also via a very specific ethical claim associated with either female vulnerability and/or empowerment that has race, class, ablest, and heteronormative dimensions. In refining feminist knowledge, politics, and tensions in this way, the space of global governance creates gender experts, even if versed in broader, complex feminist debates and politics, who are destined to find their role one of compromise. Gender experts are thus constrained

---

[60] McRobbie (n 14) 13.   [61] Davis and others (n 28).   [62] Prügl (n 15) 617.
[63] ibid 627.
[64] Clare Hemmings, *Why Stories Matter: The Political Grammar of Feminist Theory* (Duke University Press 2011).

by a structural incapacity to attend to feminist ethical and political dimensions that can be attributed to the institutions they work within. Part of the compromise arises from the dependence on gender as quantitative, measurable, and rendered understandable through indicators.

Relatedly, Buss raises three distinct feminist concerns about measurement in the context of gender equality. First, Buss identifies gaps between the measure and what it pertains to quantify. Second, Buss examines how the grammar of measurement tools shapes outcomes and possibilities. Third, Buss considers how governance measures leave off, or are inimical to, 'the complex structural dimensions of inequality not easily quantifiable in metrics'.[65] Buss also argues that the tools used to measure phenomenon, not only have unexpected effects, but can also work to inscribe hierarchies while presenting as neutral in terms of biases and hierarchies. An element of this is the reduction of strategies for change to the compilation of data and report-writing that may displace the original ethical and political agenda that promoted the development of measures in the first place. Ahmed, who records similar effects in diversity work within UK universities, finds, 'good practice is clearly a term used within a tick box approach, insofar as "doing well" is presumed to be something that can be ticked, measured, distributed and shared'.[66] Both Ahmed's and Buss's work resonates with a legal analysis of the work of gender experts and gender expertise in the international realm, highlighting the need for attention to how feminist knowledge is turned into a series of processes that produce the appearance of 'know-how' with respect to gender. This then leads the gender expert in to a trap that requires, on the one hand, attentiveness and knowledge of a feminist history and methodologies and, on the other hand, capacity to deploy this within a series of measures and tools that are far removed from feminist political and ethical claims with respect to how feminist knowledge is produced.

Merry's work on indicators further demonstrates the way that neoliberal governance tools both represent specific values and beliefs as well as ironing out the complexity of social justice projects in global governance.[67] For Merry, the consequence is a leak from corporate settings into global governance where indicators reify categories and diminish the political choices fundamental to their very design.[68] Once created the indicator becomes disconnected from the agendas that shaped it, so that the simplification and normalisation of the categories deployed by the indicator, not only promote the tick box approach analysed by Ahmed, but facilitate projects that engineer self-monitoring, that provide justification for control and interventions, or reasons not to intervene should the choice of categories measured fail to illuminate groups suffering significant harm and/or disadvantage. Again, like Buss's scholarship, Merry's work informs a study of gender expertise as her study of indicators assists recognition of the constraints imposed on gender expertise within international institutional settings and demonstrates the space between the feminist messages

---

[65] Buss (n 25) 385.
[66] Sara Ahmed, 'You End Up Doing the Document Rather than Doing the Doing' (2007) 30(4) Ethnic and Race Studies 590, 595.
[67] Merry (n 21).　　　　[68] ibid.

taken up in international agendas and the feminist methods that illuminated them in the first place.

In addition to feminist analysis of expertise in global governance, Kennedy's account of expertise within global governance further provides a useful series of insights into the relationship between the professional role of the expert and underlying ethical and political commitments of both institutions and individuals. Kennedy's analysis of the role of the expert within global governance is built upon seeing expertise as 'vocabularies of advice, implementation, technique, know-how—useful for limiting and challenging the power of others'.[69] Kennedy lays out an explanation of how expertise is produced through the work of background actors within international law, identifying the role of technical skills and techniques, the ironing out of spaces of discretion as well as the dependence on background knowledge (theories, methods, research).[70]

Understanding expertise as a technical art rather than political knowledge is further embedded in the expectation that governance techniques, or know-how, are neutral, as expertise is assumed to be built on modes and models of understanding that do not reflect politics, biases, and ethics constructing their apparent technical neutrality.[71] Kennedy develops his analysis of the methods, and questions, experts use to understand the way in which expertise functions as more than technical management,[72] and asks us to see expertise as entering global governance as political acts.[73] Kennedy's analysis relies on recognition of the distinction between background actors (the expert, applying technical, non-political know-how) and foreground actors (who bear political responsibility and authority) who require legitimacy to maintain authority. For Kennedy background actors, and the expertise associated with this role, underpin the political legitimacy of the foreground, such that Kennedy argues for a turn to exposing and acknowledging the political commitments of background actors.

To position, and thus ask questions about, gender expertise via Kennedy's analysis directs me towards a series of repeating tensions in the production of gender perspectives and/or expertise within the United Nations and its various entities, including UN Women. These tensions swirl around the modes of feminist thinking that are severed from the development of gender expertise because of the needs of institutions and the notion of expertise as one that provides concrete technical know-how. As such, attention to gender as a performative, fluid social structure and the need for gender to be understood as a power relation that intersects with other power relations within communities in ways that are diverse, both temporally and spatially, challenges the very idea of gender as something able to be deployed in the context of expertise in an institutional setting. The space within gender expertise to assert 'gender is not women or men, but rather directs us to how we come to be represented as belonging to the class of woman or man', and the intersectional dimensions of this, is undermined by a focus on measures and indicators.[74] In Ferguson's study

---

[69] Kennedy, 'Challenging Expert Rule' (n 21) 11.   [70] ibid 9.   [71] Buss (n 25).
[72] Kennedy, 'Challenging Expert Rule' (n 21) 11.   [73] ibid 23–24.
[74] Probyn (n 51).

of gender expertise in international development institutions, she challenges the gendered normativity and representations of the institutions producing expertise indicating that these must also be pulled to the foreground.[75] Ferguson, reflecting on her own work as a gender expert, concludes:

> there is clear separation between internalized versus externalized approaches to gender. As often found in many different aspects of feminist practice, it is 'okay' to talk about gender as long as nobody has to give up anything or be profoundly challenged about their assumptions, beliefs and behaviours. This can be said to function at an institutional, as well as a personal, level.[76]

International institutions cannot simply deploy gender expertise as measures, indicators, and tick boxes to be applied to a situation, community, or issue. A performative, relational approach to gender asks questions about the way gender is represented, subsumed, and produced through the working of the institution itself. This suggests gender expertise requires actors who can 'read' gender and advise on (or challenge) gender as it is constructed within global governance and institutions before any outward-looking work can be commenced.

Kennedy's analysis of the politics of expertise relies on the silencing of any explicit political stance of experts (background actors) yet gender experts might often be described as explicitly placing their political commitments in the foreground when committed to feminist politics.[77] Nevertheless gender expertise does function as a background technique that then plays an important function in legitimating the authority of, say, the Security Council and the political actors who gain authority through the Council's structures. Kennedy's account of expertise within global governance, in particular the shifting political/ethical modes within the space of expertise, might be therefore be expanded via analysis of gender expertise. Kennedy argues '[e]xperts ... influence the world through the outcomes of their active debates as well as through their shared common sense about the world'[78] so that 'within each vocabulary there will be settled matters of consensus that do not need expression, matters of consensus that seem nonetheless to require articulation or affirmation and active debates'.[79] However, recalling Scott's description of feminist theories, there is little settled in feminist knowledge as 'critical reading replaces the operations of classification, in which the relationship between past and present is not taken for granted but considered a problem to be explored'.[80] As such, the space of gender expertise, when severed from feminist methodologies that actively disrupt and interrogate knowledge production, constructs outcomes that diminish feminist political and ethical tensions and replace these with assertions of gender as stable, measurable, and settled. Or, rather, the political and ethical commitments that produce the agitation for gender initiatives within international spaces in the first place are displaced by the gender expectations and norms of the institutions rather than those of the background actors (gender experts).

---

[75] Ferguson (n 41) 4–5.   [76] ibid 13.   [77] ibid 7.
[78] Kennedy, *A World of Struggle* (n 27) 136.   [79] ibid 138.
[80] Joan W Scott, *The Fantasy of Feminist History* (Duke University Press 2011) 22.

3. Gender Effects/Gender Affects

Before progressing the analysis to (as per Prügl) 'push forward the work of feminist critics',[81] a few examples of gender expertise and its emergence across global governance are given in this section. The material underscores the fallacy with the 'feminist success' stories often reiterated in the era of UN Women, as the effects of gender expertise are realised as either segregated from the central decision-making body on a specific issue (for example, climate change) or are reliant on the appointment of specific women into high-level appointments with personal agendas for transformative gender policies (as has been seen during the African Decade for Women). Consequently, I argue that 'gender effects' make visible a series of 'gender affects', following Pedwell this includes 'affective relations and practices—including encounters of empathy, sympathy, and compassion that also frequently (re)produce cultural distinctions, social norms and political practices of exclusion'.[82] That is, I regard the larger institutional expectations with respect to gender expertise to be shaped by unacknowledged expectations of institutional actors with regard to the place and role of gender law reform. I argue this occurs in an affective register built on assumptions about gender that are not verbalised but often felt/known and that consequently fail to disrupt gender as an embedded space of privilege that operates in conjunction with other structural biases.

To explore these effects and affects I analyse the dissonance between different institutional endeavours on climate change to demonstrate how mapping gender expertise can be told differently depending on one's institutional location. I then examine how the inclusive security strategy of NATO and the deployment of gender expertise during the Ebola crisis in West Africa in 2014 both demonstrate the tendency in institutions to give an outward focus to gender expertise, ignoring the internal gender dynamics of institutions. In the final example, I examine the African Women's Decade and the role that specific individuals are expected to take with respect to championing gender. I examine how this focus on key female actors actively works against the entrenchment of lasting institutional change and relegates gender expertise as an 'add-on' to the business as usual of the institution, while promoting the access of elite women to political and institutional representations without attending to the classed consequences of this access.[83] I also provide a short discussion of the slippage between the development of gender expertise and a focus on women's issues and/or women's empowerment within institutional endeavours. I conclude that gender affects perpetuate the effect that the appointment of gender experts is the only 'gender work' institutions perform, such that this becomes a technology of governance that predisposes gender expertise towards indicators and metrics over feminist strategies for transformation.

---

[81] Prügl (n 15) 615. [82] Carolyn Pedwell, *Affective Relations* (Palgrave 2017) 1.
[83] Nic Cheeseman, Francis Onditi, and Cristina D'Alessandro, 'Introduction to the Special Issue: Women, Leadership and Peace' (2017) 7(1) African Conflict and Peacebuilding Review 1, 13.

3.1 The location of expertise

The relationship between gender expertise and climate change, and how this is understood within different international institutions, provides a good instance of how highlighting one set of gender developments might disguise a lack of action with respect to gender, on the same issue, in a different international organisation that commands the central agenda on the issue. In this section I examine the situating of gender expertise on climate change. In chapter 6 I note similar patterns in the rise of gender initiatives as an element of the counterterrorism provisions. While UN Women includes an agenda for sustainable development and the UN Sustainable Development Goals include gender equality within the list of the seventeen goals to be achieved by 2030,[84] the 2015 Framework Agreement on Climate Change mentions gender equality and women's empowerment in the Preamble to the Framework Agreement and has only two references to women or gender concerns in the Paris Agreement itself.[85]

The Paris Agreement entered into force in November 2016, having secured 174 ratifications from member states. The Agreement, in its Preamble, notes the need for implementation to respect human rights, the rights of indigenous and migrant communities, respecting the rights of disabled persons, and the need for intergenerational equity, as well as 'gender equality' and the 'empowerment of women'. Article 7 includes gender-responsiveness as a list of concerns state parties should be mindful of in implementation, and Article 11 also requires that capacity-building should be gender responsive.

The original framework also requires, in paragraph 103, that the mechanism created under Article 15 of the Agreement ('to facilitate the implementation of and promote compliance with the provisions of this agreement'), amongst technical, scientific, and regional representation 'take into account gender balance'.[86] However, this was not included in the final text of the Paris Agreement, so it remains a soft law provision connected to the implementation process. On the one hand, if the spotlight is on the work of UN Women, a space of gender expertise in relation to pressing issues of sustainability and development, including climate change, is apparent. However, the key achievement and mandate on sustainable development drafted after the creation of the Sustainable Development Goals, the Paris Agreement, is devoid of any significant attention to gender expertise, as the unclear terminology of 'gender responsiveness' is all that is referenced within the main text (Articles 7 and 11) of the Agreement.

As such, within the Paris Agreement the recognition of any gendered dimensions to climate change is incredibly narrow: state parties are not required to integrate gender into climate change work or policy, international institutions are not required to consider gender balance with regard to the composition of decision-making

---

[84] UNGA Res 70/1 (25 September 2015) UN Doc A/RES/70/1.

[85] Paris Agreement (adopted 12 December 2015, entered into force 4 November 2016) UN Doc FCCC/CP/2015/L9/Rev preamble (hereafter Paris Agreement).

[86] ibid, para 103; art 15 of the Agreement (annexed).

bodies, and gender issues need not be given attention in decision-making processes. Importantly, the gendered effects of climate change, increasingly documented, are not acknowledged or given space for analysis and development through the work of the Agreement.[87] Instead a group of twelve experts with 'recognized competence in relevant scientific, technical, socio-economic or legal fields' is to be formed with 'equitable geographical representation, with two members each from the five regional groups of the United Nations and one member each from the small island developing States and the least developed countries'.[88] After attention to these constraints within this small committee, membership processes must be mindful of 'taking into account the goal of gender balance'.[89]

It seems fair to conclude that gender expertise is not regarded as a priority within climate change decision-making at the United Nations. Indeed, the inclusion is about parity of representation for women with men (and in one small committee only) not for gender perspectives, gender expertise, gender issues, or gender analysis to be undertaken. This is in marked contrast to UN Women's toolkit for gender and climate change which advises:

When incorporated in analyses of climate change, the gender approach promotes understanding of how the identities of women and men determine different vulnerabilities and capacities to deal with climate change; such an approach can also help to attenuate the causes of climate change. Integrating the gender approach is also helpful in designing and implementing policies, programmes and projects that lead to greater equity and equality. In particular, it may contribute to building more capacity to adapt to and mitigate climate change, insofar as it affords a clearer and more complete view of the relations people have built with ecosystems.[90]

As such, the mapping of gender expertise within global institutions is destined to be an unsatisfactory task because gender perspectives appear in some but not all aspects of global governance. Critical feminist 'success' narratives highlight pockets of gender expertise and transformation within international institutions without sufficient questions about why these spaces and structures within the international order and not others require the inclusion of gender expertise. In the example above, gender expertise within UN Women on climate change and sustainable development is represented as a component of the work of the institution. It is only by turning to the spaces where decisions with regard to sustainable development and climate change are developed that it becomes apparent that the pocket of expertise developed within UN Women is isolated from the actual work being conducted on the issue. The work of gender experts, despite its detail and regardless of its quality and relevance, appears tokenistic as a result. To imagine that the structures of governance being designed to respond climate change are immune from the gender effects

---

[87] Radoslav S Dimitrov, 'The Paris Agreement on Climate Change: Behind Closed Doors' (2016) 16(3) Global Environmental Politics 1.

[88] Paris Agreement (n 85) para 103.   [89] ibid.

[90] UN Development Programme, *Resource Guide on Gender and Climate Change* (UNDP 2009) <http://www.un.org/womenwatch/downloads/Resource_Guide_English_FINAL.pdf> last accessed 31 May 2018; also see Probyn (n 51) 104–11.

that feminist scholarship have illuminated as infiltrating at the core of global governance would be naïve. Furthermore, this example demonstrates how the expertise developed within UN Women is pushed to the peripheries within institutionally specific work in a manner that suggests a poor legacy of gender mainstreaming.

3.2 Gender as external/the province of Others

Beyond the segregation of gender expertise across the different institutions of international law, a topic I return to in the following chapter, this section inquires into how gender expertise is received and understood within institutional structures. As such, I draw on the examples of gender training within NATO and the deployment of Water, Sanitation, and Hygiene (WASH) in West Africa to examine the space between the outward application of gender expertise and the inward understanding of gender affects within the institutions themselves.

In NATO the development of gender expertise across the various components of the armed forces is referred to as 'Gender Awareness Training'.[91] French Army Major, Stephanie Nichol indicates the following perspective represents the core of NATO gender training:

We need to take into consideration the gender perspective now, in the training, the preparation, and the doctrine. You need to be trained and need to have strong knowledge about what gender is, and how to deal with it in your daily work.

Nichol then gives the following practical example of the impact of this approach: '[i]n a hospital setting, for example, we need to ensure there are females available to assist with female patients and males to assist with male patients'.[92] The distinction between gender perspectives and responding differently to men and women in the field suggests the incorporation of gender expertise into a core aspect of training—even when at commander level as in this NATO example—tends to collapse back into the use of gender to refer to women. This approach underscores gender difference rather than gender as relational and performative, diverse and embedded. Hurley finds that:

gender mainstreaming initiatives are inherently disruptive. They ask new things of organisations, requiring attention to be placed on areas traditionally deemed to be unimportant. Yet, a new focus on gender competes with pre-existing organisational norms and pre-existing patterns of gender relations. What ensue are complicated and contradictory patterns of resistance and a conditioning of the 'new', disruptive, gender policies.[93]

---

[91] NATO/EAPC Action Plan for the Implementation of NATO/EAPC Policy on women, peace and security (2016) 5 <http://www.nato.int/nato_static_fl2014/assets/pdf/pdft_2016_07/160718-wps-action-plan.pdf> last accessed 31 May 2018.

[92] NATO, 'NATO Act promotes Gender Perspective Training' (NATO Allied, Command, Transformation 2013-2018) <http://www.act.nato.int/nato-act-promotes-global-gender-perspective-training > last accessed 31 May 2018.

[93] Matthew Hurley, 'Gender Mainstreaming and Integration in the North Atlantic Treaty Organisation' in Rachel Woodward and Claire Duncanson (eds), *The Palgrave Handbook of Gender and the Military* (Palgrave 2018) 403, 414.

Following Hurley, the expertise presented via gender training and gender mainstreaming can work to reinforce existing beliefs about sex difference and gender rather than challenging the affective core of gender that already exists within military institutions, as in any other institution.

This is further illustrated by an example drawn from the institutional response to the Ebola crisis in West Africa in 2014. The key states affected by the epidemic were Sierra Leone, Liberia, Mali, Senegal, and Guinea Bissau. While both the Security Council and the World Health Organisation eventually responded in establishing programmes to halt the transmission of Ebola, responsibility for the delivery of the response largely remained with NGOs who had an established history (and resources) in the region in terms of the delivery of WASH programmes. The UK development NGO Oxfam developed a WASH-Ebola programme centred on a three-tiered approach encompassing treatment, containment, and prevention. The programme was community focused and, in line with Oxfam's larger policy, included gender mainstreaming which involves advice for all staff and a gender analysis in crisis situations.[94]

Despite the commitment to gender mainstreaming and the requirement that gender analysis was undertaken in advance of the programme, reports from gender experts deployed to assist with the WASH policy reflect on the inadequate understanding of gender that was used in the design of the response to the Ebola crisis in West Africa in 2014.[95] The study of the effectiveness of gender expertise was taken by those appointed as gender experts during the crisis, who conclude that gender is 'not a one-off exercise, but recurrent, and it requires critical thinking as situations also change'.[96] The authors go on to state: 'a narrow view of gender mainstreaming meant men's and women's roles in disease prevention remained poorly understood and women's participation in response activities remained limited'.[97] As such, whether the focus is gender expertise delivered via gender training, as in the NATO example, or gender mainstreaming that is prioritised within development and health initiatives, as in the WASH example, the assumption is that gender is something impacting on behaviours external to the organisation. The need for a gender review of behaviours and attitudes within the organisations themselves remains unexplored. The consequence is the affective role of gender in organising and rewarding (or diminishing) behaviours within the institutions are ignored and perceived as universal.

One of the consequences in the WASH study was awareness that characterising women as mothers meant that the capacity of humanitarian actors to see women as agential was significantly diminished. As a result, important hygiene practices that needed to be targeted were overlooked:

A 'good' mother or wife was seen as one who cared for and provided for the sick, however, in Ebola she was explicitly told not to provide care and, in fact, told that providing care for

[94] Simone E Carter, Luisa Maria Dietrich, and Olive Melissa Minor, 'Mainstreaming Gender in WASH: Lessons Learned from OXFAM's Experience of Ebola' (2017) 25(2) Gender and Development 205, 209.
[95] ibid 208–09.　　[96] ibid 218.　　[97] ibid 209.

the sick and deceased increased risk to the outbreak and its spread. This was because they are more likely to come into contact with bodily fluids or blood which is the primary method of transmission ... Women were therefore put in a very difficult position. They risked either not fulfilling their duties as caregivers, causing significant distress to them and their family members, or risked spreading the disease if they did fulfil their role as a 'good' caregiver (wife/mother), which involved flouting the bylaws. In either case, they were exposed to stigma, and accusations of failure to fulfil expected duties.[98]

The failure to see the power of gender norms in dictating local behaviours, and that those norms might be significantly different in terms of the values and behaviours in the assessing state, was insufficiently considered within the gender analysis. Carter et al find that '[t]he campaigns were not developed together with the contribution of women, who could have provided advice on messages and images to better support the adoption of safe behaviour'.[99] Nevertheless, this conclusion still organises around gender as something to be discovered via speaking to women, betraying a continued failure to acknowledge the existing gendered assumptions that international actors carry within their own expertise.

Under current approaches the experience of gender in the developing, or crisis, state is regarded as something to be learned and observed while the gendered practices of the actors observing remain immune from scrutiny. The assumptions that the gender expert carries are rendered insignificant, as gender is imagined as external to the self and the institution—discoverable in post-conflict, developing, and/or crisis states. The impact of this will play out in the deployment of expertise, such that local iterations of gender will be read 'affectively': as given meaning and attributing relevance that is in itself gendered in line with the expert's own understanding of gender. Rather than looking for gender's effect (i.e. on women, on girls, on men) there is a need to explore its affective domain—how it creates blind spots for the expert/institution and how this undermines power in the local context in ways that may not be visible to those whose affective response to gendered cues are derived from their own gendered histories/meanings. Both the NATO and WASH examples demonstrate that from the institutional point of view the important aspect is the appointment of a gender expertise rather than any complex understanding of power relations or assumptions with respect to how gender operates.

3.3 Gender expertise as governance technology

With the increase in gender-related posts in the UN after the advent of UN Women, in militaries after Security Council Resolution 1325, and in both regional and government structures over the same period, the gender-specific assumptions about who might take up a gender mandate may no longer be prevalent, although it does open a series of further questions about what constitutes gender expertise. Haunting this discussion are the interlinked questions of why the turn to gender is so often constituted as a turn to women and why the turn to women flattens women's differences.

---

[98] ibid 211.   [99] ibid 214.

Thus, the assumption that a global sisterhood might trump local, cultural, religious, political, and economic differences effectively elides the political nature of women as actors as it assumes a biological, or even socially construed, connection between women that promotes understanding across other sites of difference.[100]

Feminist analysis of gender relations demonstrates the value of seeing gender as an analytical tool that facilitates understanding of power relations, discourses, structures, representations, the role of bodies, and assumptions regarding where power lies within a community. In the words of Moreton-Robinson,

> there are dominant subject positions in society that are implicated in relations of ruling. These subject positions are historically constituted and are represented in discourse through and beyond the activity and experience of individual subjects.[101]

As such, legal initiatives, including the development of gender expertise in international institutions, that are not mindful of how gender perspectives and gender equality projects quickly collapse into a focus on women reassert a narrow construction of gender. This reinforces the gender binary and sit too comfortably within the construction of male subjectivity that positions women as the Other and as primarily a victim who comes to law for protection. In addition, following Moreton-Robinson's argument, the consequence of the collapsing of gender into female representation will reiterate racialised, colonial, ableist, and heteronormative histories through the production of elite women as holding a universal understanding of how gender operates.

Furthermore, feminist approaches that assert gender as performative, following Butler's work, force recognition that gender expertise itself plays a role in the dynamism of gender and its specificity in institutional spaces.[102] Thus rather than simply reproducing dominant views of gender, the creation of gender expertise within international governance structures becomes the legal solution, without need for scrutiny of what that means in practice. Outside of nodes of gender expertise the institution will also be productive of gender—so the complexity of the institutional form renders a degree of impossibility in extracting either the impact of gender initiatives within the institution or the impact of the institution on the operationalisation of gender. What is useful, however, is to think of the performative dimension of gender as understood by individuals at an affective level—where sensations and emotional responses to 'how gender should be' are often deep-set and unconscious.

Consequently, both gatekeepers to and facilitators of the development and deployment of gender expertise within an institution can often transform the movement of gender through the institution—stalling, blocking, channelling—due to the way gender is expected to be represented, performed, spoken of, and who is to speak with respect to gender. For example, gender as a binary—that is, as a distinction

[100] Paul Higate and Marsha Henry, *Insecure Spaces: Peacekeeping, Power and Performance in Haiti, Kosovo and Liberia* (Zed Books 2009).

[101] Aileen Moreton-Robinson, *Talkin' Up to the White Woman: Indigenous Women and Feminism* (University of Queensland Press 2000) xxii.

[102] Judith Butler, *Gender Trouble: Feminism and the Subversion of Identity* (Routledge 1990).

between men and women—needs to be admitted, spoken to, acknowledged, and analysed as this is often assumed to be self-evident. Transgender, a-gender, and non-binary issues, and individuals, are silenced and rendered invisible when the gender binary is assumed or normalised. To speak from outside the gender binary is then challenged or unheard or without a language. Furthermore, the assumption that gender 'happens' consistently across spaces is a fiction, such that different gender cultures and beliefs need to be articulated, identified, and acknowledged; for example, the different effects and affects of femininity and masculinity within institutional communities. The complexity of any individual experience of gendering carries with it the history of gender across the communities that individual lives within. For Meenakshi the consequence is: '(m)y existence under whiteness and after colonialism is a perpetual state of being misgendered. My gender is not neutral, my gender is brown, and hairy, and lesbian. My gender transcends white concepts of the binary and thus it transcends the non-binary.'[103] Interrogation of the capacity for institutions to write out this intersectional and non-Western gendering via the investment in a specific reproduction of gender has not been part of inquiry of the gender expertise. Furthermore, the investment of those with power and privilege in maintaining the gender status quo also leads to intersectional harm for some men, which is simultaneously rendered an impossibility when the gender binary has been internalised and gender interventions are imagined, or expected, to move through the institution as women's issues.

The creation of an African Decade for Women within the African Union has pretty much gone unnoticed as a space for gender expertise in contexts outside of the African continent, likewise the coordination of ministers for gender affairs into the Directorate of Women, Gender, and Empowerment.[104] The appointment of prominent African leaders into the directorate also underscores the larger concerns of the chapter—where gender expertise is continually confused with female political leadership. In particular, the appointment of Nkosazana Dlamini-Zuma as Chairperson of the African Union in 2012 was regarded as a means to ensure the development of gender policy within the institution. Subsequent developments saw Dlamini-Zuma's political desires within the South Africa political space end her role in the AU which coincided with a general disintegration of the push for more extensive gender policy across the organisation. The impossibility of on the one hand female-ness creating an assumption of gender expertise and on the other the lack of institutional change because of the existence of female political leaders championing gender issues raises questions about how institutions regard gender expertise. Both Dlamini-Zuma and the former Liberian President, Sirleaf-Johnson have received criticism for their waning gender successes and very little commentary acknowledges the naivety of centring gender expertise on the appointment of individual

---

[103] Priyanka Meenakshi, 'My Gender is Not Neutral, My Gender is Brown, and Hairy, and Lesbian' [2016/17] Gal-dem: the Home Issue 87, 90.

[104] UN-NGLS, 'African Women's Decade (2010–2020) officially launched on International Day of Rural Women' (United Nations Non-Governmental Liaison Service, 15 October 2010) <https://www.unngls.org/index.php/un-ngls_news_archives/2010/749-african-women%E2%80%99s-decade-2010-2020-officially-launched-on-international-day-of-rural-women> last accessed 31 May 2018.

women. For Cheesman, Onditi, and D'Alessandro, in their overview of women's political leadership in Africa '[t]he current gender equality paradigm is too reductionist, thus no meaningful institutional and social transformation is expected'.[105] The focus on individual women in high-profile positions detracts from the development of entrenched strategies and responses.

The mobilisation of Hilary Clinton as an advocate for international women's rights is an additional example, where her gender credentials are assumed rather than assessed and her support for authorised force during the Obama presidency in the US is not regarded as impacting on her capacity to represent women's interests—in the US or abroad. The tensions between national political representation, which are likely driven by home state political agendas, and the international casting of female political leaders and actors as gender experts betrays the failure of gender expertise to capture feminist goals. Feminist knowledge asserts the understanding that there is no gender-free space and that different, or variant, gender discourse infiltrates and construct all communities so the sense that an expert might stand outside the biases, privileges, and blind spots of their own gender normativity to 'read' and advise on the gendered privilege, biases, and blind spots elsewhere is a dangerous approach. In particular, this risks the incorporation of a specific cultural expectation around gender that is far from expert.

Kennedy describes the capacity to work in the background (and therefore absent from the political domain) as a component of the privilege of expertise.[106] He further sees this not as a justification for the ending of expertise, but rather leading to a need for expertise to be mindful of its own biases and blind spots.[107] When examining gender expertise, there needs to be acknowledgement that an understanding of the normative structuring and positionality of the expert—and of the institution—contains gendered expectations and assumptions. The absence of recognition of the pervasiveness of gender remains a gender deficit in institutional approaches that is constructed via the failure of reflexivity on the part of the structures that seek to encompass gender as part of their external monitoring and not an aspect of internal processes.

The connecting of these descriptions with feminist theorising assists understanding of how gender expertise functions to embed and disrupt tensions within feminist histories. By this I refer to the capacity to tell the story of gender at the UN, within regional organisations, and within states, as one of arrival and success: gender expertise and the appointing of gender experts within the international order gives the impression of gender as known, of gender as discovered, and therefore easily understood and deployed as a technique of governance. The purpose of this chapter is to suggest quite the opposite: highlighting how gender is collapsed into a reference to women that eradicates the feminist understanding of gender as a power relationship, undermining the necessity that gender projects unpick and respect the diversity of women's experiences. In analysing states and institutions as gendered

---

[105] Cheeseman, Onditi, and D'Alessandro (n 83) 11.
[106] Kennedy, 'Challenging Expert Rule' (n 21).   [107] ibid 18.

frames for the workings of the international order in following chapters, I use gender as a tool for thinking, for thought, for political engagement with, and through, the normative structuring of the global order. To understand this, questions regarding the types of knowledge produced by contemporary sites of expertise help identify not only the narrow range of feminist ideas deployed within spaces of expertise but also the immunity of international institutions from self-awareness of the gendered knowledge they produce, and propagate, that ultimately mitigates against any transformative gender reform.

4. Intersectionality and the Politics of Listening

Feminist theory refines, reconsiders, and produces a complex reading of the ways gender has come to be understood as a technique, a measurement, a discourse, and a tool of expertise.[108] While I have described the appearance of gender techniques within international law as compromised, in this section I am interested in the potential of reorienting gender expertise via the contours of feminist methodologies. This prepares for my analysis in the following chapter which considers more closely the types of feminist approaches incorporated into global governance and how fragmentation/diversification within international law effectively fragments feminist gains. In this final section of this chapter I therefore reflect on the effects of gender expertise; to design an epistemology of feminist dialogues, mindful of feminist methodologies, in particular intersectionality and the politics of listening.

Shepherd describes gender as a 'noun, a verb and an adjective'[109] while Cohn describes how different feminist theories and feminist scholars might see gender as a structural power relation, gender as an important social arrangement and space of social meaning, gender as an important space where self-identity resides, gender as fluid and contested, gender as a meaning system that is drawn from expectations about femininity and masculinity, and institutions as gendered.[110] Gender is also central to the production of heteronormativity, certainly in mainstream Western configurations of gender, in many cases creating heteronormativity as invisible in social, institutional, structural, and symbolic systems of meaning and ordering. This creates a significant risk of the reassertion of heteronormativity through the work of gender expertise, if the relationship between sexuality and gender is not configured within institutional accounts of gender. As such, if gender is understood as a tool for understanding different layers of power and meaning then it is important that in approaching the deployment of gender expertise within the international realm that attention is paid to the various structures where gender norms are assumed,

---

[108] Carol Cohn, 'Women and Wars: Toward a Conceptual Framework' in Carol Cohn (ed), *Women and War: Contested Histories, Uncertain Futures* (Polity Press: 2013) 3–16.

[109] Laura J Shepherd and Laura Sjoberg, 'Trans-bodies in/of War(s): Cisprivilege and Contemporary Security Strategy' (2012) 101 Feminist Review 5, 7.

[110] Cohn (n 108).

including the anchoring of heteronormativity in the gender binary. Intersectionality as feminist methodology, and account of power, also troubles gender through the relationship between gender and race, gender and able-bodiedness, gender and cisprivilege, and gender and class—demanding gender expertise that is mindful of the potential co-optation of gender projects in the perpetuation of other sites of disadvantage and harm.

Prügl's identification of gender as something that is produced and reinforced by international organisations, rather than transformed, aligns with Charlesworth's understanding of the relationship between feminist methods and feminist messages, and therefore propels this aspect of my discussion. I am interested in asking how international institutions situate and produce gender norms, as well as the effect this has on the turn to gender expertise and the work of gender experts in those institutions. In analysing the placement of gender expertise, I argue for a feminist methodology that is mindful of the diverse and complex ways gender is theorised in feminist projects and that seeks to disrupt a sense that gender has a simple meaning. This approach requires a shift away from the reduction of gender projects via the focus on women, women's visibility, and women's participation because the focus on women risks a reasserted institutional projection of gender norms where the complexity of power relationships, the entrenchment of a heteronormative gender binary, and the writing out of women's differences function to displace feminist methodologies and fail to create transformative gender work within international law. Gender expertise, and the manner in which it is framed within international institutions, is an important starting point to think differently about how feminist approaches to international law might engage with and within institutions.

In addition to gender emerging as a process of indicators, tick sheets ,or factored as the appointment of gender expertise (rather than the transformative potential of that expertise), gender initiatives within the global arena construct a series of normative assertions about gender that are deeply implicated in the production of global hegemony and the spread of neoliberalism. Drawing on Connell, there is a need to understand that '[l]ocal gender orders now interact not only with the gender order of other local societies but also with the gender order of the global arena'.[111] This 'global gender order' appears to be transfixed by the heteronormative binary of gender, readily collapsing gender initiatives into a focus on women and largely disregarding the production of masculinity through the everyday operations of international institutions, transnational business,[112] and international relations.[113] Consequently, the limited feminist approaches that filter through to international gender projects are continually circumscribed

[111] RW Connell, 'Change Among the Gatekeepers: Men, Masculinities, and Gender Equality in the Global Arena' (2005) 30(3) Signs 1801, 1804.

[112] RW Connell, *The Men and the Boys* (Cambridge University Press 2000).

[113] Charlotte Hooper, *Manly States: Masculinities, International Relations and Gender Politics* (Columbia 2001); Swati Parashar, J Ann Tickner, and Jacqui True, *Revisiting Gendered States: Feminist Imaginings of the State in International Relations* (Oxford University Press 2018).

by the existing gender norms within international institutions which are strengthened rather than transformed.

Therefore, the assumption that gender is a study and response to women's lives leaves unresolved the means through which masculinity, in particular, hegemonic masculinities, reproduce and are reproduced—in all their diversity. Important to the analysis in this chapter then is recognition, in the words of Connell, that unless there is 'change amongst the gatekeepers' and projects to 'remake masculinities to sustain gender equality', the production of gender expertise within the global order will be limited in terms of transformative political or legal change.[114]

To ask for no adaption to the practices and beliefs of those who benefit from existing gender relations perpetuates a sense that a measurable, women-focused gender agenda can be meaningful. Or, in the words of Ferguson, 'when gender can only be discussed as being external to an institution, it seems that gender expertise comes up against a wall'.[115] This takes away from a question of 'who are the gender experts' and why are they not producing (enough or sufficient) feminist outcomes, to a series of questions on how gender expertise, circumscribed by the structures it is permitted to flourish within, produces an unconscious heteronormative gender order that relies upon a male and/or masculine norm and worldview as the starting point while diminishing feminist accounts of difference.

The turn to gender expertise within global governance consequently compresses debates on gender—prioritising harm experienced by women in some spaces (primarily developing states) without seeing the co-optation of institutional structures and masculinities in the perpetuation of this harm. Ferguson reflects:

> While it is broadly acceptable for gender experts to highlight gender inequality in 'developing' countries, it is more problematic to do so in reference to the headquarters of international institutions. It is particularly difficult to challenge male privilege in the management structures of international organizations, as well as to highlight the high prevalence of young women working as interns and in secretarial jobs therein, and the levels of harassment to which they are often subjected.[116]

In addition to the institutional limitations of where and how gender can be mobilised as a form of expertise, there have been specific initiatives to engage men in gender politics in the global arena. For example, the UN Women 2014 'HeforShe' campaign that was led by UN Special Envoy Emma Watson.[117] This campaign underscores how an approach to gender equality hinged on sex difference reifies stereotypical and essentialist constructions of men and women that are co-opted into additional power structures. Furthermore, the use of celebrity endorsements reinforces a very specific account of gender that is Western focused, while reinforcing

---

[114] Connell (n 112).   [115] Ferguson (n 41) 13.   [116] ibid 8.

[117] Susan Hopkins, 'UN Celebrity "It" Girls as Public Relations-ised Humanitarianism' (2018) 80(2) The International Communication Gazette 273; Emma Watson, 'Gender Equality is Your Issue Too' (*UN Women*, 20th September 2014) <www.unwomen.org/en/news/stories/2014/9/emma-watson-gender-equality-is-your-issue-too> last accessed 31 May 2018.

gender harm and discrimination as something that happens outside of the West and not within the structures of the global order itself.[118] Consequently, the focus on engaging men does little to disrupt the legacy of the global gender order which reproduces specific intersections of race, gender, ableism, cis-privilege, and sexuality. Hopkins argues

UN Women celebrity ambassadors call for global gender equality, while simultaneously profiting immensely from gendered norms and feminine stereotypes in their 'day jobs' as corporate brand ambassadors. Moreover, through the commercial PR packaging of humanitarian celebrity, female audiences are being sold not just a PR-ised version of feminist activism, but a particular, privileged, white and Western interpretation of ideal femininity and heteronormativity.[119]

The role of celebrity campaigns serves to further illustrate the troubling gender binaries that gender operates through within international law, such that the gender binary's nexus to heteronormativity within Watson's plea in the HeforShe campaign need not even be articulated.[120] Furthermore, the inference that gender expertise can be deployed and developed by anyone—including Hollywood actors—undermines the in-depth understanding of feminist methodologies and messages that feminist activists, globally, contribute to international institutions.

Gender expertise and the work of gender experts are filtered through the political and ethical frameworks that institutions are constructed around. Consequently, the creation of spaces for gender expertise, as well as the outputs of gender experts, look more like the work of the institution than the outcomes of feminist knowledge projects. It is important to contemplate a richer understanding of gender, with all the tensions and dialogues feminist accounts offer within that space, to consider feminist approaches to international law as requiring a series of fundamental transformations. Attention to the complexity of gender as a power relation and the need for centring intersectionality is required; I take this up in the remainder of the discussion in this chapter. As indicated above, the hyper-attention to gender 'elsewhere' quickly collapses into a failure to regard local gender knowledge as relevant and a failure to see the performative dimensions of gender in powerful institutions. In turn this not only reproduces the affective dimensions of gender in Western contexts but attempts to deploy Western and elite accounts of gender norms via the work of the gender experts as if they were experienced in a universal fashion. Through centring intersectionality, I contribute to Prügl's challenge to move beyond critiquing the outputs of gender expertise to thinking through mechanisms for exposing and understanding the internal gender workings of international institutions. At the heart of this remains a feminist approach propelled via dialogues, difference, and

---

[118] BS Chimni, *International Law and World Order: a Critique of Contemporary Approaches* (2nd edn, Cambridge University Press 2017).

[119] Hopkins (n 117) 2.

[120] Karen Engle, 'Celebrity Diplomacy and Global Citizenship' (2012) 3(1) Celebrity Studies 116.

multiple tools that mirror the entrenched feminist understanding of intersectional harm and the role of institutions and power in perpetuating intersectional privilege as an invisible constant.

Throughout this chapter I have elaborated an argument on the transference of feminist messages into the institutionalised role of gender expertise as both promise and compromise. The promise lies in the transformational feminist politics and ethics that challenged and positioned gender in international spaces as it has become today. The compromise is usefully summed up in Charlesworth's distinction between feminist methods and feminist messages; where the methods of feminisms become the casualty, or cost, of feminist 'successes' in institutional spaces, action, and dialogues. I have also argued that gender expertise, or the appointment of gender experts, becomes a technology of global governance such that the legal strategy is the appointment of gender expertise, without the incorporation of a space or the tools for the actor appointed to materialise a feminist politics within the institution—rather their very presence is intended to indicate the receptivity of feminist agendas into international institutions. This subsumes and dislocates the transnational feminist histories, which demand more than liberal feminist strategies of inclusion, while also maintaining the intractability of complex feminist methods, such as intersectionality, to international law because of the preoccupation with women and sex difference within the strategies deployed. The importance of gender as interlocked with other structures of oppression, the multiple mechanisms through which this is manifest, and the amenability of gender to co-optation into imperialist legal endeavours then become criticisms of gender expertise and leave unchallenged the gender structures and mechanisms reproduced by international institutions themselves.

I have tried to both admit the radical transformation of specific sites within international institutions, so as to recognise the feminist labour that produced these transformations, while acknowledging the very limited feminist outcomes that are produced via these changes. This leads me to focus on and examine sites of feminist knowledge that have not travelled into the international and which have been resisted within global governance: intersectionality, gender as a mechanism to understand the construction, performance, and representation of masculinity and femininity, and the need for postcolonial feminist approaches that engage race and imperialism within international institutions. In this final section, I revisit these components of my argument considering in detail the consequences of extending beyond gender expertise to further understand feminist politics and ethics as a series of methods and methodologies that sit less comfortably within the current regimes of global governance. This opens up the text to think beyond the critiques of gender expertise and feminist successes within international law to commence dialogues on next steps and routes to action.

4.1 Intersectionality

While the term intersectionality originated within the critical legal work of Crenshaw, it is a concept and idea that emerges in a range of contexts and in a cross-disciplinary fashion.[121] In 2000, Crenshaw's report on gender and racial discrimination for the UN recognises the necessity for intersectional approaches, yet this has had little impact within gender law reform. For example, the Security Council's eight resolutions on women, peace, and security have a limited approach to the intersectional nature of gender discrimination. In 2000, Crenshaw reported to the UN that:

[d]iscrimination emanating from categorical distinctions on the basis of sex and race have historically intersected in multiple and diverse ways, and have taken specific forms during particular historical conjunctures, such as in the contexts of slavery and colonialism. The dominant structures of power often relied on violence to sustain their patriarchal and racial boundaries.[122]

In contrast, Security Council resolutions on women, peace, and security demonstrate no recognition of women's diversity, other than the inclusion, in resolution 2122, of the need to include 'socially and/or economically excluded groups of women' and, in 2015 in resolution 2242 where a reference to 'cross-geographical representation' is acknowledged in relation to the appointment of women to senior leadership posts.[123] The failure to address intersectionality, that is the embedded structures of power within our communities and how this compounds gender discrimination and harm, has created a series of Security Resolutions that work from the assumption that women are a uniform group, with largely uniform needs both across and within societies. In addition, the failure to instrumentalise intersectional understandings of gender discrimination has allowed the term 'woman' to be deployed throughout Security Council reports and resolutions without attention to the different types of harm different women experience, different access different women have to social justice initiatives, and the different costs to women of speaking out against gender-based harm.

In other institutional endeavours the capacity for an intersectional approach to gender expertise has been varied. Significantly, the CEDAW Committee has attempted to use intersectionality to challenge states for their treatment of women from rural and migrant communities, as well as in examination of the experiences of lesbian, poor, and disadvantaged women, to acknowledge discrimination and harm is 'more than' gender plus an additional site of disadvantage.[124] While the Convention does not include reference to intersectionality, in General Recommendation 28 the CEDAW Committee identified intersectionality as 'a

[121] Kimberle Crenshaw, 'Mapping the Margins: Intersectionality, Identity Politics and Violence against Women of Colour' (1991) 43(6) Stanford Law Review 1241; Combahee River Collective, 'The Combahee River Collective Statement' in Barbara Smith (ed), *Home Girls: A Black Feminist Anthology* (Kitchen Table: Women of Color Press 1983) 272–83; Jennifer Nash, 'Rethinking Intersectionality' (2008) 89 Feminist Review 1; Beth Goldblatt, 'Intersectionality in International Anti-discrimination Law: Addressing Poverty in its Complexity' (2015) 21(1) Australian Journal of Human Rights 47.

[122] Kimberley Crenshaw, *Gender Related Aspects of Race Discrimination* (UN Division of the Advancement of Women 2000) UN Doc EGM/GRD/2000/EP1; UN [DAW, OHCR, UNIFEM], Report of Expert Group Meeting (Zahgreb, 2000) <http://www.un.org/womenwatch/daw/csw/genrac/report.htm> last accessed 31 May 2018.

[123] UNSC Res 2122 (18 October 2013) UN Doc S/RES/2122 para 7(a).

[124] Meghan Campbell, 'CEDAW and Women's Intersecting Identities: A Pioneering Approach to Intersectional Identities' (2015) 11(2) Direito GV Law Review 479, 480.

basic concept for understanding the scope of the general obligations' and further enhanced this approach through additional general recommendations, such as General
Recommendation 26 on women migrant workers and General Recommendation
27 on older women, as well an explicit invoking of intersectionality in General
Recommendation 35, on violence against women, to acknowledge intersecting
harms.[125] In General Recommendation 30 the CEDAW Committee explicitly
links its work with the UN Security Council's women, peace, and security agenda,
described by O'Rourke and Swaine as a mechanism for 'productive interactions'
between the two institutions.[126] In terms of intersectionality, as an approach and
method for feminist framing of gender approaches, the interlocking of these two
spaces of gender expertise is yet to be productive. Crenshaw's original articulation of
intersectionality was centred on US anti-discrimination law so the integration into
international anti-discrimination law is recognition of the amenability of this specific type of law as a means to address and respond to intersectional harm.

The continued segmenting of intersectional harm (into specific categories of
women) is usefully disrupted by General Recommendation 28, which Campbell
describes as 'pioneering a new and fluid approach to intersectional discrimination
that more successfully integrates theory and practice'.[127] Both the limits and potentials of law as an intersectional feminist tool are thus encapsulated in the approach
of the CEDAW Committee. At one level the CEDAW approach risks the collapsing
into identity categories and an additive approach to intersectionality, rather than the
integrated development of responding to the complexity of intersectional harms.
However, at the same time that the CEDAW Committee 'misreads' the Convention
and then develops this misreading through the general recommendations, through
individual communications to States, and through inquiry procedures in an increasingly innovative fashion. These misreading lie in reading the direction of CEDAW
to apply to 'all women' as an intersectional claim, as well as the necessity that the
CEDAW Committee have both a political commitment to intersectionality and
feminist understanding of the different types of methodologies required to produce
outcomes that are attentive to intersectionality. This highlights the risks inherent in
the deployment of gender expertise, outlined above, that the expertise aspect is often
underplayed, so that specialist knowledge required by gender experts is undervalued.

---

[125] Committee for the Elimination of All Forms of Discrimination against Women (CEDAW),
'General Recommendation No 26 on Women Migrant Workers (5 December 2008) UN Doc
CEDAW/C/GC/26; Committee for the Elimination of All Forms of Discrimination against Women
(CEDAW), 'General Recommendation No 27 on Older Women and the Protection of Human Rights'
(16 December 2010) UN Doc CEDAW/C/GC/27; Committee for the Elimination of All Forms of
Discrimination against Women (CEDAW), 'General Recommendation No 28 on the Core Obligations
of State Parties under Article 2 of the Convention on the Elimination of All Forms of Discrimination
Against Women' (16 December 2010) UN Doc CEDAW/C/GC/3; Committee for the Elimination
of All Forms of Discrimination against Women (CEDAW), 'General Recommendation No 35 on
Gender-Based Violence Against Women, updating General Recommendation 19' (26 July 2017) UN
Doc CEDAW/C/GC/35.
[126] CEDAW, 'General Recommendation No 30 on Women in Conflict Prevention, Conflict and
Post-Conflict Situations' (18 October 2013) UN Doc CEDAW/C/GC/30; O'Rourke and Swaine
(n 39) 169.
[127] Campbell (n 124) 483.

As a result, the appointment of a gender expert becomes the solution and expertise in feminist methodologies may or may not be an element of the job description.

While the CERD Expert Report, with Crenshaw as rapporteur, implicitly acknowledges race theory as a specific body of knowledge of relevance to international legal structures, contemporary focus on gender, absent race, or sexuality, or ableism, cis-normativity, or class privilege, fails to recognise that gender experts will also reflect specific cultural understandings of race, gender, sexuality, ableism, cis-genderism, and class, as well as of religion. The tools, the dialogues, the tensions, the limitations, and the possibilities of intersectional approaches have been well theorised and developed despite their non-appearance in contemporary sites where women's issues (now gender perspectives) emerge in global governance.[128] The limited voicing of intersectional politics within the international realm[129] functions to refine the range of expert knowledge that emerges within the international and to cast a specific framing of feminist messages (rather than feminist methodologies) as the goal of feminist politics.

Race, in particular, but also sexuality and ableism, are only present insomuch as specific assumptions about gender, race, sexuality, and ableism are raised by, engaged with, and given space by gender experts and tools. That is, race and the differentiated harm race constructs for women of colour or for minority groups within communities are not represented within the spaces of gender expertise in global governance. However, like the gender expectations of institutions, racial privilege and harm are not absent within the space of gender expertise; rather, gender is produced through institutional practices, and certain assumptions are normalised. For example, when specific groups of women are given access to participation in institutional structures, race and class privileges also operate within these institutional structures and tend to be reproduced along with gendered expectations. As such, Ferguson's claim that 'it is "okay" to talk about gender as long as nobody has to give anything up or be profoundly challenged about their assumptions, beliefs and behaviours'[130] carries within it the intersection of gender with race, class, ableist, cisgendering, and heteronormative power structures. This has resonance for feminist approaches to international law as it challenges the idea that the creation of spaces of expertise on gender can be transformative in isolation from attention to these interlocking power structures.

If institutions have this nested gender agenda, then strategies for gender law reform and the deployment of gender expertise require further design that is attentive to feminist methodologies. Some beginnings might lie in following the work of the CEDAW Committee, for example, the conscious 'misreading' of the framing in the treaty as applying to all women as a stimulus for developing jurisprudence

---

[128] Nira Yuval-Davis, 'Power, Intersectionality and the Politics of Belonging' in Wendy Harcourt (ed), *The Palgrave Handbook of Gender and Development* (Palgrave 2016) 367; Nira Yuval-Davis, 'What is Transversal Politics?' (1999) 12 Soundings 94; Lola Okolosie, 'Beyond "Talking" and "Owning" Intersectionality' (2014) 108 Feminist Review 90; Gail Lewis, 'Presence through Violence' (2017) 117 Feminist Review 1.

[129] Crenshaw, *Gender Related* (n 122).   [130] Ferguson (n 41).

with mindfulness of intersectionality and different women's lives and needs. Alternatively—or perhaps simultaneously—greater recognition of the possibilities and limitations of gender expertise, circumscribed by the agendas of institutions but nevertheless holding some value, even if only as place markers before feminist methodologies might be embedded alongside feminist messages in legal forms. Finally, greater recognition of the pervasiveness of the intersectional effects of gender might lead to new dialogues, which in turn lead to new spaces to listen to those who experience gender discrimination and harms yet feel unheard and unrepresented within contemporary gender law reforms. I return to these strategies across the following chapters of the book.

To think about gender as the production of dominant masculinities and femininities, there is a need to note that although gender experts are identified to work on issues of equality, participation, or protection in relation to gender, there is an underlying tension within international institutions if those roles are focused on identifying and responding only to gendered harm as it is experienced by women. Feminist approaches identify a range of approaches to theorising the construction of masculinities and femininities that has implications in terms of the assumption of women as feminism's subject: the risk of producing rather than recognising heteronormativity as complicit in gendered harms and a denial of the importance of masculinity as a powerful social construction and organising structure. It is important not to simply identify these as deficiencies in the global order and global governance but to also consider possible alternative renderings of feminist approaches to international law that are mindful of masculinity, essentialism, and sexuality. One methodology, which I enlarge in the subsequent chapter, is theorising the recognition of diverse subjectivity as integral to feminist projects. Rather than arguing for this as a move to accept and acknowledge intersectionality as a description, I work to shift this as a core organising knowledge. The plural subjectivity theorised then requires gender expertise to be grounded in a theory of difference that incorporates the politics of listening to be with, rather than for, others. For Gill this requires a ' "speaking with" approach (that) involves engaging in more than simple dialogue … through the locations, sensations and actions of our bodies that we interpret perceptual information in order to understand the world; this embodied knowledge is, in turn, manifested in our socio-cultural performances'.[131] This is an epistemological shift from the theorising of feminist methodologies through the subject of woman/women towards theorising a methodology that is articulated through plural subjects and recognition of their worldview as world-shaping.

As argued above, across international documents the use of the term gender as interchangeable with the term women presents a series of feminist dilemmas. Feminist projects are built from a political and ethical identification of the harm and discrimination that women experience in the world and an acknowledgement that feminist scholarship is linked to the lived experiences of women. This extends into understandings of gender and theories of embodiment that are relevant to

---

[131] Aisha Gill, 'Feminist Reflections on Researching so-called "Honour Killings" ' (2013) 21 Feminist Legal Studies 241, 247.

legal accounts of subjectivity, drawn from feminist methods centred on the relation between the gendered body and dominant discourses on gender and sex within communities. Nevertheless, the deployment of the term gender, from a feminist perspective, acknowledges, at least implicitly, that the production of gender is a knowledge that pertains to the lives, experiences, and expectations of men and women, masculinities and femininities, as well as the entrenching of cis-genderism, allowing for gender to be perceived as fluid, existing on a continuum, and constructed.

Although in 1998 the word gender still caused considerable consternation in the drafting of the Rome Statute for the International Criminal Court, the word 'gender' subsequently seems to have congealed into international legal code for 'women'.[132] For example, across the eight Security Council resolutions on women, peace, and security there are references to gender in a multitude of ways, including: gender perspectives, gender-sensitive, gender-based violence, gender considerations, gender dimensions, gender mainstreaming, gender equality, gender issues, gender guidelines, gender issues, gender advisors, gender entities, gender expertise, gender advisors, gender training, gender related issues, and gender experts. At the same time, although there are many references to women in these resolutions, men are mentioned only twice across the eight resolutions. The first mention is in Security Council resolution 2106 where men and boys are noted in the Preamble as victims of sexual violence in armed conflict.[133] The second mention is in Security Council resolution 2242, again in the preamble, where men and boys are noted as partners for promoting women's participation.[134] The resolutions are, of course, addressed to *women*, peace, and security so it is possible to argue not only is an absence of men and references to men entirely appropriate but that, following the CEDAW Committee, this does not foreclose an intersectional approach. Nevertheless, feminist theorising that engages intersectionality queries the unitary production of the term 'women' or, in the words of Kapur the 'hegemonic use of the word gender'—allowing alternative histories and readings of gender, the gender binary, and the intersectional experience of gendered lives.[135] For feminist legal theorists, balancing the need for legal clarity with intersectional feminist methodologies is not straightforward. When reflecting on gender expertise, disrupting gender's hegemonic deployment requires new dialogues within feminist legal frames that surfaces these tensions and speaks to them as method. A possible outcome of an intersectional approach to developing gender expertise in the international realm would be to centre Kapur's ideas on peripheral subjects and use this to understand where gender expertise lies. That is, when speaking on how gender operates in a specific context, how gender interlocks with other sites of privilege, and the best means to see the gender norms of institutions, there is a need to promote serious dialogue through listening to the actors that speak within a local community. This is a conscious shift from a feminist methodology

---

[132] Louise Chappell, *The Politics of Gender Justice at the International Criminal Court: Legacies and Legitimacy* (Oxford University Press 2016) 46.

[133] UN Security Council Resolution 2106 (24 June 2013) UN Doc S/RES/2106.

[134] UN Security Council Resolution 2242 (13 October 2015) UN Doc S/RES/2242.

[135] Ratna Kapur, *Erotic Justice: Law and the New Politics of Postcolonialism* (Glasshouse Press 2005) 5.

theorising difference that, in contrast, pivots around the experience/expertise of white, Western, and elite women. As such, my approach to intersectionality, in addition to theorising a model of plural subjectivity addressed in the following chapter, stems from a feminist politics of listening.

4.2 The politics of listening

The conclusion of the prior text seems somewhat unoriginal—listen to local voices. So, in this section I want to draw out precisely what this might mean when voiced as a feminist methodology. My claim is, first and foremost, a methodological one. I mean this in the sense that active listening and hearing what the meaning of gender is, how gender harm emerges, and is sustained, and how international institutions bring their gendered assumptions into gender expertise is drawn from Kapur's challenge to take seriously the normative commitments, the knowledge production, and the views of those who are most affected by the changes feminism may wish to operationalise.[136] This includes, by definition, an acceptance that changes might be asked of actors within academic and international institutions in the Global North and other spaces of power and privilege; change that disrupts, is uncomfortable, and may even be silencing of these actors. Importantly, Kapur's methodology interlocks with Otto's views on the politics of listening.[137] In particular, I draw on Otto's description of her experience as an Expert Panellist at the Asia-Pacific Regional Women's Hearing on Gender-Based Violence in Conflict, held 10 –11 October 2012, in Phnom Penh, Cambodia, to inform my understanding of listening, which Otto describes as a politics of listening that avoids 'engaging in a process of consumption that confirms my own humanity, rather than acting on a politics of listening that looks to realising justice in and beyond the law'.[138] As such, Otto speaks of requiring strategies 'to draw those of us listening ... directly into the frame of responsibility'.[139] To embark on and appreciate a politics of listening in this text I spent considerable time reflecting on whose voice informs and shapes the conclusions drawn. As the text advances I work to actively bring myself into the 'frame of responsibility'.[140] This, I argue, asks for a specific, personal listening on my part to the racialised histories of the colony that I benefited from in my own history. The politics of listening might also be applied and thought through in relation to gender expertise as a methodology for transforming who is engaged as an expert and what tools gender experts are assumed to work with: not measures or indicators but feminist methodologies that start from a premise of difference and power as produced through gendered forms.

Otto writes of the role of experts at the hearings in Phnom Penh, noting the space between the acts of listening during the testimonies in the hearings and the contributions of experts. Otto concludes:

---

[136] ibid.
[137] Dianne Otto, 'Beyond Legal Justice: Some Personal Reflections on People's Tribunals, Listening and Responsibility' (2017) 5(2) London Review of International Law 225.
[138] ibid.   [139] ibid 243.   [140] ibid.

Although the experts spoke with passion and commitment, there was very little resonance between what they had to say and the survivors' testimonies of their quotidian struggles for survival in the present realities of post-conflict (in)justice. For me, it was an object lesson in how agendas, understood as universal, can not only fail to connect with the local, but can also dictate how the problem is presented and addressed at the local level.[141]

For Otto part of the solution is to build practices that make clear the connection between listening and responsibility. This approach offers no simple reformation of feminist work in the global order as, at its heart, is an understanding of the co-optation of feminist accounts of law into the continued production of specific types of legal interventions and a challenge to what feminist actors within international spaces think they know. Consequently, there must be attention to where race and other forms of privilege integrate into feminist knowledge production to reinforce the status quo when transformed into institutional outcomes.

To return to the examples of gender expertise discussed across this chapter it is useful to commence dialogues on how a joint process of attentiveness to intersectionality and to the political responsibility of listening, as articulated by Otto, might suggest different approaches to gender expertise. In the discussion of the Paris Agreement I analysed how gender expertise was minimised in the outcome document. Attention to intersectionality and political listening would require not only the adding of gender expertise: attention must be given to which expertise is important in addressing climate change via a feminist methodology. MacGregor writes that the

overarching theme in gender and climate change research is that climate change is not gender-neutral but has gender-differentiated causes and effects. The main arguments are not only that climate change will be experienced by men and women differently, but also that women will be more severely hurt by the impacts than men.[142]

MacGregor goes on to argue, however, that approaches to gender and climate change need to shift from the focus on identifying gendered differentials in effects towards 'the cultural and symbolic (that is, ideational) dimensions of climate change or to the ways in which gendered environmental discourses frame and shape dominant understandings of the issue'.[143] Drawing on the approach argued for in this book, MacGregor's approach would require an intersectional understanding of gender as the tool to interrogate dominant approaches to climate change and, drawing on political listening as feminist method, simultaneously ask Western feminists and gender experts in the Global North to recognise their own political responsibilities to act and to change when listening to the accounts of those living with the impact of climate change. This would require not the production of new gendered victims to save but the use of feminist methodologies to ask about the privileges attendant to those who shape and speak dominant discourses on climate

---

[141] ibid.
[142] Sherilyn MacGregor, ' "Gender and Climate Change": From Impacts to Discourses' (2010) 6(2) *Journal of the Indian Ocean Region* 223, 226.
[143] ibid 228.

changes while simultaneously creating spaces for peripheral subjects to speak and inform the contours of climate change law. This would require attention to who is permitted to be expert—on gender, on climate change, and on gender and climate change.

In returning to the approach to gender expertise found in the examples from NATO and WASH, an intersectional response to the transformation of institutions would require feminist methodologies that ask how political listening is mobilised in the design of expertise. For example, that the women, peace, and security resolutions articulate a need for consultations with local women's groups, although I have criticised this as limited, might be reflected on as providing a framework for feminist misreading. In the most recent Security Council resolution on women, peace, and security there is recognition of the need for 'broad consultation, including with civil society, in particular women's organizations' and a request that 'the hosts of such meetings give due consideration to facilitating a cross representation of civil society participants'.[144] Drawing on the strategic 'misreading' described in the CEDAW Committee's approach to intersectionality, a feminist methodology that draws out dialogue on how these provisions might stimulate new approaches to gender expertise—who speaks and who listens—and might be productive. With such an approach, the framework for gender expertise might begin consultations with existing local expertise to assess and understand where gender expertise already exists and to actively listen to who feels silenced by current institutional arrangements, as well as to listen to how the history of international interventions, whether colonial, regional, or via the United Nations, shape the reception for any subsequent interventions. These seem important feminist dialogues to have with regard to military engagements, such as those undertaken by NATO under the women, peace, and security agenda—and beyond—as well as interventions undertaken by development organisations, such as occurred in the WASH response to the Ebola outbreak in West Africa in 2014. The necessity of seeing and hearing, actually listening to, local gender expertise to inform the construction and design of intervention would be an imperative element of these misreadings, even if this displaces the appointed gender expert's knowledge.

The final example, drawn from the example of the African Women's Decade, questions the assumption that the appointment of high-profile women will translate into lasting gender law reform. This reduces gender expertise into a technique of governance that is void of feminist methodologies through an assumption that women are feminists and that all feminisms are the same. Transformation beyond this requires multi-tiered listening that asks where best practices occur (and does not assume Western democracies have an enlightened approach to gender expertise), while also engaging local, regional, and transnational conversations that at once share practices yet does not dictate the deployment of gender expertise in a given context, noting the further requirement to listen to the specific intersectional privileges and harms that occur within in a community.

---

[144] UNSC Res 2242 (13 October 2015) UN Doc S/RES/2242 paras 1, 2.

The development of gender expertise within the international institutions and structures of the twenty-first century remains the product of hard fought feminist battles and interventions that should be celebrated. The modes in which that knowledge now circulates in contemporary institutions, underscoring and enhancing the institution rather than feminist agendas, gives reason for a rethinking of how feminist knowledge is fashioned in the international sphere. To take seriously and consider the problems with the desire for an international institution to cloak approval on feminist interventions potentially undoes the feminist possibilities for reimagining how power operates. Alternative mechanisms would permit feminist law-making and feminist judging—for example, as occurs in people's tribunals or strategies for engaging international (transnational?) spaces of protest and activism that do not need an international institution to mobilise their potential. These are thoughts I return to across this book. Without attention to how feminist politics arrive at international institutions, the transformative nature of gender expertise will continue to lie in the empowerment of actors who look like and have access to the same knowledge histories as the actors who already function and work in global institutions. Setting forth a feminist methodology that challenges how knowledge is reinforced through the working of gender expertise must be developed to mobilise transnational feminist networks that have histories of work against existing structures and which already speak alternative feminist knowledge practices. In this way race politics, ableism, cis-genderism, class, and heteronormativity will also be configured as intersecting with stories of gender privilege. Feminist methods, feminist critique, and feminist action that are critical of their own biases, and attentive to the biases and privileges carried through international institutions, that seek new ways of speaking to power, that listen with a consciousness of their own political responsibilities, and that sometimes choose, simply, to work outside of existing power/institutional arrangements to achieve feminist space/gains, are consequently knitted into the role of the gender expert.

To return to the synthetic Palmyra Arch in Trafalgar Square and the technology that permits the creation of a replica that is but is not: a similar understanding can be given to the development of gender expertise within global governance. To stand, in Syria, before the remains of the Palmyra Arch is to marvel at a specific history and a specific series of acts that have both survived and mutated over time: the history and the creation are part of the object. Likewise, feminist histories lie interwoven with the creation of Security Resolution 1325, the birth of the International Criminal Court, the life of CEDAW, and the creation of UN Women: stories of activism and agitation, of transnational connection and disagreements inform the feminist content that arrives at the institutions of international law. However, gender expertise within international law 'must take account of divergences from the canon—understood as differing interpretations, resistances and subversions—particularly, as these manifest in the Global South, which tends to be marginalized at the international level'.[145] The current structure of gender expertise and the mechanisms to

---

[145] Soumita Basu, 'Global South Write 1325 (too)' (2016) 37(3) *International Political Science Review* 362.

measure gender do the same work as the synthetic monument—capturing a form and a shape without incorporating the diverse and complicated acts behind the image, the measure, the technical know-how. At stake is the entrenched violence in gender histories and ongoing violence of the structural bias of institutions that remains unchallenged when feminist dialogues and tensions are remade as a series of measures, indicators, and techniques or expertise.

3

Fragmentation

1. Introduction

Engaging feminist dialogues on contemporary issues within international law, outside of a focus on women's issues, is one of the key objectives of this book. At the same time, I am interested to move beyond critique and consider what comes after the analysis of foundational components of the international order. In this chapter I develop a discussion on fragmentation in international law, mapping the articulation of fragmentation by scholars and analysing the impact of fragmentation on gender law reform. To move beyond critique and description, I articulate plural legal subjectivity as a feminist methodology that accounts for and sees the plural legal structures in contemporary international legal arrangements. I draw on alternative accounts of subjectivity in feminist theories to articulate a normative starting point for future feminist dialogues. In addition, I approach the tension between resistance and compliance within feminist approaches to international law through imagining spaces where compliance might be enhanced and transformed through feminist dialogues with critical legal accounts of contemporary global governance.

Critical legal scholarship on international law has brought to the fore important debates on the consequences and effect of fragmentation on the discipline. Fragmentation is understood as an effect of the rise of the sub-disciplines and regimes within international law and the effect of multiple forums for the resolution of international disputes.[1] This chapter examines the impact of fragmentation on global governance from a feminist legal perspective, contributing an understanding of the structural limitations of existing scholarship on fragmentation and of the impact of the fragmentation and diversification of international law on gender law reform.[2] I argue that the diversification of sites of international law contributes to the fragmentation of gender law reform—both across spaces of global governance and from the rich dialogues on gender, sexuality, race, legacies of empire, and class that inform wider feminist dialogues than those that surface in gender law reforms. Consequently, regardless of whether fragmentation is perceived as a strength of, or

---

[1] Anne Peters, 'The Refinement of International Law: from Fragmentation to Regime Interaction and Politicisation' (2017) 15 International Journal of Constitutional Law 671 672–73.

[2] Gina Heathcote, 'Fragmented Feminisms: Critical Feminist Thinking in the Post-Millennium Era' in August Reinisch, Mary E Footer, and Christine Binder (eds), *International Law and ... (Select Proceedings of the European Society of International Law 2014)* (Hart 2016).

Feminist Dialogues on International Law. Gina Heathcote. © Gina Heathcote 2019. Published 2019 by Oxford University Press.

risk to, international law, the structural limitations and biases of law demand a different feminist engagement with global governance than the current liberal/radical/cultural feminist law reforms can affect. The chapter concludes that a feminist approach that is attentive to plural subjects has the potential to dramatically reorientate feminist engagements with international law. I draw on the plurality of legal forms produced via fragmentation to engage mechanisms for theorising difference as a feminist epistemology.

As with the previous chapter, I examine some of the spaces within international law where gender law reform has been permitted to flourish and examine the feminist approaches that have characterised these innovations.[3] This chapter builds on the analysis of how gender expertise has been deployed within global governance to interrogate the substantive contributions to international law that I describe as drawing on largely liberal, radical, and cultural feminist modes of law reform. Gender law reform focused on women's empowerment or increased participation reflect liberal feminist arguments for inclusion, while reforms centred on protecting women and prosecuting those responsible for sexual violence against women reflect US radical feminist preoccupations with carceral law and prosecution strategies.[4] Ironically the latter also often invoke cultural feminist tropes, centring women's different experiences from men in a manner that often solidifies gender difference.

In identifying specific feminist approaches as central to the production of gender law reform I argue that this fragments feminist knowledge and further disrupts the claim of feminist successes within international law.[5] Drawing out the claims on the relevance of intersectionality as a normative starting point in the previous chapter, I introduce feminist theorising of the nomad, the migrant, and peripheral subject to explore the value of attention to plural subjectivities as a feminist method shaping future gender law reform. In articulating a feminist method attentive to plural subjectivities, I interrogate critical legal responses to fragmentation that re-centre fragmentation as refinement and as promoting the consolidation of international law in the era of globalisation.[6] I argue that plural subjectivities, in addition to an understanding of the plurality of international institutions, is a necessary structural (rather than descriptive) mechanism to expose persistent biases and hierarchies that continue to be unexamined within international law and international legal

---

[3] Dianne Otto, 'The Exile of Inclusion: Reflections on Gender Issues in International Law over the Last Decade' 10 Melbourne Journal of International Law 11; Dianne Otto, 'Power and Danger: Feminist Engagement with International Law through the UN Security Council' (2010) 32 Australian Feminist Law Journal 97; Hilary Charlesworth, 'Talking to Ourselves: Feminist Scholarship in International Law' in Sari Kouvo and Zoe Pearson (eds), *Feminist Perspectives on Contemporary International Law: Between Resistance and Compliance* (Hart 2011) 17.

[4] Catherine Powell, 'Gender Indicators as Global Governance: Not Your Father's World Bank' (2016) 17 Georgetown Journal of Gender and Law 777, 805–06.

[5] Halley and others indicate governance feminism refers to 'the incremental but by now quite noticeable installation of feminists and feminist ideas in actual legal-institutional power': Janet Halley, Prabha Kotiswaran, Hila Shamir, and Chantal Thomas, 'From the International to the Local in Feminist Legal Responses to Rape, Prostitution/Sex Work and Sex Trafficking: Four Cases Studies in Contemporary Governance Feminism' (2006) 29 Harvard Journal of Law and Governance 335, 340.

[6] Margaret Young (ed), *Regime Interaction in International Law: Facing Fragmentation* (Cambridge University Press 2012).

writing. The chapter builds an understanding of feminism that expands feminist possibilities within international spaces and that can develop feminist approaches to international law—within and across feminist, critical, and mainstream dialogues.

Fragmentation scholarship engages the emergence of varied legal spaces, structures, and concepts while also theorising legal pluralism as a distinct mechanism for transforming law and legal relationships. How pluralism manifests in legal writing is varied, as this may signal a commitment to understanding the multiple legal models contained by a single system or an understanding of the plurality of legal orders, constituted globally. Twining describes legal pluralism as embodying both descriptive accounts of alternative legal structures and normative accounts that embrace legal pluralism as an integral legal form (as opposed to a space for the study of 'other' legal systems).[7] An attachment to legal pluralism might engender a passion for the diversity of international legal arrangements across spaces and structures or a commitment to uncovering legal forms outside of the dominant Western legal liberalism—and its colonial histories. In this chapter I draw on the latter as a mechanism to re-imagine the foundations of international law through theorising diverse understandings of subjectivities. The chapter outlines a commitment to legal pluralism as an engagement with plural and wandering subjectivities to inform the conceptualisation of legal subjectivity. This is a conscious turn away from the masculinist subject of international legal histories.[8] In the rendering of feminist work on subjectivities visible I analyse the potential for nomadic, migrant, and peripheral subjects to provide a normative template, extending legal pluralism via a feminist model of plural subjectivities.

I present plural subjectivities as a normative grounding for future feminist analysis of international law. An emergent method of feminist legal inquiry, that draws on the bodies and subjects that populate feminist and gender theories, is then proposed as a mechanism to bring together feminist writing on transnationalism and critical international legal approaches to plurality. In particular, the nomad,[9] the migrant,[10] and the peripheral subject[11] are introduced as forms of subjectivity that reorientate contemporary accounts on the fragmentation of international law and reassess the focus of feminist approaches to international law. In taking this framework forward in the text I also respond directly to past critiques of structural bias

---

[7] William Twining, 'Normative and Legal Pluralism: A Global Perspective' (2009) 20 Duke Journal of Comparative and International Law 473.

[8] Rosemary Hunter, 'Contesting the Dominant Paradigm: Feminist Critiques of Legal Liberalism' in Margaret Davies and Vanessa E Munro (eds), *The Ashgate Research Companion to Feminist Legal Theory* (Routledge 2013) 13; Ngaire Naffine and Rosemary Owens (eds), *Sexing the Subject of Law* (Law Book Company 1997); Yoriko Otomo 'Searching for Virtue in International Law' in Kouvo and Pearson (n 3) 33; Gina Heathcote, 'War's Perpetuity: Disabled Bodies of War and the Exoskeleton of Equality' (2018) 44(1) Australian Feminist Law Journal 71.

[9] Rosi Braidotti, *Nomadic Subjects: Embodiment and Sexual Difference in Contemporary Feminist Theory* (2nd edn, Columbia 2011).

[10] Avtar Brah, 'Diaspora, Border and Transnational Identities' in *Cartographies of Diaspora: Contesting Identities (Gender, Racism, Ethnicity Series)* (Routledge 1996) 178.

[11] Ratna Kapur, *Erotic Justice: Law and the New Politics of Postcolonialism* (Glasshouse Press 2005).

feminisms that draw attention to the need for approaches drawn from outside of Western feminist legal histories.[12]

The following section opens with an analysis of the literature and international reports on fragmentation, demonstrating the relevance of this to contemporary feminist work within the discipline of international law. Section 3 analyses the fragmentation of gender law reform: practically, within the institutional apparatus and intellectual framing of international law, and substantively, through the segregation of diverse currents within feminist and gender theories from the developments that have materialised within international law. I offer this as an alternative to some of the existing feminist critiques of 'governance feminism' (or GFeminism) and argue that an understanding of the structural limitations of international law is vital to any critique of (so-called) feminist 'successes' within the international realm.[13] Thus while critiques of GFeminism centre on describing gender initiatives within international law as at the mercy of a narrow range of (Western) feminist approaches, I demonstrate the need to appreciate the role fragmentation within international law and the global order plays in constraining the potential for inclusion of diverse feminist approaches in a system which mitigates against the very possibility of structural change at the level required. The final section of the chapter offers specific feminist tools for reframing approaches, emphasising a diversity of feminist approaches as a necessary mechanism for a feminist dialogues and as leverage for a transformative feminist politics and ethics within international law. This avoids the closing off of feminist thinking that occurs through either hyper-attention to specific gender law reforms or, as international institutions tend to do, assuming feminisms as singular and universal in a manner that deploys gender as a reference to women in problematic and, ultimately, retrogressive ways. Plural subjectivities as a methodology within feminist legal theory, I argue, is a mechanism premised on dialogue and difference as coordinating methodologies for transformative legal change, that has the capacity to draw in intersectionality and the politics of listening.

2. On Fragmentation and International Law

In this section I review the various dialogues within international law on fragmentation, from early accounts warning of the risks of fragmentation to more recent scholarship that perceives a refinement of international law as an expected consequence of diversification.[14] Noting claims for an emergent global constitutional function,

---

[12] Karen Engle, 'International Human Rights and Feminisms: Where Discourses Keep Meeting' in Doris Buss and Ambreena Manji (eds), *International Law: Modern Feminist Approaches* (Hart 2005).

[13] Halley and others (n 5).

[14] Young (n 6); Martti Koskenniemi and Päivi Leino, 'Fragmentation of International Law: Postmodern Anxieties?' (2002) 15 Leiden Journal of International Law 553; Eyal Benvenisti and George W Downs, 'The Empire's New Clothes: Political Economy and the Fragmentation of International Law' (2007) Stanford Law Review 595; Anne-Charlotte Martineau, 'The Rhetoric of Fragmentation: Fear and Faith in International Law' (2009) 22 Leiden Journal of International Law 1.

as well as the relevance of legal pluralism with discourse on fragmentation, I conclude that the fragmentation scholarship provides useful descriptive accounts of the wherewithal of global governance. At the same time approaches to fragmentation insufficiently engage with the persistence of entrenched bias and the interlocking perpetuation of power relations. It is striking, for example, that references to plurality rest with identification of the plurality of international institutions and do not consider pluralism as a mechanism to re-evaluate and understand the multiplicity of legal arrangements and conceptualisations. In examining this material, I introduce the approaches to fragmentation articulated by critical legal scholars, such as Koskenniemi and Peters, as well as mainstream approaches within international law. I conclude with a review of arguments that find fragmentation provides a mechanism for the refinement of international law, and demonstrate how, across approaches to fragmentation, the search for a better description of the global order displaces robust engagement with the power structures that prop up the institutions of global governance.[15]

Scholarly understanding of the impact of legal fragmentation on international law has spawned critical, and mainstream texts. Across scholarship, fragmentation within international law is perceived to exist in at least two registers and with multiple consequences (positive and negative) for the discipline. First, fragmentation is a reference to the rise of specialist regimes,[16] often characterised as transnational laws, which govern and regulate concerns as diverse as human rights, trade, sport, technology, environment, maritime law, and health, and the search for an overarching mechanism to coordinate development and conflict across these regimes.[17] Second, fragmentation is also used to refer to the rise of specialist institutions, in particular international courts and tribunals, with different and overlapping spheres of practice that resolve disputes in both international and transnational legal regimes and that, potentially, contribute to the development of international law across diverse forums. Early understandings of fragmentation from successive ICJ judges described the rise of new courts and tribunals as 'jeopordi[sing] the unity of international law',[18] 'exacerbat[ing] risk'[19] and lacking an 'overall plan' thus 'fragmented and unmanageable'.[20] The original fear of uncertainty, due to the lack of court hierarchy within the international realm, was voiced by successive Presidents of the International Court of Justice and was ultimately responded to through the creation of the directive from the UN General Assembly to the International Law

---

[15] Peters (n 1).   [16] Young (n 6) 4–5.

[17] I use the transnational law/s to refer to those that rules evolve through specialised regimes, and by definition can be characterised as *lex specialis*, and can be contrasted from the general rules of public international law.

[18] Speech by HE Judge Gilbert Guillaume, President of the ICJ, to the General Assembly, 30 October 2001.

[19] Speech by HE Judge Gilbert Guillaume, President of the ICJ, to the General Assembly, 26 October 2000.

[20] Robert Y Jennings, 'The Role of the International Court of Justice' (1997) 68 British Yearbook of International Law 58, 59–60.

Commission (ILC) to take up the matter.[21] This enlarged the scope of inquiry from the proliferation of courts and tribunals to an engagement with specialised regimes and substantive concerns, including conflict of laws issues debated under legal pluralism. This developed into a broader scholarly inquiry centred on the plethora of specialised regimes within international law that necessitated a need to understand the interlocking, overlapping, and divergent components of these structures.

In response to scholarly and institutional arguments on fragmentation, the ILC, in 2002, found:

> fragmentation can be seen as a sign of the vitality of international law ... the proliferation of rules, regimes and institutions might strengthen international law ... the increasing scope of international law means that areas that were previously unaddressed by international law are now being addressed. Similarly, there are advantages in increased diversity of voices and a polycentric system in international law.[22]

In the same report the ILC identified its own role as 'to assist international judges and practitioners in coping with the consequences of the diversification of international law'[23] and to provide 'what could be called a "toolbox" designed to assist in solving practical problems arising from incongruities and conflicts between existing legal norms and regimes'.[24] Each of these goals infers a sense of challenges brought by fragmentation, whilst still describing fragmentation as a site of renewal in terms of identifying the potential of the international legal system to respond to its own inadequacies.[25] In the academic literature, Koskenniemi and Leino encourage acceptance of the manner in which global 'political communities have become more heterogenous, their boundaries much more porous, than assumed by the received images of sovereignty and the international order, and that the norms they are express are fragmentary, discontinuous, often ad hoc and without definite hierarchical relationship'.[26] Debates on fragmentation thus emerge as stories of international law at risk and as stories of international law as reflecting changing global patterns and arrangements.

By 2006, Koskenniemi's report to the ILC demonstrated the increased nexus between developments in critical legal scholarship and their currency within the mainstream of international law.[27] With Koskenniemi taking the lead on the ILC's work on fragmentation, earlier anxieties with regard to the fragmentation of international law were tempered with a sense of latent potentiality.[28] From a critical perspective,

---

[21] International Law Commission, 'Fragmentation of International Law: Difficulties arising from the Diversification and Expansion of International Law: Report of the Study Group of the International Law Commission—Finalized by Martti Koskenniemi' (13 April 2006) UN Doc A/CN4/L682 (*Fragmentation of International Law*); also see ILC, 'Report of the International Law Commission 58th Session' (May–9 June and 3 July–11 August 2006) UN Doc A/61/10, para 251; ILC, 'Summary Record of the 2468th Meeting' (23 July 1996) UN Doc A/CN4/L528.

[22] ILC, 'Fragmentation' (n 21) para 2.1.   [23] ibid.   [24] ibid, para 21(e).

[25] Rosalyn Higgins, 'A Babel of Judicial Voices? Ruminations from the Bench' (2006) 55(4) International and Comparative Law Quarterly 791.

[26] Koskenniemi and Leino (n 14) 558.

[27] BS Chimni, *International Law and World Order: A Critique of Contemporary Approaches* (2nd edn, Cambridge University Press 2017).

[28] ILC, 'Fragmentation' (n 21) para 7.

the practical issues connected to fragmentation debates (proliferation of courts, conflict of laws issues, substantive diversification) interlink with a deep rooted series of concerns about the purpose and potential of international law as a global legal structure. The solution, for Koskenniemi and Leino, is to characterise fragmentation as postmodern in such a manner that the anxieties experienced by other commentators are better understood as inevitable and malleable rather than a site of potential dissolution of international law.[29] Beyond Koskenniemi and Leino's argument that fragmentation is a marker of postmodern law and life, broader critical inquiries have looked to theories of constitutionalism[30] and models of global administrative law,[31] to move away from the 'crisis' stories of fragmentation, towards a sense of understanding the structural possibilities of a diverse yet unified system, or structure, of global, transnational, and international laws, both public and private. For Peters this yields a sense that fragmentation is best understood as diversification that ultimately leads to refinement. Peters concludes: 'The lens of "refinement" allows accepting and reassessing diversity, conflict, and even contradiction as a positive condition which manifests and facilitates the realization of the values of critique and contestation within international law.'[32] Fragmentation, for Peters, can be 'successfully managed' and thus is a feature for the refinement rather than the diffraction of international law, with the diversity of global governance an important component of the contemporary international legal framework.[33]

Fragmentation debates, beyond inquiries into whether it constitutes a risk or opportunity, centre on how specialised regimes and institutions create a diffusion of international legal norms, as different regimes develop specialised practices and approaches to the application of law. Furthermore, debates on fragmentation highlight the intersection of public and private international law, drawing attention to new issues that extend beyond traditional approaches to the conflict of laws and to the transformative role of non-state actors, including international institutions and multinational corporations. Debates on, and analysis of, global constitutionalism and legal pluralism are of specific relevance to fragmentation scholarship,[34] with recognition that new sites of conflict—between specialised transnational regimes and national laws, between overlapping specialised regimes, and between transnational and indigenous legal structures—require a set of meta- or secondary rules when regime conflict occurs.[35] Nevertheless, for Peters, fragmentation creates the condition

---

[29] Koskenniemi and Leino (n 14).

[30] Nico Krisch, *Beyond Constitutionalism: The Pluralist Structure of Postnational Law* (Oxford University Press 2010).

[31] Benedict Kingsbury, 'The Concept of 'Law' in Global Administrative Law' (2009) 20 European Journal of International Law 23.

[32] Peters (n 1) 704.

[33] ibid 672 (where Peters at 702 states: 'it is time to bury the f-word').

[34] Colin Murray and Aoife O'Donoghue, 'A Path Already Travelled in Domestic Orders? From Fragmentation to Constitutionalism in the Global Legal Order' (2017) 13 International Journal of Law in Context 225, 247: 'The global legal order's current, fragmented state evidences a legalised and differentiated governance order primed for constitutionalisation.'

[35] Gunther Teubner and Peter Korth, 'Two Kinds of Legal Pluralism: Collision of Transnational Regimes in the Double Fragmentation of World Society' in Margaret Young (ed), *Regime Interaction in International Law: Facing Fragmentation* (Cambridge University Press 2012) 23.

for international law to be strengthened through the resolution of conflict between regimes.[36]

An alternative critical account emerges in the work of Teubner, whose development of Luhmann's larger work on autopoietic systems attempts to map a broader understanding of fragmentation through the embedding of fragmentation within social realities.[37] Teubner argues for 'particular constitutions for each of these global fragments—nations, transnational regimes, regional cultures—connected to each other in a constitutional conflict of laws'.[38] Teubner's sociological approach to global constitutionalism, which prioritises the social and functional differentiation of the various systems, structures, and regimes within transnational law, thus proposes a new way of describing the existing system to resolve the anxieties expressed by jurists. Teubner's work, however, never addresses the power and inequalities reproduced by each system. Likewise, Craven describes fragmentation as a

continuous feature of international legal thought and practice in its attempt to overcome difference and diversity that assail the discipline both from within and outside. 'Fragmentation' is simply a way of expressing, with certain obvious overtones, a concern that the disciplinary centre can no longer hold the forces of diversity in check. What goes for 'centre' or indeed 'diversity', however, remains the central point of debate.[39]

These critical framings are largely absent of what Koskenniemi and Leino describe as an anxiety and fear of postmodern diversification, as they regard the embedded structures of international, transnational, and global laws as requiring better description and mapping. Consequently, little attention is given to how the global order—fragmented or diversified—produces and replicates power structures. Craven does conclude with a reference to power relations and the legacy of imperial histories—among states—as usefully managed via the growing diversification of international law but avoids interrogation of the complexity of gender as intersectional, and thus the additional power differentials also reproduced within the international system, whether fragmented or diversified, refined or disorderly in its developments.[40] In this chapter I extend this understanding of diversity to draw in feminist theorising on difference, in particular intersectionality, so as to theorise pluralism in relation to understanding subjectivity as equally as specialised regimes.

Similar to Craven, Koskenniemi and Leino acknowledge the imperial history of international law, and the legacy of inequality between states, yet affirm that 'a politics of tolerance and pluralism, [is] not only compatible with institutional fragmentation, but its best justification'.[41] Elsewhere Koskenniemi writes, '[t]he point of the emergence of something like "international criminal law" or "international human

---

[36] Peters (n 1) 61: 'the resulting regime collisions are praiseworthy because they manifest and further promote pluralism, contestation, and politicization'.

[37] Gunther Teubner (ed), *Autopoetic Law: A New Approach to Law and Society* (Walter de Gruyter 1988); Gunther Teubner, *Constitutional Fragments: Societal Constitutionalism and Globalisation* (Oxford University Press 2012).

[38] Young (n 6) 15.

[39] Matthew Craven, 'Unity, Diversity and the Fragmentation of International Law' (2003) 14 Finnish Yearbook of International Law 3, 32.

[40] ibid.   [41] Koskenniemi and Leino (n 14) 579.

rights law" (or any other special law) is precisely to institutionalise the new priorities carried within such fields'.[42] Koskenniemi highlights how the fears of the international court are connected to older fears of the diversification of international law articulated within traditional, formalist accounts of the discipline. Identifying how this fear gradually subsides into an acceptance of the inevitabilities and potentialities of fragmentation for international law as a discipline, Koskenniemi does consider the structural biases of the various regimes within international law where more than one specialist regime might operate as a forum for decision-making in disputes, so that '[t]he choice of the frame determined the decision. But for determining the frame, there was no meta-regime, directive or rule.'[43] Similarly, Koskenniemi and Leino address the critical uncertainty regarding the latent imperial trends found in arguments for humanitarianism, human rights, and so forth, that is associated with a cosmopolitan, Kantian form of instrumentalism.[44] Nevertheless, while Teubner, Craven, and Peters or Koskenniemi and Leino all provide useful descriptions and insight into fragmentation, as do the ILC Reports, none address the perpetuating of inequalities within the international legal system associated with race, class, ableism, sexuality, or gender, including cis-genderism, or the legacies of colonialism and the prior destruction of indigenous socio-political and legal structures. The limited engagement with these internal biases of law undermines the implicit, and explicit, embrace of legal pluralism within writing on fragmentation and international law, as the reassertion of the status quo remains.

At the same time, despite the mixture of critical and mainstream international legal scholarship that emerges on fragmentation, as well as the diverse range of topics drawn in, the substantive and structural complexity of gender and women's rights is not a component of the inquiries that have emerged. Halley describes an awareness of the potential of fragmentation as key to governance feminism (here GF) strategies, such that,

GF-as-a-strategic-enterprise, in our examples anyway, shares with these very complex moments an understanding of legal power as highly fragmented and dispersed; they deemphasize the politics/law distinction in order to work not only in the spectacularly legal domains of litigation, legislation, and policymaking, but also in personal pressure campaigns, consciousness raising, and highly discretionary legal moments such as prosecutorial charging strategy.[45]

The recognition of the plural sites, and actors, that GFeminism works through, however, has not spawned sufficient feminist scholarship or attention, nor has the impact of fragmentation on gender law reform generally. O'Rourke and Swaine argue that advocates for increased gender law reform should use fragmentation to develop 'ongoing processes of cross-regime dialogue, to facilitate practical cooperation, and inter-regime accountability, in which each regime seeks to hold the other to account for its activities'.[46] O'Rourke and Swaine give the example of the cross-fertilisation

---

[42] Martti Koskenniemi, 'The Fate of Public International Law: Between Technique and Politics' (2007) 70 Modern Law Review 1.

[43] ibid 6.   [44] Koskenniemi and Leino (n 14).

[45] Halley and others, 'From the International to the Local' (n 5) 341.

[46] Catherine O'Rourke and Aisling Swaine, 'CEDAW and the Security Council: Enhancing Women's Rights in Conflict' (2018) 67 International and Comparative Law Quarterly 167, 172.

of approaches to human rights and women, peace and security. For O'Rourke and Swaine this:

effectively brought the two systems of accountability and thematic activity on gender and conflict into conversation with one another and addressed the specifics of their relationships, thereby signalling the realignment of the WPS and broader international women's rights agendas. Whether and how their shared concern for thematic areas of interest, and for accountability on the same, is taken forward from this point will largely determine whether fragmentation across the regimes is entrenched, or the opportunity for enhanced synergy maximized, for common advancement of women's rights in conflict and peacebuilding.[47]

O'Rourke and Swaine indicate the cross-fertilisation of the women, peace, and security and CEDAW agendas functions to enhance the legitimacy of the Security Council resolutions, describing the General Recommendation as 'an effort to give retrospective legal status to the UNSC resolution 1325 and its successors'.[48] Not surprisingly the links between the two sites of gender law reform therefore reinforce the narrow models of feminist messages already consolidated within each specialised regime. For O'Rourke and Swaine the cross-regime articulations ultimately demonstrate a mechanism for ensuring continuities in gender law reform across different institutions[49] On this account, feminist 'messages' are not integrated into global governance; nevertheless fragmentation offers the opportunity for checks and balances in a manner assumed to represent global and transnational feminist voices.

The embrace of plurality by contemporary international legal scholars is then a space for recognition of the multiple forums and regimes that exist within international law, rather than recognition of multiple legal forms or structural transformation. These debates are undertaken with limited feminist interventions and with attention to a specific understanding of plurality within law. For example, the identification of plurality initiates a turn to functionalism that asserts that this is how the system works rather than sufficiently exploring the privileges and biases the functioning of the global order further perpetuates. The plurality asserted fuses attention to international law's own multiplicity via respect for dominant legal traditions, globally, while other sites of difference, particularly as experienced by indigenous and non-Western communities, peoples, and individuals, is erased from the discussion. To understand, and incorporate, renderings of diversity, renewed attention to legal pluralism, drawn from an understanding of diverse legal arrangements, is required. Further, to dislodge the masculine legal subject that forms the basis for understanding the international legal subject of the state, attention to plural subjectivities is required to avoid entrenching gender law reform that fails to see gender as embedded and connected to further power relations. Thus, I argue in this chapter that the failure to attend to theories that posit plural legal modes and subjectivities perpetuates the reassertion of the status quo that pivots on a version of humanity and subjectivity drawn from the Western enlightenment man that haunts legal liberalism. This analysis complements the study of gender law reform

---

[47] ibid 192.   [48] ibid 194.   [49] ibid 199.

commenced in the former chapter, adding to the analysis of gender experts a study of the diversification of gender law reform across different international institutions.

With these thoughts in mind, this chapter expands the legal pluralist project within international law to explore how legal pluralism informs potentially trans-formative feminist projects. I argue that there is value in identifying feminist legal accounts that shift away from examination (or assumption) of liberal and Western legal structures to understand the potential of legal pluralism as a feminist tool. For example, Davies' work on flat law embeds all legal relationships and struc-tures within larger networks of norms that recognise horizontal forms of regula-tion and overlap.[50] Her account of law is enriched by an ability to disregard the vertical register of common law traditions in favour of one that recognises law as one of a series of normative structures within (and across) communities.[51] Similar to Teubner, Davies looks to engage the relationship between the law and the social. While Teubner's goal in approaching fragmentation through systems theories is to provide a better description of international legal systems, Davies's goal is to avoid the process of inclusion and exclusion that underpin legal relationships and legal hierarchies.[52] Davies argues that 'a horizontal perception of law places the value of relations, contiguity and subject empowerment at the heart of what law is'.[53] It is this aspect of feminist legal theorising—which overlaps with my perception of plural understanding of subjectivities within gender theories—that I wish to insert into fragmentation debates and use to move beyond *re-description* of the global order towards spaces for *re-imagining* the foundations of legal arrangements and possi-bilities. Central to this project are the shifting plural legal subjects found within gender and feminist theories and the feminist epistemological expectations of law as plural in the sense of law's normativity embedded in broader structures of meaning, in particular, the theorisation of diversity and difference (rather than universality) across global, regional, and local spaces. This recalls Arendt's articulation of human sameness existing within the human capacity for difference; that is, plurality is the 'condition of human action because we are all the same, that is, human in such a way that nobody else is ever the same as anyone who ever lived, lives, or will live'.[54] I argue that the recognition of plural legal forms opens questions around who the subject of law is, disrupting the very possibility of a singular notion of the legal sub-ject in favour of diverse subjectivities.

In the next section I argue that expanding feminist understanding of fragmenta-tion is important because the take-up and exploration of both gender and women's rights within institutional and academic spaces provides an excellent case study of the impact of fragmentation on both the practical and substantive development of international law. Furthermore, the continued framing of fragmentation as refine-ment (or consolidation) by scholars and institutions alike is ultimately unhelpful,

---

[50] Margaret Davies, 'Feminism and the Flat Law Theory' (2008) 16(3) Feminist Legal Studies 281.
[51] Robert Cover, 'Nomos and Narrative' (1983–84) 97 Harvard Law Review 4.
[52] Davies (n 50) 281.   [53] ibid 301.
[54] Hannah Arendt, *On Violence* (Harcourt 1970) 8; Gina Heathcote, *The Law on the Use of Force: A Feminist Analysis* (Routledge 2012) 176.

as this remains a reassertion of the status quo of international law, through the turn to functionalism, and leaves unquestioned the foundational components of international law that perpetuate inequalities. A broader feminist and gender framework (in the sense of non-legal) can be used to better understand fragmentation, and its consequences, and this is an approach that connects to the rejection of a specifically (and largely Western) masculine history of international law. The fragmentation of feminist approaches within international law is an important signifier of the poverty of mainstream approaches to fragmentation. That is, the perpetuation of bias, in this case gendered biases, reproduced by the fragmenting (or the refining) of international law is indicative of the perpetuation of the structural inadequacies of the discipline per se. I argue that legal pluralism provides an important conceptualisation and recognition of difference at an epistemological level. Plural legal subjects then advance a specifically feminist framing of difference.

As the study of 'women's issues' or 'gender issues' within international law immediately identifies, an extremely partial (and fragmented) account of international law emerges (primarily centred on international human rights law, collective security and international criminal law) and, while admittedly these spaces represent a series of useful developments within specific international legal spaces, they remain insufficient developments within gender perspectives or in terms of transforming the field of international law more generally. Unlike O'Rourke and Swaine's promotion of the use of diversified structure of global governance as a check and balance system for the implementation of gender law reform, my interest is to consider how the institutions and structures of international law themselves dictate and produce circumscribed outcomes.[55] The chapter thus posits and imagines feminist dialogues on plural subjectivities as integral to any future gender law reform, drawn from transnational feminist projects that both theorise and enact feminist understandings of difference as a starting point for feminist methodologies.

3. Fragmented Feminisms

Review of Koskenniemi's report to the International Law Commission sees no reference to 'women' or 'gender' within the study. Nonetheless the impact of fragmentation on gender perspectives within international law is of considerable importance, demonstrating how changes within the constitution of legal structures create specific outcomes and how various initiatives by a range of women and feminist actors targeted specific sites of global governance. Women's human rights and the CEDAW process,[56] the women, peace, and security framework within the Security Council,[57]

---

[55] O'Rourke and Swaine (n 46); Mona Lena Krook and Fiona MacKay (eds), *Gender, Politics and Institutions: Towards a Feminist Institutionalism* (Palgrave 2011).

[56] Marsha A Freeman, Christine Chinkin, and Beata Rudolf (eds), *The UN Convention on the Elimination of all Forms of Discrimination Against Women: A Commentary* (Oxford University Press 2012); Loveday Hodson, 'Women's Rights and Periphery: CEDAW's Optional Protocol' (2014) 25 European Journal of International Law 561.

[57] Gina Heathcote and Diane Otto (eds), *Rethinking Peacekeeping, Gender Equality and Collective Security* (Palgrave 2014).

developments within international criminal law with respect to gendered crimes,[58] as well as gender and development initiatives,[59] all rely on some (assumed) shared goals and, yet, function with considerable fragmentation, being located across the various institutional arms of the UN, and within a range of sub-disciplines and specialised regimes. Not surprisingly at the same time that Koskenniemi developed the institutional engagement with fragmentation, Kennedy's work on expertise within the international order as an additional feature of twenty-first-century global governance mirrored the rise of the gendered expert in global institutions. In the previous chapter I mapped how the critical legal engagement with expertise benefits from attention to practical and theoretical feminist developments over the same period. Here I reflect on the capacity for useful dialogue between critical legal scholars and feminist scholars on the legacy and effects of fragmentation.

The practical segmentation and division of work on women and gender across the institutions of the United Nations, and throughout the various legal structures within international law, has had specific impact on the development of the feminist thinking and gender law reform within international spaces. First, the continued focus of gender reform on issues centred on women's lives consolidates the assumption that gender perspectives focus on women.[60] Fragmentation contributes to this through creating pockets of isolated reform on gender that are effectively directed at women's issues rather than at the discipline of international law. This highlights 'the long-overdue need to move beyond an understanding of gender as relating only to women's vulnerability'.[61] Even when men are considered as subjects within gender initiatives, for example in work around male victims of conflict-related sexual violence, a reassertion of a gendered binary between men and women occurs rather than any serious attempt to reflect the sophisticated understanding and diversity of gender politics or an understanding of gender as varied within and across communities.[62] Second, as discussed in chapter 2, the work on gender within the United Nations appears to have been ghettoised into the umbrella body of UN Women, where gender mainstreaming is expected to be conducted by gender experts and institutions, so that individuals and laws that are not directly focused on gender/women remain untouched by gender law reforms. As such, gender issues remain occasional and special interest topics rather than knitted into the structures of international law. The next generation of feminist scholarship must take this fragmentation as a serious indication of the politics behind the turn to gender in (select) international spaces, which are often predicated on the legitimation of specific

---

[58] Alona Hagay-Frey, *Sex and Gender Crimes in the New International Law* (Brill 2011).

[59] Ambreena Manji, 'The Beautyful Ones of Law and Development' in Buss and Manji (n 12) 159.

[60] Judith Gardam and Dale Stephens, 'Concluding Remarks: Establishing Common Ground between Feminism and the Military' in Heathcote and Otto (n 57) 265, 270–71.

[61] Simone E Carter, Luisa Maria Dietrich, and Olive Melissa Minor, 'Mainstreaming Gender in WASH: Lessons Learned from Oxfam's Experience of Ebola (2017) 25(2) Gender and Development 205, 212.

[62] Dianne Otto, 'A Sign of "Weakness"? Disrupting Gender Certainties in the Implementation of Security Council Resolution 1325' (2006–07) 13 Michigan Journal of Gender and the Law 113; Chloé Lewis, 'Systematic Silencing: Addressing Sexual Violence against Men and Boys in Armed Conflict and Its Aftermath' in Heathcote and Otto (n 57) 203.

actors and institutions, rather than a commitment to the development of feminist law. Gender law reform, in the era of fragmentation, is not only fragmented across specialist regimes, 'gender law reform' becomes a specialised regime itself. Likewise, feminist method and feminist messages are fragmented from the institutional outputs, so that gender law reforms is refined to appease existing structures of global governance and the institutions they emerge within.

Understanding gender law reform as entrenched in the workings and limitations of the global system (for example, via critical approaches to fragmentation or expertise) rather than outside the system (and 'within' feminist dialogues) is crucial to theorising beyond the current limited model of gender law reform. Without this linkage of feminist approaches to contemporary critical work on the evolving international order it seems inevitable that feminist law and policy initiatives within the international will continue to appear to legitimate and consolidate, rather than transform, the global order. In this section I document the two aspects of gender law reform within international law that underscore the impact of fragmentation on gender initiatives. The two concerns I document in this section tally with the types of description Charlesworth, Chinkin, and Wright document in 1991, and again in 2005, regarding the practical and substantive (normative) exclusions of women from the international sphere.[63] However, in contrast to these earlier accounts highlighting both the practical and normative design of international law as spaces of exclusion, I argue for recognition of the post-millennium shift towards partial inclusion of gender law reform which ultimately fragments feminisms and reduces the impact of feminism on the structures and processes of international law. Gender law reform, like fragmentation debates, then risks reaffirming the status quo and existing inequalities rather than a realisation of the transformative potential of feminist approaches to international law. Unless feminist legal inquiries and projects develop their theorisation of the global order it seems inevitable that the global order will dictate the terms of feminist engagement and thus produce spaces of co-optation rather than transformation via gender law reform strategies.[64]

In examining the first concern, the practical, and most visible, effects of fragmentation exist in the organisation of 'gender issues' within international law. The real consequences of this are perhaps best understood by picking up and thumbing through any international law text book in pursuit of an understanding of either feminist approaches or gender law reform. Despite the multiple sites of gender law reform, gender perspectives, and the concrete legal developments in relation to gender, the topics of women and gender remain structurally invisible from the purview of the mainstream international lawyer. Gender is thus both present and absent in international law's self-representations. There are acknowledged sites where gender 'happens' and most, if not all, of these pertain to women's rights (and men's

---

[63] Hilary Charlesworth, Christine Chinkin, and Shelly Wright, 'Feminist Approaches to International Law' (1991) 85(4) American Journal of International Law 613, 631; Christine Chinkin, Shelley Wright, and Hilary Charlesworth, 'Feminist Approaches to International Law: Reflections from Another Century' in Buss and Manji (n 12).

[64] Sara Ahmed, 'Close Encounters: Feminism and/in "the globe"' in Sara Ahmed, *Strange Encounters: Embodied Others in Post-Coloniality* (Routledge 2000) 161.

accountability for the violation of these rights in the most extreme cases) but these are not regarded as foundational to international law. As a result, both scholarly accounts and policy documents only pay attention to gender from within the spaces that are labelled as focused on women, in particular within and via the CEDAW Committee and/or UN Women. This constructs a practical fragmentation of gender law reform across the sub-disciplines of international law, that also establishes segregation of feminist approaches from international law as a discipline and the international legal institutions that develop the law and its application.

The practical fragmentation of gender law reform from the everyday work of international institutions happens within specific sites where gender law reforms have occurred, for example, international criminal law and collective security, as equally as it happens across the discipline as a whole. While there is significant jurisprudence, and academic commentary, on gender within international criminal law,[65] as well as significant legal developments and scholarship on collective security via the women, peace, and security framework developed by the Security Council,[66] mainstream articulations of either international criminal law and/or collective security pay little heed to gender reforms. For example, within international criminal law this has resulted in a corpus of literature and jurisprudence on gender-based violence, specifically conflict-related sexual violence, and little feminist engagement with the nature, form, and operation of international criminal law. At the same time the gender 'successes' within international criminal law remain fragmented from mainstream developments and emerge predominantly through the work of specialist gender actors and scholarship rather than, as early articulations of gender mainstreaming envisaged, as a concrete and embedded component across the breadth of the discipline and institutions.[67]

The fragmentation of gender initiatives within the global order emerges, on the one hand, from a feminist scholarly and practitioner focus on these specific sites as equally as, on the other hand, from the larger disciplinary fragmentation and (perhaps) avoidance of feminist content in non-feminist scholarship.[68] Despite the coordination of gender affairs through the creation of UN Women in 2010,[69] the gender mainstreaming of international law and institutions remains one where specialised actors and gender experts within UN Women are expected to undertake

---

[65] Louise Chappell, *The Politics of Gender Justice at the International Criminal Court: Legacies and Legitimacy* (Oxford University Press 2016); Doris Buss, Joanne Lebert, Blair Rutherford, Donna Sharkey, and Obijiofor Aginam, *Sexual Violence in Conflict and Post-Conflict Societies: International Agendas and African Contexts* (Routledge 2014); Louise Chappell and Andrea Durbach, 'Special Issue on the International Criminal Court: A Site of Gender Justice?' (2014) 16(4) International Feminist Journal of Politics 533.

[66] Heathcote and Otto (n 57); Laura Shepherd and Paul Kirby, 'Special Issue on the Futures of Women, Peace and Security' (2016) 92 International Affairs 275; Nicola Pratt and Sophie Richter-Devroe, 'Special Issue Critically Examining UNSCR 1325' (2011) 13(4) International Feminist Journal of Politics 489.

[67] Karen Hall and Stacey Fox, '"Favourite Footnote"? Hilary Charlesworth on Feminism and International Law' (2006) 13 Limina: A Journal of Historical and Cultural Studies 1.

[68] Chimni (n 27); Andrea Bianchi, *International Law Theories: An Inquiry into Different Ways of Thinking* (Oxford University Press 2016).

[69] General Assembly Resolution 64/289 (2 July 2000) UN Doc A/RES/64/289.

gender work without the tools to deploy feminist methodologies as a component of gender law reform. As seen in the study of expertise, the appointment of a gender expert becomes the gender law reform rather than engaged and sustained gender mainstreaming within international legal structures. What is important for the purposes of engaging fragmentation debates is an understanding that there remains a segmentation of 'gender work' from UN work and a segmentation of gender issues from international law issues, that is, perhaps, at some levels attributable to the larger fragmentation of the discipline and its institutions. Furthermore, this practical fragmentation of gender work within the discipline has also steered feminist scholarship away from engagement with the structures of the global order and centred feminist scholarship within international law on a small range of issues largely drawn from human rights, collective security, and international criminal law initiatives. The consequence, within work on gender in international institutions, is the development of a tendency to assume that the gender biases and discrimination are experienced similarly by women globally and a narrow set of issues (primarily gender-based violence and conflict-related sexual violence). The casualties of this approach, then, are engagements with (or appreciations of) the diverse manifestations of gender arrangements, the interaction of gendered harms with other sites of discrimination, and biases within the system as well as a general neglect of strategies to transform the structures of international law and the global order. The preference instead is the development and incorporation of some initiatives on women's issues within the existing international legal system.

The disconnection of gender perspectives from the larger structures and foundations of international law alongside a fragmentation of women, gender, and feminist issues across the sub-disciplines of international law mirrors the rise of sub-disciplines explored in the ILC reports. As such, while Halley argues against the rise of GFeminism for its 'near seamless performance of consensus'[70] and the production of an 'overwhelmingly ... structuralist feminist worldview'[71] her work does not explore the potential for feminist engagement within international law beyond GFeminism or the structural constraints through which existing feminist projects have gained, in the words of Otto, footholds within international law.[72] While Halley's work centres on uncovering the political commitments of the specific 'brand' of feminist politics that has influenced international criminal law, an exploration of the two key additional sites where feminist influence can be perceived, collective security and human rights, suggests that even with recognition of the valuable work these sites of knowledge produce this ultimately exists as a tiny, fragmented space of international law as a discipline.

I examine the politics and ethics, or 'brand' of feminist successes within international law, below; however, I think it is important to first map the (serious lack

---

[70] Janet Halley, 'Rape at Rome: Feminist Inventions in the Criminalization of Sex-Related Violence in Positive International Criminal Law' (2009) 30 Michigan Journal of International Law 1, 6.

[71] ibid.

[72] Dianne Otto, 'The Exile of Inclusion: Reflections on Gender issues in International Law over the Last Decade' (2009) 10 Melbourne Journal of International Law 1.

of) magnitude of these successes to demonstrate the fra they present.
This is in distinction to Halley's approach which documen velopments in
international criminal law as including GFeminism as 'a participant'.[73]
In contrast, Chappell describes feminist advocacy and agenoarticipant'.[73]
criminal law as providing a 'mixed gender justice record', that dnternational
ness to gender discourses in the earlier stages in the developmentes an open-
Criminal Court followed by limitations connected to the legacternational
ance norms.[74] This is a fragmented space within international crinal govern-
more so within international law as a whole. Consequently, rather tand even
international criminal law as wholly subsumed by feminist politicstructing
to identify the subset of international criminal laws that have contaiportant
of feminist engagement with the sub-discipline of international crimirextent
institutions. nd its

The establishment of the International Criminal Court and the pr orial
choices of the court demonstrate this: the 1990s moved towards gender ive-
ness via the responsiveness of the ad hoc tribunals, which laid the grol rk
for an endorsement of gender justice strategies within the Rome Statute, he
ICC. Chappell describes the inclusion of provisions to prosecute sexual vic
to have women and gender experts included in International Criminal Court
cesses and the reparations model as 'groundbreaking'.[75] However, Chappell
finds the 'implementation record in regard to gender justice has been partial a
inconsistent'.[76] To move beyond Halley's thesis that 'GFeminism learnt to walk th
halls of power' and understand these inconsistencies, fragmentation can be used as
a means to demonstrate that the halls that opened to feminist actors in the 1990s
were located within specific, constrained spaces rather than within the larger international legal structures.[77] The limited halls that were open to feminist engagement
mitigates and fragments the feminist outcomes within international criminal law
and, arguably, within the discipline of international law as a whole. Furthermore,
the absence of successful sexual violence prosecutions in the ICC is an important reminder that the 'feminist' spaces within international criminal law were discursively
limited to conflict-related sexual violence not the function and scope of the tribunals. Sellers argues that gender justice nevertheless provides the potential for a means
to 'reconceptualize redress under international criminal law', although the contours
of this reconceptualisation have thus far been minor.[78] Chappell also writes of the
nestedness of institutions, such that even relatively new institutional structures like
the ICC establish their legitimacy and absorb the practices within the global order
which retains powerful gender ideologies. The footholds of power thus become
tenuous cracks in a much larger global project on individual criminal liability.

---

[73] Halley (n 70) 12.   [74] Chappell (n 65) 4.   [75] ibid 2.   [76] ibid.
[77] Halley (n 70).
[78] Patricia Visuer Sellers, '(Re)considering Gender Justice' in Fionnuala Ní Aoláin, Naomi Cahn, Dina Haynes, and Nahla Valji (eds), *The Oxford Handbook on Gender and Conflict* (Oxford University Press 2018) 211, 222.

In addition to in criminal law, the Security Council, post-2000, also
became a space wh st involvement was both sought and developed. The
history of women vism as a component and agitator within international
law can be traced e 1915 Hague Peace Conference.[79] The subsequent creation of the Wo rnational League for Peace and Freedom (WILPF) then
situated the or appropriately to respond to the call to develop an agenda
on women, p security in 2000. The groundbreaking drafting of Security
Council reso 25 came about as WILPF heeded the call of the Bangladesh
President of rity Council in March 2000 to help draft the text of Security
Council re 1325.[80] However, the final text was adapted by the Council,
and not W that specific feminist concerns, namely demilitarisation and the
arms tra not part of the final text.[81] In the years immediately after the mil-
lenniu little 'feminist' documentation from the Security Council until the
Secreta eral's reports take an annual form after 2003 and the Council issues
its sec olution on women, peace, and security in 2008, followed by two more
in 20 Although feminist influence can be regarded as 'within' the work of the
Secu ouncil after 2000 and with the landmark drafting of resolution 1325, it is
no after 2008 that the expansive work on women, peace, and security is visible
wi the broader outputs of the Security Council.

2018 with eight resolutions on women, peace, and security and references to
drawn from the resolutions increasingly emerging in additional thematic reso-
ons and in some situation-specific resolutions, as well as over ten years of annual
cretary-General's reports on women, peace, and security, the feminist-motivated
utputs on collective security are considerable.[83] Despite the focus of the Security
Resolutions across the four pillars of participation, protection, prevention, and re-
lief/recovery, the resolutions centre on a narrow approach to gender law reform,
with attention to issues related to conflict-related sexual violence the primary site
of these outputs and with limited capacity for feminist methods to guide developments.[84] Furthermore, specific periods of activity, for example the drafting of the
High-Level Report released in 2015, have also been followed by periods of waning
interest from the Council such that in the two subsequent calendar years, regardless
of the comprehensive approach demanded by Security Council resolution 2242 in
2015, the Council's women, peace, and security outputs have diminished rather
than increased.

[79] Otto, 'A Sign of "Weakness"?' (n 62).

[80] Security Council Resolution 1325 (31 October 2000) UN Doc S/RES/1325.

[81] Felicity Ruby, 'Security Council 1325: A Tool for Conflict Resolution?' in Heathcote and Otto
(n 57).

[82] Security Council Resolution 1820 (19 June 2008) UN Doc S/RES/1820; Security Council
Resolution 1888 (30 September 2009) UN Doc S/RES/1888; Security Council Resolution 1889 (5
October 2009) UN Doc S/RES/1889.

[83] Security Council Resolution 1960 (16 December 2010) UN Doc S/RES/1960; Security Council
Resolution 2106 (24 June 2013) UN Doc S/RES/2106; Security Council Resolution 2122 (18 October
2013) UN Doc S/RES/2122; Security Council Resolution 2242 (13 October 2015) UN Doc S/RES/
2242.

[84] Heathcote and Otto (n 57); Ní Aoláin and others (n 78) chs 8–14.

Similar to the outputs on conflict-related sexual violence that emerged in the ad hoc tribunals, gender law reforms within collective security are fragmented from larger international concerns and fragmented from wider feminist issues so that neither foundational international legal issues nor foundational issues within collective security are required to seriously respond to feminist thinking. An example is the 2015 Security Council report on the Responsibility to Protect which has no incorporation of gender perspectives and initiatives, despite being drafted as the Council embarked on its own High-Level review of the women, peace, and security successes.[85] Likewise, resolution 2250—issued less than two months after resolution 2422 which '[r]ecognizes the ongoing need for greater integration of resolution 1325 (2000) in its own work'—has no reference to women, girls, or gender perspectives, despite being titled 'the maintenance of international peace and security' and focusing on youth and security.[86] New situations on the Security Council's agenda, such as the tensions and violence in Ukraine post-2013, have no references to the gender dimensions of the violence effectively undermining the Security Council's own assertion of the intrinsic link between women, peace, and security.[87] This is despite resolution 2422 including the decision to 'integrate women, peace and security concerns across all country-specific situations on the Security Council's agenda'.[88] In other situations, for example in the post-conflict reconstruction in Libya, the Council reasserts its position on combatting conflict-related sexual violence with little, if any, attention to the local manifestations of gender violence or provision of tools for any broader gendered analysis of security and violence in Libya.[89]

Beyond collective security and international criminal law, the additional space where feminist strategy has informed legal outputs have been within the realm of human rights law and, in particular, the work of the CEDAW Committee.[90] Even more so than developments within international criminal law and collective security, the work of the CEDAW Committee remains segmented from the larger work of the UN—working as it does on women's issues via the state reports on issues derived from CEDAW. It has only been when the CEDAW Committee itself has enlarged the scope of its own remit that potential for cross-fertilisation of CEDAW into conflict[91] or larger strategies around combatting violence against

---

[85] *Report of the Secretary-General: A vital and enduring commitment: implementing the responsibility to protect* 13 July 2015, UN Doc S/2015/500.

[86] Security Council Resolution 2250 (9 December 2015) UN Doc S/RES/2250; Security Council Resolution 2242 (13 October 2015) UN Doc S/RES/2242 para 5.

[87] 7476th Meeting of the Security Council 11 December 2015, UN Doc S/PV7576 (on Ukraine).

[88] Security Council Resolution 2242 (13 October 2015) UN Doc S/RES/2242 para 5(b).

[89] Security Council Resolution 1973 (11 March 2011) UN Doc S/RES/1973; Security Council Resolution 2380 (5 October 2017) UN Doc S/RES/2380; Gina Heathcote, 'Humanitarian Interventions and Gendered Dynamics' in Ní Aoláin and others (n 78) 199.

[90] Convention on the Elimination of All Forms of Discrimination against Women (CEDAW) 18 December 1979, 1249 UNTS 13.

[91] Committee for the Elimination of All Forms of Discrimination against Women (CEDAW), 'General Recommendation No 30 on Women in Conflict Prevention and Post-Conflict Situations' (18 October 2013) UN Doc CEDAW/C/GC/30 (hereafter General Recommendation 30).

women[92] gains potential for realisation. In terms of legal developments, attention to CEDAW is confined to its value as a specific human rights regime and it is not perceived as fundamentally transforming international law and its operationalisation. Rather CEDAW functions as a specialised regime (on women's human rights) within the larger specialised regime of human rights institutions. As discussed in chapter 2, while the work of the CEDAW Committee has been innovative in the means through which the purposes and objects of the treaty have been used to develop a broad engagement with a range of issues, this is ultimately constrained by the terms of the CEDAW constituent document. One important aspect of the work of the CEDAW Committee is the attempt, via general recommendation 30, to link the Security Council agenda on women, peace, and security with established human rights practices.[93]

The emergence of attention to women and gender issues within the Security Council and within international criminal law, as well the preoccupation with sexual violence in armed conflict, and the model of women's rights law that the CEDAW document permits, therefore suggest, rather than feminist 'successes', gender law reform is indicative of a very selective process of legitimation of vulnerable international institutions. This positions these feminist developments as fragmented if they are viewed from the perspective of international law—for example from the foundational structures of the discipline, which attend to the role of states, the sources of international law, the subjects of international law, and cross-cutting topics such as jurisdiction, immunities, state responsibility, and global institutions. Consequently, despite being described as feminist successes and evidence of feminists walking the halls of power, gendered understandings have developed little traction in global governance beyond these institutional endeavours. The feminist successes that have occurred, despite being described by Halley as structural in the type of feminism deployed, have not influenced the structures at all.

Even within the sub-disciplines—international criminal law, collective security, and human rights laws—these gender initiatives pertain to a discrete range of developments rather than constituting any structural transformation of the disciplines they are situated within. Both Halley and Engle identify this as a structural feminist strategy in reference to the specific US radical feminist history that sees gender as a structure of dominance rather than a project of engaging with the structures of international law.[94] This US radical/liberal/cultural feminist agenda informs the range of international developments that have occurred: characterising these as unbridled feminist successes, however, risks reifying US feminisms as the central or only feminist approach. This risks further writing out the complex, varied, and ongoing

---

[92] Committee for the Elimination of All Forms of Discrimination against Women (CEDAW), 'General Recommendation No 19 on Violence Against Women' (30 January 1992) UN Doc CEDAW/C/GC/19.

[93] O'Rourke and Swaine (n 46).

[94] Halley and others, *Governance Feminism* (n 13); Karen Engle, 'Feminist Governance and International Law: From Liberal to Carceral Feminism' in Janet Halley, Prabha Kotiswaran, Rachel Rebouché, and Hila Shamir (eds), *Governance Feminism: Notes from the Field* (University of Minnesota Press 2018).

non-US and non-Western feminist activism and theory that can be developed to construct dialogues on alternative feminist approaches within international law. Consequently, the need to engage with the foundations of international law, and the uncovering of bias within those structures, requires considerably different feminist approaches than the liberal, cultural, and radical models prevalent in the feminist success stories found within international criminal law, collective security, and human rights.

At a more practical level, it was the creation of UN Women in 2010 that was, at some levels, intended to coordinate a space to disrupt the fragmented developments on gender and women's issues within the UN. The focus of UN Women, thus, is across eight areas of concern with offices in member states across regions and with the organisation placed within the Secretary-General's office.[95] However, somehow the coordination of gender affairs within UN Women constructs the organisation as a specialised regime that reflects the larger fragmentation of the global order, discussed above, and actively dismantles early ideas around gender mainstreaming as a project to infiltrate all areas of the global order with gender sensitive approaches. The practical fragmentation of feminist approaches to international law thus happens twice: first in the fragmented pockets where developments have been permitted and, second, within the specialised regime, structures, and spaces that UN Women ultimately facilitates, potentially in isolation from large global initiatives and in parallel to other specialised regimes in the global order.

In addition to the practical fragmentation, an additional split occurs at a substantive level. This aspect of feminist approaches is less apparent from the international legal plane and concerns the diversity of feminist approaches, gender theory, and even understandings of women's rights. Despite the practical divisions in the fragmented international legal frameworks on gender, there is an astounding consistency in the 'brand' of feminist politics that is taken up by international institutions. Not surprisingly, this can, at least on the surface, be associated with the history of US feminist legal work associated with the second wave. MacKinnon's approach to radical feminism, first articulated in the 1980s, is influential although a very specific blending of US radical, cultural, and liberal feminisms would be a better description of contemporary international law on women and gender.[96] However, it is important to stress that feminist organising and influence within international forums is influenced by transnational feminisms beyond these US approaches and that US approaches to law, including international law, are—and always have been—considerably more diverse than liberal/radical/cultural approaches. My purpose is to highlight the narrowing of international approaches in the post-millennium period, as well as the writing out of non-US feminisms (what I would loosely describe as transnational feminisms) within the space of global governance. The selective pick-up of dominant US feminist approaches is remarkably consistent across different spaces where international legal developments have occurred, and this has

---

[95] The eight areas are: Leadership and Political Empowerment; Economic Empowerment; Ending Violence against Women; Peace and Security; Humanitarian Action; Governance and National planning; Sustainable Development; and HIV and AIDS.
[96] Catherine Mackinnon, *Feminism Unmodified: Discourses on Life and Law* (Harvard University Press 1988).

the consequence of fragmenting feminisms in numerous ways, including in terms of which feminist issues are 'picked up' within international law, which voices are permitted to 'represent' women (and gender issues) and how women and gender reforms are 'received' within non-Western communities.

Reminiscent of Riles's analysis of the view from the international plane in colonial politics, where she examines how specific local issues are transposed as international problems, a narrow form of feminist approach is asserted (or taken up) within international legal structures.[97] The selective take-up of feminist issues is well demonstrated through the example of sexual violence initiatives which has its roots in US radical feminist approaches that identify female sex difference and women's sexual vulnerability as the core of gender inequality. The US radical feminist preference for criminal regulation and prosecutions as a mechanism to challenge gendered violence also re-emerges within international developments. The international developments with respect to sexual violence, tend to mirror US national responses to sexual violence and violence against women that have been criticised as a form of 'carceral feminism':

While its adherents would likely reject the descriptor, carceral feminism describes an approach that sees increased policing, prosecution, and imprisonment as the primary solution to violence against women.[98]

The Security Council approach to women, peace, and security, although not without its wider initiatives, has gained considerable traction with respect to the regulation and prohibition of conflict-related sexual violence, leading to the development and imposition of specific legal structures within post-conflict states, a preoccupation with naming and shaming strategies, the emergence of targeted sanctions for perpetrators of conflict-related sexual violence, and an exceptionalising of sexual violence in armed conflict while sexual violence in states experiencing peace remains outside of the purview of global governance.[99] In addition, the complexity of women's insecurity in conflict and post-conflict states where economic concerns, access to resources, representation, and gender-based violence (not just sexual violence) are all indicators of both ongoing insecurity and women's specific experience of insecurity remains significantly under-responded to by the international community.[100]

---

[97] Annelise Riles, 'View from the International Plane: Perspective and Scale in the Architecture of Colonial International Law' (1995) 6 Law and Critique 39.

[98] Victoria Law 'Against Carceral Feminism' in Sunkar and Bhaskar (eds) *Jacobin*, (17 October, 2014) <https://www.jacobinmag.com/2014/10/against-carceral-feminism/> last accessed 31 May 2018; Engle, 'Feminist Governance' (n 94); Elizabeth Bernstein, 'Militarized Humanitarianism Meets Carceral Feminism: The Politics of Sex, Rights, and Freedom in Contemporary Antitrafficking Campaigns' (2010) 36(1) Signs 45.

[99] Gina Heathcote, 'Naming and Shaming: Security Council Resolution 1960 (2010) on Women, Peace and Security and Human Rights Accountability' (2012) 4(1) Journal of Human Rights Practice 82; Gina Heathcote, 'Robust Peacekeeping, Gender and the Protection of Civilians' in Jeremy Farrell and Hilary Charlesworth (eds), *Strengthening the Rule of Law through the Security Council* (Cambridge University Press 2016) 150.

[100] Heathcote and Otto (n 57).

As argued above, the preoccupation with the imposition and creation of a legal response to conflict-related sexual violence is then understood as fragmenting the range of feminist voices influencing international legal developments and the range of topics developed as international. This also develops, within the work of the Security Council and within international criminal law, a feminist project centred on regulating perpetrators of sexual violence rather than halting or preventing violence, providing health and security for survivors of sexual violence, or understanding conflict-related sexual violence, for example, as structurally connected to gendered expectations and behaviours produced in peace and conflict. O'Rourke's study of the interaction between local women's organisations and international actors in three post-conflict states demonstrates how the preoccupation with incarceration of specific perpetrators of conflict-related sexual violence from the global community shapes funding for women's organisations in post-conflict states. O'Rourke argues that the carceral focus of gender law reform can disrupt the provision of services (policing, health, economic security) for non-conflict related gender violence and reinforces a 'web of harms' that genders security from the personal to the public for women in post-conflict spaces.[101]

While Halley differentiates between the liberal and radical registers within US feminism (in terms of the influence on international criminal law), the range of feminist footholds across the international system encompasses a combination of radical, cultural, and liberal feminist approaches.[102] As such, alongside the focus on 'saving' women and prioritising women's vulnerability to specific types of sexual violence (in conflict and/or in public spaces) there is also attention from the Security Council to facilitating women's participation within public bodies at the national level. The latter is premised on a liberal feminist framework of equality that includes the capacity for temporary special measures to address unequal representation. However, a liberal inclusion approach fails to consider women's existing participation, often regarded as informal labour and disconnected from formal decision-making structures, as well as the diversity of women's lives and experiences of gendered harm. Ongoing feminist tensions are easily deployed to critique the liberal moves within the UN, including critique of a universal understanding of women's lives that renders women of colour, racial and religious minority women, indigenous women, trans women, non-heterosexual women, and disabled women's lives as potentially abject and invisible unless they are able to 'look like' the female subject of liberal feminist approaches or as victim subjects that adhere to radical feminist approaches. The Security Council's approach to representation and participation—also framed through liberal inclusion models—can be linked in this way to the wider remit of CEDAW and its application within the global order.

At one level the text of CEDAW has always been circumscribed by a liberal feminist ethic, centred as it is on discrimination against women, and the life of the convention and the CEDAW Committee represent a pushing at the possibilities of liberal

---

[101] Catherine O'Rourke, *Gender Politics in Transitional Justice* (Routledge 2013).
[102] Halley (n 70).

feminism that demonstrate the possibilities and potential of working within existing legal paradigms. Nevertheless, the centring on rights will always be circumscribed by the structures of international law and international human rights law. Therefore, the rights discourse that CEDAW is drawn from persists as a liberal feminist account that seeks to reveal 'the gender exclusions within liberal democracy's proclamation of universal equality, particularly with respect to law, institutional access, and the full incorporation of women into the public sphere'.[103] The necessity of working within the pre-exiting, largely liberal, structures of international institutions mutes alternative feminist strategies and, potentially, lends gender equality strategies as amenable to neoliberal co-optation.[104] The CEDAW Committee's General Recommendation 30 on women in conflict prevention, conflict, and post-conflict situations brings together the work on collective security and human rights.[105] In addition, Security Council resolution 2212 acknowledges CEDAW's nexus to the women, peace, and security framework asserting its relevance in the first paragraph of the preamble.[106] It is in these resolutions that the dual liberal–radical feminist approach becomes visible as the Security Council twins a programme for women's participation with a need for women's protection from (primarily) sexual violence. As such, paragraph 4 of Security Council resolution 2122 'reiterates [the Security Council's] ... intention when establishing and renewing mandates of United Nations missions ... to include provisions to facilitate women's full participation and protection'.[107] This hinged project that centres on women's insertion into existing post-conflict processes alongside mechanisms for protection from sexual violence during armed conflict plays out the project of liberal and radical feminism in their most diluted form, without any sense of the diversity of approaches within feminisms let alone feminism across transnational spaces and temporalities.

The thin conception of liberal–radical feminism within international institutional legal tools has consequences both in terms of the scope of possibilities for realisation and in terms of how those documents become received in non-Western contexts. This can be demonstrated through attention to the development of these same strategies in the rule of law projects that the Security Council links to its gender equality and empowerment of women agenda. As such, in resolution 2122, paragraph 3 links the Security Council's women, peace, and security work to further thematic areas including

Protection of civilians in armed conflict, Post-conflict peacebuilding, The promotion and strengthening of the rule of law in the maintenance of peace and security, Peace and security

---

[103] Catherine Rottenberg, 'The Rise of Neoliberalism Feminism' (2014) 28 Cultural Studies 418, 419.

[104] ibid. [105] General Recommendation 30 (n 91).

[106] Security Council Resolution 2122 (18 October 2013) UN Doc S/RES/2122 (issued on the same day as General Recommendation 30 (n 91)); Security Council Resolution 1820 (19 June 2008) UN Doc S/RES/1820 (Preamble); Security Council Resolution 1888 (30 September 2009) UN Doc S/RES/1888 (Preamble); Security Council Resolution 1889 (5 October 2009) UN Doc S/RES/1889 (Preamble).

[107] Security Council Resolution 2122 (18 October 2013) UN Doc S/RES/2122, para 4.

in Africa, Threats to international peace and security caused by terrorist acts, and the maintenance of international peace and security'.[108]

This crossing over of the women, peace, and security framework into the broader thematic work of the Council, on the one hand, represents an interesting expansion of the Security Council's work. At the same time, the choice of agendas the women, peace, and security framework is to be extended into, and the very limited model of liberal–radical feminist approaches within the Security Council's existing women, peace, and security resolutions, further defines the substantive (or normative) closure of this approach.

The reception of the women, peace, and security framework in non-Western spaces, not unexpectedly, can have serious consequences for local women's organisations. First, the agenda-setting from 'above' dislodges local concerns, requiring local needs and expectations be 'repackaged' into a form that accommodates the approach to gender equality articulated from the Security Council. Second, the association of gender equality with something foreign can create real risks for local and regional women's feminist networks which can be regarded as importing Western traditions at the expense of local understandings, even when strong local feminist histories are entrenched within a community. This fragments the diverse and changing sites of feminist and gender theory, constructing a largely liberal–radical model as the universal feminist approach and others, in particular postmodern, postcolonial, and critical race, queer, and crip feminisms, as particularised fragments belonging in spaces outside of the international. Additionally, the rich histories of transnational feminist activism and theory are often erased from accounts of the emergence of women's rights and gender initiatives within international law.[109] There is a need to actively seek to re-engage international law with feminist 'Others' to engage with fragmentation as a reimagined site latent with the potential of intersectional, diasporic, peripheral, and nomadic subjects that utilise transnational spaces to direct and transform knowledge production.

The complex movement of transnational feminist politics requires understanding of the non-vertical transplantation of ideas and their relevance, structurally, to both international law and feminist approaches. In this manner Knop's transnational legal feminism can be developed as a normative framework for attention to diverse forms of knowledge, subjectivity, and being.[110] The three specific ideas I draw into this discussion in this chapter are peripheral subjects, nomadic subjects, and the gendering of migrant/diasporic subjects: all theorisations of gender that take intersectionality as a normative starting point for understanding the complexity of gender relations. The conclusion, in line with Knop, is that each of these models has resonance both across and within specific communities and yet their translation into political and

[108] ibid, para 3.

[109] Aili Tripp, 'The Evolution of Transnational Feminisms: Consensus, Conflict and New Dynamics' in Myra Marx Ferree and Aili Tripp (eds), *Global Feminisms: Transnational Women's Activism, Organizing and Women's Rights* (New York University Press 2006).

[110] Karen Knop, 'Here and There: International Law in Domestic Courts' (2000) 32 International Law and Politics 502.

feminist knowledge relies on an understanding of the particular within any space or place.

4. Fragmented Subjects

The discussion, above, on the fragmentation of feminist approaches separates the descriptive and the normative components of gender law reform. In this section I highlight the approach of Knop which reconsiders the foundational structures of international law via transnational legal feminism and a conflict of laws approach. Knop's attention to legal pluralism then leads me towards additional feminist dialogues where subjectivity is reimagined—in particular, Kapur's identification of peripheral subjects as a normative starting point,[111] Braidotti's conception of the nomadic subject,[112] and the study of migration via the framing of diaspora spaces in the work of Brah.[113] These become normative accounts of plural legal subjectivities which I argue offer a specifically feminist intervention into legal pluralism that has the potential to reconceive and reimagine feminist approaches to international law. As such, I understand legal pluralism as an approach that starts from the diversity of legal forms and I use feminist methodologies to query whether diverse subjectivities should also be an aspect of plural legal approaches, dislodging the notion of a unified and autonomous legal subject prized in Western legal theories.

Knop's perception of transnational legal processes, a form of transnational legal feminism, considers the translation of legal rules, principles, and norms between systems as an important theoretical and normative component of the international that has previously been misunderstood.[114] Knop analyses the movement of international law into domestic law and describes the process through attention to translation practices. Knop explores theories of translation as a means to respect difference within international law, acknowledging translation (of language) as more than a literal interpretation, as 'creativity' and 'uncertainty' exist within the process.[115] This normative recognition of difference across domestic legal spaces, and Knop's exploration of how this can be accommodated by and in fact shape international law, is what is of interest to me. In focusing on the translation of laws in a transjudicial form, Knop's approach permits and realises the development of a larger feminist commitment to diversity and understanding of intersectional politics. Knop's work thus develops an understanding of law where persuasive rules are understood as integral to the development of universal structures, such as human rights, within specific legal contexts, that emerge across temporal spaces and thus are attended to differently in various times and spaces. The juxtaposition of the development of global—or transnational—patterns with an understanding of local renderings of those same rules reflects an understanding of the complexity of international law and a unique means to understand a range of false binaries within international law, including universalism and cultural relativism, monism and dualism, rules and

---

[111] Kapur (n 11).   [112] Braidotti (n 9).
[113] Brah, *Cartographies of Diaspora* (n 10).   [114] Knop (n 109).   [115] ibid 506.

norms. Knop's attentiveness to difference might be developed further: the identification of a need for translation across communities might be extended to also identify the plural subjects who speak across those same communities.

In constructing an understanding of international law, developed locally through translation into local rules that in turn speak across and through legal forms to reimagine the international, Knop embeds a commitment to legal pluralism in her project that I wish to extend into recognition of the diverse subject as a necessary and transcendental or meta-figure within the international legal system. In disrupting the expectation that legal norms filter down into the local/domestic space or that legal rules filter up into the larger international normative order, Knop equally facilitates recognition of the poverty of contemporary understandings of legal subjectivity. Knop's project functions as a challenge to versions of legal subjectivity constructed on stories of masculine closure and unencumbered subjects, through recognition of the need for developing dialogue across different domestic legal forms.[116] The consequence is a shifting towards recognising the legal subject as always in relationship with other legal subjects, be they states, non-state actors, international organisations, regional bodies, or individuals. Feminist theories then provide useful accounts of diverse subjectivity that feed into the analysis of the foundations of international law, reasserting the capacity for a model of sources and authority within international law that is drawn from an expansive, changing understanding of subjectivity and that can thus be attentive to power relationships, inequalities, and imperial histories. Knop's transnational legal feminism takes as its starting point recognition that legal systems, states, and legal subjects, like individuals, function as separate and connected subjects, embedded in a network of legal forms facilitating cross-fertilisation and translation of ideas as equally as the legal structure, like individuals, asserts its separateness and individuality. In this final section of the chapter, I explore three different articulations of subjectivity from diverse feminist writers to imagine the types of conversations on international law that might commence if subjectivity was reconfigured as plural. This approach builds on the commitment to a feminist epistemology of intersectionality and the politics of listening articulated in the previous chapter.

In the work of Kapur, via the articulation of the peripheral subject as a normative starting point for feminist theorising, a robust critique of feminist approaches to international human rights law, and violence against women strategies within the international, is presented.[117] Kapur's approach hinges on acknowledging the victim subject of liberal–radical feminist approaches to human rights asking how feminism constructs its subject/s and thus its theories of knowing.[118] The peripheral subject is akin to transnational legal feminism, which acknowledges non-dominant legal forms as relevant to the rendering of international/global laws. The peripheral subject acknowledges the perspective, agency, and voice—as a normative force—outside of the masculine, Western unencumbered subject imagined in liberal projects and often reproduced within gender law reform. Kapur demonstrates

---

[116] ibid 533.   [117] Kapur (n 11) 131.   [118] ibid 107.

how contemporary approaches to challenging violence against women under international human rights law constructs a non-Western subject in need of 'saving' and elite women within global arenas as 'agents' (best placed to undertake the job of saving). The binary discounts the capacity of those cast as victim to articulate feminist legal approaches, or solutions, given the necessity that they be saved. Kapur challenges feminists to attend to the normative agenda of peripheral subjects as a mechanism for disrupting the victim–agent binary.[119] Through bringing Kapur's work together with Arendt's work on the politics of natality, the peripheral subject emerges as a mechanism for engaging political consciousness in the foundations of international law through attention to global inequalities and their gendered manifestations. That is, the peripheral subject asks difficult questions with regard to whose interests are represented in gender law reform and, given her location outside of the Global North, is a reminder to articulate gender as embedded in racialised, heteronormative, and colonial histories. Gender law reform might look very different if this were the normative starting point, informing feminist methodologies within international law.

My methodology, however, is not to presuppose the position and needs of those on international law's peripheries—that would undermine the drawing in of Kapur's project. Instead feminist dialogues must attend to peripheral subjects, listen to her, and consider her normative universe a legitimate starting place for engaging the international. However, in order not to construct a new particular parading as a universal the peripheral subject must be placed in dialogue with others, for example, Braidotti's nomadic subject. The nomadic subject enters Braidotti's work as a cross boundary, stateless post-human whose subjectivity 'reflects the existential situation of the multicultural individual, a migrant who turned nomad'.[120] At the core of Braidotti's project is a commitment to 're-thinking the bodily roots of subjectivity' that acknowledges both the diversity of lived bodily experiences and the epistemological projection of identity onto bodies in a manner that 'Others' specific subjects. Braidotti's account is then able to engage directly with the construction of subjectivity both through and within identity politics, across differentiations, to release understandings of subjectivity into the ranging, temporally shifting, and geographically mobile subjectivity of the nomad. Braidotti's work centres on the individual subject within philosophical work, transferring and reimagining this within the context of the international may thus seem counter-intuitive unless a return to understanding the sexed and gendered state is prefigured in our understanding of the state within international law.[121] That is, in recalling feminist accounts of the sexed and gendered meanings of legal subjectivity, the pursuit of alternative framings of subjectivity is required. This approach is disruptive of the agenda of existing gender law reform which are addressed within the contemporary formations of international law.

---

[119] ibid.   [120] Braidotti (n 9) 21.
[121] Hilary Charlesworth, 'The Sex of the State in International Law' in Ngaire Naffine and Rosemary Owens (eds), *Sexing the Subject of Law* (Law Book Company 1997).

Despite early feminist work on international law directly addressing the sex and gender of the state there has been a general decline in attention to this type of foundational concept within international law, from contemporary feminist and critical scholars alike. Braidotti's project is akin to Kapur's focus on subjectivity, although where Kapur draws on postcolonial subjects to frame a subject of resistance to the imperial legacy of international endeavours, Braidotti uses an account of postmodernism (as the contemporary temporal account rather than an ahistorical theory) and psychoanalytical accounts to explore the role of the affective and the role of desire in the formation of subjectivity.

In terms of fragmentation debates, Braidotti's nomadic subject indicates a need to frame the fragmentation of international law as repressing the key affective and bodily accounts within the assumed spaces of international law. In particular, the state within fragmentation scholarship is insufficiently interrogated in accounts that fall back onto a series of expectations connected to legal formalism. That is, approaches to fragmentation tend to concentrate on demonstrating how international rules work and function despite the fragmentation of the overarching structure, reinforcing the underlying model of state sovereignty regardless of the growth of new specialised regimes of global governance. The transference from a defined and closed understanding of subjectivity (as the state is assumed to be via its defined territory) to attention to nomadic subjectivity questions key assumptions that remain embedded within international law as a discipline, including within debates on fragmentation. The persistence of difference as a marker of inequality so that, in the words of Braidotti, 'the nomadism in question here refers to the kind of critical consciousness that resists settling into socially coded thoughts and behaviours' can be developed as a normative project that challenges the assumptions that inform legal thinking.[122] Traversing of boundaries (between states, between ideas, between fragmented forms of law) is grounded on understanding what it means to be human—and, reflecting changing contemporary conceptions of subjectivity, post-human. Braidotti imagines a version of subjectivity that considerably transcends philosophical traditions that have placed the male body and experience of powerful men as the archetype of the human condition. If feminist engagements with international law seek to move beyond the dominant spaces of gender law reform that have emerged thus far, and accepting that these law reforms tend to reproduce gendered bodies and sexed subjects, a fluid and dynamic account of subjectivity is necessary. This extends understanding of gender and sexuality as fluid into the re-conceptualisation of international law from a feminist perspective and unsettles the continued reproduction of a female subject in gender law reforms.

To Braidotti's and Kapur's projects, centred on subjectivity, Brah's work on diaspora furthers understanding of the failure of categories of belonging within dominant philosophical-political accounts. The closure of identity politics and limited perspective offered when mapping the world through the national state (or nationalism) destroys significant appreciation of the migrant's multi-located sense of belonging and the capacity for human empathy, memory, and difference

---

[122] Braidotti (n 9) 26.

to be the site of our sense of belonging. Like Braidotti and Kapur, Brah's account commences a project of acknowledging fractured subjectivity that has resonance within international legal accounts of fragmentation. But, rather than seeking a means to understand fragmentation within an (assumed) hermeneutically sealed world of legal relationships, rules, and principles, Brah's work asks for a consideration of fragmentation as the space to know and understand the 'Other'. Such that the international human rights lawyer, perhaps, might know and understand the theoretical and practical constraints of the international trade lawyer, that the humanitarian actor might hear and see the narratives of the environmental activist, that the development policymaker might engage within the sanctions body, and in each case vice versa, to see maps of belonging and home, of language and law, as similar in their differences. In contrast, fragmentation is a story of individualising and dividing international legal regimes in a manner that reasserts the need for the state and the organisations within international law to function within the current foundational paradigms and without attention to how assumed stories of the origins of international law retell themselves as without particularisation or home.[123] Furthermore, Brah's critical contributions remind feminist methodologies that their messages need not look to the Global South to 'find' gendered harm and discrimination, and that intersectional harm configures and produces all spaces, even those we imagine as home. Brah's articulation of the migrant, in dialogue with peripheral and nomadic subjects, suggest the starting points for feminist dialogues might be plural subjectivities, which continually open out their invitation to those who are to speak.

Kapur, Braidotti, and Brah all present challenges to the feminist and the international lawyer alike—they demand a reassessment of the engagements with gender law reform, both practical and substantive, that have evolved and emerged since the early 1990s. The expectation that legal arrangements might embrace contemporary gender theorists' formation and engagements with multiple, wandering subjectivities in the first two decades of feminist approaches to international law is unrealistic. The types of feminist developments within international law have instead mirrored the types of larger development within the discipline, including that of fragmentation. The consequence is a reassertion and acceptance of the sexed and gendered foundations of international law. To shift beyond this a broader and more complex feminist encounter within international law is required. This in turn feeds back into larger debates on fragmentation to conceive of a post-fragmentation period in international law where fragmentation is perceived as a starting point for understanding a transnational legal framework. Thus, knowledge is able to traverse legal structures, in a nomadic fashion, with attention to (assumed) peripheral accounts of legal arrangements as normatively equivalent to the core. This also produces a central questioning of any sense of belonging, or home, that is derived from a nationalist politics and deprived of the multi-consciousness of the migrant.

In sum, this chapter turns from the debates on fragmentation to further feminist engagements with the foundational structures—and developments—of

---

[123] Ruth Buchanan and Rebecca Johnson, 'The "Unforgiven" Sources of International Law: Nation-Building, Violence and Gender in the West(ern)' in Buss and Manji (n 12) 135.

international law and to map the development of feminist legal work within the international sphere. My initial impetus to undertake this study was driven by a sense of encountering two different spaces where legal pluralism and plurality were emergent themes and to ask what they might productively offer each other. The first site is work within critical legal scholarship which at once acknowledges and theorises legal pluralism and connects this to the fragmentation debates within international law but does not read, or see, or tell, stories of gender and the connection between understandings of legal pluralism with feminist and gender theories. As such, feminist writing on plural subjectivities, or in the case of Knop, on transnational legal models, is the second set of scholarship I am interested in and I have demonstrated the relevance of this to fragmentation discussions throughout this chapter. That is, feminist understandings of transnational legal approaches, the shifting between the spaces and planes of legal knowledge, and the need for an understanding of the complexity gained through attention to plurality contribute a counter-hegemonic theory of knowing the international sphere. Complexity, fluidity, choice, and closure are demonstrated as at once outside the legal and eternally constructed by the legal via a transnational feminist legal approach. Acknowledging this drives recognition that there is, and must be, an explicit engagement with ethical commitments within feminist legal projects. The unspoken ethical commitment of the current fragmented approach to feminist legal advances within the international—where the non-Western woman is constructed and reconstructed as damaged, in need of protection, without voice, and eternally cast as an actor defined through her assumed feminine body—is reassigned a problematic gender ethic. The binary of m>f retold in the stories of international law as one of female sexual and bodily vulnerability juxtaposed against the invisible normal subject that is male and intersects with other sites of power, including race, class, able-bodiedness, cisgenderism, and sexuality needs to be placed as a topic for feminist dialogues on gender law reform. In the following chapter, in an effort to move beyond the limitations of gender law reform, I reimagine legal subjectivity without the assumed gender binary and through the motif of split subjects.

Feminist projects within international law must actively work to disrupt this sense of knowing, or assuming gender politics, to use and develop plural understandings as a mechanism to intervene and disrupt precisely what we think international law *should* be. It is in stories of plurality that the knowledge to disrupt the intersecting power relations, that persist in telling the particulars of international legal history as a universal, are made visible. In this chapter, I have used the debates on fragmentation to demonstrate how, from a feminist perspective, the fractal metaphor of international law is a repeating pattern that would benefit from the disruptive spaces of knowing that are spoken by the peripheral subject, the nomad, the migrant, and bodies that defy the binaries of Western gender norms. In the prior chapter I developed a response to feminist 'successes', or gender law reform, within international law through analysis of the rise of gender experts and expertise, using critical legal understandings of expertise to develop an argument about the complex feminist ethics and political agendas that are both stymied and advanced through the work of gender experts in global governance. The final three chapters will build on a feminist politics of plural subjectivities, political listening, and intersectionality in relation to the foundations of international law reviewing sovereignty, international institutions, and authority as a means to move beyond the stagnation perpetuated through gender law reform that is constrained by Western liberal, radical, and cultural feminist agendas. As such, the text embraces the productive tensions within feminist legal dialogues—and beyond—through a broader incorporation of feminist methods and thus, in the words of Otto, developing 'footholds' for feminist futures.[124]

---

[124] Dianne Otto, 'Power and Danger: Feminist Engagement with International Law through the UN Security Council' (2010) 32 Australian Feminist Law Journal 97, 121.

4

Sovereignty

1. Introduction

Ghouta, Syria, February 2018. Five hundred people killed in airstrikes from the Syrian military over four days. As I write I force myself to watch and read the incomprehensible. I already know what is happening in Syria. I have followed the legal and political ramifications as well as the very personal accounts of colleagues and friends. Yet the violence unleashed by the Syrian state this weekend, as I write, against the Syrian people seems to sever perceptions and understanding of humanness. In the UN Security Council over the same four days there is no discussion of a military intervention by the collective security apparatus, dialogue is stalled on whether a resolution creating a ceasefire and sending humanitarian aid will be agreed to by permanent members. The draft resolution, proposed by Kuwait and Sweden on 21 February 2018, 'follows a marked intensification of violence as the conflict nears its seventh anniversary' and was finally agreed on 24 February 2018.[1] In the final text, Security Council resolution 2401 establishes a thirty-day ceasefire and demands access for weekly aid convoys, alongside medical evacuations. The ceasefire was broken on the same day the resolution was issued. Importantly, resolution 2401 begins by '[r]eaffirming its strong commitment to the sovereignty, independence, unity and territorial integrity of Syria'.[2] I have searched for academic feminist analysis of the political and legal dimensions of the seven-year Syrian conflict and have found only a handful of publications, largely from NGOs.[3] The Security Council resolution

---

[1] Security Council Report, 'Syria Possible Vote on Humanitarian Draft Resolution and Meeting on Eastern Ghouta' (*What's In Blue*, 21 February 2018) <http://www.whatsinblue.org/2018/02/syria-possible-vote-on-humanitarian-draft-resolution-and-meeting-on-eastern-ghouta.php> last accessed 31 May 2018.

[2] UNSC 2401 24 February 2018 UN Doc S/RES/2401, Preamble; Alex J Bellamy, 'When is a Ceasefire Not a Ceasefire? In Syria, where Most of the Killing is Allowed' 28 February 2018, *International Global Observatory* <https://theglobalobservatory.org/2018/02/ceasefire-syria-ghouta/> last accessed 31 May 2018.

[3] Laila Alodaat, 'No Women, No Peace in Syria' *The Huffington Post* (9 December 2016) <https://www.huffingtonpost.com/laila-alodaat/no-women-no-peace-in-syri_b_8762904.html> last accessed 31 May 2018; Jane Freedman, Zeynep Kivilcim, and Nurcan Özgür Baclaioğlu, *A Gendered Approach to the Syrian Refugee Crisis* (Routledge 2017); Khuloud Alsata and Anuj Kapilashrami, 'Understanding Women's Experience of Violence and the Political Economy of Gender in Conflict: The Case of Syria' (2016) 24(47) Reproductive Health Matters 5; Laila Alodaat and Sarah Boukhary (eds), *Violations against Women in Syria and the Disproportionate Impact of the Conflict on Them: NGO Summary Report UPR of Syrian Arabic Republic* (WILPF November 2016); Laila Alodaat, 'The Armed Conflict in Syria

Feminist Dialogues on International Law. Gina Heathcote. © Gina Heathcote 2019. Published 2019 by Oxford University Press.

makes no mention of the gender dimensions of this permanent site of crisis in the 2018 resolution.[4] This is despite the prior dialogue of the Security Council with the Syrian Women's Advisory Board by the Council.[5] I force myself to click the links on social media and to bear witness to the continued violence.

Charlesworth's analysis of humanitarian intervention debates concludes:

> we should consider our own personal and professional investment in crises. We need to ana-
> lyse the way we exercise power, and who wins and who loses in this operation. In asking this
> question, we will undermine that pleasurable sense of internationalist virtue that comes with
> being an international lawyer, but perhaps in the end contribute something to countering
> the injustices of everyday life.[6]

Charlesworth's larger argument is that international law functions through a crisis mentality, where legal change is developed as a heroic response to crises that are extracted from the histories of violence they are permitted to flourish within.[7] The violence in Syria has become a permanent crisis. Later in 2018 alleged chemical weapon attacks perpetrated by the Syrian state result in the use of force by Western states. The deadlock in the Security Council leads to the use of force without authorisation. Before the Security Council, the sovereign rights of the Syrian state remain affirmed and protected through the Syrian state's political alliance with Russia. Other than acknowledging the Russian right to veto Security Council resolutions, the relationship between Russia and Syria is no business of international law. This strange state of affairs where sovereignty is always relational and yet constructed as autonomous, unencumbered, is the focus of this chapter. Drawing on the conceptualisation of plural subjectivities in the prior chapter, I examine the relational structure of interstate relations and the splits that precede the acknowledgment of legal subjectivity on the international plane. I am mindful throughout of the deadly, violent reality of the fraternal bonding of states that defines international relations as equally as the assertion of sovereign right/might.[8]

As a feminist analysis of sovereignty, I seek to fill the space that remains if the unencumbered, masculine legal subject is accepted as a legal fiction. In filling that space I commence a discussion and analysis of subjects as split, splitting, and relational. To undertake this, I consciously refocus feminist thinking within international law

---

and its Disproportionate Impact on Women' (2014) Focus Gender InfoBrief <https://www.fes.de/gender/infobrief5//pdf_content/FES_IL5_FOCUS02.pdf> last accessed 31 May 2018.

[4] UNSC 2401 24 February 2018 UN Doc S/RES/2401; Simon Tisdall, 'Amid Syria's Horror a New Force Emerges: The Women of Idlib' *The Guardian* (London, 26 May 2018) <https://www.theguardian.com/world/2018/may/26/syria-idlib-women-children-society> last accessed May 2018.

[5] Zedoun Alzoubi, 'Syrian Civil Society through Peace Talks in Geneva: Roles and Challenges' (2017) 29(1) New England Journal of Public Policy <https://scholarworks.umb.edu/nejpp/vol29/iss1/> last accessed 31 May 2018.

[6] Hilary Charlesworth, 'International Law: A Discipline of Crisis' (2002) 62(3) Modern Law Review 377, 392.

[7] ibid; Anne Orford, *Reading Humanitarian Intervention: Human Rights and the Use of Force in International Law* (Cambridge University Press 2003).

[8] Yoriko Otomo, 'Searching for Virtue in International Law' in Sari Kouvo and Zoe Pearson (eds), *Feminist Perspectives on Contemporary International Law: Between Resistance and Compliance* (Hart 2011) 33.

on to the foundations of the discipline through an analysis of the gendering of state sovereignty, with consideration of transformations in the late twentieth century and through the first decades of the twenty-first century. I focus on better reflecting humanity within foundational thinking on international law and, thus, thinking through conceptions and perceptions of what it means to be human (or in Wright's terminology 'becoming human'), without assertion of traditional male models of legal subjectivity.[9] Building on the attention to intersectionality and the articulation of plural subjectivities in the previous chapters, I contemplate a model of split subjectivity as a useful redescription of how state sovereignty functions within global governance. I also consider the importance of gendered experiences and histories of law as informing legal knowledge while rejecting a feminist message centred on woman as subject.

The twentieth century saw adaptations to the meaning of state sovereignty under international law and understandings of state sovereignty have continued to change in the post-millennium period.[10] In this chapter, state sovereignty is analysed through a feminist lens as a means to reframe and rethink approaches to sovereignty while also expanding the parameters of feminist thinking on international law. I contribute to mainstream debates on the changing nature of sovereignty from a feminist perspective, so as to address the limitations of contemporary accounts of state sovereignty. State sovereignty has been invoked within feminist scholarship as a barrier to the full realisation of gender equality, yet—as discussed across this book—in the early twenty-first century, feminist approaches to international law have increasingly avoided engagement with foundational concepts, including state sovereignty.[11] Feminist scholarship has emerged, instead, with a predominant focus on specific issues, such as the prosecution of sexual violence under international criminal law and women's experiences in conflict and post-conflict periods.[12] Within this literature disproportionate focus on the harm women experience during armed conflict often fails to engage or question foundational concepts within international

---

[9] Shelley Wright, 'The Horizon of Becoming: Culture, Gender and History after September 11' (2002) 71 Nordic Journal of International Law 215.

[10] Christine Chinkin and Freya Baetens (eds), *Sovereignty, Statehood and State Responsibility: Essays in Honour of James Crawford* (Cambridge University Press 2015).

[11] Hilary Charlesworth and Christine Chinkin, *The Boundaries of International Law: A Feminist Analysis* (Manchester University Press 2000) 170.

[12] Debra Bergoffen, 'Toward a Politic of the Vulnerable Body' (2003)18(1) Hypatia 116; Doris Buss, 'Performing Legal Order: Some Feminist Thoughts on International Criminal Law' (2011) 11 International Criminal Law Review 409; Binafer Nowrojee, ' "Your Justice is Too Slow": Will the ICTR Fail Rwanda's Rape Victims?' (2005) Occasional Paper #10, UN Institute for Social Development; Marsha Henry, 'Peacexploitation? Interrogating Labor Hierarchies and Global Sisterhood Among Indian and Uruguayan Female Peacekeepers' (2012) 9(1) Globalizations 15; Christine Bell and Catherine O'Rourke, 'Peace Agreements or Pieces of Paper? The Impact of UNSC Resolution 1325 on Peace Processes and Their Agreements' (2010) 59(4) International and Comparative Law Quarterly 941; Fionnuala Ní Aoláin, Dina Haynes, and Naomi Cahn, *On the Frontlines: Gender, War and the Post Conflict Process* (Oxford University Press 2011); Machiko Kanetake, 'Whose Zero Tolerance Counts? Reassessing a Zero Tolerance Policy against Sexual Exploitation and Abuse by Peacekeepers' (2010) 17 International Peacekeeping 200; Deniz Kandiyoti, 'Between the Hammer and the Anvil: Post Conflict Reconstruction, Islam and Women's Rights' (2007) 28 Third World Quarterly 503.

law and potentially reifies the foundations of international law as a result.[13] Detailed analysis of what it means to challenge, reconstruct, or revert to sovereignty as a technique of ordering within transnational spaces is important not only because of the changing nature of sovereignty, but also because gender law reform, focused primarily on women as subjects for inclusion within and/or requiring protection by the law, is likely to reproduce sex difference rather than disrupt it.[14]

Scholarship on feminist approaches within international law, in the analysis of a tension between resistance and compliance or of the risks of governance feminism, analyses the role of gender law reform in legitimating international institutions and law.[15] The legitimating effect of gender law reform has its roots in the civilising discourse that early gender law reforms likewise produced, such that the imperial history of sovereignty and the role of gender law reform in disciplining non-European states require the combined attention of international lawyers and actors. Anghie concludes 'the basic assumptions that structure the more traditional histories of the discipline need to be reassessed. Rather than viewing colonialism as peripheral to the discipline, I would argue that colonialism is central to the formation of international law'.[16] Given the commitment across this book to an understanding of plural subjectivities as necessary to reimagine the normative contours of international law, I argue that the indigenous communities and colonised peoples that have been required to earn sovereignty or settle for less-than sovereign models of subjectivity must be an aspect of the re-conceptualisation/s of state sovereignty within feminist dialogues on international law. Thus, in this chapter I draw on Anghie's argument that:

'civilised' states were sovereign; uncivilised states were not sovereign and hence lacked membership in the family of nations. Sovereignty, then, might be viewed as containing within itself a series of mechanisms by which exclusion and discrimination can be effected, and these mechanisms were developed for and animated by the purpose of disempowering the non-European world.[17]

From this understanding, it is possible to better understand how gender law reform strategies always risk being/becoming a mechanism of exclusion and a means to identify civilised states from uncivilised, rogue, or failing states. The Women, Peace and Security Index 2017–18, for example, ranks states across three categories that successfully replicate older colonial models of power.[18] To avoid this type of imperial

---

[13] Felicity Ruby, 'Security Council Resolution 1325: A Tool for Conflict Resolution?' in Gina Heathcote and Dianne Otto (eds), *Rethinking Peacekeeping, Gender Equality and Collective Security* (Palgrave 2014) 173.

[14] Yoriko Otomo, 'Of Mimicry and Madness: Speculations on the State' (2008) 28 Australian Feminist Law Journal 53; Clare Hemmings, *Why Stories Matter: The Political Grammar of Feminist Theory* (Duke 2011); Charlesworth and Chinkin (n 11) ch 5.

[15] Sari Kouvo and Zoe Pearson (eds), *Feminist Perspectives on Contemporary International Law: Between Resistance and Compliance* (Hart 2011); Janet Halley, Prahba Kotiswaran, Rachel Rebouché, and Hila Shamir, *Governance Feminism: An Introduction* (Minnesota University Press 2018).

[16] Anghie Anthony, 'Western Discourses on Sovereignty' in Julie Evans, Ann Genovese, Alexander Reilly, and Patrick Wolfe (eds), *Sovereignty: Frontiers of Possibility* (University of Hawai'i Press 2013).

[17] ibid 23.

[18] Jeni Klugman, *Women, Peace and Security Index 2017/18* (Georgetown Institute for Women, Peace and Security 2017) <https://giwps.georgetown.edu/wp-content/uploads/2017/10/WPS-Index-

reproduction, gender law reform must attend to the foundational elements of global governance through the reimagining of core concepts such as state sovereignty rather than simply propping up existing legal structures.

Importantly, Knop's seminal article called for feminist analysis of state sovereignty in 1993 and acknowledged:

Feminist scholarship in international law has not yet set itself the task of rethinking State sovereignty, preferring to work within or—perhaps more aptly—around it. While criticizing the premise of the State as bounded, it has nevertheless accepted the premise of the State as unified. I have attempted to show that such an approach does not and cannot yield a clear direction for rethinking State sovereignty.[19]

Knop further developed her thinking on sovereignty in her book, *Diversity and Self-determination in International Law*, while simultaneously providing an integrated understanding of the intersection of race and gender politics through a study of the exclusion of groups within international law. [20] In this chapter, I return to the questions Knop posed, surrounding the relationship between feminist political goals, critiques of sovereignty, and critical legal understandings of sovereignty. Early feminist writings on international law, such as the work of Knop but also Charlesworth,[21] considered and critiqued the foundations of international law, including the definition of statehood and feminist perceptions of sovereignty which were then further elaborated in the work of Charlesworth and Chinkin.[22] Beyond these seminal texts, there has been a general neglect of this aspect of international law from feminist scholars despite early feminist texts on international law acknowledging that 'major reordering of international legal doctrine and institutions would be required to accommodate women'.[23]

To commence a process of reordering, I focus this chapter on how feminist methods might open up dialogue for reimagining sovereignty through the motif of the split subject. I develop the split subject as a relational understanding of legal subjects that incorporates the temporal and territorial implications of inter-, cross-, and regional-state relations. The split subject is intended to engage international law at its foundations via feminist critique and to displace the masculine subjects implied in mainstream conceptions of state sovereignty. Inspired by feminist philosopher Kristeva's musings on pregnancy as a 'radical splitting of the subject', this

---

Report-2017-18.pdf> last accessed 31 May 2018.; Anu Mundkur and Laura Shepherd, 'How (Not) to make WPS Count' (*LSE WPS Blog*, 23 January 2018) <http://blogs.lse.ac.uk/wps/2018/01/23/how-not-to-make-wps-count/> last accessed 31 May 2018.

[19] Karen Knop, 'Re/Statements: Feminism and State Sovereignty in International Law' (1993) 3 Transnational Law and Contemporary Problems 293, 332. NB: Knop capitalises the first letter in state throughout her text; I have replicated this in the quotations taken from her work but have not capitalised this in my own text.

[20] Karen Knop, *Diversity and Self-determination in International Law* (Cambridge University Press 2002).

[21] Hilary Charlesworth, 'The Sex of the State in International Law' in Ngaire Naffine and Rosemary Owens (eds), *Sexing the Subject of Law* (Law Book Company 1997) 251.

[22] Charlesworth and Chinkin (n 11) ch 5.

[23] Karen Engle, 'International Human Rights and Feminisms: When Discourses Keep Meeting' in Doris Buss and Ambreena Manji (eds), *International Law: Modern Feminist Approaches* (Hart 2005) 53.

chapter confronts the complexity of understanding the international legal subject in the early twenty-first century through feminist and critical lens.[24] Throughout the chapter, I provide a reflection on the possibility of personification of the state through the motif of the split and the splitting of the legal subject, which at its core identifies subjects, even when acting autonomously and independently, as in relation to other subjects. I consider the potential and limits of a split subject as the legal subject imagined by international law, ultimately offering the split subject as a meta tool drawn from the real-world connections, relations, and splits that define subjects to develop understanding and imagining of new frameworks rather a specifically feminised form of subjectivity.

For example, the late twentieth and early twenty-first centuries can be described as a period when the international legal subject was split in numerous ways: as new subjects (states) emerged in the aftermath of conflict and during secession struggles, via decolonisation processes, or as the consequence of international interventions, as well as through the rise of non-state entities such as self-governing territories and UN territorial administrations, as equally as through the consolidation of international institutions and regional networks as spaces of international cooperation. Furthermore, as understandings of home and belonging have been disrupted by virtual and physical movement across territories, previous markers that constituted the boundaries of international subjectivity have struggled to contain the diversity of actors moving through and with access to any given territory. Brah's work on the cartographies of diasporas draws out the epistemological shift required to see the cross-border associations, memories, and meanings that fixation on the nation as being closed territorially and conceptually rule out.[25] The imagining of community and belonging that diaspora communities both configure and draw attention to highlights the need for re-evaluating structures which reify difference such that Brah asks:

How can a project such as feminism or anti-racism, or a class movement, mobilise itself as a potential force for change if it did not start by interrogating the taken for granted values and norms which legitimate dominance and inequality by naturalising particular differences?[26]

Inequalities divide communities—pushing and constructing which knowledge is regarded as central to the organisation of political and legal, amongst other, structures. State sovereignty plays a central role in dividing international communities in a manner which does not reflect the transnational dimensions of human experiences. This chapter uses the split subject as a means to better encapsulate this range of approaches within feminist approaches to international law.

In the following section I will introduce the key feminist works that I draw on, in particular the work of Otomo with respect to feminist methodologies and

---

[24] Julie Kristeva (Alice Jardine and Harry Blake tr), 'Women's Time' (1981) 7 Signs: Journal of Women in Culture and Society 13; Julie Kristeva, 'Motherhood According to Giovanni Bellini' in Leon S Roudiez (ed), *Desire in Language* (Columbia University Press 1980) 237, 238.

[25] Avtar Brah, *Cartographies of Diaspora: Contesting Identities* (Routledge 1996).

[26] ibid 116.

international law, alongside a return to Knop's article on state sovereignty.[27] Together with Kristeva's articulation of the split subject and Arendt's politics of natality, this material sets the parameters for my thinking through state sovereignty from a feminist perspective in the remainder of the chapter.[28] In the third section I join feminist approaches with a conversation drawn from critical legal scholarship on the responsibility to protect and international law on secession, to explore the value of state sovereignty perceived through the notion of a split (rather than bounded) subject. In the final section of the chapter, I connect the three sites of knowledge explored in the chapter: feminist approaches to state sovereignty, critical legal approaches with a specific focus on the imperial histories of the discipline, and scholarship on the changing nature of international law to draw conclusions about the potentialities of feminism in post-millennium international law and theory beyond women as subject or actor within international law.

2. Feminist Approaches to State Sovereignty

For Otomo, the call for a new vocabulary in approaching international law is developed as an argument against the development of strategies of compliance that fail to engage in revolutionary feminist practices. In an argument that resounds with Charlesworth's approach, Otomo counsels:

> The answer ... is to hold on to both resistance and revolution as feminist telos, but to distinguish in our minds between the institutional *structures* of international law (which we must continue to engage with and resist in order to achieve our political goals), and the *space* created by failures of masculinist international law discourse which we can fill with revolutionary readings, writings, speaking and beings.[29]

If contemporary scholarship on the work of the international criminal court, women's human rights, and the Security Council's women, peace, and security agenda falls into Otomo's first category (engagement and resistance within the institutional structures of international law) the goal in this chapter is to reassert a dialogue on 'the space created by failures of masculinist international law discourse'.[30] In returning to state sovereignty I am interested in the failure of the 'body bag' built on a Kantian ethic of unpierced, closed subjects within the international realm.[31] The responsibility to protect doctrine, for example, is built around the premise that state sovereignty is not a closing off of the domestic space of the state. The reimagined state in responsibility to protect dialogues is one which has territorial control that is conditional and negotiable. Likewise the emergence and acceptance of non-state

---

[27] Knop, 'Re/Statements' (n 19).
[28] Kristeva, 'Woman's Time' (n 22); Hannah Arendt, *The Human Condition* (2nd edn, Chicago 1998) 9.
[29] Otomo, 'Searching for Virtue' (n 8) 35.   [30] ibid.
[31] Ngaire Naffine, 'The Body Bag' in Ngaire Naffine and Rosemary Owens (eds), *Sexing the Subject of Law* (Law Book Company 1997) 79.

entities as international legal subjects is no longer refutable.[32] The partial personality granted to international organisations fragments the discipline of international law and the nature of state sovereignty.[33] Similarly the emergence of earned sovereignty[34] and the movement away from the Montevideo Convention as providing the criteria for statehood, so that human rights standards, economic policy, and international cooperation increasingly fill the test for statehood[35] suggest the masculinist discourse constructed within international law, taught in mainstream international law courses, and articulated in formalist accounts of the discipline,[36] have long been jettisoned both in practice and in scholarship.[37] Yet, the feminist scholarship that engages with these developments remains sparse, under-discussed, and limited in terms of creating new spaces to replace the failure of masculinist accounts of law and legal subjectivity. Furthermore, the masculinist construction of the isolated, autonomous legal subject continues to pervade Western understandings of the baseline definition of state sovereignty—even at the very moment of acknowledging its demise.[38]

Drawing inspiration from Otomo's twofold project, I consider the split subject as conceptual apparatus to fill the space created by the poverty of masculinist state discourse. Otomo thus finds '[w]e may, for example, remain within a maternal metaphor, but rather than writing it into the sacrificial fraternal economy, hold onto the more nuanced (parasitic, symbiotic, combative) relations between mother and child when thinking about regulation of such relations'.[39] Similarly, I am not advocating the transference from a masculinist conception of law to a feminine conception of law—rather I propose a project of seeing the diversity of bodies and personhood derived from the recognition of plural subjectivities. As such, the split subject, or the pregnant body, is understood as difference, as potentiality, as the natal moment which connects what it means to be human (rather than female or male). Focus on the split subject also permits attention to the instability of borders, the changing and the porous nature of sovereignty, and nomadic, migrant, and peripheral subjects as knowledge-makers. This seems an important adjunct to the discussion of plural subjectivities, allowing the feminist legal dialogue to excavate further into the structures of law and ask questions about its ontology.[40]

Prior to considering the split subject, I revisit Knop's analysis of feminism and state sovereignty picking up and exploring the resonance this analysis has in the post-millennium international legal arena. Before proceeding, a note on terminology: I

---

[32] Reparations for Injuries Suffered in the Service of the UN (Advisory Opinion) [1949] ICJ Rep 174.

[33] Cecilia M Bailliet (ed), *Non-State Actors, Soft Law and Protective Regimes: From the Margins* (Cambridge University Press 2012) 4.)

[34] Paul R Williams and Francesca Jannotti Pecci, 'Earned Sovereignty: Bridging the Gap between Sovereignty and Self-Determination' (2004) 40 Stanford Journal of International Law 347.

[35] Joseph Weiler, 'Differentiated Statehood? "Pre-States"? Palestine@the UN' (2012) 24(1) European Journal of International Law 1.

[36] Anthony Aust, *Handbook of International Law* (2nd edn, Cambridge University Press 2007).

[37] Weiler (n 35).

[38] Gina Heathcote, *The Law on the Use of Force: A Feminist Analysis* (Routledge 2012) ch 3.

[39] Otomo, 'Searching for Virtue' (n 8) 44.   [40] Charlesworth and Chinkin (n 11) 18.

have largely directed the discussion as an analysis of state sovereignty under international law, following Knop who also directs her analysis at state sovereignty. This choice was made over an analysis of the legal definition of a state,[41] or a broader inquiry into sovereignty, to facilitate a focus on the legal personality of states as originating, within international law, through the principle of sovereign equality[42] and the analogy of individual legal subjectivity within domestic law.[43]

In her account of state sovereignty, Knop laments the failure of feminists to

become conscious of their own assumptions about State sovereignty, to understand its potential as a strategy of empowerment, and to critically examine the ways in which State sovereignty sets the functional and allegorical parameters of international law.[44]

Knop goes on to focus on both the functional, which she frames in terms of women's participation in governance institutions, and the allegorical parameters of international law, which she frames through a discussion of the personification of the state.[45] In examining the personification of state sovereignty Knop argues against the analogy between state and individual legal personality describing the analogy as being built on assumptions about individual and state sovereignty that she considers unsustainable. Knop argues, drawing on the work of Henkin[46] and Lauterpacht,[47] that scholarship centred on understanding the state as composed of individuals and of groups has greater purchase than that evoking the analogy between individual sovereignty under domestic law and state sovereignty under international law.[48] Knop's rejection of the analogy between individual and state sovereignty rests on the claim that '[s]tates are not like individuals in the significant respect that they are not unified beings … irreducible units of analysis'.[49] Knop is then critical of feminist approaches that shift between the two different conceptions of state sovereignty (conceptual and participatory) and remain articulated without attention to the different constructions of international law from which they derive. Knop is particularly critical of accounts that use the domestic analogy to then attempt to transform the perceived masculine nature of state sovereignty via a (feminine) ethic of care.[50]

Knop's account gives, thus, a sophisticated feminist rendering of state sovereignty through attention to 'difference and diversity, voice and representation'[51] made possible through disregarding the analogy and concentrating on acknowledgement that the relationship between state sovereignty and individuals is a real

---

[41] Charlesworth, 'The Sex of the State' (n 21).

[42] UN Charter Art 2 (1); Gerry Simpson, *Great Powers and Outlaw States* (Oxford University Press 2004).

[43] Naffine (n 31).   [44] Knop, 'Re/Statements' (n 19) 294–95.   [45] ibid 298.

[46] Luis Henkin, 'The Myth of Sovereignty' in State Sovereignty: The Challenge of a Changing World: New Approaches and Thinking in International Law. *Proceedings of the 21st Annual Conference of the Canadian Council on International Law* (Ottawa 1992) 15, 18.

[47] Hersch Lauterpacht, *Private Law Sources and Analogies of International Law* (2nd edn, Law Book Exchange 2012) 27.

[48] Knop, 'Re/Statements' (n 19) 319.   [49] ibid.

[50] Sara Ruddick, *Maternal Thinking: Towards a Politics of Peace* (Beacon Press 1995).

[51] Knop, 'Re/Statements' (n 19) 343; Emmanuelle Tourme-Jouannet, 'The International Law of Recognition' (2013) 24 European Journal of International Law 667.

(rather than an analogous) one. Knop focuses on the knowledge that states comprise of individuals and groups whose nuances, differences, and multiplicity are central to understanding and, consequently, developing 'women's perspectives on sovereignty theory'.[52] Despite Knop's article as an important early attempt to develop a feminist analysis of the foundations of international law, the subsequent decades have seen little feminist scholarship emerge on international conceptions of state sovereignty, while the vehicle of the state as a mechanism for guaranteeing women's rights continues to be accepted uncritically in a considerable amount of feminist writing.[53] Significantly, both Otomo and Charlesworth interrogate aspects of state sovereignty, as do authors such as Riles,[54] yet these are peripheral claims within their larger projects on gender mainstreaming, revolution, and legal histories, as well as the war on terror,[55] state building,[56] or even humanitarian intervention.[57] The centring of feminist scholarship on the state, its legal definition and meaning as the primary legal subject within international law, has been less common.

In returning to Knop's project I wish to reassert the analogy between state sovereignty and individual sovereignty,[58] precisely because of the understanding that states are 'not unified beings'. Knop's claim that states are not unified beings mirrors the claims about domestic legal subjects in feminist accounts, for example, writing on intersectionality. As such, understandings of sovereignty can persist as fractured and split in a manner that can lend credence to the analogy where both individuals in domestic legal systems and states within the international legal system are analogous in the legal status given to each. In both cases the error and persistence of a masculine subject can be reframed as a split subject, not only without gender/ sex but both relational and autonomous. The analogy thus requires understanding of individuals and states as sovereign entities that experience a range of splits, fracturing, connections, and relationships that make the boundaries of the subject inherently messy, whether the subject is the individual or the state.[59] In framing state sovereignty through the split subject the feminist focus on diversity and difference

[52] Knop, 'Re/Statements' (n 19) 343: Knop's use of the terminology 'women's perspectives' is taken to be a reference to feminist approaches rather than a literal invocation of women's perspectives while at the same time acknowledging that an aspect of Knop's scholarship is the political project of utilising the diversity of women's voices as a feminist method.

[53] Doris Buss, 'Racing Populations, Sexing Environments: The Challenge of Feminist Politics in International Law' (2000) 20(4) The Journal of The Society of Public Teachers in Law 463; Ratna Kapur, *Erotic Justice: Law and the New Politics of Postcolonialism* (Glasshouse Press 2005); Sari Kouvo, 'The United Nations and Gender Mainstreaming: Limits and Possibilities' in Sari Kouvo and Zoe Pearson (eds), *Feminist Perspectives on Contemporary International Law: Between Resistance and Compliance* (Hart 2011); Bailliet (n 33); Swati Parashar, J Ann Tickner, and Jacqui True, *Revisiting Gendered States: Feminist Imaginings of the State in International Relations* (Oxford University Press 2018).

[54] Annelise Riles, 'View from the International Plane: Perspective and Scale in the Architecture of Colonial International Law' (1995) 6 Law and Critique 39.

[55] Vasuki Nesiah, 'From Berlin to Bonn: Militarization and Multilateral Decision-Making' in Hilary Charlesworth and Jean-Marc Coicaud (eds), *The Faultiness of International Legitimacy* (Cambridge University Press 2010) 146.

[56] Kouvo (n 53).   [57] Heathcote, *The Law on the Use of Force* (n 38) ch 5.

[58] Otomo's work draws heavily on psychoanalytical theories in a manner I only touch on this chapter; the influence of this scholarship should nevertheless be apparent: Otomo, 'Searching for Virtue' (n 8).

[59] Patricia J Williams, *The Alchemy of Race and Rights* (Harvard 1991).

embedded within the plural subjectivities is then opened forth. As split subjects are inherently mutable and built around notions of difference and dynamism they draw out the previous discussion of plural subjectivities and assist description of how states function, with histories and relationships across borders, within the global order. I use the examples of the responsibility to protect doctrine and secession to underscore this claim, below, and to highlight how the split subject has the capacity to acknowledge and disrupt the imperial history of global governance. Recalling Syria, above, noting and understanding the splits and cohesions as integral to the persistent violence might be useful in disrupting the protection that state sovereignty has offered the Assad government.

Although Knop directly rejected the personification of state sovereignty, my approach resonates with two important additional aspects of Knop's 1993 argument.[60] First, I take seriously Knop's identification of the need to identify power as more than the capacity for coercion toward understanding power via the ability to act in concert— a conception she draws from the work of Arendt.[61] Second, Knop's continual assertion of the nexus between difference and diversity within the population of a state and informing the conception of state sovereignty resurfaces in the modelling of the split subject analogy. Taking the split rather than the masculinist subject as the starting point opens state sovereignty to the acceptance of diversity because recognition that the capacity for the subject to split away from itself to create new entities as central to the normative ordering of international law is recognition of legal subjectivity as both relational and separate. The latter claim then takes us back to the former: that power is born of the capacity to work in concert, that is, across difference and with others. Consequently, the propensity of powerful states to rely on coercion to achieve outcomes within the international law is recognised as reliant on a perception of subjectivity that is constrained by masculine perceptions of how power, and change, operate. Reconfiguring sovereigns as split conceives of the possibilities of joining and splitting as part of the status quo of existence, something understood in a very real manner in the UK in 2018 as I write in the wake of the Brexit referendum.[62]

It is important to anchor the discussion of the split subject with that which it is not intended to be. This is not an ethics of care politics centred on using women's difference or feminine forms as the normative foundation for a new (or old!) international order. Nor is this built around the body that is primarily sexed female.[63] Neither is the split subject constructed as an approach aimed at giving the ultimate answer to conceptions of the international: this would negate the attention to feminist method attested to earlier which specifically rejects the notion of 'grand theories'

---

[60] Knop, 'Re/Statements' (n 19); V Spike Paterson (ed), *Gendered States: Feminist Revisions of International Relations Theory* (Lynne Reiner 1992).

[61] Hannah Arendt, *On Violence* (Harcourt 1970) 44; Knop, 'Re/Statements' (n 19) 313.

[62] With thanks to Dr Louise Hood for pointing this out.

[63] Carol Gilligan, *In a Different Voice: Psychological Theory and Women's Development* (Harvard University Press 1982); Hilary Charlesworth, 'Feminist Reflections on the Responsibility to Protect' (2010) 2(3) Global Responsibility to Protect 232.

supplying complete 'answers' to complex legal and political projects.[64] Drawing on Charlesworth's use of Gunning and world travelling, the notion of the split subject is drawn not from a universal feminine form but rather the knowledge that all humans emerge from a splitting from the pregnant body.[65] This is reflective of an approach where feminist messages are attentive to the complexity and the diversity of women's experiences of the world. The pregnant body is used as a symbol for the reality of sovereignty as intimately and originally concerned with a breaking away, a separation and natal potential rather than an entering of the world as a fully formed and unified subject.[66] This occurs for individuals, whether through the process of being born or through the growth from childhood to adult that requires variations in dependence on central carers, as well as for states which require some form of separation from previous arrangements and independence from previous community structures to assert sovereignty.

Kristeva's split subject is articulated in the context of her reflections on the emergence of a second generation of women's movements in Europe that had occurred by 1981.[67] Kristeva considers the split between feminist co-optation into state or socialist projects and, what she labels, an 'avant-garde feminism' that is focused on female utopias. The former (early forms of governance feminism within European state structures) she challenges for the co-optation into non-feminist structures that Kristeva considers ultimately reappropriating feminist messages for their own ends. The latter ('avant-garde' feminisms), Kristeva is particularly critical of for their dependence on the category woman. Kristeva, then questions whether

having started with the idea of difference, feminism will be able to break free of its belief in Woman, Her power, Her writing, so as to channel this demand for difference into each and every element ...[68]

For Kristeva addressing feminism's 'belief in Woman' is linked directly to the linear temporality of both modernity and the nation. Kristeva notes that 'pregnancy seems to be experienced as the radical ordeal of splitting the subject'.[69] As a comment drawn after an analysis of Freud's construction of the female subject as one of lack, or envy, Kristeva proposes a model for imagining a de-gendered subject, where the split subject is the radical moment rather than the sexed body. This aligns with scholars such as Scott, who, in her account of the legacy of thinking on sex difference, considers the need for feminist scholarship 'to simultaneously insist on and refuse the identity of "women"'.[70] The split subject at once acknowledges the incompatibly of the masculine legal subject as a universal while simultaneously rejecting the feminine, or

---

[64] Nicola Lacey, 'Feminist Legal Theory and the Rights of Women' in Karen Knop (ed), *Gender and Human Rights* (Oxford University Press 2004) 13.

[65] Hilary Charlesworth, 'Talking to Ourselves? Feminist Scholarship in International Law' in Sari Kouvo and Zoe Pearson (eds), *Feminist Perspectives on Contemporary International Law: Between Resistance and Compliance?* (Hart 2011) 17; Isabelle Gunning, 'Arrogant Perception, World Travelling and Multicultural Feminism' (1992) 23 Columbia Human Rights Law Review 189.

[66] Otomo, 'Searching for Virtue' (n 8) 71–72.   [67] Kristeva, 'Women's Time' (n 24) 19.

[68] ibid 33.   [69] ibid 31.

[70] Joan W Scott, *The Fantasy of Feminist History* (Duke University Press 2011) 10.

female experience, as substitute or alternative. Central to this is an understanding of the exclusions feminine universals have carried into feminist scholarship, resulting in the amenability of feminist scholarship to very limited gender law reform agendas while alienating and undermining women from outside of elite women and Western women's experiences of gendered lives. As such, a plural understanding of subjectivity, first, grounds the diversity of women's experiences—and men's—and, second, accommodates the split subject as a motif of humanness where to be human is to be born into difference (and, via Arendt, this is what makes humans the same).

At the same time the split subject can hold the knowledge that 'the relationship posited between male and female, masculine and feminine, is not predictable; we cannot assume that we know in advance what it is'.[71] As such, the split subject need not be fixed to dominant gender arrangements through recognising gender as a power relationship that, in coordination with other power structures, enacts on, shapes, and is shaped by subjects. For Kristeva, the split subject is linked to understanding of the 'subject in process/in question/on trial'.[72] To bring this knowledge to international legal understandings of state sovereignty allows the conceptualisation of state sovereignty to commence with difference, fluidity, and the capacity for multiple subjectivities as the starting point rather than the deviation: it this which I explore throughout this chapter.

To emphasise the non-gendered component that I imagine when speaking of the pregnant body or the split subject, Arendt's politics of natality is a relevant additional tool for framing the split subject. Arendt's politics of natality focuses on the understanding that that which makes us human is our capacity to be born anew, both physically and in our relationships or actions, and our capacity thus for difference. Rather than natality as intimately connected to the feminine, Arendt addresses natality as that which connects each human subject as the same at birth yet acknowledging that each new human being has infinite potential for difference. As such, Arendt advocates that:

[n]atality; the beginning inherent in birth can make itself felt in the world only because the newcomer possesses the capacity of beginning something anew, that is, of acting. In this sense of initiative, an element of action and therefore natality, is inherent in all human actions. Moreover, since action is the political activity par excellence, natality, and not morality, may be the central category of political [thought].[73]

Bringing together these components of Kristeva and Arendt's scholarship is, below, utilised to consider what it means to imagine the non-sexed, non-masculine (or non-feminine) international legal subject of the state via the lens of the split subject. I use this as a tool to reimagine feminist dialogues on state sovereignty and legal subjectivity that can accommodate and respond to contemporary feminist and gender theories. In the following section, I consider the potential and limits of such a project through an analysis of contemporary critical scholarship on the responsibility to protect and secession. Alternative projects might imagine different conceptions

---

[71] ibid 11.   [72] Kristeva, 'Women's Time' (n 24) 31.
[73] Arendt, *The Human Condition* (n 28).

of the subject, international or individual, or address additional sites within the international arena where the fluidity and difference of legal subjectivity is clearly marked: for example, debates on earned sovereignty, or early twenty-first-century exercise of extraterritorial control.

The rejection of feminine and masculine forms is also a reaction to psychoanalytic accounts that identify fraternal tendencies within masculinist imaginings of sovereignty.[74] The bounded subject not only functions as a tool for isolating the state from interventions into its internal processes, it also functions to perpetuate global inequalities between states. A psychoanalytical rendering of the relationship between sovereign equals demonstrates how the construction of state sovereignty as closed permits fraternal bonding between states that encounter each other as equals alongside a rejection of states that are perceived as unable to demonstrate sufficient closure on internal affairs.[75] Thus the fractured, splintering, or porous state is constructed as the 'Other' to the closed, bounded state in a manner that feminises some states and opens them to the interventions (monetary, military, prosecutorial, and otherwise). The split subject, in rejecting the gendered or sexed representations of subjectivity, requires attention and acceptance of the porous, fractured, and split moments, across temporal, geographic, virtual, and conceptual spaces, which all sovereigns exist within.

My reading of the pregnant body is thus framed as the splitting of the subject from whom we are born and thus builds an understanding of individual sovereignty (autonomy) that comprehends the complexity of connection, relationship, affect, desire, separation and merging, fragmentation, and, the focus of this chapter, shifting understandings of state sovereignty. I have previously considered and analysed the construction of the legal subject as a category imbued with human traits in relation to the law on the use of force,[76] and a necessary offshoot of that work seemed to be a return to the legal subject to use it as a vehicle to push forward and develop feminist methods within international law while interrogating foundational legal categories.[77] One way to reimagine state sovereignty is to let go of the masculine framework that earlier legal thinking has been built on, towards conceptualising the non-sexed body as a metaphor for understanding the changing nature of sovereignty and, I would add, changing understandings of gendered bodies. I am not propelled by a desire to replace a masculine construction of legal subjectivity with a feminine motif and therefore deploy the pregnant body as a means to understand the very possibility of the split subject, rather than as a gendered or sexed subject. Furthermore, I argue that in accepting the split subject as within the realms of the possible, international law is better able to account for and describe contemporary transformations to the international legal subject, as well as the existing inequalities perpetuated through the sense of reproducing state sovereignty as closed via its territory and domestic jurisdiction. The split subject also accommodates the

---

[74] Otomo, 'Searching for Virtue' (n 8) 37.   [75] ibid.

[76] Heathcote, *The Law on the Use of Force* (n 38).

[77] Gina Heathcote, 'Feminist Reflections on the "End" of the War on Terror' (2010) 11(2) Melbourne Journal of International Law 277.

complexities of transnational, non-state entities as part of the international order in a manner that may allow international lawyers to lose their attachment to state sovereignty as a secure and necessary space, in exchange for recognition of the fluid, the relational. In the following section I demonstrate the value of recommencing feminist dialogues on state sovereignty under international law via conversations on split subjectivity, through a reading of critical understandings of the responsibility to protect and secession.

3. Contemporary Debates on State Sovereignty

In this section I examine two sites impacting on state sovereignty that give the appearance of significantly shifting away from masculinist conceptions of international legal personality, yet continue to reinforce state sovereignty as a unified or closed space.[78] The first is the doctrine of responsibility to protect and, in drawing on the work of Orford and Mgbeoji, I consider the space for feminist analysis of the responsibility to protect doctrine.[79] My analysis, in line with Otomo's thinking, is directed at the doctrine itself rather than at women's experiences of responsibility to protect policy via international institutions.[80] I follow this with an analysis of international engagements with the process of secession: both its denial and reluctant acceptance by international legal scholars, as well as the split subject confronted within mainstream conceptions of international law through the reality of secession. Throughout I consider the limited engagement with legal subjectivity in contemporary feminist writing and thus open the space to imagine, in the words of Otomo, 'a new feminist language and lexicon within international law': constructing a mechanism to consider the advantages of seeing the split over the bounded subject.[81]

3.1 Responsibility to protect

The responsibility to protect doctrine was originally articulated by the Independent Commission on Intervention and State Sovereignty (ICISS), a team of independent experts appointed by the Canadian government to respond to concerns at the end of the millennium regarding the apparent failure of international legal conceptions of sovereignty and the non-intervention into the domestic space of sovereign states during humanitarian crises. To answer the growing disquiet around the paralysis of

---

[78] Charlesworth, 'Feminist Reflections' (n 63) 248.

[79] International Development Research Centre, *Responsibility to Protect: Report of the International Commission on Intervention and State Sovereignty* (International Development Research Centre 2001) <http://responsibilitytoprotect.org/ICISS%20Report.pdf> last accessed 31 May 2018; Anne Orford, *International Authority and the Responsibility to Protect* (Cambridge University Press 2011); Ikechi Mgbeoji, *Collective Insecurity: The Liberian Crisis, Unilateralism and the Global Order* (University of British Columbia Press 2004).

[80] Sara E Davies, Zim Zowoka, Elis Stamnese, and Sarah Tuitt (eds), *Responsibility to Protect and Women, Peace and Security: Aligning the Protection Agendas* (Brill 2013).

[81] Otomo, 'Searching for Virtue' (n 8) 35.

the international community in the wake of events in Rwanda[82] and the Former Yugoslavia,[83] followed by the documentation of continued human rights abuses in the Serbian province of Kosovo that ultimately led to the unauthorised intervention by NATO,[84] the ICISS articulated sovereignty as a responsibility that imposes duties on states. Bellamy and Reike note the twofold nature of this aspect of the responsibility to protect doctrine.[85] The first, the responsibilities that states owe to the individuals and groups that reside within its territory, for Bellamy and Reike, are 'responsibilities [that] are deeply embedded in existing international law, much of which is considered *jus cogens*'.[86] The second component, the responsibilities of other states to respond to a state's failure to protect its population, Bellamy and Reike argue 'are much less well defined legally' (an apt description of the continued international response to the current situation in Syria).[87] Bellamy and Reike add that the responsibility to protect foreign populations may be driven by a moral or political imperative but currently does not exist, within international law, as a legal rule although they suggest this may be *lex feranda* especially in relation to the prevention of genocide.[88] The World Summit Outcome Document, issued by the General Assembly in 2005, further acknowledges that humanitarian interventions outside of the collective security structure have not emerged as law, a position strengthened in 2011 when member states waited for Security Council authorisation prior to intervening in Libya.[89] Although states have indicated that the responsibility to protect doctrine would justify the use of force in Syria without authorisation and states have used unilateral force against terrorist actors, no state has relied on the responsibility to protect to justify military force on the Syrian territory: the legal status of responsibility to protect doctrine remains *lex feranda*, at most, as a result.[90] In April 2018 an increase in unilateral strikes by a range of Western actors mirrored the use of force by the US in 2017 against Syria on the grounds that the Syrian government was using chemical weapons against its own people. The legality of these actions remains unestablished; given the long-term failures of foreign states to protect Syrian civilians it would be difficult to argue that these strikes constituted action justified under the responsibility to protect.

Bellamy and Reike's focus is predominately concerned with pretexts and justifications for the use of force or humanitarian interventions as a mechanism for halting state-led or state condoned violence against the population. Feminist analysis of

---

[82] Fred Grunfeld and Anke Huijeboom, *The Failure to Prevent Genocide in Rwanda: The Role of Bystanders* (Brill 2007).

[83] Christine Gray, 'Bosnia and Herzegovina: Civil War or Interstate Conflict? Characterisation and Consequences' (1996) 67 British Yearbook of International Law 155.

[84] Christine Chinkin, 'The Legality of NATO's Action in the Former Yugoslavia (FRY) under International Law' (2000) 49(4) International and Comparative Law Quarterly 910.

[85] Alex J Bellamy and Ruben Reike, 'The Responsibility to Protect and International Law' (2010) 2 Global Responsibility to Protect 267.

[86] ibid 269.   [87] ibid.   [88] ibid.

[89] UNSC Res 1973 (11 March 2011) UN Doc S/RES/1973.

[90] UK Prime Minister's Office, 'Chemical Weapons by Syria Regime: UK Government Legal Position' (Government Digital Service 29 August 2013) <https://www.gov.uk/government/uploads/system/uploads/attachment_data/file/235098/Chemical-weapon-use-by-Syrian-regime-UK-government-legal-position.pdf> last accessed 31 May 2018.

humanitarian interventions, including via the responsibility to protect claims, indicates that military interventions have low success rates in terms of transforming women's security[91] and in terms of disrupting the sexed nature of legal authority and relationship between law, gender, and violence.[92] In contrast, Orford's study of the responsibility to protect considers the manifestations of the doctrine in arenas within international law and practice, as well as how the notion of sovereignty as protection is neither novel nor neutral.[93] Orford identifies the masking of executive power that the responsibility to protect doctrine constructs and considers responsibility to protect as 'constructing a significant shift in thinking about the lawfulness of authority in the modern world'.[94] In doing so the responsibility to protect not only creates new sites of executive power under the guise of protection; further consequences flow for prior understandings of authority, in particular that vested in state sovereignty. As such, responsibility to protect constructs two tiers of sovereignty. Existing within the first tier are states with capabilities for intervention, identified through the bounded nature of their own borders as well as their capacity to influence the executive powers that Orford identifies.[95] In the second tier are states whose capabilities (and thus sovereign power) are diminished through internal fracturing and splitting that ultimately permits those identified as capable (states in the first tier) to intervene: militarily, economically, politically.[96]

In terms of conceptions of state sovereignty, the porous nature of state sovereignty— for some states but not others—within responsibility to protect doctrine reinforces difference and inequalities and ultimately leaves the masculinist, bounded, and powerful state as unchallenged. Responsibility to protect doctrine similarly leaves unchallenged and unobserved in law the fraternal bonds that are developed between powerful states to maintain the status quo. If, instead, state sovereignty is understood as vesting in split subjects then the combined unified and porous nature of all international legal subjects requires emphasis and understanding. Consequently, even with a legal commitment to sovereign equality, the spaces where some subjects experience cross state interventions as power and where other subjects experience interventions as violations are understood as within the relational nature of states, linked to their histories and productive of their vulnerabilities and might. Macro differences (that is, between states rather than within them) when considered from an understanding of subjects as created through splitting and existing through continued splits, then require incorporation into understanding and perceptions of how state sovereignty operates within international law. For example, approaching Syria not only requires understanding of internal splits (including both the creation of Rojava as a separate Kurdish enclave and the control of some Syrian territory by the so-called Islamic State, or ISIS) but equally of historical splits, such as the Treaty of

---

[91] Charlesworth, 'Feminist Reflections' (n 63).

[92] Ruth Buchanan and Rebecca Johnson, 'The "Unforgiven"' in Doris Buss and Ambreena Manji (eds), *International Law: Modern Feminist Approaches* (Hart 2005) 135; Heathcote, *The Law on the Use of Force* (n 38).

[93] Orford, *International Authority* (n 79) 25.   [94] ibid 41.   [95] ibid.

[96] Rose Parfitt, 'Book Review of Brad R Roth Sovereign Equality and Moral Disagreement: Premises of a Pluralist International Legal Order' (2012) 23 European Journal of International Law 1175, 1185.

Sveres and Syria's relations with mandate powers, as well as the relationships with regional actors including Iran, Israel, and Lebanon and the cross-border incursions from Turkey, alongside recognition of the flow of Syrian refugees into neighbouring states. Viewed with these splits visible, the notion of relationality between states seems important and an aspect international law needs to be able to better comprehend and respond to. This can be understood regardless of whether difference is experienced through constructions of race, ethnicity, culture, or via economic disparities between states. In the acceptance of subjects as split, splitting, or able to be fractured in multiple ways, diversity is placed at the core of defining legal subjects with temporal dimensions also rendered visible. This adheres to the commitment to plural subjectivities theorised in the previous chapter and addresses the fiction of the bounded state.

Additional splitting occurs between sovereign states and emergent executive spaces that demonstrate the further fallacy of the bounded subject as a legal entity. That is, the use of regional and international mechanisms, where states might choose to work in concert, are understood through the lens of split subjectivity, again, as within the conditions of legal subjectivity rather than as exceptions to the sovereign power of the state. The choice of the permanent members of the Security Council, thus, to work through the Council to respond to violence in Libya in 2011 is understood as the capacity of legal subjects to work in concert. The split subject does not address the excesses of power and colonial legacies that play out in the authorisations of force (and failures to authorise) by the Security Council but does facilitate recognition that the history of vulnerable, and rogue, states has always functioned in relation to colonial and economic power arrangements.[97] This echoes the account of Mgbeoji when he considers the intervention into the Liberian conflict during the late 1990s and early twenty-first century.[98] Mgbeoji challenges dominant Western intervention strategies and policies that ignore regional, as well as local understandings of violence and political unrest, for ultimately perpetuating rather than halting the vulnerability of states that are unable to protect their population. For Mgbeoji the solution is greater recognition of the authority and potential of regional structures: an account that could be developed within the idea of a split subject.[99]

The vulnerable or violent state is never an isolated, bound masculine legal subject because the state at risk of internal conflict, through either state-led or state-condoned violence, is a subject that splits in multiple fashions. Acknowledging this splitting is temporally connected to previous splits disrupts the distinction between 'rogue' and 'powerful' states to consider the interconnections, dependencies, mirroring, mimicry, and rejections that exist in state relations as equally as they exist within relations between individuals.[100] Not only will attention be drawn to recognise past splits and configurations (such as colonialism), so too will current relationships with other international subjects that contribute to the conditions fermenting humanitarian crises. The split subject does not normalise these splits and relations but facilitates heightened attention to the range of splits that occur, and

---

[97] Orford, *International Authority* (n 79) 212.   [98] Mgbeoji (n 79).   [99] ibid 143.
[100] Otomo, 'Searching for Virtue' (n 8).

that have occurred, within international law in a manner preferable to their continued denial. Orford's earlier work, on the consequences of monetary interventions into the former Yugoslavia can, under this analysis, be re-invoked as part of a complex story of violent and non-violent interactions.[101] These interactions occur between subjects that the international legal system can only be fully cognisant of through recognition of the archetype subject of law as the split subject rather than the masculinist conception of the bounded, unified subject of law.

Contemporary conflicts, such as the violence in Syria, are then understood in terms of historical splits as well as existing relationships between legal subjects. Responsibility to protect, in this manner, is understood as extending the status quo of liberal legalism.[102] Responsibility to protect preserves the fiction of bounded sovereignty as the norm within international relations,[103] permitting powerful states closure with regard to their internal legal structures while disrupting/overriding the boundaries of some, but not all, weaker states. The perpetuation of different standards for sovereign equals then permits a host of one-way interventions, while ignoring others such as the flow of refugees out of a territory during a humanitarian crisis: a splitting of the population of a state in a manner that creates new relations between different sovereign entities. Feminist theories that enter dialogue on split subjects, and plural subjects, see the refugee population through constructions of home and belonging that create communities—imagined and real—and that do not observe the international demarcation of state borders.

Under the analysis above, the split subject raises questions about the responsibility to protect doctrine. This is because the responsibility to protect permits, or at least promotes, working in concert for states that identify in a fraternal fashion, while rejecting the autonomy of states unable to mirror the sites of closure projected by masculinist state sovereignty. This is reminiscent of Anghie's description of the nineteenth-century construction of sovereignty as a tool to deny legal subjectivity during colonisation.[104] The split subject, in contrast, exists in a normative universe of both potential and existing dependencies across legal subjects that need not be denied as it is the capacity for the subject to split that constructs what it is to be a sovereign subject.

The radical potential of this form of reimagining of the legal world may be difficult to comprehend and, equally, in a world heavily drenched in gender norms and thinking, risks (in the words of Otomo) 'acknowledging, or even venerating a maternal feminine, that we transform that body into an icon'.[105] The project, then, is to adapt the underlying thinking to contemplate what it means to see bodies, subjectivity, and sovereignty as non-gendered and non-sexed. The possibility of conceiving

[101] Anne Orford, 'Muscular Humanitarianism: Reading the Narratives of the New Interventionism', (1999) 10 European Journal of International Law 679.

[102] David Chandler, 'The Responsibility to Protect? Imposing the "Liberal Peace"' (2004) 11(1) International Peacekeeping 59.

[103] Mgbeoji (n 79) 248.

[104] Antony Anghie, 'Finding the Peripheries: Sovereignty and Colonialism in Nineteenth Century International Law', (1999) 40(1) Harvard International Law Journal 1.

[105] Otomo, 'Searching for Virtue' (n 8).

of subjects that exist in the moment of natality where sameness, in that this is where all humans originate, and difference, in the uniqueness of each subject, seems to accurately capture the conditions of becoming (a non-gendered) human.[106] This raises questions about what is at stake if gendered and sexed forms of knowledge are jettisoned. In relation to the modification of sovereignty proposed via the responsibility to protect, this would require attention to the specifics of human violence and abuses of sovereignty, as well the multiple and diverse interactions between states, that create the conditions for humanitarian crisis. That is, the relations between past splits, current fractures within the state, and the possibility of interventions (military, humanitarian, economic) from foreign states and interventions. This mode of thinking requires a rejection of masculinist discourse on state sovereignty to better see state sovereignty as grounded in moments of splitting and pregnant communities of understanding and action. Critical projects, such as Orford's or Mgbeoji's, are then complemented by feminist methods to further consider the difference between coercion and concert, methods and messages, and the spaces for seeing and understanding diversity both within and across states. It is not necessary to look to states experiencing conflict to find relevance for the split subject. My home in Australia is born in a foundational moment of splitting from the United Kingdom, at the moment of federation in 1901, established via an Act of the UK Parliament.[107] Likewise, the forceful splitting of the Australian territory from the indigenous community's understanding of their sovereignty of the land had to occur for the Australian state to come into existence. Britain, where I currently reside, exists in constant flux as it denies and retells its own histories of occupation and annexation; splitting from the entities created through colonialism. These histories raise new questions about the capacity of responsibility to protect to reimagine sovereignty when the relational nature of sovereignty has sustained the gendered privilege of the unencumbered state.

3.2 Secession

The second example I draw on to explore the usefulness of understanding legal subjects as split subjects is that of secession. As both present and absent legal rule (or principle) in international law, secession haunts state sovereignty as both illegal and holding the potential to split the legal subject of the state. Indeed, it might be argued that all states are pregnant with the potential split that secession represents. Although not clearly recognised as a legal right of groups within a state, examples of secession abound in the history of the international order—from the break-up of the Former Yugoslavia, the creation of Bangladesh, the claims of the people of Kashmir, the dismantling of the USSR, the transformation of Micronesia into sovereign states, the emergence of South Sudan as a sovereign state, and to the creation of many self-governing territories globally. Secession exists as potentiality and reality in the global order despite (or in spite of) the absence of a clear international

---

[106] Wright (n 9).   [107] Commonwealth of Australia Constitution Act (UK) 5 July 1900.

legal framework governing secession.[108] International law, while accommodating the emergence of (some) new states via the process of decolonisation in the latter half of the twentieth century, has attempted to avoid establishing law on secession through the containment of self-determination to pre-existing colonies or non-self-governing territories.[109] In 1991 the Badinter Commission described secession as an internal matter for states and therefore not a component of international law.[110] These approaches centre on the role of state consent in international law, such that secession, defined as the breaking away from the parent state without consent, is regarded as a significant challenge to the coherence of the international system as a whole.

Kohen describes the approach of contemporary international law toward state secession: '[t]he emergence of a new State to the detriment of an older sovereign disrupts the composition of international society and challenges the very foundations of its main actors'.[111] Yet this traditional view of international law deriving its legitimacy from state consent has increasingly been eroded to accommodate the reality of interstate relations where coordination and compliance can be achieved via a range of methods including arbitration, judicial settlement, non-binding agreements, and the acts of non-state actors, in particular international organisations as well as non-governmental organisations. Events such as the breakdown of the former Soviet Union and the former Yugoslavian Republic, as well as the emergence of Eritrea as an independent state, the achievement of self-governing status in Bougainville and Kosovo, have led to acknowledgment that secession is not a wholly internal process and that international law plays a role in the transition to statehood or any other status.[112] Kohen describes this as 'international law play[ing] the role of the "midwife" providing legal justification for the creation of new states'.[113] This changing understanding of the role of secession within—rather than external to—the processes of international law is indicative of the factual circumstances in which, once functioning as a sovereign state and with recognition of the older sovereign state, international law has had to accede secession as a political process if not a legal one.

Secession remains an international legal reality that the international community, tied to the notion of state sovereignty, has had difficulty accommodating. Yet the split subject dismisses the difficulties of attempting to preserve state sovereignty when the facts no longer reflect this. The focus on a model appreciative of the existence of split and splitting subjects allows for the capacity of subjects—emerging, and those in existence—to work in concert to produce and accommodate change and diversity within communities. Central to this reconception of international law, then, is preservation of diversity that is also centred on the rejection of coercive measures

---

[108] Marcelo G Kohen, *Secession: International Law Perspectives* (Cambridge University Press 2006) 3.

[109] Declaration on the Granting of Independence to Colonial Territories and Peoples, UNGA Res 1514 (XV) (14 December 1960) (adopted by 89 votes to none; 9 abstentions).

[110] Badinter Commission (for the former Yugoslavia) Opinion No 9 (Settlement of problems of state succession) in European Community: Declaration on Yugoslavia and on the Guidelines on the Recognition of New States (1992) 31 International Legal Materials 1485; James Crawford, *The Creation of States in International Law* (Oxford University Press 2006) ch 9.

[111] Kohen (n 108) 1.   [112] Crawford (n 110) 418.   [113] Kohen (n 108) 4.

to produce (or avoid) change. The split subject therefore undoes the legal fiction of states as bounded entities, acknowledging the relational histories of states as well as the potential for states to split into new formations.

This is important because the veil of sovereignty—as a closed space that grants the domestic government authority over territory and citizens—has been used to deny the rights of peoples and to maintain the legal fiction of unity. A shift to recognise the different ways in which the subject is split, creates a space for recognition of difference while preserving the autonomy of the legal subject. That autonomy, acknowledged as born of past splits and connections, requires attention to those actors who are not part of the sovereign authority but who are impacted upon by the sovereign's decision to support or deny secession. I draw out methods of interruption as a means for inclusive decision-making in the following chapter; here, it is useful to give examples of what the split subject offers peoples within a state to articulate their needs. For example, border territories in any state, but significantly in states where borders have been artificially imposed via colonialism, will always have communities who have entrenched histories of flow back and forth across the border. This produces different understandings of belonging and connection in the border territories than in the metropole, away from the border. In postcolonial states cross-border movement has often consolidated pre-colonial identities and lead to fracturing and conflict. In the ICJ case between Nigeria and Cameroon, the dispute over Bakassi territory meant that a decision was destined to overlook the ties of a significant number of the peninsula's inhabitants in favour of recognising the sovereignty of a single state over the territory. In awarding the territory to the Cameroon, residents whose attachments remained to Nigeria ultimately faced persecution and returned to Nigeria, despite lacking citizenship in Nigeria.[114] If the starting point is to recognise the split, and thus relational element of sovereignty, then the end of dialogue does not rest with allocating control of the territory because the people in the territory are recognised as having connections to both states. The responsibility of both states is then to work in concert in response to the shared consequences. A failure to work in concert cannot be blocked by the veil of sovereignty because state sovereignty is recognised as relational. Consequently, the splits and ruptures in the history of territory are understood as creating shared stories, needs, and relations that also require legal understanding and responses and, potentially, a space for international law to recognise the impact of its own colonial history.

The shift to understanding state sovereignty as born of a split is an attempt to re-conceptualise sovereignty with a reimagined international law grounded in the reality of common diversity. As such, secession is both embraced as potential and a space for considering power as defined through acting in concert rather than via coercive action. Recalling Arendt, there is a need to see political action as a space conceived via a politics of natality where individuals (or states or the individuals that constitute the population of a state) are understood as having their diversity in common. This directly disrupts the construction of sovereignty as implicitly

---

[114] Oreva Olakpe, 'State Sovereignty and Migrations: Straddling Human Rights and Security in a Globalised World' (PhD, SOAS University of London, forthcoming 2019) [on file with author].

invoking the 'Other' to sustain existence and/or power. For secession, this means acting in concert can surpass coercion as a response to secessionist claims. This is also a closer reflection of existing practice, where non-coercive secession claims have become recognised and renamed as devolved power or even as the creation of new states.[115] Consequently, using the split subject within international law acknowledges the legal histories that construct the discipline where secession has occurred, allowing scholars and practitioners to work toward diminishing the use of coercion to achieve (or halt) secessionist claims.

4. Splitting the Subject

The task for the future, therefore, is to map out some of the characteristics and determinants of state identity in a way that takes into account not merely the formal properties of statehood, but also the sense of 'self', 'singularity' and 'community' that justifies the attachment of international legal obligations to particular territories and social groups.[116]

In this section I connect feminist approaches to state sovereignty, critical legal approaches, and the changing nature of international law to draw conclusions about the place of feminist thinking on post-millennium international law and theory. I review the split subject and the tensions within feminist thinking that it skirts and consider the need to move beyond 'a belief in Woman, Her power, Her writing' to focus on difference and projects that discard gendered and sexed forms to look beyond traditional, masculinist accounts of personhood, sovereignty, and legal structures.[117]

Showalter understands gender theory as follows:

Rather than seeking to repair the historical record by adding women's experiences and perceptions, gender theory challenges basic disciplinary paradigms and questions fundamental assumptions in the field.[118]

A similar approach is found in the work of Scott, who contends that it is the methodologies of feminist thinking that propel feminist thinking forward.[119] Across the book, I have argued, for feminist analysis of international law to remain relevant, feminist methodologies require greater attention. Within this, however, the message of feminist histories and knowledge retains a space: this is because the project of recognising and seeing women's experiences is connected to the process of challenging and understanding the limits of discursive structures. Yet the focus on women's experience potentially leads feminist legal approaches into disciplinary quandaries

---

[115] Kohen (n 108).

[116] Matthew Craven, 'The Problem of State Succession and the Identity of States under International Law' (1998) 9 European Journal of International Law 142, 162.

[117] Kristeva, 'Women's Time' (n 24) 31.

[118] Elaine Showalter, 'Hysteria, Feminism and Gender' in Sandra Gilman, Helen King, Roy Porter, Gilman S Rosseau, and Elaine Showalter, *Hysteria Beyond Freud* (California Press 1993) 288.

[119] Scott (n 70).

born of the subject of woman.[120] In addition, Charlesworth and Chinkin warn of the role abstractions of personhood play in legitimising specific gendered laws.[121]

In this section I consider the tensions apparent in splitting the subject, returning to Charlesworth and Otomo's conceptualisations of feminist approaches to international law to think through the nexus between women's experiences and the theoretical engagement with legal categories. In doing so I revisit the examples above to consider the limits and risks of conceiving of state sovereignty via split subjects. I conclude the strength is not to reconceive the world as configured through split subjects, rather to use the notion of pregnant bodies and split subjects to demonstrate the confines of masculinist thinking and to demonstrate the potential to productively reimagine known categories. This an important corrective to the construction of split subjects as a feminist 'answer', as I regard the split subject as a device to ask new feminist questions. My approach is conceived to join feminist and critical projects in moving beyond the formal characteristics of statehood and develop feminist thinking toward recognising that 'international personality has always been experienced differently by different states'.[122] To address these concerns, I have argued, feminist methodologies require tools that theorise gender and diversity.

In returning to the relationship between feminist methods and feminist messages, in her response to the responsibility to protect doctrine, Charlesworth develops an understanding of the need for a twofold approach. Charlesworth identifies the risks of only focusing on methods (as opposed the earlier critique of institutional pick up of messages and not methods).[123] For Charlesworth, a focus only on method is potentially as counterproductive as legal strategies only focused on the messages of feminist approaches. While the latter often results in liberal reform strategies, the former risks real paralysis in both critical and feminist projects as foundations and structures can be usefully deconstructed and critiqued while concrete reform strategies remain muted or utopian.[124] For Charlesworth, feminist messages are intimately connected to feminist method and she writes elsewhere of developing an international law of everyday that develops through both critique and practice.[125] In relation to the responsibility to protect, Charlesworth identified flaws in the development of the doctrine, particularly as this was 'without attention to the lives of women',[126] and flaws in the conceptualisation of responsibility to protect because it 'depends on gendered accounts of military intervention'.[127] These two separate claims identify the space between feminist political projects (centred on women's experience or feminist messages) and feminist methods (centred on understanding how structures are sexed and gendered). Reading across Charlesworth's scholarship

---

[120] Denise Riley, *'Am I that Name?': Feminism and the Category of Women in History* (Palgrave 1988).
[121] Charlesworth and Chinkin (n 11).   [122] Parfitt (n 96) 1185.
[123] Charlesworth, 'Feminist Reflections' (n 63).

[124] I use the term utopian, in the sense of an imagined feminist future, rather than in the mode it is often used in international legal theory to identify a specific approach within mainstream international legal approaches: see Martti Koskenniemi, *From Apology to Utopia: The Structure of Legal Argument* (2nd edn, Cambridge University Press 2005).

[125] Hilary Charlesworth, 'International Law: A Discipline of Crisis' (2002) 65 Modern Law Review 277.

[126] Charlesworth, 'Feminist Reflections' (n 63) 233.   [127] ibid.

the central importance of seeing methods and messages intertwined is crucial. However, in terms of developing concrete outcomes a dual feminist method and feminist message strategy demonstrates the complexity of working forwards, especially if transformation of global governance structures is perceived as part of the solution.

Similarly, True asserts the central role of the nexus between women's experience and feminist theory in feminist methods.[128] True's work looks to the need for attention to economic and social rights as a component of feminist projects, specifically in post-conflict and transitional justice settings, that utilise feminist method grounded in women's lived experiences to articulate international practice and policy.[129] The articulation, in this chapter, of a project centred on international legal discourse over international legal practices, and their consequent impact on lived experiences, risks a split between mind and body (doctrine and practice) that would be antithetical to feminist projects. Both Otomo and Charlesworth use the split between message/method and resistance/revolution to illustrate gaps in contemporary international legal engagements from feminist scholarship engaged within mainstream dialogues. Yet both build their engagement with method (Charlesworth) and revolution (Otomo) through praxis within feminist scholarship that is precisely concerned with the relationship between theory and practice.

Drawing from the work of Lacey, there is a loop between critique—utopia—reform that understands the necessity for work in each space rather than isolation in understanding the various components of feminist scholarship.[130] As such, while for the most part attending to the spaces of critique/utopia throughout this book, I am mindful of the real world implications of both masculinist discourses on international law—which contribute to the failure of international law to construct feminist outcomes—and a feminist focus on the critique of international law. As such, centring on the re-conceptualisation of state sovereignty requires further development to consider the meaning in terms of the lived reality of gendered subjects that feel the impact of international institutional practices. While it may be possible to imagine the split subject devoid of gendered expectations and qualities, this does not equate with the lived experiences of bodies which remain sexed and gendered in their encounters in the real world. The split subject becomes a project to be reinserted in feminist engagements within international law and institutions to consider the possibilities for remoulding known legal categories as a component of feminist messages. The split subject demonstrates how understanding human diversity requires a reframing of practices and that in terms of concepts and categories gendered knowledge needs to be jettisoned. This leads us back to Otomo's understanding of the need for revolutionary spaces that shift beyond masculinist categories within international law.

---

[128] Jacqui True, 'The Political Economy of Gender in UN Peacekeeping' in Gina Heathcote and Dianne Otto (eds), *Rethinking Peacekeeping, Gender Equality and Collective Security* (Palgrave 2014) 243.

[129] Doris Buss, Joanne Lebert, Blair Rutherford, Donna Sharkey, and Obijofor Aginam (eds), *Sexual Violence in Conflict and Post-Conflict Societies* (Routledge 2014).

[130] Lacey (n 64).

Throughout I have configured the split subject as an imagined subject that accommodates diversity both within and across sovereign subjects. This resonates with the work of Wright who attends to what it means to become human and theorises that as a species we have only begun to embark on the project of becoming human.[131] The pregnant body is a theory of the possible, acknowledging the self as always Othered in some form. To be diverse, or different, is consequently engrained in what it means to be human.[132]

In line with Charlesworth and True, Otomo identifies two problems/risks with attempts to reconfigure international law through feminist method precisely because of the nexus between method and message—thus she pushes beyond acceptance of the need for method/message nexus to consider the risks of this approach. First, Otomo warns that 'the writing over of others must be negotiated at every turn'.[133] That is, attention to difference will not erase inequalities or difference and each assertion of inclusion will necessarily construct exclusions. Second, as highlighted above Otomo acknowledges '[t]here lies a risk, in acknowledging, or even venerating a maternal feminine, that we transform that body into an icon'.[134] For Otomo, then, the powerful assumption of gender onto bodies and categories of knowledge must be attended to. In de-gendering the split subject I have attempted to attend to both of these aspects to assert difference as the central quantity of being human and to reject the gendered, or sexed, body as the central ordering to understand primary human difference.

I have endeavoured to identify the split subject as a non-gendered space, that is, an acknowledgment that individuals commence through a splitting from the pregnant body and that the process of rupture and splitting, as equally as the continuation of connection, are never finalised.[135] Of course, the pregnant body is culturally conditioned/structured as a vessel for female iconography and feminine behaviours, but my attention is not on the pregnant body rather on the subject that splits from it which is neither female nor male merely human. This then creates space for asking what it means to be human and, in following Arendt, I have developed the thesis that to be human is to be born and in being born is to be the same as others in our capacity to be different.[136] Throughout I have used this model of individual subjectivity to consider the analogous shaping of the subjectivity of states, as sovereign entities, under the global order. State sovereignty is thus reconceived as created via a splitting from a prior entity and the focus is on the potential for further splitting, for the need for relationships and connections, as well as development of autonomy and a sense of self/identity. State sovereignty is understood as analogous to individual sovereignty in the sense that legal subjects are never whole, closed, or unified; instead they are diverse, fractured, connected, singular, and fluid all at once. This opens international law and legal analysis to a politics of potential rather than a model that

---

[131] Wright (n 9).
[132] Martha Fineman, 'The Vulnerable Subject: Anchoring Equality in the Human Condition' (2008) 20 Yale Journal of Law and Feminism 8.
[133] Otomo, 'Searching for Virtue' (n 8) 40.   [134] ibid 41.
[135] Kristeva, 'Women's Time' (n 24).   [136] Arendt, *The Human Condition* (n 28).

continually reasserts its static, closed, and bounded nature, as has been the case with models of state sovereignty conceived in relation to the masculine body. As such, this is Otomo's project of imagining revolutionary spaces and lexicons with an attention to opening up categories rather than shutting them into preconceived and gendered forms. I have used an analogy between state sovereignty and individual sovereignty to understand that states are 'not unified beings', nor are individuals.[137] In arguing that the analogy can persist, the attempt is to understand how both individuals and state sovereignty can be regarded as fractured and split in their relations with other legal subjects.

As has been seen in this chapter, the responsibility to protect doctrine emerged precisely in response to the notion of state sovereignty as inviolable. At the same time secession has remained an exception rather than a rule of international law despite varied state practices that have permitted the splitting of states into different types of legal subjects and entities. Throughout this chapter, I have argued that the split subject has the capacity to better accommodate our knowledge of the reality of sovereignty. The project of seeing and imagining the split subject is intimately connected to the release of law from its masculinist origins and the exclusionary legal order derived from this model. At the same time the approach of this chapter is not intended to be prescriptive, as my project has been to reimagine state sovereignty through a lens where diversity and difference are central to the legal project and where power can be understood as the capacity to act in concert rather through coercive measures. The power of international law to function through compliance and agreement rather than coercion is in many ways a good description of the manner in which the majority of international laws work. As such, the split subject is proposed not as an alternative or as a necessary component of the international order, it is simply a framework, a language, a reimagining of what we cannot see if we restrict our thinking to known descriptions of the world around us.

Returning to the beginning of the chapter and the continued violence in the Syrian state, Alodaat provides an analysis of the gendered configurations of law and violence in the Syrian state.[138] While focused on the impact of the conflict on women's lives, Alodaat also questions the complicity of Syrian law in perpetuating the forms of gendered insecurity the Syrian people endure. Alodaat entrenches intersectionality in her analysis of law, gender, and violence in Syria, as well as the impact of conceptions of sovereignty on Syrian women's security. As such, although centred on women's experiences Alodaat articulates the consequences of, for example, disability in armed conflict, and the gendered burdens it creates:

the survivors of explosive weapon attacks suffer from long-term challenges such as physical disabilities, psychological harm, and thus, social and economic exclusion. These challenges have a greater impact on women who live in a society where, compared to the men, they already have less access, more social restrictions and limited freedom of movement[139]

---

[137] Otomo, 'Searching for Virtue' (n 8).
[138] Alodaat, 'The Armed Conflict in Syria' (n 3).   [139] ibid 14.

Local community networks, such as the white helmets (Syrian Civil Defence) in the Idlib region of Syria similarly use female actors to deliver medical support to women in the region, acknowledging the complex, gendered reality of the lives of women in the region.[140] Likewise, Alodaat identifies the ongoing effect of a history of gender discriminatory laws in Syria on women's security in peacetime and conflict:

Personal Status laws do not grant women custody of their children or the right to make decisions related to their livelihood without the approval of the child's father, and in his absence, the father's male relatives or a judge. Finally, traditions put many constraints on women when it comes to working outside of the house, and the spread of arms and use of explosive weapons in populated areas have added a massive burden to their freedom of movement. These restrictions turn into an absolute ban when sexual violence becomes a weapon of war—turning women's refuge into a de-facto detention facility.[141]

Furthermore, the failure of the Syrian state to grant citizenship to children via their mother's nationality, creates gendered conditions for women who cannot leave Syria, despite the violence, because of these gendered legal arrangements. As such, although centred on women's experiences in Syria, Alodaat leads the way in conceptualising the gendered effects and consequences of conflict, highlighting the need for both women's participation and women's protection via decision-making spaces that prioritise the need for knowledge of the intersection of law, gender, and insecurity in the region. This remains in contrast to the Security Council's approach, which sees a general silence in official documents and, where informal consultations have occurred, criticisms for the failures with regard to inclusions. I return to the issue of women's participation in the following chapter; here it is enough to acknowledge the complexity Syrian women raise in relation to the conflict, through the use of a gender lens to build their analysis demonstrating at once a need for a feminist message (on the insecurity in women's live) and a feminist method (to challenge the entrenched gender relations).

I derived the split subject from the work of Kristeva and associated it with, by analogy, the pregnant body, yet it is not configured as a gendered, or sexed, body. The strength of the analogy is in the acknowledgement of our own births as a process of splitting from the pregnant body and thus, drawing on Arendt, recognises the human sameness in our capacity to be born. The sameness that is difference thus becomes that which makes us human and is arguably a useful capturing of what it means to be a sovereign individual. In analogy we can use the split subject to better describe the nature of state sovereignty. I have played with and explored this notion throughout this chapter, by no means interrogating it to its limits or exploring the split subject sufficiently to understand where the analogy might unstick or, akin to masculinist understandings of state sovereignty, be ultimately inadequate due to the anthropomorphic universe it confines us to. As a tool to demonstrate the need for imagination and openness in our international legal writing, the split subject emerges as feminist, as attentive to difference, and as latent, nay pregnant, with possibilities.

---

[140] Tisdall (n 4).   [141] ibid 15.

Postscript

As I conclude the writing of this chapter I am reading Moreton-Robinson's text *Sovereign Subjects* and reflecting on the privilege of history that has enabled me, literally, to write this chapter.[142] To my mind come two different issues related to sovereignty and my life. First, in my current home, Brexit dominates the news as the UK state attempts to split from the European Union; the necessity of future intertwined relations tells the story of sovereignty as one that rests in the paradox of connection and difference. Second, the white settler status of my birth state unsettles the confidence with which I write this chapter. Moreton-Robinson writes of the 'security of white, patriarchal sovereignty', unsettling the focus on gendered histories as my pivot for a feminist dialogue on sovereignty and reasserting the need to recognise plural subjectivities—as motif of international and domestic legal subjects and the nexus (not just analogy) between the domestic and the international.[143] Acknowledging the contested histories and contested present of state sovereignty that I benefited from/benefit from, dislodges the stories of split subjects in this chapter. I have derived the split subject from a Western perception of subjectivity, which does not hear those whose experience of sovereignty is one of dispossession and thus never split but was instead rendered unreadable, silent, and unknowable. The interplay between the legal status of indigenous Australians—that had to be gained—and the legal status of indigenous Australia—which is never regarded as a possibility except as an adjunct to white possession of sovereignty in Australia—identifies the continuum that, on the one hand, gives me the assured status as citizen (of both the UK and Australia) and assured status as authority to write on meanings of state sovereignty that ultimately betray the privilege that needs to be spoken. I write because my birth state awarded me uncomplicated status as legal subject. Unspoken in that sentence is my whiteness (and even more embedded is the histories of European migration to Australia in my family tree). I write because the uncomplicated status of Australia as a state under international law is an Australia that I benefit from. As a white Australian woman citizenship was granted to my foremothers in 1901 as the federal state was conceived; this considerably precedes the granting of citizenship to indigenous Australians in 1967.[144] Citizenship for non-indigenous Australian women, while threaded within the patriarchal and colonial origins of the state, remains unquestioned and I have been able to assume its mantle as a passport to facilitate significant intellectual and physical global travelling. In contrast, citizenship for indigenous Australians remains a space of dispossession connected to the absence of sovereignty. Moreton-Robinson writes:

---

[142] Aileen Moreton-Robinson, 'Writing Off Indigenous Sovereignty' in Aileen Moreton-Robinson (ed), *Sovereign Subjects: Indigenous Sovereignty Matters* (Allen & Unwin 2007).

[143] ibid 102.

[144] However, note that not all Australian states gave women the right to vote at this time.

What indigenous people have been given, by way of white benevolence, is a white-constructed form of 'Indigenous' proprietary rights that are not epistemologically or ontologically grounded in indigenous conceptions of sovereignty.[145]

While Moreton-Robinson here writes in reference to sovereignty over the territory of Australia, the links between individual sovereignty and collective sovereignty, individual self-determination and collective self-determination, are apparent—the language for both citizenship and sovereignty derives from the settler-colonial model that displaces indigenous ownership and reimagines indigenous citizenship and sovereignty as the same as, or a derivative of, the settler-colonial model. This is the model that I have taken for granted throughout this chapter and which I have sought to better describe via the motif of the split subject. Indigenous voices ask something different:

Our sovereignty is embodied, it is ontological (our being) and epistemological (our way of knowing), and it is grounded within complex relations derived from the intersubstantiation of ancestral beings, humans and land. In this sense, our sovereignty is carried by the body and differs from Western constructions of sovereignty which are predicated on the social contract model, the idea of unified supreme authority, territorial integrity and individual rights.[146]

As such, the split subject written into this chapter requires that indigenous voices be interjected as a frame for future dialogues. Gender without historicity writes gender into power relations in raced and colonialising fashions, economically exploitative and ableist in the imagined histories and presents embedded within, and with the lived and remembered violence that are integral to knowing the world at risk of re-iteration rather than undoing. I return to the implications of this, my positionality and my privilege, in chapter 6. It is attention to feminist methodologies that prompts me to ask these questions (both intersectional and postcolonial feminisms) but the consequences are for all critical legal scholars, mainstream international lawyers, and feminist scholars working on international law.

---

[145] Moreton-Robinson (n 142) 4.   [146] ibid 2.

5

Institutions

[W]e all have a deep stake in the operation of norms and the power relations of normalization, and... to understand these, we need to understand how disability plays into this, especially through the intertwined dynamics of culture and law.[1]

Communities based on queer kinship ties offer us hope that human solidarities and loyalties can break free of the bonds of the nation-state and extend to include others, particularly those most disadvantaged by the brutal heteronormative order that states impose.[2]

1. Introduction

In recognising feminist approaches to law as encompassing a series of feminisms, and thus dialogues, this chapter considers how different and differing dialogues might be incorporated via a feminist epistemology of plural and split subjects that draws in the critiques of crip and queer theories alongside a diversity of feminist methodologies. The chapter builds on the analysis of expertise and fragmentation that illuminates the risks for feminist engagements with global governance and law, to consider further strategies of reconstruction (and disruption) within the structures of the global order. I pay particular attention to international institutions, as non-state actors wielding legal power of sorts within global governance. While the previous chapter centred on state sovereignty and examined the potentialities of conceptualising a split subject, in this chapter I take dialogues from contemporary feminist approaches—the configuring of maternal subjectivity as interruption and feminist approaches to political economy—as initiating plural dialogues on international institutions from a feminist perspective. My objective is to prioritise specific tensions within feminist dialogues (essentialism, imperialism, materiality) as leaping off points that can be used as productive tools for the analysis *and transformation* of international law. In doing so this chapter approaches international institutions, and their role as non-state actors within the global order, via feminist dialogues without presupposing or asserting the existence of a single feminist approach to international

---

[1] Gerald Goggin, Linda Steele, and Jessica Robyn Cadwaller, 'Normality and Disability: Intersections among Norms, Law and Culture' (2017) 31(3) Continuum 337, 339.

[2] Dianne Otto (ed), *Queering International Law: Possibilities, Alliances, Complicities, Risks* (Routledge 2018) 257.

Feminist Dialogues on International Law. Gina Heathcote. © Gina Heathcote 2019. Published 2019 by Oxford University Press.

law. Along the way, and through drawing on the maternal subject as inspiring a politics of interruption, the chapter plays with the idea of interruption through the interventions of crip and queer theories that are interjected into the chapter.

In acknowledging that co-optation of some feminist ideas within international institutions illuminates the dangers of endorsing and legitimating institutions, I argue that examining how international institutions are gendered at a foundational level is necessary. At the same time, in recognising the potential impossibility of projects of gender law reform, I use queer and crip scholarship to disrupt any feminist sense of knowing. This allows me to approach the epistemological concerns of the book as open to the unsettling knowledge of thinking about thinking differently.[3] Nevertheless I also develop the feminist inquiry into the lawmaking capacity of institutions and analyse the trajectories future feminist dialogues might take within institutional structures. I rely on feminist articulations of the maternal,[4] feminist politics of location,[5] and political economy approaches[6] to build on the examination of legal subjectivity as plural, as split and grounded in diverse relationality, as articulated across the book. I explore how relationality is felt and lived differently in the material lives of specific bodies and communities and how recognition of temporal, as well as classed, situated, and sexualised, Othering disrupts relationality, subject formation, and recognition. As such, this chapter provides an argument in favour of dialogues and spaces via feminist engagements within international law that are not only attentive to the biases of the international legal system but that also engage openly with the colonial genealogies of international law, the embedded heteronormativity of law, and the gendered normalising of bodies through analysing what it means to reconfigure the dialogues on feminist knowledge, action, and engagements within international law.

In legal scholarship only limited feminist engagement with international institutions is apparent, although the adjunct field of international relations has seen the emergence of feminist institutionalism as a field of study.[7] In addition, important critical legal accounts of international institutions do not address either the gendered structures or the gender outputs of international institutions.[8] International legal writing on soft law and non-state actors has links to feminist writings and does include specifically feminist interventions; however, this has not produced a significant corpus of feminist engagements with international institutions.[9] As noted

---

[3] Lisa Baraister, *Maternal Encounters: The Ethics of Interruption* (Routledge 2008) 5.

[4] Irene Gedalof, 'Interruptions, Reproduction and the Genealogies of Staying Put in Diaspora Space' (2012) 100 Feminist Review 72.

[5] Sara Ahmed, *Strange Encounters: Embodied Others in Postcoloniality* (Routledge 2000).

[6] Jacqui True, *The Political Economy of Violence against Women* (Oxford University Press 2012).

[7] Mona Lena Krook and Fiona Mackay (eds), *Gender, Politics and Institutions: Towards a Feminist Institutionalism* (Palgrave 2011); Swati Parashar, J Ann Tickner, and Jacqui True, *Revisiting Gendered States: Feminist Imaginings of the State in International Relations* (Oxford University Press 2018).

[8] Jan Klabbers, *An Introduction to International Organisations Law* (3rd edn, Cambridge University Press 2015).

[9] Alan Boyle and Christine Chinkin, *The Making of International Law* (Oxford University Press 2007); Cecilia M Bailliet (ed), *Non-state Actors, Soft Law and Protective Regimes: From the Margins* (Cambridge University Press 2012); Gina Heathcote, 'Fragmented Feminisms: Critical Feminist Thinking in the Post-Millennium Era' in August Reinisch, Mary E Footer, and Christina Binder (eds), *International Law and ... (Select Proceedings of the European Society of International Law 2014)* (Hart 2016) 309.

throughout this book, feminist legal texts and feminist strategies within the United Nations tend to examine specific institutions, such as the Security Council[10] or the International Criminal Court,[11] and the outputs of these institutions, such as the resolutions on women, peace, and security or the jurisprudence on gender crimes, as opposed to working to develop feminist methodologies.[12] In contrast, I develop this chapter through consideration of the powers, authority, and structures of international institutions, as well as opening feminist dialogues to the discussion of power, authority, and structures reproduced by gender law reform.

I provide a gender analysis of the constitutive powers and structures of three international institutions, selecting organisations with different structures and remits to capture the different settings of international institutions and to think about what a feminist dialogue on the tools and formations of those institutions might lead towards. In examining the structures and the constitutive powers of international institutions, I draw on Charlesworth and Chinkin's articulation of feminist approaches within international law as requiring attention to the organisational and the normative.[13] However, to move beyond a critique of existing gendered arrangements within international institutions, I look outside feminist legal theories to the wider fields of gender, queer, and crip theories to articulate new feminist epistemologies on international law.[14] Throughout this chapter I draw on non-legal feminist scholarship that is specifically concerned with the parameters of knowledge production, the politics of location, and the political economy of gender, to examine the potentialities of international institutions, while drawing these into dialogue with queer and crip theories.

The chapter continues the kaleidoscope approach of the book, rather than preferring or embracing a single approach, to evidence conversations, starting points, tensions, and, indeed, dialogues on international law that emerge from attention to varied spaces of feminist theorising. I do appreciate that tensions in feminist dialogues are not always pleasant/welcoming and the notion of dialogue can be fraught for feminists who find their voice absent in mainstream feminist spaces and histories, including feminists of colour, crip, trans-, and queer feminists.[15] Disengagement might be preferred over dialogue by those who enter feminist spaces with histories different from mainstream voices: this is something that has received insufficient response from feminists working on international law as scholars, policymakers, and experts. I argue this is a dialogue and a tension that needs to be surfaced for any

[10] See further, Gina Heathcote and Dianne Otto (eds), *Rethinking Peacekeeping, Gender Equality and Collective Security* (Palgrave 2014).

[11] Louise Chappell, *The Politics of Gender Justice at the International Criminal Court: Legacies and Legitimacy* (Oxford University Press 2016) 2–15.

[12] Sari Kouvo and Zoe Pearson (eds), *Feminist Perspectives on Contemporary International Law: Between Resistance and Compliance* (Hart 2011).

[13] Hilary Charlesworth and Christine Chinkin, *The Boundaries of International Law: A Feminist Analysis* (Manchester University Press 2000) ch 6.

[14] Otto, *Queering International Law* (n 2).

[15] Alyosxa Tudor, 'Dimensions of Transnationalism' (2018) 117 Feminist Review 20.

future gender law reforms to develop as feminist methodologies rather than just taking up feminist messages.

This chapter also considers the centrality of listening—in particular, the need for listening by feminists who might otherwise be expecting to claim a space a speak. In the words of Otto: 'the politics of listening challenges us all to take responsibility for justice based on our interconnectedness as people and our shared political and legal institutions'.[16] In this chapter I have tried to hold the politics of listening (over speaking) as a key to thinking about which feminist knowledge is introduced into international institutions. In the process I consider how a feminist understanding of tensions—between activism and academic spaces, between theory and practice, between core and peripheral subjects, between different modes of feminist thinking, as well as in addressing essentialism, imperialism, and materiality—might be used to undo the manner in which the global order, and its institutions, rebuild their own power beyond the limited and curtailed approach to knowledge and location that is often (also) embedded within traditional, critical, and mainstream approaches to international law (including gender law reform). Gill writes of a process of learning to 'speak with' as a postcolonial feminist technique. Written in the context of qualitative research, Gill finds 'the ethics of speaking with participants requires sensitivity, reflexive and reflective examination, relationship building, and ethical accountability between researchers and their research participants'.[17] In the context of qualitative research this has significance; my approach has been to consider, drawing on both Gill and Otto, how to 'speak with' and 'listen' in a manner that actively transforms the text without disrupting the capacity to contribute to the existing body of literature and field of research. As with the prior chapter, this chapter therefore unfolds with its own interruptions and spaces of self-reflection to actively undo the privileging of certain knowledge histories alongside a consciousness of which authors are quoted and represented in the text.

In particular, I both engage crip theory and attend to some of the critiques from disability theorists of crip theory. Crip theories are generally regarded as originating in the work of McRuer who developed a study of the convergences of queer and disabilities studies to question and voice approaches to the non-normative. McRuer argues for a crip theory that is a subset of queer theories and that forms 'an identity politics that resists the normative construct of able-bodiedness'[18] — drawing disability studies and queer theories into dialogue, or 'inviting conversation, searching out community, and wondering aloud what the word could do or mean'.[19] Crip theory has also received rigorous critique from disability studies and

---

[16] Dianne Otto, 'Beyond Legal Justice: Some Personal Reflections on People's Tribunals, Listening and Responsibility' (2017) 5(2) London Review of International Law 225.

[17] Aisha Gill, 'Feminist Reflections on Researching so-called "Honour Killings"' (2013) 21 Feminist Legal Studies 241, 245.

[18] Kirstin Marie Bone, 'Trapped Behind the Glass: Crip Theory and Disability Identity' (2017) 32(9) Disability and Identity 1297, 1303; Robert McRuer, *Crip Theory: Cultural Signs of Queerness and Disability* (New York 2006).

[19] Merri Lisa Johnson and Robert McRuer, 'Introduction: Cripistemologies and the Masturbating Girl' (2014) 8(3) Journal of Literary & Cultural Disability Studies 245, 248.

critical disability studies scholars who describe the approach as limited in that it 'authorizes anyone to speak on behalf of the disabled rather than prioritizing actual disabled voices'.[20] For Bone the consequence is that crip theory 'fashions a theoretical glass closet in which the disabled community is kept on display rather than being allowed to speak for themselves'.[21] The debates that unfold thus look at issues of personhood, normativity, identity, and speaking for/with through a dialogue that interlocks with many of the concerns of this book. Following my methodology of using tensions to underline and engage important and persistent dilemmas, crip theories, disability studies, and queer theories—in conversation—add to the dialogue on institutions. This is not only a series of correctives with respect to how the body and its experiences of the world are insufficiently engaged with by feminist approaches to international law, this is a dialogue that demands listening, particularly in the spaces of tension, to provoke new kinds of reflections on the limits and possibilities of both gender law reform and feminist approaches. Thus, while for McRuer, crip 'functions as a moniker that can be used to indicate a coalitional identity that resists normative constructions of personhood',[22] from a disabilities studies perspective this resistance functions to silence the everyday struggles and encounters, let alone normative contributions, of those living with disability. I am interested in how this at once alerts feminist theories to the failures in terms of engaging queer, disabled, and queer, disabled lives into dialogue, and how this debate mirrors tensions between activist and academic accounts on gender law reform. Likewise, the feminist dialogues presented in this chapter that challenge imperialism, essentialism, and re-engage materialism both mirror some of the tensions and might be further articulated through the approach of both crip and disability studies. The chapter thus imagines ways to move beyond dialogue as methodology, to ask who speaks, how space for speaking within a dialogue is conceived, and what prior acts might be necessary to foreground feminist dialogues.

To elaborate the feminist dialogues identified, the chapter provides an analysis of the Human Rights Council, the World Health Organisation, and the Peacebuilding Commission. The choice of institutions was driven by a desire to reflect different types of international institutions: a large subsidiary organ, the Human Rights Council (HRC); a specialised agency, the World Health Organisation (WHO); and a smaller, intergovernmental advisory body, the Peacebuilding Commission (PBC).[23] The subject matter across the three institutions is notably diverse and the lifespan of each institution varied. The Human Rights Council is the newest entity amongst the three, dating from 2007, and has a broad mandate with respect to the review of state compliance with international human rights law.[24] The WHO was

---

[20] Bone, 'Trapped Behind the Glass' (n 18) 1309. [21] ibid. [22] ibid 1303.

[23] For an introduction to the creation of the HRC and the PBC, see CSR Murthy, 'New Phase in UN Reforms: Establishment of the Peacebuilding Commission and Human Rights Council' (2007) 44 International Studies 39; on WHO, see Theodore M Brown, Marcos Cueto, and Elizabeth Fee, 'The World Health Organization and the Transition From "International" to "Global" Public Health' (2006) 96(1) American Journal of Public Health 62.

[24] On the Human Rights Council see: http://www.ohchr.org/EN/HRBodies/HRC/Pages/HRCIndex.aspx last accessed 31 May 2018; Bertrand G Ramcharan, *The UN Human Rights Council* (Routledge 2011).

created in 1948 and centres its work on directing global health initiatives.[25] The PBC dates from 2005 when it was created via Security Council resolution 1645 and General Assembly Resolution A/RES/60/180.[26] The PBC brings together a range of actors to advise and propose strategies in relation to UN peacebuilding while supporting peace efforts for states emerging from conflict.[27] The diversity of form and function across the three institutions discussed in this chapter allows me to draw out some persistent patterns within international legal structures that would benefit from future feminist dialogues on their adaptation towards transformation.

Queer analysis of international law demonstrates similar interrogation of the feminist tension between approaching international institutions and the power of the institutions to co-opt and remake those approaches through the language and structures of the institutions. For Kapur,

queer engagement with human rights has taken the radicality out of queer rather than resulting in the queering of human rights. While there are undoubtedly temporal moments when the radicalism of the project emerges, these are quickly quenched by the lure of normativity and glitter of respectability.[28]

Drawing queer approaches, such as Kapur's, into dialogue with feminist approaches to institutions, I argue, requires attention to the diverse feminist accounts that might engage the various structures of international institutions. Within the various dialogues that feminist accounts on international law have already commenced, writing from disability studies theorists or engagement with crip theories has been almost invisible.[29] In the context of the jurisprudence, on gender and disability, from the CEDAW Committee, Campbell writes of the very different methodology intersectionality draws into legal work:

Under CEDAW, if sex and gender is one of the bases for the discrimination, it is necessary to examine how other identity and factors contribute to the discrimination. This transcends the discontinuities between intersectionality theory and practice. It moves intersectionality beyond a ground-based approach and approaches multiple identities from a fluid, expansive and integrated perspective.[30]

Campbell's reflections on methodologies within the realm of international expertise not only dovetail with many of the ideas expressed across this text, they also illuminate the ongoing attentiveness to both method and messages within feminist knowledge production that opens dialogue to queer, crip, and disability studies.

---

[25] The Constitution was adopted by the International Health Conference held in New York from 19 June to 22 July 1946, signed on 22 July 1946 by the representatives of sixty-one States and entered into force on 7 April 1948.

[26] UN Security Council Resolution 1645 (30 December 2005) UN Doc SC/RES/1645; UN General Assembly Resolution 60/180 (30 December 2005) UN Doc A/RES/60/180.

[27] Vladimir Kmec, 'The Establishment of the Peacebuilding Commission: Reflecting Power Shifts in the United Nations' (2017) 24(2) International Peacekeeping 304.

[28] Ratna Kapur, 'The (Im)Possibility of Queering International Human Rights Law' in Dianne Otto, *Queering International Law* (n 2) 132.

[29] Meghan Campbell, 'CEDAW and Women's Intersecting Identities: A Pioneering Approach to Intersectional Identities' (2015) 11(2) Direito GV Law Review 479.

[30] ibid 499.

A feminist epistemology that commences from the knowledge of plural subjectivities, that starts from the premise that bodies and projects are different, have different world views and needs, and yet equal capacity to contribute to dialogue, must open to the challenge of hearing the contributions of crip and disability theories, to recognise that '"compulsory" heteronormativity and able-bodiedness merge at sites of domination such as the family, the school and the workplace'.[31] To this, law might be added to further develop feminist dialogue on the articulation of gendered bodies as a mechanism for normalising subjects. I am determined not to let the difficulty I encounter in drawing existing scholarship from crip and disability studies onto the page as a mechanism for silencing; or a reason to rely on a footnote as merely a wave to those who are Othered in gender law reform. Nevertheless, the arrival of crip, disability, and queer writing in a text on feminist dialogues on international law is an interruption in and of itself, requiring a concerted effort to make space, listen, and stay with the troubles.[32]

I begin the following section with a short introduction to the legal organisation and powers of international institutions alongside a short review of key feminist and critical accounts of the potential and the limitations of international institutions, including recent feminist international relations scholarship on feminist institutionalism. I conclude the section with an analysis of gender mainstreaming, given the central place this has held as a mechanism for gender law reform across diverse international institutions. Drawing on the work of Clisby and Enderstein, I note the universalisms and blunt features of gender mainstreaming as a cross-institutional tool, ultimately arguing rigorous feminist engagement with core institutional structures is required 'to shift from tokenistic inclusivity of gendered discourse at the policy level to genuine "engendering"' of development processes.[33] Throughout, I work to intersperse these descriptions with contributions from critical disability studies, queer and crip theories—mostly to interrupt but also to highlight the need for these additional dialogues to be heard within feminist approaches to international law.

In section 3 I analyse the HRC describing its powers and remit before deploying an analysis of the practical and normative exclusions/inclusions that the HRC operates through. I argue for a politics of interruption to transform approaches to representation from being centred on women to shift towards embracing a feminist methodology. I follow this with analysis of the WHO and the production of soft laws, in particular with regard to the right to maternal health, highlighting the diversity of feminist approaches and their potentialities as a dialogue of relevance to international law and institutions. I argue that the entrenched essentialism of approaches to women's health requires new feminist methodologies that are attentive

---

[31] Dan Goodley, 'Dis/entangling Critical Disability Studies' in Anne Waldschmidt, Hanjo Berrensem, and Moritz Ingversen (eds), *Culture–Theory–Disability* (Verlag 2017) 85.

[32] Donna Haraway, *Staying with the Trouble: Making Kin in the Chthulucene* (Duke University Press 2016).

[33] Suzanne Clisby and Athena-Maria Enderstein, 'Caught Between the Orientalist–Occidentalist Polemic: Gender Mainstreaming as Feminist Transformation or Neocolonialism Subversion?' (2017) 19(2) International Feminist Journal of Politics 231.

to plural subjectivities. The section concludes with an examination of the PBC, centring on how the mandate for the PBC was established and the contours of its work since its inception. In some ways the PBC is an interruption to the manner in which international institutions are configured, functioning as a hybrid creation of the UN General Assembly and UN Security Council. I examine the different feminist critiques of the PBC and ask what it means to hold the tension between some of these accounts, rather than attempting to resolve or write out the tensions within feminist dialogues. At the same time, given the imperialist and essentialist co-optation of feminist messages within global governance, I argue for a queer-crip-feminist methodology, built on recognition of plural subjectivities and dialogue, as a method to approach security through the lives of those whose bodies feel least able to move freely through public spaces. Through analysing the contours of these three institutions, the final section of the chapter demonstrates the productive space of feminist tensions and the necessity of feminist difference to develop dialogues that are able to reimagine and critique international institutions, and by extension the international order, in new and thoughtful feminist ways.

2. Approaching Institutions

This section provides a short introduction to key debates with respect to the nature and role of international institutions within international law. Mainstream approaches to international institutions tend to centre on three enquiries: the source of the institution's authority, the scope of the powers of the institution, including both soft and hard law capacities, and the structure and membership of the institution, including the role of states and non-state actors.[34] I review each of these aspects in this section of the chapter and also introduce gender mainstreaming as a key institutional initiative, established after the Beijing conference on women. In observing the limits of the gender mainstreaming project, I examine the legacy of state consent as defining the very possibility of legal subjectivity for non-state actors.[35] Returning to the descriptions of split and plural subjects from prior chapters, I argue that the emergent and dynamic quality of the legal personality of institutions under international law further emphasises the need for a configuration of legal subjectivity beyond masculine forms, of autonomous, bounded actors.[36] The chapter thus approaches institutions in the terms expected by mainstream approaches to international law whilst ultimately working to disrupt this same set of knowledge.

My understanding of international institutions is influenced by Klabbers's description of international organisations as producing a 'tension between formality and informality' driven by the nature of international institutions as not-states and

---

[34] See further Dapo Akande, 'International Organisations' in Malcolm Evans (ed), *International Law* (Oxford University Press 2014) 248; Klabbers, *International Organisations Law* (n 8); Ian Hurd, *International Organisations: Politics, Law, Practice* (3rd edn, Cambridge University Press 2018).

[35] Cedric Ryngaert, 'Non-state Actors: Carving Out a Space in a State-Centred Legal System' 63 (2016) Netherlands International Law Review 183.

[36] ibid 186–88.

yet of central importance in the continuation and existence of global governance.[37] Klabbers's approach is also an inquiry into the limits of functionalism, so that he is able to recognise the technical aspects of the work of international institutions (requiring an acceptance of functionalism) alongside the political drivers that continue to influence and produce the outcomes, structures, and scope of international organisations.[38] Through the law on international organisations, I present an understanding of existing critical inquiry in this area of international law, which I argue is relevant to feminist dialogues on international law.[39] As such, the chapter, while consciously bringing expanded feminist dialogues to international organisations law, also considers the potential for dialogues between critical legal and critical feminist engagements within law.

Klabbers places functionalism as a better description of the nature of international organisations, over formalist or instrumentalist accounts.[40] While formalist projects inevitably return to the powers of states to explain the powers (and limits) of international organisations, instrumentalist accounts retain an implicit normative role for international law, beyond the political agendas of states, that can be achieved through the use and workings of international organisations. The tensions between formalist and instrumentalist tendencies of the international legal order help explain the apertures where gender law reform have been received: given the soft law outputs of international organisations under a formalist account gender law reform rarely creates binding obligations for states, while the specific feminist agendas contained by gender law reform are usually amenable to recognising values of the system, in particular human rights, democracy, and justice without any thick or complex description or challenge to their meaning. A functionalist account, as offered by Klabbers, avoids the need to align with either formalist or instrumentalist approaches, through recognising that these might be part of the problem, focusing instead on both recognising and separating political—or normative—drivers within international law to engage the working practices of international structures, including organisations.[41]

Feminist approaches to law have thus far insufficiently theorised sustained dialogues in response to tensions between instrumentalism and formalism.[42] My own preference is to follow Klabbers's functionalism, which opens a dialogue on instrumentalism and formalism as well as leaving an openness to understanding the political drivers behind global governance while retaining space for an epistemology

---

[37] Jan Klabbers, 'International Institutions' in James Crawford and Martti Koskenniemi (eds), *The Cambridge Companion to International Law* (Cambridge University Press 2012) 235.

[38] Klabbers, *International Organisations Law* (n 8).

[39] Study and recognition of the role of institutions within international legal scholarship is often aligned with the emergence of the New Haven School. The instrumentalism apparent in New Haven approaches often emerges in critical legal approaches: Martti Koskenniemi, 'The Fate of Public International Law: Between Technique and Politics' (2007) 70 Modern Law Review 1; Anne Orford, *Reading Humanitarian Intervention: Human Rights and the Use of Force in International Law* (Cambridge University Press 2003) ch 6 where the recognition of a normative role for international law, beyond formalism, is often implicit.

[40] Klabbers, *International Organisations Law* (n 8) 35.   [41] ibid.

[42] Charlesworth and Chinkin (n 13) 26–36.

of difference; plural and split subjects; as functioning to challenge the underlying political configurations of global governance. That is, recalling Otomo's challenge to write outside of the masculine history of international law, functionalism looks to what works and why, without portending a normative commitment to the continuation of the status quo.[43]

2.1 Constitutive powers

The powers of international institutions are established via the constituent document and evolve via the practice of the institution. The Human Rights Council was established via General Assembly Resolution A/RES/60/251 (15 March 2006), with its members elected via General Assembly votes. The WHO was established via a treaty agreement between United Nations member states in 1948, with membership open to all UN member states. The Peacebuilding Commission was established through Security Council resolution 1645 (2005) and General Assembly Resolution A/RES/60/180 (30 December 2005), with its members elected or selected from the Security Council (seven members selected), General Assembly (seven members elected), ECOSO (seven members elected), UN missions (five top providers to missions), and from UN funders (five top funders, including the peacebuilding fund). Each of these organisations, therefore, function as specialised agencies (WHO) and secondary organs (HRC, PBC) of the United Nations, such that their powers are also circumscribed by the authority of the principle organs that created them and any law-making powers are soft law powers. The exception is the WHO, which, as a treaty body can issue agreements, via its Assembly, on matters within its remit that are binding on states. All three institutions under discussion have limited powers to construct legally binding obligations under international law: however, each has the capacity, in varying degrees, to influence future law-making and state practice via recommendations and inquiry processes, as well as soft law powers through the creation of non-binding resolutions. In all cases, including the hard law-making power of the WHO, the capacities of the institution are limited to the object and purpose of the organisation.

The changing relationship between states and institutions is reflected in the role of constituent documents in establishing the parameters of an institution's powers. While institutions are not permitted to act *ultra vires*, or outside the powers given to them via the constituent document, the meaning of this is always subject to the necessity that institutions be guided by the object and purpose of the institution rather than a rigid adherence to the precise terminology of the constituent document. This is most obvious in the life and practice of the Security Council, which has expanded its remit via practice.[44] The Nuclear Weapons Advisory Opinion before the International Court of Justice found it necessary to maintain a restraint on the

---

[43] Yoriko Otomo, 'Searching for Virtue in International Law' in Sari Kouvo and Zoe Pearson (eds), *Feminist Perspectives on Contemporary International Law: between Resistance and Compliance* (Hart 2011).

[44] Gina Heathcote, 'Women and Children and Elephants as Justification for Force' (2017) 4(1) Journal on the Use of Force and International Law 66.

expansion of institutional remits, although this has not been without criticism.[45] In addition, the practice of international organisations in transforming the action of states, over time, and thus contributing to the crystallisation of customary international law remains impossible to quantify and yet an important, significant site of interplay between states and institutions within international law. At the same time, the role of states in creating, defining, acting through, and implementing the work of international organisations curtails the possibility of international institutions challenging the state-centric nature of international law. The dynamic interplay between states and institutions remains insufficiently analysed within feminist scholarship: importantly, feminist scholarship can, through attention to plural subjectivities, challenge the flip-flopping between state consent as block to the work of institutions and institutions as potentially unrestrained lawmakers. To do so requires recognition of the need for structural transformation of international institutions, so that the stranglehold of states on the constitution and outputs of international institutions is tempered via restraints on the role of states that ultimately dislodge masculine notions of subjectivity; to embed relationality that is attentive to historical interactions and assumed knowledge about how different voices are included in institutional apparatus.

Early feminist writing on international law indicated that the solidifying of institutional power into spaces of hard law-making (Security Council, International Criminal Court), reflected, to a degree, a sense from feminist scholars that state consent remained the key barrier to the realisation of women's rights and/or gender justice within the global order.[46] Consequently, the turn to institutions to pursue gender law reform has been a specific strategy for feminist actors within international law; not so much bypassing the states as instrumentalising the goodwill of states open to gender law reform and ignoring the role gender law reform plays in supporting fledging institutions. The persistent focus on women in institutional approaches ignores dialogues with queer theories that already exist within feminist spaces, suggesting a shameful neglect of the breadth of feminist histories (both in the West and well beyond). As has been reviewed in prior chapters, if the naming of the feminist subject as woman is the strategy required for inclusion, it is a poor feminist project—creating the conditions for its own facsimile of feminism in the pursuit of gender law reform.

Within the field of international relations the study of feminist initiatives within global governance has led to the development of 'feminist institutionalism' as a field of inquiry which proposes to 'bring to the study of institutions a specific lens that makes visible constitutive, gendered power relations and the processes that support and undermine them'.[47] Drawing on new institutionalist approaches within international relations, feminist institutionalism accepts the larger structural and

---

[45] *Legality of the Use by a State of Nuclear Weapons in Armed Conflict* (Advisory Opinion) [1996] ICJ Rep 2 para 21.

[46] Charlesworth and Chinkin (n 13); Karen Knop, 'Here and There: International Law in Domestic Courts' (2000) 32 New York University Journal of International Law and Politics 501.

[47] Krook and MacKay, *Gender, Politics and Institutions* (n 7) xi.

political restraints of international organisations while studying the impact and consequences of institutional policy and action.[48] Considered as a bridge between realist and constructionist approaches within international relations theory, new institutionalism focuses on the processes and interactions both within and amongst institutions as a site of knowledge production in contrast to a focus on either states or individuals. Within international legal theories, process-orientated theories provide a similar approach: they highlight the processes and decisions of institutions as able to embed and develop ideals such as democracy, justice, or human rights.[49] Within international legal theories, feminist alignment with new institutionalism has been less influential, although specific authors have developed nuanced critiques from within specific institutional spaces.[50]

Feminist institutionalism as a project that focuses on processes and outputs of international institutions influences some of the claims articulated in this chapter. For example, True's writing on the political economy of gender addresses international institutions as a space where women's livelihoods might be transformed through developing a feminist political economy approach to challenge the structure and rationale of international institutions directly. True's work thus raises a series of important dilemmas for feminist dialogues on international institutions and asks important questions with regard to how feminist methods might be transformative from within those institutions without avoiding the corollary need for disengagement from the 'projects' of global governance as a simultaneous feminist strategy (as developed by Otomo).[51] For Chappell, addressing these same questions from a feminist institutionalist position and as a feminist legal scholar, there is a need to acknowledge:

If gender justice advocates withdraw from engagement with powerful institutions—be they courts, state bureaucracies, or legislatures—these institutions won't stop regulating our lives. However, in the absence of feminists holding them to account, such institutions may well do a much worse job of addressing gender injustices manifested through misrecognition, misrepresentation and maldistribution.[52]

In this mode, the feminist institutionalism emergent within international relations re-emerges within some contemporary feminist legal writing, such as Chappell's work on the International Criminal Court, as an important corrective to both critical feminist accounts of the dangers of pursuing gender reforms within international

---

[48] ibid 8–13.

[49] Rosalyn Higgins, *Problems and Processes: International Law and How We Use It* (Oxford University Press 1994).

[50] Chappell, *The Politics of Gender Justice* (n 11); see also Natalie Florea Hudson and Anne-Marie Goetz, 'Too Much that Can't Be Said: Anne-Marie Goetz in Conversation with Natalie Florea Hudson' (2014) 16 International Feminist Journal of Politics 336; Valerie Oosterveld, 'Evaluating the Special Court for Sierra Leone's Gender Jurisprudence' in Charles C Jalloh (ed), *The Sierra Leone Special Court and its Legacy: The Impact for Africa and International Criminal Law* (Cambridge University Press 2013) 234.

[51] Otomo (n 43) 35.

[52] Louise Chappell, 'Authors Response: Addressing Gender Justice at the ICC: Legacies and Legitimacy' (22 December 2016) *EJIL Talk!* <http://www.ejiltalk.org/authors-response-the-politics-of-gender-justice-at-the-icc-legacies-and-legitimacy/#more-14704> last accessed 31 May 2018.

institutions and with the goal of addressing the larger blindness of the institutions themselves to gender justice beyond women's issues. The tensions between critical feminist accounts of institutions, such as Nesiah or Otto's work, is resolved by Chappell through a recognition of 'critical feminist friends' as vital, while distinct from, feminist institutionalism.[53] In this sense a clear tension in feminist legal writing, between scholars critiquing the limitations of institutional engagement and scholars engaged in understanding and expanding gender justice within institutional settings, is dismissed rather than confronted directly.

This chapter explores whether this tension between inside/outside approaches within feminist scholarship can be productively owned as a dialogue that is not without disagreement or difference. However, my approach differs from Chappell's which accepts the status quo of institutions with respect to the design of their powers, their relationship with states, and the structure and foundations of international institutions within the global order. I shift from Chappell's approach because the image of 'critical friends' as adjunct rather than constitutive of feminism places the dialogues with race, queer, and crip voices within the critical agenda as outside of the dialogues on feminist institutionalism. Feminist institutionalism instead prioritises gender and accepts institutional reorientating of gender law reform as inevitable.

Consequently, this chapter ultimately finds the focus on 'gender justice' and 'feminist' approaches within feminist institutionalism as offering an insufficient account of the range of dialogues and tensions that inform feminist methods, approaches, and scholarship outside of legal or international relations scholarship. For example, True's work on political economy and institutions is significant but should also be placed in dialogue with gender's intersections with additional structures of power and privilege (beyond economic differentials). Likewise, a turn to institutions that overlooks the authority with which those institutions were created, including the role of the legal structures institutions operate within—and through—and which perpetuate the status quo, will ignore the gendered forms of that authority. The consequence for gender law reform is the legitimation of the institution rather than transformative gender strategies. Therefore, this chapter takes the work of True, and feminist institutionalists, as an aspect of a series of feminist accounts that must be placed in dialogue with an approach to international institutions that is attentive to the interlocking privilege and power institutions reproduce, from their constitutive documents and powers through to the contours of their outputs.[54] This approach acknowledges the value of existing gender justice projects within institutions while raising additional dialogues with respect to the fundamental nature of the organisations themselves via an array of feminist accounts of power, of gender, and of privileged knowledge within feminist approaches, as well as within global governance.

---

[53] ibid; Dianne Otto, 'The Exile of Inclusion: Reflections on Gender Issues in International Law over the Last Decade' (2009) 10 Melbourne Journal of International Law 11; Vasuki Nesiah, 'The Ground Beneath Her Feet: "Third World" Feminisms' (2003) 4(3) Journal of International Women's Studies 30.

[54] Krook and MacKay (n 7).

For example, a turn to the HRC is in part a discussion of the gendered division between first and second generations of rights.[55] However, feminist dialogues on the HRC must also assess how the promotion of rights, by necessity, reproduces a liberal model that itself represents a tool of privilege and sustains that privilege at the level of knowledge production such that alternative histories, stories, livelihoods, and knowledge practices are devalued through the constituent structure of the organisation itself. This is sustained through the objects and purpose of the organisation and the remit of the HRC, as well as the soft law nature of the constituent document itself. The position of the organisation is such that not only is it inimical to feminist projects that are not framed within liberal contours (ie rights), the intersectional nature of gender harm will be reproduced by the constitutive structure of the organisation as a series of identity tropes (gender plus race plus class plus sexuality etc) rather than recognition of rights as an interlocking platform for the sustaining of existing power relations. In particular, the historical role of gender as civilising force and of rights as the persistent silencer of non-masculine forms of knowledge is unavailable as a means to critique international institutions when the knowledge that creates the object and purpose held within the constitutive document, in this example human rights themselves, remains closed to critique. Feminist approaches to institutions and institutional reform that ignore the need for a feminist critique of rights are destined to reproduce the constituted inequalities the institution is designed through rather than disrupt these assumptions.

In the extended examination of the HRC, below, I analyse how a maternal theory of interruption might be regarded as a contributor to feminist dialogues that address the histories of knowledge production and privilege reproduced within contemporary international institutions. As a tool for change I draw on accounts of maternal subjectivity that transpose maternal essentialism for a politics of interruption, following Gedalof's account of the politics of interruption as encompassing social reproduction via understanding of the intersection of race and gender. I reimagine the HRC and the capacity for embracing interruption as a means for transformative feminist dialogues, open to an epistemology of plural subjectivities. I regard Gedalof's politics of interruption as a mechanism for further dialogues that approach the history of human rights as complicit in civilising missions, including through the deployment of gender justice, that leaves the HRC in need of a different level of critique than is currently offered within feminist dialogues.

2.2 Structural matters

The structure of international organisations will vary from institution to institution—including with respect to funding, representatives, decision-making processes, and review mechanisms. In referencing the structure of international organisations, I am interested in the residual role of states in the decision-making, funding, and

---

[55] True, *Political Economy* (n 7); Celina Romany, 'Women as Aliens: A Feminist Critique of the Public/Private Distinction in International Human Rights Law' (1993) 6 Harvard Human Rights Journal 87.

functioning of international organisations, as well of that of non-state actors (such as independent experts and NGOs). Fundamentally, although international organisations are non-state actors the nexus to states remains through the requirement that states create and function as the members of the institution. As such, Ryngaert describes the state/non-state relationship as one in which '[s]tates, or states assembled in international organizations, are still pulling the strings, and arguably only accept NSAs [non-state actors] insofar as these serve the purposes of the state or organization'.[56] The acknowledgement, then, of non-state actors, such as international institutions, contributing to and shaping contemporary international law, as well as the recognition of the qualified legal subjectivity of international institutions, is always tempered with the role of states as both creators and actors that realise the obligations and rights constructed. This knowledge holds the paradox that international institutions are not states and yet are constructed by and through the acts of states. Exploring the consequences of this for feminist projects within international law is likewise filled with paradox—as it is clear that advances with respect to gender justice within global governance have been achieved through the strategic turn to international institutions and yet those institutions remain circumscribed both by the limited powers granted to them by states and the role of states in enacting the contours of institutional outputs. International institutions recall the split subjectivity of states insomuch that as equally as international law is constructed through the sovereign equality of states, international law is also dependent on the capacity of states to work in concert through international institutions; states thus diffuse (split!) their powers through the relational spaces of institutions.

A feminist dialogue on international institutions must, therefore, not only regard the outputs of international institutions but also engage with the nature and structure of international institutions that perpetuates the power and privileges embedded in international legal histories because of the role of states as necessary to give effect to institutional outputs. As such, while a feminist institutionalist approach works to celebrate small gains in gender justice that often have the potential to effect 'subtle and small shifts over time'[57] that may ultimately work towards 'something more significant and transformative',[58] a feminist legal project must be mindful of the feminist dialogues neglected by such an approach. In particular, activating incremental change within international institutions leaves untouched and unchallenged the underlying knowledge projects that produce and set the conditions for the institution's operation while also neglecting the colonial and imperial histories that international law emerged through. The type of feminist knowledge and knowledge on gender justice amendable to institutional pick-up will be those that do not challenge the status quo and functioning of the institution itself, in particular the entwined histories of gender, race, sexuality, ethnicity, and ableist power that the institutions, and the states behind them, require to exist and remain unchallenged. Consequently, gender justice projects that work within international institutions

---

[56] Ryngaert (n 35). [57] Chappell, *The Politics of Gender Justice* (n 11) 18.
[58] ibid 10.

and identify these as spaces for gender law reform must be held in dialogue with the spectrum of dialogues that inform feminist accounts—and the plural subjects who dance, speak, listen, articulate, paint, sing, and challenge feminist self-cohesion.

The WHO's structure and organisation is a useful example of how feminist dialogues must expand beyond either the inclusion of gender justice provisions or policies centred on women's lives. The structure of the WHO, as with other specialised agencies, was established via the constitution of the organisation, signed in 1946 by sixty-one member states at the International Health Conference in New York. The Constitution establishes the WHO as composed of three bodies: the World Health Assembly, the Executive Board, and the Secretariat. The Executive Board's membership comprises of experts and the Secretariat functions as the administrative arm of the Organisation. The Assembly is the only body with law-making powers (although these may be delegated to the Board when relevant)[59] and its members are state representatives, usually health specialists.[60] As a treaty-body the WHO is given a law-making function such that, '[t]he Health Assembly shall have authority to adopt conventions or agreements with respect to any matter within the competence of the Organization'[61] and that '[e]ach Member undertakes that it will, within eighteen months after the adoption by the Health Assembly of a convention or agreement, take action relative to the acceptance of such convention or agreement'.[62] The WHO is established via and through the ongoing agreement of states, as well as funded via state (and philanthropic) contributions.[63]

The combination of health expertise—rendering the knowledge deployed as largely technical and scientific—paired with the central role of states at the foundation of the WHO structure produces a model that is unlikely to be a transformative site of gender knowledge. For example, the structure of the various committees and programmes on gender and/or women within the WHO are not geared around a gender-mainstreaming or inclusiveness across health issues but segment women's health from core concerns of the organisation. For example, the primary gender sub-body is within the Committee on Information and Accountability which produces annual reports on Accountability for Women and Children's Health under the motto of 'Leave no Woman, Child or Adolescent Behind' and is linked to the 'Every Woman, Every Child' campaign launched by Ban Ki Moon in 2014.[64]

Underlying the initiatives on women's health within the WHO is a very specific series of understandings with respect to the role of women's health within global governance. In particular, given the many projects, committees, and programmes instigated by the WHO the very specific, separate attention to women's health appears to leave unchallenged that any and all health initiatives must attend to women's health, just as it must attend to the health of men, trans, and of non-gendered individuals. Furthermore, the coupling of women's health with children

[59] Constitution of the World Health Organisation New York (adopted 22 July 1946, entered into force 7 April 1948) 14 UNTS 221 Article 29 (hereafter *Constitution of the WHO*)

[60] ibid art 10.   [61] ibid art 19.   [62] ibid.

[63] For the funding contributions of member states and others see <http://www.who.int/about/finances-accountability/funding/voluntary-contributions/en/> last accessed 31 May 2018.

[64] See <http://www.everywomaneverychild.org/about/> last accessed 31 May 2018.

and adolescent health, while useful from a child's rights perspective through the implicit acknowledgement of women's dominance, globally, as primary carers for children, appears to reassert women as less than men (who would be, it is assumed, the focus of non-women specific programmes) and women's health as aligned with children and adolescents. Rather than dislodging existing preferences for male bodies to be constructed as normal bodies, the foundational knowledge of these projects reproduces this mindset, while essentialising the female body as the Other to 'normal' medical subjects and as primarily a reproductive body, via the association with child-rearing.[65] Far from being knowledge produced via the institution, this is knowledge that reflects the knowledge practices of those states whose political structures influenced and continue to influence the contours of international law—where states are designed and understood via a 'monoglossian' model that values the individual as a rational, unencumbered actor that forms interactions within the public sphere of the commons separate to the private, domestic space of the home/domestic sphere of political arrangements.[66] The association of the state as subject that is built on a male history of political ordering infiltrates the assumed knowledge structures of international law, and its institutions, to this day, including in the nature and arrangement of gender law reforms.

The project of redefining international law through what is not male must therefore begin at the foundational structures of the discipline. The plural subject called into theory via disability studies speaks to this aspect of the dialogues presented here, writing theories of the body into feminist dialogues:

Our collective cultural consciousness emphatically denies the knowledge of vulnerability, contingency, and mortality … The body is dynamic, constantly interactive with history and environment. We evolve into disability. Our bodies need care; we all need assistance to live. An equality model of feminist theory sometimes prizes individualistic autonomy as the key to women's liberation. A feminist disability theory, however, suggests that we are better off learning to individually and collectively accommodate bodily limits and evolutions than trying to eliminate or deny them … This kind of theoretical intertextuality inflects familiar feminist concepts with new resonance.[67]

In the further study of the WHO, below, I consider how maternal health is articulated via the institution. I argue for alternative knowledge forms that enter into dialogues about the locations, histories, and assumptions reproduced about gender, bodies, and institutions.

2.3 Gender mainstreaming, quotas, and women's participation

The Fourth World Conference on Women, hosted in Beijing in 1995 produced a Platform for Action that prompted the notion of gender mainstreaming. Although

---

[65] Janice MacCormack, Reiner Kirkham, and Virginia Hayes, 'Abstracting Women: Essentialism in Women's Health Research' (1998) 19(6) Health Care for Women International 495.

[66] Ryngaert (n 35) defines this as 'one-person narratives'.

[67] Rosemarie Garland-Thomson, 'Integrating Disability: Transforming Feminist Theory' in Kim Q Hall (ed), *Feminist Disability Studies* (Indiana University Press 2011) 13, 34.

the Platform for Action does not specifically mention gender mainstreaming, paragraph 197 (and the section on Institutional Mechanisms for the Advancement of Women generally) requires 'mechanisms and institutions to promote the advancement of women as an integral part of mainstream political, economic, social and cultural development'.[68] The holistic approach to gender equality embedded within the Beijing Platform for Action led to gender mainstreaming as an aspect of the work of the United Nations by the end of the millennium. As a soft law, endorsed in agreed conclusions of the Economic and Social Council, gender mainstreaming was defined as:

the process of assessing the implications for women and men of any planned action, including legislation, policies or programmes, in all areas and at all levels. It is a strategy for making women's as well as men's concerns and experiences an integral dimension of the design, implementation, monitoring and evaluation of policies and programmes in all political, economic and societal spheres so that women and men benefit equally and inequality is not perpetuated. The ultimate goal is to achieve gender equality.[69]

As an institutional strategy gender mainstreaming is utopian—and proved to ultimately be unsustainable in an organisation that has a history of articulating gender equality via the development of specific agendas on women's rights that tend to essentialise women and to reinforce a gender binary, rather than dismantle the gender binary and its hierarchical history. Charlesworth describes gender mainstreaming as both over- and under-inclusive: over-inclusive as the definition from the Economic and Social Council, requiring the assessment of implications for men and women is not clearly differentiated as 'different from standard policy considerations', yet under-inclusive because '[i]t does not address the complex ways that gender is created and sustained by social and power relations'.[70] Furthermore, gender mainstreaming, post-Beijing, quickly became less about an integration of gender perspectives across all aspects of the UN's work and instead a strategy to count the women and/or require gender experts within the organisation to consult across an increasing array of the UN's work.[71]

By 2010 the language of gender mainstreaming seemed to have withered away in UN documents; at this time the key initiative became the coordination of gender affairs across the institution via the establishment of UN Women, as discussed in chapter 3. In their analysis of international institutions, Charlesworth and Chinkin focus on women's participation in institutions and sketch out the key feminist concerns regarding the manner in which institutions function. Charlesworth and Chinkin's analysis of international institutions finds: 'While increasing the

---

[68] 'Beijing Declaration and Platform for Action' UN Fourth World Conference on Women (Beijing 4–15 September 1995) UN Doc A/CONF177/20/Rev1 para 197.

[69] ECOSOC Agreed conclusions 1997/2 (18 July 1997) UN Doc E/1997/66; ECOSOC resolution 2001/41 on gender mainstreaming (July 2001) UN Doc E/RES/2001/41.

[70] Hilary Charlesworth, 'Talking to Ourselves? Feminist Scholarship in International Law' in Sari Kouvo and Zoe Pearson (eds), *Feminist Perspectives on Contemporary International Law: Between Resistance and Compliance* (Hart 2011) 29.

[71] Sari Kouvo, 'The United Nations and Gender Mainstreaming: Limits and Possibilities' in Doris Buss and Ambreena Manji (eds), *International Law: Modern Feminist Approaches* (Hart 2005).

participation of women in the UN is only one aspect of the broader project of enhancing the UN's future, it is essential for increasing the UN's effectiveness and accountability.'[72] As discussed in chapter 3, in terms of (future feminist) strategies, Charlesworth and Chinkin consider both practical and substantive gender concerns which, almost two decades later, might still be raised with respect to contemporary international institutions.[73] Charlesworth and Chinkin's study of the composition of international institutions, with respect to women's representation, remains an important issue and one that came to the fore during the election of the new Secretary-General in 2016.[74] Nevertheless, it is clear that women have increasingly been selected for roles within institutions, for example within the HRC, through appointments as experts under the Special Procedures, and through the very specific gender strategy on women's representation at the International Criminal Court. Yet mapping women's representation within international institutions is influenced by where attention is focused. Thus, in 2016, across the 41 thematic topics under the Special Procedures mechanisms of the HRC, 24 Special Rapporteurs, out of a total of 64, were women—so roughly thirty-seven per cent. This represents a significant development compared to the representation of women across senior roles at the UN since Charlesworth and Chinkin's analysis in 2000.[75] Nevertheless, attainment of a gender balance with respect to women's participation in international institutions is yet to be achieved. At the most senior levels, '28 women have chaired one of the UN's six main committees (compared to 424 men); 3 women have served as General-Assembly President (compared to 68 men); and zero have ever held the position of Secretary-General'.[76] However, it is worth noting that Yancopoulos provides a temporally elongated analysis—looking across the life of the United Nations rather than a time slice of gender representation at the time of writing—so that historical inequalities with respect to gender balance are captured and prioritised in the description.

Within key institutional entities the representatives of states will be selected by member states and there is no requirement for member states to send a gender balance amongst its representatives within institutions, such as the General Assembly, Security Council, or HRC. Radical democratic models, such as that employed by the Democratic Party of the Regions (DBP) in South Eastern Turkey,[77] which require a system of co-representation, would be relatively simple to implement across key international institutions within the United Nations. A co-representation model could be established to require each member state to send at least one female and one

---

[72] Charlesworth and Chinkin (n 13) 198.

[73] ibid; Gina Heathcote, 'Humanitarian Intervention and Gender Dynamics' in Naomi Cahn, Dina Haynes, Fionnuala Ní Aoláin, and Nahla Valji (eds), *Oxford Handbook on Gender and Conflict* (Oxford University Press 2018) 237.

[74] Ourania Yancopoulos, 'Does the United Nations Have a Real Feminist in the Next Secretary-General, António Guterres?' (*Ethics and International Affairs*, 25 October 2016) <https://www.ethicsandinternationalaffairs.org/2016/united-nations-real-feminist-next-secretary-general-antonio-guterres/> last accessed 31 May 2018.

[75] Charlesworth and Chinkin (n 13) 174–79.   [76] Yancopoulos (n 74).

[77] Ofra Bengio, 'Game Changers: Kurdish Women in Peace and War' (2016) 70(1) Middle Eastern Journal 30, 36–37.

male representative to any treaty body, specialised agency, or subsidiary organ. This could be an important and effective move with respect to women's representation and participation across the United Nations. Nevertheless, there are additional feminist concerns that would not be addressed by such a move: in particular, the model assumes a female–male dichotomy with respect to gender relations and appears unable to recognise more than two genders. In addition, a co-representation model, like quotas, is likely to lead to the appointment and participation of elite women whose further privilege is, for the most part, similar to male representatives in the same institutions. These would not necessarily be reasons not to advocate for a co-representation model within international institutions, rather this is indicative that co-representation is a first rather than a final step in transforming representation and participation in international institutions from a feminist perspective.

It is hoped that co-representation immediately opens further dialogues on who is silenced by the focus on gender as an organising structure. Seuffert examines international law's histories to ask who is able to be at 'home' in international law, arguing:

> Questions central to international law today, who may travel, invade and conquer, invaders and outsiders, arise from the shapes provided . . . Sedimented in these shapes and bounds of hospitality and international law are questions of homophobia and misogyny in the recognition of humanity and rationality, and of worthiness in the provision, and punishment for breaches, of hospitality . . . I want to promote further inquiry into the extent to which the heirs to homophobia and misogyny in these traditions, facing the challenge of embracing the law of hospitality, opening our home to other . . .[78]

The shift to expand women's participation within international institutions, if feminist, must also address and create space for these dialogues, welcoming into the spaces created those traditionally excluded from global governance.

Failure to use gender participation as a mechanism for further dialogues on inclusion and exclusions within international law perpetuates the tension inherent in quotas and agendas. That is, to increase women's participation within decision-making and institutional spaces highlights a series of underlying feminist tensions that have not adequately been addressed in feminist scholarship on international law. The tension revolves around the placement of women as the subject of feminist and gender reforms, as discussed across this book, such that broader feminist conceptions of gender that examine gender as fluid, gender as performative, and/or gender interconnected to other spaces of power and privilege are insufficiently addressed if the agenda revolves around the increased representation of women. Mindfulness of which women gain access to international institutions and how damaging gender binaries might be reinforced by such an approach requires discussion. Empirical work on the impact of increased representation of women in governing structures adds further strands of thinking that challenge the notion

---

[78] Nan Seuffert, 'Queering International Law's Stories of Origins: Hospitality and Homophobia' in Dianne Otto (ed), *Queering International Law: Possibilities, Alliances, Complicities, Risks* (Routledge 2018).

that increased participation of women, on its own, is a fruitful feminist strategy. For example, Yadav's study of female MPs in Nepal demonstrates the necessity to understand institutional and political histories (in this case the legacy of the Maoist movement) in their local context to understand the purchase and effect of female leadership and representation on institutional outcomes.[79] For scholars advocating gender balancing within international institutions, similar understandings of the nestedness of institutional regimes to recognise how security, human rights, or health each produce specific types of expert knowledge that further silence and suppresses alternative accounts and knowledge practices is also important.

Beyond the issue of representation, however, Charlesworth and Chinkin identify the structures of international institutions as maintaining gendered forms that are ultimately inimical to the development of a transformative feminist politics. The starting point for Charlesworth and Chinkin in 2000 was a need to challenge 'the sexed and gendered character of international institutions' through 'a revision of the division of labour that confines women and men to different spheres of activity'.[80] In this chapter, I wish to understand the role of feminist thinking in the way international institutions might be approached at a deeper level than a recognition of the continued impact of a gendered division of labour on women, and men's, livelihoods. Although attention to the gendered division of labour remains an important task, the remaining discussion asks a deeper structural question with regard to how knowledge is organised and perceived within international institutions, with the Human Rights Council, the World Health Organisation, and the Peacebuilding Commission as case studies. Charlesworth and Chinkin prefigure this task when they assert 'international power structures themselves must be challenged and reconstructed to accommodate the half of humanity currently on their margins'.[81]

3. Three Institutions

In order to think through the feminist dialogues, I have argued for an appreciation of feminism that foregrounds a series of interlocking and diverse dialogues. In this section I examine the three international institutions, the Human Rights Council, the World Health Organisation, and the Peacebuilding Commission, in detail and with reference to a diverse set of feminist dialogues drawn from inside and outside of contemporary feminist accounts of global governance. Throughout I work to disrupt any sense of comfort derived from attention to these dialogues through the interjections of feminist, crip, and queer theories as necessary contributors at an epistemological level.

---

[79] Punam Yadav, *Social Transformation in Post-Conflict Nepal: A Gender Perspective* (Routledge 2016).
[80] Charlesworth and Chinkin (n 13) 199.   [81] ibid 198.

3.1 Human Rights Council

… 'nested newness' alerts us to the ways in which 'old' gender practices, norms, and expectations often underpin new institutions in ways which can blunt their reformist potential.[82]

This section considers the Human Rights Council, describing the Council's powers and remit before embarking on an analysis of the practical and normative exclusions (and inclusions) that the HRC operates through. In taking a feminist lens to the HRC, I explore the continued impact of the colonial genealogy of the international order on the contours of international institutions. I begin by examining the source of the HRC's powers, the nature of those powers, and its membership and scope.

I am concerned to unearth the gendering of the practical and normative structures of the HRC—not for the production of legal tools (gender law reform) but rather as a structure embedded within the organisation and production of knowledge. The HRC is a good choice for this inquiry because it was created after the establishment of all the key women's rights instruments, including CEDAW, DEVAW, and the Beijing Platform for Action, as well as being created after the work within the Security Council on women, peace, and security that has increasingly been articulated as functioning through and alongside approaches to women's rights.[83] Notwithstanding the various criticisms of the HRC, and its relatively weak legal power, I analyse how the constitution and structure of the HRC itself is gendered; this allows me to identify the layers of gendered normativity that operate within international institutions. Consequently, I argue that despite the practical steps towards women's inclusion, via legal instruments such as the CEDAW regime, there remains value in drawing out and emphasising the space between the application of feminist methods and the reception of feminist messages in international institutions. In particular, I use the HRC to demonstrate the continued impact of the colonial genealogy on the international order as a gendered intersection of power and privilege that disrupts and creates distrust amongst states and actors within international institutions, limiting the capacity for the institution to fulfil its objectives. My starting point is to acknowledge that the study of gender absent of recognition of colonial legacies produces institutional outcomes that perpetuate rather than undo these inequalities.

The Human Rights Council was established in 2006 via General Assembly resolution 61/251.[84] As such, the HRC's constituent document is itself a soft law established through the coordination and cooperation of member states via the General Assembly. As the successor to the much-criticised Human Rights Commission, the HRC's key responsibility is the promotion and protection of human rights, globally, through the Universal Periodic Review (UPR) process, the work of an Advisory

---

[82] Louise Chappell, 'Nested Newness and Institutional Innovation: Expanding Gender Justice in the International Criminal Court' in Mona Lena Krook and Fiona Mackay (eds), *Gender, Politics and Institutions: Towards a Feminist Institutionalism* (Palgrave 2011) 163.

[83] UNSC Res 2242 (13 October 2015) UN Doc S/RES/2242 Preamble.

[84] UNGA Res 60/251 (15 March 2006) UN Doc A/RES/60/251.

Committee, and a complaints mechanism, as well as the capacity to undertake fact-finding missions and commissions of inquiry.[85] The UPR process instigates a system for review of all state human rights records every four years. In terms of membership, the HRC comprises of representatives from forty-seven UN member states, with representatives elected every three years. Member states can only sit on the HRC for two consecutive terms and the HRC was designed with regional representation requirements.[86] No gender requirements with respect to representation have been instituted.

The Human Rights Council, far from shaking off the criticisms of its predecessor, the Human Rights Commission, continues to attract criticism, primarily with respect to member states with records of human rights abuses being elected onto the Council.[87] The membership model raises persistent questions regarding what the participation of states with poor human rights records in the HRC signals in terms of tolerating and ignoring widespread and systematic human rights abuses, and remains a persistent challenge to the HRC's legitimacy and authority.[88] For example, the election of China, Saudi Arabia, and the Russian Federation to join the HRC in 2014 drew criticism on the grounds that these states have continuing poor records in terms of the promotion and protection of human rights.[89] Claims that Saudi Arabia advanced its system of capital punishment through beheadings during its term on the HRC, as well as alleged violations of human rights perpetrated by Saudi Arabia in the Yemen, China supressing minority rights protest, and Russia's highly visible state repression of non-heterosexual individuals were highlighted by states and by civil society actors as representing areas of considerable international concern.

The underlying political and geographical splits that are apparent in these criticisms of the HRC, notwithstanding the significant human rights abuses of the governments in these member states, illustrate some of the impossibilities of a global institution, with membership comprising of states, to address human rights, when membership requires state representatives rather than independent experts. The US has often been at the forefront in terms of voicing criticisms of membership bids, despite the US's own poor human rights record on a number of issues, from Guantanamo Bay to police violence against black citizens. At the time of writing, after criticisms of human rights failings in the US in the UPR, the Trump administration withdrew

[85] Philip Alston, 'Reconceiving the UN Human Rights Regime: Challenges Confronting the New Human Rights Council' (2006) 7(1) Melbourne Journal of International Law 185.

[86] Seats are distributed as follows: African States 13 seats, Asia-Pacific States 13 seats, Latin American and Caribbean States 8 seats, Western European and other States 7 seats and Eastern European States 6 seats.

[87] Rosa Freedman, *The United Nations Human Rights Council* (Routledge 2013).

[88] The challenges to the HRC's authority and legitimacy can be contrasted with the limited challenges to the Security Council's legitimacy and authority, as discussed in the following chapter.

[89] Human Right Watch, 'UN: Suspend Saudi Arabia from Human Rights Council: "Gross and Systematic" Violations in Yemen Threaten Council's Credibility' (29 June 2016) <https://www.hrw.org/news/2016/06/29/un-suspend-saudi-arabia-human-rights-council> last accessed 31 May 2018; Tom Batchelor, 'Saudi Arabia Should Be Dropped from UN Human Rights Council, Say British Lawyers' *The Independent* (London, 1 February 2018) <http://www.independent.co.uk/news/world/middle-east/saudi-arabia-human-rights-council-un-yemen-lawyers-shrouded-in-secrecy-a8188511.html> last accessed 31 May 2018.

from their seat on the HRC. By definition, the international human rights regime addresses states as violators and, as no state comes to the Council with a 'clean' human rights record, it is inevitable that a state-driven human rights entity comprising of states as members that do not abuse human rights is an impossibility—the global violation of women's rights is an excellent indicator of this reality.

My approach is informed by Gedalof's understanding of the maternal as a motif for reconceiving the way we imagine knowledge production occurs. For Gedalof, inspired by the work of Baraister, there is a need to acknowledge 'from the perspective of a subject who mothers, interruption is both productive and normal, that it marks and defines the everyday experiences and subjectivities of individual mothers'.[90] Unlike Baraister, Gedalof examines a theory of interruption via a study of race and gender. Gedalof's attentiveness to Brah's work significantly shifts the temporal and geographic assumptions with regard to mothering that Baraister does not address.[91] In positioning Gedalof's approach as a starting point for understanding international institutions, a series of dialogues with regard to how knowledge develops and what knowledge is required to contain might be imagined. In using Gedalof's theory of interruption, mothering is embedded as a space of knowledge or, to use Gedalof's words, 'the "normal", the "familiar", the everyday, is in fact the work of persisting in the face of, in tandem with, being interrupted, so that what is repeated is never in fact the same, because its conditions are always being changed, being interrupted'.[92] This rethinking of how knowledge is, and should be, perceived is potentially powerful for feminist dialogues on law because of the way objective knowledge and impartial truth claims are repositioned in a political-philosophical space that asks about interruptions, discontinuities, and their connection to processes of social and cultural reproduction.[93]

In returning to the HRC, where the production of 'truth' and 'objectivity' is precisely what seems at risk when member states are permitted to participate (or withdraw support) despite their own poor human rights record, a turn to a dialogue that holds interruption and change within its modes of operation would be powerful at a number of levels. First, a theory of interruption might pursue the very simple participation claim that co-representation of member states could be pursued to create a gender balance within the HRC (and other international institutions).[94] That is, member states might be required to send two representatives to the Council, one identifying as male and one not identifying as male. This would not only be an interruption in the way things have been done previously but also

---

[90] Gedalof (n 4) 79.   [91] Baraister (n 3) 23.   [92] Gedalof (n 4) 79.

[93] This is not a call to embrace, essentialise, or prioritise mothering as the universal female experience. I deploy and discuss mothering as a motif that might offer an alternative or different knowledge encounter that is presupposed on its iterative, creative, changing, evolving, and non-permanence as well as grounding this knowledge in experiences of the everyday. I use the term 'maternal', and regard similar terms, such as 'mum' or 'mothering' as constructed terminologies that give meaning to a series of practices. While these are often associated with a biologically female body in dominant Western political philosophies, I do not regard a biological connection or a biologically female body to be necessary to enact practices of mothering/the maternal/to be a mother.

[94] The co-representation model is drawn from Kurdish local government structures in Turkey: Bengio (n 77).

ask member states to interrupt the status quo of their own representation policies, consider how things might be done differently and how this might transform cultural expectations with respect to gendered participation. While some states might wish to argue that there are insufficient qualified women available to fill a co-representation strategy, when argued as a space of interruption and a politics of interruption, co-representation requires member states to inquire as to what is in effect being interrupted by such a policy and why women in decision-making positions leads to repetition of anxiety by those in power and within political groups.

Commencing a strategy of co-representation on gender grounds would hopefully lead to further dialogue on additional mechanisms to diversify who states chose to represent them within international organisations. Further opportunities for interruptions might be offered to survivor groups within states who, for example, might be consulted by human rights representatives, and placed as formal advisors, or indeed as state representatives. States with consistent poor performance in a specific area might only be given the opportunity to bid for a seat on the HRC if they interrupt their own histories through incorporating advisors from specific groups into their delegation. For example, settler colonial states, such as Australia (a member of the HRC as I write in 2018), who have a long record of human rights abuses against the indigenous population, might be required to interrupt their own participation through the incorporation of indigenous representatives into the delegation they would send to the HRC as a condition of bidding for a seat.

Likewise, if feminist theory and approaches already, always, recognise a dialogue with crip theories, then gender law reform strategies, including those that are centred on increased participation for women, must, by definition, ask how disabled and queer voices are represented and given access to decision-making forums. This might be the very practical reality of checking and demanding inclusive physical spaces, as well as an intellectual shift that questions how communities within international institutions construct and obstruct the capacity to belong and participate within global governance.

Second, the politics of interruption asks for a rethinking of the substantive forms and the working structures of international institutions. The purpose of the UPR, therefore, is precisely to embark on an interruption into state practice and to disrupt the reproduction of certain practices as normal, routine, and expected. Similarly, shadow reports by human rights and survivor's groups further interrupt the state's representation of its own practices through the creation of alternative records and repositories of knowledge. This process, however, is slow in achieving change due to the soft law nature of the institutional outcomes that leave no compulsion for states to respond or to change their behaviour. As such, a feminist project that not only regards soft law tools, such as the UPR, as important 'interruptions' into the cycles of knowledge production requires a fundamental rethinking of the substance and structures of international institutions themselves. To interrupt the structural components of the HRC gender co-representation and advisory structures that specifically attend to that state's past human rights abuses as requirements for state representatives would be starting points.

Within the HRC's practices the process of UPR functions as a disruption and an interruption into the state's everyday mode of functioning. Importantly, the UPR asks states to interrupt persistent practices. Yet as a soft law tool UPR is a weak mechanism that cannot compel states to change their behaviours, despite the report and investigative processes producing knowledge and perspective—both at a formal and informal level. I argue, drawing on Gedalof, that the process of reproduction and interruption must go further and, in pursuing gender justice, interrogate the knowledge the Council relies on as assumed and accepted, and that this is necessary to fully interrupt the continued abuses that states, whether on the Council or outside it, continue to perpetrate.

The starting point for this interruption is the gendered histories of human rights. My concern is that international institutions reproduce stories of human rights that place women's human rights as an aspect of the triumphal emergence of human rights—from CEDAW to Beijing to the protection of women's rights under the guise of military force in Afghanistan—without consideration of the co-optation of human rights in the intersectional harm women experience. This can be understood through examining the specificities of women's human rights, for example the attempt to 'deliver' women's human rights to the women of Afghanistan after the end of the Taliban rule, and through examining 'general' human rights, for example the right to be free from torture. A feminist turn towards international institutions that is absent of dialogues established to disrupt the assumed knowledge produced within those institutions will continue to reproduce, rather than disrupt or interrupt, the gendered imperialism that international law was produced through and continues to reproduce.

The US decision to use military force in Afghanistan in 2001, after the attacks on the World Trade Centre in New York, was—from a legal perspective—articulated as the right to self-defence.[95] Popular accounts articulated in Western states used the Taliban's gender apartheid as a mechanism to ferment support from Western populations and, to this day, relay stories of the 'empowerment' and 'agency' of Afghan women brought about by US, and NATO, presence in Afghanistan. Lamb writes of her experience in Kabul, after the fall of the Taliban:

There were French lawyers arriving to draw up the constitution. Feminists setting up gender awareness classes, a women's bakery and a beauty school for which American beauty editors sent make-up. There would even be estate agents, as the so many aid agencies coming pushed the rents up sky high. Elections were planned for the coming spring. But when I talked to my Afghan friends no one mentioned democracy or women's rights. They wanted security and food and speedy justice.[96]

Likewise, Kandiyoti's study highlights a gap between women's livelihoods and the women's rights rhetoric employed by Western states in narratives of Afghanistan

---

[95] Gina Heathcote, *The Law on the Use of Force: A Feminist Analysis* (Routledge 2012) ch 4.
[96] Christina Lamb, *Farewell Kabul: From Afghanistan to a More Dangerous World* (William Collins 2015) 42.

post-2001.[97] For Nesiah, the pull of human rights as a civilising mantra for third world women invokes a binary between secularism and the religious while ignoring how human rights approaches have already framed the debate, and the knowledge parameters.[98]

The colonial histories of human rights must be seen as histories that are specifically linked to the role of gender, producing women's bodies as classed, raced, and sexed bodies. In constructing key tropes in civilising discourses, women's human rights knowledge contributes to the spectre of the Afghan woman's body, confined to the private sphere and under the blue burka that quickly became, after 9/11, a global symbol of the brutality of religious fundamentalism. Consequently, when Kubra Khademi walked through the streets of Kabul in armour as a performance piece in 2015 to protest against the sexual harassment of Afghan women this was not reported as art, or a statement on gender based violence, but as a statement on the uncivilised nature of gender affairs within Kabul, and the region more broadly.[99] That sexualised street harassment is a common, global occurrence is overlooked by the need to assert that 'gender equality is still in its infancy' in Kabul.[100] Recalling Lamb's comment above, Khademi's performance art appears to be a story of security and insecurity rather than gender: Kubra Khademi subsequently left Afghanistan, after death threats that lead her to continue her career as an artist in Paris, France.[101] The media narratives and reportage do not speak of women's security or gender-based violence but rather emphasises, again and again, the uncivilised and regressive public space in Kabul and by extension Afghanistan. Women's rights are reinforced as different from mainstream security concerns and as simultaneously a key indicator of the failure of state-building in Afghanistan that is assumed to be a consequence of local mindsets and not the international community, who ultimately offer Kubra Khademi refuge.

To speak of human rights and the assumptions the HRC works from, about the nature, histories, and patterns of human rights abuses, requires attention to the intersection of gender and colonial histories in the production of this knowledge. Developing new feminist dialogues on the potentiality of the HRC as a space for future gender law reform also requires the opening of dialogues to read sexuality, able-bodiedness, race, and colonial histories as written into accounts of gender. In this sense, feminist dialogues must listen to queer projects that examine how '[c]itizenship in a country of the global North and its attendant entitlements (rights, welfare) are privileges that are contingent on conformity with these normative

---

[97] Deniz Kandiyoti, 'Between the Hammer and the Anvil: Post-Conflict Reconstruction, Islam and Women's Rights' (2007) 28 Third World Quarterly 503.

[98] Nesiah (n 53).

[99] Ben Tufft, 'Woman in Armour Protesting Against Sexual Harassment in Kabul pelted with Rocks' *The Independent* (London, 8 March 2015) <http://www.independent.co.uk/news/world/asia/woman-in-armour-protesting-against-sexual-harassment-in-kabul-pelted-with-rocks-10093830.html> last accessed 31 May 2018.

[100] ibid.

[101] Kubra Khademi, Multidisciplinary Artist <www.kubrakhademi.org> last accessed 31 May 2018.

identity categories and subject positions'.[102] At the same time recognising a queer attention to non-normativity raises the need for additional dialogue with crip and disability studies. A theory of interruption that refuses to settle the parameters of gender law reform and instead defines a method for continued interruptions and dialogues seems a useful feminist dialogue on international institutions. As such, a study on feminist approaches to participation must ask who is silenced in the process of achieving gender balance within institutional representation. This has numerical and knowledge components and, in the words of Wilkerson, encompasses a project of thinking 'the unthinkable, to sacrifice comfort and abandon respectability to work for genuine inclusion. Perhaps the first step is to face the challenge of asking, when such coalitions have not materialized, why they have not'.[103]

3.2 World Health Organisation

This section examines the WHO and the production of soft laws, in particular with regard to the right to maternal health. I link the diversity of feminist approaches and their potentialities as dialogues of relevance to international law and institutions to the WHO. I analyse the risks and value of institutional production of soft law from a feminist perspective prior to examining contemporary feminist engagements with the politics of location. I consider feminist dialogues on the politics of location as sites of important knowledge and methodologies that might inform future feminist approaches to international institutions.

I analyse the WHO as illustrative of specialised agencies within the international order. Other specialised agencies include the World Trade Organisation, the Food and Agriculture Agency, the International Civil Aviation Organisation, the International Labour Organisation, the World Bank Group, and the Universal Postal Union, amongst others. Each specialised agency is established via a multilateral treaty and thus membership comprises of signatory states, while the scope of the organisation will be limited to the object and purposes of the agency established in the constituent document. Most have some form of law drafting power and, even if producing soft law, influence law-making through their specialised knowledge. Contemporary international legal scholarship on both expertise and fragmentation invokes these regimes as evidence of both the technical specialisations required and of the rise of sub-regimes, especially where dispute mechanisms have emerged, such as the WTO Dispute Settlement Body. The attention to gender, and gender perspectives, varies considerably across the various specialised agencies. The World Bank Group, for example, undertakes and commissions a prolific series of gender analyses and policy papers; other regimes, imagined as largely technical in scope, such as the Universal Postal Union do not contribute to the contours of gender law reform

---

[102] Bina Fernandez, 'Queer Border Crossers: Pragmatic Complicities, Indiscretions and Subversions' in Dianne Otto (ed), *Queering International Law: Possibilities, Alliances, Complicities, Risks* (Routledge 2018).

[103] Abby Wilkerson, 'Disability, Sex Radicalism and Political Agency' in Kim Q Hall (ed), *Feminist Disability Studies* (Indiana University Press 2011) 193.

within the global order. The WHO has developed some gender specific agendas, while other aspects of its work remain immune from any gender analysis and/or policy, so it constitutes a good example of a specialised agency for the purposes of this chapter.

As the WHO is a large institution I focus on the accommodation of the Millennium Development Goal on maternal health.[104] I reflect on how soft laws produced via specialised agencies can be considered important arenas for feminist law reform. Returning to Charlesworth and Chinkin's identification of soft law as feminised and yet potentially feminist I analyse the risks and value of institutional production of soft law from a feminist perspective.[105] In examining the production of soft laws on maternal health I also consider feminist dialogues on the maternal as analytical tools to demonstrate how feminist knowledge that is incorporated into international endeavours tends to downplay the politics of location. The prevalence of human rights as a 'catch all' within the maternal health discourse is a good example of how the politics of location, and thus an understanding of the variance of gender, human rights, and other types of knowledge, are not integrated into the knowledges drawn on to articulate gender within the WHO. The focus of this section is distinct from the previous one. In the study of the HRC I have examined the politics of interruption and motherhood as interruption as a corrective to dominant knowledge projects in Western states that often inform global governance. In this section I examine the maternal as situated as a specifically women-centred policy and the risks of incorporating a very narrow understanding of maternal experience within the current form of expertise, policy, and law. Within this account I am interested in the role of human rights as a motif and agenda that is incorporated in an unexamined fashion, in terms of holding various truths about human experience that are, for example, gendered.

To undertake such a project and open this dialogue it is necessary to first dislodge Western feminist assumptions regarding the universal experience of mothering and the production of mothering in the Global North as invisible alongside mothering in the Global South as a hyper-visible health risk, to consider this as a gendered space of knowledge production rather than simply reproduction. The continued imagining of motherhood as uniform and as experienced in the same way by women within and across communities is not only dismissive of cultural variations in meaning and understanding of maternal subjectivity but also silences the different experiences of disabled, migrant, lesbian, and trans people as mothers. Gedalof's account of the politics of interruption, drawing on Baraister, accepts such a possibility and engages difference through the recognition of social reproduction and the necessity of sameness to build stories of nation and belonging, arguing that 'something new and different arrives to make us stop and look around a space that has been invisible in its apparent repetitiveness, something that takes us outside of ourselves and could make

---

[104] For information on the Millennium Development Goals and Sustainable Development Goals, see <http://www.who.int/topics/millennium_development_goals/maternal_health/en/>; <http://www.unwomen.org/en/news/in-focus/women-and-the-sdgs/sdg-5-gender-equality> last accessed 31 May 2018.

[105] Charlesworth and Chinkin (n 13) 66; Bailliet (n 9).

us look at ourselves anew'.[106] Furthermore, a feminist dialogue designed around a politics of interruption, it is hoped, is also open to the interruption of its own expectations with respect to the production of knowledge.

The eight Millennium Development Goals (MDG), focused on specific strategies to alleviate the impact of poverty, globally, included MDG Five to improve maternal health. This incorporated the specific goals of reducing levels of maternal mortality by three-quarters and to achieve universal access to reproductive health between 1990 and 2015. Over this period maternal mortality fell by forty-five per cent and universal access to reproductive health services was not achieved. In 2015 the MDGs were superseded by the Sustainable Development Goals (SDG)—targeting 2030—which contain seventeen goals, including gender equality, but no longer specifically address maternal health improvements. SDG Three, however, includes maternal health within the larger goal of ensuring healthy lives and promoting well-being for all at all ages. The WHO asserts SDG Three contains the goal 'to reduce the global maternal mortality ratio to less than 70 per 100 000 births, with no country having a maternal mortality rate of more than twice the global average'.[107] Consequently, the 2018 WHO Recommendation, Intrapartum Care for a Positive Childbirth Experience, 'highlights the importance of woman centred care to optimize the experience of labour and childbirth for women and their babies through a holistic, human rights-based approach'.[108] The emphasis on human rights and individual choice present a specific understanding of health encounters. I analyse the WHO's approach to maternal health in this section to centre and assess the role of soft law documents within international institutions and to consider the tensions in development projects that 'carry' Western perceptions of gender, sex, and sexuality.

The intrapartum care guidelines are good evidence of the discussion on both expertise and fragmentation. As a site of health expertise, the guidelines ignore a presentation of a directly political or ethical agenda. For example, recommendation number three asserts: 'A companion of choice is recommended for all women throughout labour and childbirth.'[109] The evidence-based account given to explain the inclusion of this provision refers to global economic differences through references to women from HIC (High Income Countries) and LMIC (Low and Middle Income Countries) but is unable to capture the impact of sexuality, local gender expectations, and/or intimate partner violence as well as variations in access to resources within a state to really address the complex reasons around who a women might choose as a companion during the period of giving birth.[110] A feminist dialogue on plural subjectivities would commence by asking about different women

[106] Gedalof (n 4) 79.

[107] WHO, 'Maternal Mortality: Key Facts' (WHO November 2016) <http://www.who.int/mediacentre/factsheets/fs348/en/> last accessed 31 May 2018.

[108] World Health Organisation, *WHO Recommendations: Intrapartum Care for a Positive Childbirth Experience* (WHO 2018) <http://www.who.int/reproductivehealth/publications/intrapartum-care-guidelines/en/> last accessed 31 May 2018.

[109] ibid 3.

[110] NN Sakar, 'The Impact of Intimate Partner Violence on Women's Reproductive Health and Pregnancy Outcomes' (2008) 28(3) Journal of Obstetrics and Gynaecology 266.

(and men) and the different needs required in terms of identifying birth companions. Instead, under the current regulations the combination of a focus on choice (as in the companion of choice) and a human rights based approach centres the specific legal subject of Western liberal discourses—as a rational choosing actor whose rights are defined through their identity as an individual subject.

Feminist dialogues on mothering, across feminist spaces, demonstrate a series of alternative understandings of knowledge.[111] I am less interested in how these dialogues configure motherhood and more interested in how different locales often produce knowledge in a manner that seems inconceivable in dominant articulations of 'universals' within the global order. The two universals I appraise here are human rights and mothering. Both are invoked as mechanisms for knowing that do not require specific iteration or discovery of the diversity that they might hold. Gedalof's account of the role of interruption as a form of social reproduction illustrates the counter-knowledge that might emerge and how gender might be thought through differently. This type of conversation, I argue, is the type of dialogue on international law that is relevant to future feminist international legal endeavours, including those that engage international institutions as a space of gender law reform. I therefore use the example of maternal health to look beyond the notion of specific gender law reforms towards transformative dialogues on international law that engage feminist methods.

Gedalof, drawing on Brah, writes of how

the figure of the mother in the history of Western thought stands as a metaphor for sameness. Physical reproduction—birth—is generally seen as the mere ground for the more important productive things that happen after we are born, and separation from the sameness of the mother is seen as crucial to developing as distinct individual selves.[112]

Both human rights and the individualism on which the WHO approach to maternal health centres, rely on precisely this type of underlying assumption about subjectivity. Recognising that the mother is more often produced as motif for sameness, theorising alternative subjectivities has the potential to raise feminist dialogues that admit plural subjectivities, acknowledge relational subjects, and open space for dialogues that are premised on interruptions. Gedalof develops her account in response to the construction of Britishness within the UK and through drawing on Baraister's approach to thinking about difference.[113] For Gedalof this requires moving beyond seeing 'birth as a mere repetition' or that 'the mother stands as the abject figure, as that which must be excluded and transcended, in order for the masculine subject to bring himself into being'.[114] In exchange Gedalof theorises:

... might the mother—rethought, reframed, wrenched away from this logic of the same that ties reproduction to statis—be more of a disruptive, 'post-humanist' figure for tracing an alternative narrative or genealogy...[115]

---

[111] Oyèrónké Oyèwùmí, *What Gender is Motherhood: Changing Yorùbá Ideals of Power, Procreation, and Identity in the Age of Modernity* (Palgrave 2015); Wendy Chavkin and JaneMaree Maher (eds), *The Globalisation of Motherhood: Deconstructions and Reconstructions of Biology and Care* (Routledge 2010).
[112] Gedalof (n 4) 73.   [113] ibid 79.   [114] ibid 73.   [115] ibid 74.

Gedalof's account, thus, requires a recognition of the encounter with strangers and an appreciation of social reproduction defined through interruption. The encounter with strangers, in Gedalof's work, is a reference to the knowledge processes encountered in the diasporic subject which for Gedalof disrupts the uninterrupted notion of Britishness to reconfigure difference as an element of belonging that is both present and historical.

Similarly, Ahmed theorises the incompleteness of the Beijing Conference through attention to strangers and the encounter with the Other, as stranger, constructed in the Beijing Platform for Action:

the constitution of women as global actors involves forms of differentiation, where various 'other' women are named as yet to fulfil their debt to modernity. The ideal, then, of the document is the *becoming women of all women*: it is the development of all women into modern individuals, who are able to reproduce not only the family, but the global space as familial space. In such a model, women who are marked as different to those women who are already 'modernised' must be brought into the international community.[116]

Ahmed's articulation of strangers in transnational feminist spaces adds to Gedalof's dialogue on social reproduction in Britain with an appreciation of global divisions of labour and difference that are reproduced within the structures of global governance. The WHO intrapartum study undertakes and reproduces a similar series of assumptions, where maternal health requires a becoming of the self-disciplining liberal subjects, protected via human rights norms and exercising choices in relation to health care that are predicated on an understanding of mothering and birthing configured in the global north.

To return to the WHO companion of choice recommendation in the intrapartum policy, discussed above, the imagining of a women in labour travelling to a clinic and exercising choice with regard to her labour partner provides an expectation for women outside of Western/HIC to become modern women, who give birth in hospital and clinics, who are accompanied by their partner when giving birth, and, if the further notes and evidence are to be acknowledged, aspire to be able to pay for a companion in the ideal scenario. Home or community births are not considered, despite evidence of the positive effect this has on birthing experiences and the core ideology of choice betraying an individualism akin to Western liberalism and capitalist systems. The recommendations note that '[i]n many countries, particularly HICs, women who want doulas pay for them privately. Extending companionship of choice to underprivileged women in these settings would increase equity'.[117] The assumption of privately outsourced birth care as a standard produces the perceptions of maternal health drawn from Western and HIC as desirable to constitute a familial global standard of intrapartum care. This approach ignores best practices derived through understanding local needs and the impact of an underlying liberal subject, created via the technical, medical recommendations in the report, as not uniformly representative of legal subjects.

---

[116] Ahmed (n 5) 177.   [117] WHO, *Intrapartum Care* (n 108) 32.

Both Gedalof and Ahmed centre dynamic approaches where cultural and social reproduction require, and are defined by, interruption. Gedalof develops this in response to accounts of mothering in Britain and the racialised and classed narratives interrupted by diaspora communities that construct 'interruptions that both require and enable repeatedly "going over the same ground as a way of bringing something new into being"'.[118] Ahmed takes up a similar reconfiguration of knowledge in the space of global governance, arguing that

> the possibility of something giving—not me or you—but something giving in the very encounter between a 'me' and a 'you', begins only with a recognition of the debts that are already accrued and which assimilate bodies, already recognised as strange or familiar, into economies of difference.[119]

This approach to feminist theorising grounds difference as the space for feminist knowledge production—where attention to who is made strange by universal categories and moments of assumed knowledge are the indicators of tensions and exclusion that demand further dialogue. Furthermore, identifying the politics of location as shaping knowledge production draws out the need to disrupt and interrupt knowledge production within international institutions.

Analysis of the work of the WHO demonstrates the various layers of feminist inquiry into the foundations of international law that are required. The intrapartum care document on the one hand proposes an evidence-based set of recommendations and, on the other hand, incorporates specific assumptions with regard to appropriate outcomes that would benefit from feminist dialogues that are drawn from plural accounts. This requires an account and interrogation of the assumed knowledge with respect to international standards, such as human rights and the terms of liberal subjectivity, as well as attention to the processes that permit identification of whose knowledge is important and in what ways.

3.3 Peacebuilding Commission

The United Nations Peacebuilding Commission is something of an interruption to the structure and design of international institutions. The PBC, or an institution like it, was first proposed in the General Assembly Summit Outcome Document in 2005 as a means to provide a 'coordinated, coherent and integrated approach' to peacebuilding in post-conflict communities.[120] While originally envisaged as an expert group with the Security Council and peacebuilding donor states as key actors, this was adapted after the interventions (interruptions?) of coalitions such as the G-77 who challenged the Western configuration of early proposals.[121] The final design of the institution was such that it is a joint subsidiary body of both the

---

[118] Gedalof (n 4) 82, quoting Baraister (n 3).   [119] Ahmed (n 5) 154.
[120] UN General Assembly Resolution 60/1 2005 World Summit Outcome (24 October 2005) UN Doc A/RES/60/1, para 97.
[121] Torunn L Tryggestad, 'The UN Peacebuilding Commission and Gender: A Case of Norm Reinforcement' (2010) 17(2) International Peacekeeping 159.

UN General Assembly and UN Security Council. The PBC comprises of thirty-one members, drawn from the member states on the Security Council as well as member states representing the General Assembly, the Economic and Social Council, and key donor and troop contributing states. The structure of PBC incorporates an Organisational Committee, country-specific committees, and a Working Group for Lessons Learned. The PBC was subject to review of the larger peacebuilding architecture within the UN in 2015 and this lead to a strengthening of the PBC's mandate in 2016, via the simultaneous release of Security Council and General Assembly resolutions that recognise the continuities between pre-conflict states and post-conflict states.[122] Both resolutions also incorporate women's participation as integral to peacebuilding processes.

Due to its relatively recent creation, the PBC has always included a gender mandate. Tryggestad's analysis of this finds:

the 'women, peace and security' agenda fell victim to larger political and procedural disputes that stemmed mainly from power struggles between the G-77 majority in the General Assembly and the dominant powers of the Security Council. However, once gender issues were put on the agenda their relevance to peacebuilding was acknowledged without much resistance.[123]

Tryggestad identifies a distinction between the take-up of gender norms in the PBC and the flow into the acts of member states, such that 'the norm that women and women's concerns are vital to sustainable peacebuilding cannot yet be said to have cascaded sufficiently among member states to influence policy as a matter of course'.[124] Shepherd's study of the PBC focuses primarily on the incorporation of women, peace, and security at policy levels and finds a combination of techniques at policy level that limit the effectiveness of the institution incorporating a response to gender as a power dynamic.[125] Shepherd's study of the embeddedness of the language of gender alongside the meanings given within the structures and workings of the PBC links to the discussion of expertise in chapter 2. Gender as a technology in and of itself, is underscored by Shepherd's analysis of the continual reframing of gender to work as a signifier of women and as a mechanism for increasing women's participation. Shepherd concludes that the legitimacy of peacebuilding is heavily gendered and raced in ways that frustrate and infiltrate any turn to 'local' or bottom-up initiatives.[126]

Shepherd's analysis of the gendered frames within peacebuilding policy chimes neatly with many of the arguments of this text. At the same time Shepherd's focus on text and discourse highlights a persistent set of tensions within feminist dialogues that I have not, I would argue, thus far paid sufficient attention to. Shepherd recognises this in her own methodology and writes, '[t]here is no doubt another project,

---

[122] UN Security Council Resolution 2282 (27 April 2016) UN Doc S/RES/2282 and UN General Assembly Resolution 70/262 (27 April 2016) A/RES/70/262.
[123] Tryggestad (n 121) 168.   [124] ibid.
[125] Laura J Shepherd, *Gender, UN Peacebuilding, and the Politics of Space: Locating Legitimacy* (Oxford University Press 2017) 160.
[126] ibid 168.

the ghost-twin of the project at hand, from which my ghost-twin travels to Burundi, or Liberia, or Guinea-Bissau and does engage directly with the women about whom the UN writes so copiously'.[127] However, Shepherd simultaneously challenges the framing of gender as centred on women, describing this as constraining 'that which can be imagined or implemented'.[128] In contrast, True centres women's lives and looks at the impact in the lives of women in post-conflict communities to argue for expanded rights and access to resources for women.[129] Both authors write on the PBC and ask for more than the PBC has thus far been able to achieve, through their different contributions to the dialogue on gender in peacebuilding. True, how-ever, concludes that '[w]omen's capacity to participate in peacebuilding is closely linked to their enjoyment of economic security and rights'.[130] I am interested in this tension between gender and women in feminist dialogues, as both True and Shepherd add important knowledge to the existing debates of gender law reform in global governance. True uses the experiences of women, and the gendered neglect of socioeconomic rights in peacebuilding to demonstrate the complicated struc-tural restraints on peacebuilding missions. Shepherd challenges the focus on women to ask what places and spaces gender projects hold within the larger discourses of peacebuilding. Each is looking at different aspects of peacebuilding practice and yet by placing their work in dialogue a key feminist tension is brought to the surface and given space. In following the larger methodologies explored in this chapter, further interruptions might also be sought to ask how peacebuilding practices operate if a feminist methodology can hear and listen to the differences in True's and Shepherd's approaches as a starting point for further interruptions.

For example, True's account of the political economy of peacebuilding illumin-ates the operation of gendered practices within international structures shifting dia-logues toward recognition of the underlying structural dimensions of inequalities within communities, whether international and local. True defines her approach as requiring that 'we address the physical/political and economic/livelihood inse-curities as part of the same framework for bringing about peace'.[131] As such, she examines the 'lack of coherence' within the different components of peacebuilding alongside their gendered impact in post-conflict societies.[132] True's project therefore centres on women's experiences of peacebuilding practice and the economic effect on women's livelihoods. The material effect of peacebuilding activities on women's lives thus speaks back to the limited discourse on gender identified by Shepherd; although the two pieces of research deploy different feminist methodologies they both indicate a dissatisfaction with the account of gender in peacebuilding practice. Both approaches are echoed in the independent review of gender and peacebuilding, commissioned by the PBC in 2014; amongst the conclusions drawn the author argues that '[t]he purpose and use of gender analysis is currently caught up in a distracting debate of woman-centred versus gender relations whereby tensions exist

---

[127] ibid 4.   [128] ibid 163.
[129] Jacqui True, 'The Political Economy of Gender in UN Peacekeeping' in Gina Heathcote and Dianne Otto (eds), *Rethinking Peacekeeping, Gender Equality and Collective Security* (Palgrave 2014) 243.
[130] ibid 257.   [131] ibid 244.   [132] ibid.

in the interpretation of UNSCR 1325 among peacebuilding actors in terms of women's rights versus the use of gender analysis'.[133]

Drawing in a feminist account of dialogues and interruptions, even alongside my near-constant assertion that a feminist analysis ought to focus on gender, not women, the challenges drawn by these differing accounts might be instrumental in thinking through how to address feminist tensions. That is a series of tensions around essentialism—that is, a focus on women over gender—and tensions around the material effect of gendered knowledge practices and the discursive engagement with those practices materialise. Leaving this as a tension, rather than trying to smooth over ruptures in feminist approaches, might open the way to new sorts of knowledge practices, interruptions, and dialogues. For example, rather than focusing on the need to resolve this tension, perhaps there is a necessity to examine what further knowledge is excluded in centring feminist dialogue on the choice between women-centred and gender-centred methodologies. This would, of course, be an interruption to the central arguments of the book. The consequence, however, might be to explore how the prioritising of gender, and women, in feminist work silences specific accounts of gendered lives, gendered violence, and gendered intersections, such as elaborated by differently abled and queer voices, amongst others. Furthermore, these dialogues might also be interrupted by attention to the layers of historical interventions that have deployed gender as a means to civilise non-Western communities and to write out/over local knowledge practices.

A focus on how social and economic inequalities are embedded in international and national practices thus draws in an understanding of class but might also be used as a means to further address the intersectional privileges that are rendered invisible through an account of gender in isolation. This converges with Shepherd's account of hierarchies of power and the role of gender as one manifestation of the hierarchy. Once difference is foregrounded through the examination of power and intersectionality, a feminist methodology that undoes the primacy of identity politics is required. Queer voices that look to the non-normative organisation of political arrangements, the role of different forms of kinship, and a kaleidoscope of possibilities are then identified as additional imperative dialogues, as are the underscoring of meanings given to normalise bodies in terms of ableist and sexuality norms that both crip and queer theorists speak to.

As an institution that interrupted the perceived manner in which institutions were established and designed, and then was further interrupted via the engagement of the G-77, the Peacebuilding Commission demonstrates both the limits of institutional gender law reforms and their continued potential to be interrupted, again, and again (and in a valuable way). In peacebuilding practice the voices of queer, LGBTi, and differently abled have not, as yet, been given an arena where they might be listened to, although the PBC has invested considerable resources in understanding the intersection of gender and youth.[134] A feminist dialogue that

---

[133] Eleanor O'Gorman, *Independent Thematic Review on Gender for the UN Peacebuilding Support Office (PBSO)—Final Report* (UN Peacebuilding Support Office, March 2014) 7.

[134] See, further, the Peacebuilding Fund (PBF) Gender and Youth Peacebuilding Initiative: <https://www.pbfgypi.org/> last accessed June 2018.

asks why and how emerges: one that engages how gender is both co-opted into silencing differently gendered and sexed others and why the role of gender functions to normalise specific accounts of bodies and minds. This is a dialogue with queer, crip, disability studies, and the individuals who have found sanctuary in the intellectual and actual homes created within these research communities.

4. Dialogues, Interrupted, as Feminist Methodology?

In this section I reflect further on dialogues and listening as feminist methodologies that build plural subjectivities and split subjectivities into the foundations of legal knowledge. Taking a feminist political economy approach, a maternal theory of interruption, and knowledge of colonial genealogies, I reflect on the types of dialogues necessary for future feminist approaches to international law. At the same time, I open the text to interruptions from queer and crip readings of international law to further disrupt the unencumbered and single subject of contemporary liberal legalism. I do not imagine the creation of space for this range of feminist dialogues to be either simple to create or without tensions. I am interested in how the tensions between these various accounts—as equally as between activists and academics, between critical feminist projects and legal/policy agendas, between core and peripheral subjects, and between those with access to power and those challenging the perpetuation of existing power relations—hold the potential for future feminist dialogues on international law through the very process of surfacing those tensions.

In drawing these different perspectives and methodologies into dialogue I am interested in rendering the impossibility of a static, knowable feminist theory. Instead I consider spaces of situated knowledge that are in dialogue with each other and others, and that conceive of subjects as plural and split—in terms of relationality and differences. These dialogues are situated in cultures, communities, economies, political configurations, and legal processes, and reflect gendered lives and livelihoods that are temporally and geographically fluid. In bringing attention to the material, the legacies of empire, and a maternal theory of interruption simultaneously I map different and alternative mechanisms for interrogating and shaping international law. I use crip and queer theories to illuminate how each interrogation constructs a specific location and epistemology. I do not wish to advocate for a regression into the infinite varieties of humanness but do wish to ground the relational and uniqueness of human experiences, that I regard as defining a universal experience of humanness that derives from the particular.

The turn to crip theory is not, however, self-evident. For Bone, '[b]ased in the rhetoric of queer theory, "crip" seeks to challenge constructions of able-bodiedness and be politically generative through the fracturing of key systems of oppression'; however, for Bone, 'crip theory continues a cycle of silencing and marginalization that widens the divide between disability studies and the lived experiences of the disabled rather than bridging those critical gaps in meaningful ways'.[135] The

---

[135] Bone (n 18) 1298.

debates between crip, critical disability studies, and disability studies more broadly, as well as interventions such as those attending to debility or social models of disability, draw out considerable tensions in the field of study. Bone's argument that non-disabled-identifying individuals in expounding the language of crip theories displace disabled voices risks an essentialised version of disability and yet cannot be ignored. How can a crip theory be articulated as an incorporation of a challenge to embedded assumptions with regard to able-bodiedness rather than a re-silencing? At some point a theory of interruptions, and dialogues, must attend to who is given space to speak, and at what cost to the speaking of those who continue to not be given an opportunity to speak. A parallel example in the work of international institutions is the UN response to the pursuit of self-determination by the Sahrawi peoples. In supporting negotiations between Morocco and the Sahrawi, international institutions have effectively supported the status quo rather than creating a space for the Sahrawi to exercise their right to self-determination.[136] On the surface the continued support of negotiations (dialogue) might be preferred to more violent or coercive methods of dispute resolution. However, the placing of the Sahrawi peoples and Moroccan state as equals in negotiations permits the status quo, drawn from the additional privileges granted to states as the primary subjects of international law, to accommodate and support the continued violence of the Moroccan state. This draws out an important critique of the focus of the book as a whole on feminist dialogues. In centring dialogues, I have proposed an imagined space of kind, feminist interactions able to challenge their own existing exclusions. The debates in crip and disability studies identify the naivety of imagining the constructions of the conditions for speaking as equally accommodating. Mindfulness of this flaw informs the contours of the following chapter on authority, in which I endeavour to look behind the dialogues produced throughout the text. The plural and split subjects, the politics of location, and the lived experiences of gendered lives thus continue to emerge as important interruptions and, I would argue, the form of feminist dialogue I have argued for must always be open to, indeed expect, interruptions to its own perceived knowledge practices. Thus: dialogues, interrupted.

In identifying feminist approaches as encircling a series of dialogues and interruptions, this chapter considers how diverse and divergent dialogues might be merged via plural and split subjects that draw in crip and queer theories. As a chapter attendant to the politics of interruption, the chapter struggles to contain—to listen to—the many dialogues within. However, the chapter also demonstrates how a politics of interruption, that permits plural and split subjects to speak and be listened to, can aid the development of change. I focused on gendered participation within international institutions, such as the HRC, to demonstrate how this different means to frame knowledge potentially moves beyond identity politics and

[136] Raquel Ojeda-Garcia, Irene Fernández-Molina, and Victoria Veguilla (eds), *Global, Regional and Local Dimensions of Western Sahara's Protracted Decolonization: When a Conflict Gets Old* (Palgrave 2017); Karen Jacobsen, *A Frozen Conflict and a Humanitarian Program the Works: UNHCR's Confidence Building Measures in the Western Sahara* (Feinstein International Center 2017).

approaches participation claims with a mindfulness of who is given access and the role of gendered privilege in sustaining other forms of privilege—and harms. Gender quotas or programmes of co-representation, thus, in following a feminist methodology would examine the intersectional gender arrangements to use gender law reform to include women as merely a first step to change the way participation in global governance occurs. The knowledge project underlying this approach is further explored in the example of the WHO and the limits of the collapsing back onto an unexamined acceptance of human rights and liberal legal model they endorse. Finally, the third institution under review, the PBC, demonstrated an interruption into my own thinking to regard the material effects and political economy dimensions of gender law reform—the discussion brought together the methodologies of both interruption and dialogue to identify the necessity of gender projects surfacing tensions rather than avoiding them.

To further interrupt the knowledge presented in this chapter I introduced a range of theorists who develop queer and crip theories as mechanisms for challenging the status quo of knowledge. To avoid these interruptions from circling and joining as some form of meta-theory I wish to think through the politics of location as an additional tool, relevant to feminist thinking and instrumental in the history of gender law reform. I regard the consequent attentiveness to the geographical and temporal histories of knowledge and knowledge about gender as raising additional questions for feminist scholars within global governance. Attention to gender mainstreaming as a vehicle for interventions into some states—and not others—or some institutions—and not others—demonstrates the continuity of empire in the formation of international institutions and naivety in feminist strategies that assume they work outside of this frame.

As the chapter, and the knowledge it holds, fragments across these different interruptions and dialogues, I am reminded of the critical legal response to the charges of fragmentation of the discipline of international law, that settle for praise of diversification over the risks of fragmentation. This chapter therefore asks after the diversity of feminist methodologies, how the plural subject, intersectional and split, provides the conditions for different, and alternative voices to be ushered in via feminist methodologies to provide a continual, dynamic reshaping that is always open to its own interruption.

The chapter thus accounts for multiple interruptions, including parenting ones—invisible and yet deeply implicated in the writing, such that as I wrote the final thousand words I was called to pick someone up from school. Frustrated by a break in writing about interruptions to be actually interrupted, I tried to reframe this as a moment to 'sit' with the knowledge and to reflect on it, to adapt it a little, to ask myself whether interruptions as a methodology form a conceivable feminist methodology. I reflected on what was feminist about the politics of interruption and the potential risks of losing women as subjects, I thought about who might be alienated by the knowledge in the chapter, and I wondered if I was writing a project of impossibility. I recalled that colonialism presented an interruption that was violent and thus functions to highlight the need to frame power relations as producing different meanings for differently situated peoples. I thought about

Scott's conceptualisation of gender as a critical methodology that, in refusing to accept sex difference as a primary and settled organising model, continues to ask questions of itself.[137] I thought about the gender actors, academics, and thinkers I knew who would interrupt me on this point and wondered on what authority I was speaking.

---

[137] Joan W Scott, *The Fantasy of Feminist History* (Duke University Press 2011).

6

Authority

The 'no-person' personification of now you see it, now you don't, the black woman pops in and out of presence in the statistical snapshots of the social topography, perceptible in the peripheral vision of governmental calculus but not to be brought into fleshy, embodied and complex presence, despite being scarred by increasing inequality and 'new hierarchies of belonging'.[1]

1. Introduction

Black women in Britain die at the hands of the state in the complex intersection of austerity, racism, and gendered harms: outside of the attention of international law and institutions. Likewise, outside of the attention of feminist writing on international law are Black British feminisms: a substantial and central knowledge formation on transnational feminist histories and conversations, across the Atlantic and beyond. Lewis writes of the complicity of the UK state in the deaths of black women, under conditions of austerity, within the legacy of colonialism and empire, and as victims of gender-based violence.[2] The UK state that fails to provide security for Black women is the same UK state that grants me citizenship and the capacity to move in public (and private) spaces without threat or fear.[3] This is the same UK state with the authority to veto Security Council resolutions and with the authority to lead on the resolutions on conflict-related sexual violence in the Security Council.

This chapter is focused on seeing the complexity of legal authority and the privileges that manifest in the perpetuation of power; both state power and feminist power, as legal acts, knowledge acts, and acts of displacement and silencing. Feminist approaches to international law have identified the nexus between the domestic acts of states and the failures of the international community to address gender-based violence; whether as a product of state failures or as acts attributable to the state, most prominently in post-conflict states.[4] Yet, there is a general silence

---

[1] Gail Lewis, 'Questions of Presence' (2017) 117 Feminist Review 1, 11.　　[2] ibid.
[3] Gina Heathcote, 'I am an Immigrant' (2017) 5(2-3) Poem: International English Language Quarterly 241.
[4] Rhonda Copelon, 'Recognizing the Egregious in the Everyday: Domestic Violence as Torture' (1993–1994) 25 Columbia Human Rights Law Review 291; Tamara Tawfiq Tamini, 'Violence against Women in Palestine and Mediocre Accountability' (2017) 5 UK Law Student Review 75.

Feminist Dialogues on International Law. Gina Heathcote. © Gina Heathcote 2019. Published 2019 by Oxford University Press.

within international law on the intersectional violence within peacetime states that silences alternative knowledge practices and histories and ignores the wilfulness of state structures in harming specific groups.

As such it tests a capacity to use naming as a doorway towards the other in an attempt to make present in a meaningful way the things brought together under the sign of the name—Sarah Reed #Say her name.[5]

In the UK in 2016, Sarah Reed took her life while in prison after continual failures by state officials to recognise and treat her history of serious mental health needs.[6] Sarah Reed had previously been the victim of racist police violence and traumatic medical care that triggered her mental health decline.[7] The intersectional dimensions of gender-based violence, the colonial ideologies that infiltrate state violence, the racist legacies, and the heteronormative tropes within gender-based violence have not been sufficiently placed as an aspect of feminist dialogues on international law. Feminist approaches to international law involve decisions about which violence is prioritised, pursued, and rendered visible—this authority to both speak and frame international debates on gender law reform requires increased feminist dialogues that I examine in this chapter.

My approach continues to pivot around pondering the conditions and possibilities for feminist dialogues and an analysis of authority within international law to question feminist agendas for gender law reform within the spaces of global governance.[8] The chapter was originally envisaged as an analysis of how gender law reform engages, ignores, and props up forms of authority within global governance, through a study of the convergences of the women, peace, and security agenda and the counterterrorism agenda. While this study is still included in the chapter, my approach has mutated somewhat towards thinking through what is involved in the turn to law to develop feminist agendas: what authority is given to specific feminist actors to speak and what authority is imagined lying within the domain of legal acts. In addition, and in response to the texts encountered in my everyday, and the larger theme of the book as a feminist dialogue, the chapter evolved into a study of how different discourses converge to give my own voice authority, questioning whose silences that authority depends upon. Throughout the chapter and especially in the final section, I draw upon the voices of Black British feminists and indigenous Australian authors to question my own complicity in the production of privilege and to explore the preceding steps that are necessary to genuinely open feminist dialogues on international law:[9]

---

[5] Lewis, 'Questions of Presence' (n 1) 8.

[6] Damien Gayle, 'Woman Assaulted by PC Who Lost His Job Found Dead in Holloway Prison' *The Guardian* (London, 3 February 2016).

[7] ibid.

[8] Anne Orford, *International Authority and the Responsibility to Protect* (Cambridge University Press 2011); Vanja Hamzić, 'International Law as Violence: Competing Absences of the Other' in Dianne Otto (ed), *Queering International Law: Possibilities, Alliances, Complicities, Risks* (Routledge 2018) 77.

[9] Lewis, 'Questions of Presence' (n 1); Joan Anim-Addo, Suzanne Scafe, and Yasmin Gunaratnam (eds), *Feminist Review Special Issue on Black British Feminism: Many Chants* (Palgrave 2014); Aileen Moreton-Robinson, *Talkin' Up to the White Woman: Indigenous Women and Feminism* (University of Queensland Press 2000).

This then requires inhabitation of a different kind of triangular space—a space understood as part of psychic structure, which requires acknowledgement of one's own location in a field of relationality; in which there is an understanding that one is not always at the centre and has no automatic entitlement to be so; and in which one can look on without being a participant, is the mode of being-in-relation.[10]

The self-reflexivity that shapes the chapter also questions the feminist desire for law to respond to feminist knowledge; drawing on global counterterrorism strategies as examples of the gendered, homophobic, economic, and racialised violence that international law maintains, and that feminist dialogues on international law risk complicity in. I also assert non-legal feminist action as a legitimate and important component of future dialogues on international law; exploring how protest and micro-level interventions must be rendered present in feminist approaches to global governance to shift from strategies for gender law reform to dialogues on feminist methodologies. I argue that, for Western feminists, white feminists, and feminists with access to privilege, some uncomfortable listening is the first step to feminist dialogues on international law.

Vital to the dialogues I have drawn on in this book has been the need to develop feminist thinking through a 'politics of natality'.[11] I defined a politics of natality, following Arendt, as political action, where action is conceived in the plurality of human individuality and the intrinsic capacity for new ideas. Arendt defines the capacity for new ideas as that which makes us human.[12] Arendt's model of natality concentrates on the capacity within us all, as humans, for new ideas, rebirth, and creative ownership.[13] I have argued that Arendt's natality provokes a reconceptualisation of feminist ethics and a challenge to the current development of radical, liberal, and cultural feminist-inspired gender law reforms within UN institutions.[14] However, I am wary that looking for new ideas denies those sites of knowledge that are continually dismissed, silenced, and obliterated: not new but ignored and undermined in histories of knowledge, subjectivity, and law including feminist histories and feminist subjectivities.

My imagining of dialogues, amongst feminist and critical scholars on international law, envisions a neutral and safe space of encounter that assumes that the making of space for dialogue is accommodating to all. This raises for me the question of how to attend to a politics of natality while knowing that the political encounters of black women, in the space in which I live, in the UK, in London, are intimately entwined with violent encounters with the state that refuse to name her, to render her presence as meaningful. In the words of Lewis:

[10] Lewis, 'Questions of Presence' (n 1) 15; Moreton-Robinson (n 9).

[11] Hannah Arendt, *The Human Condition* (2nd edn, Chicago 1998).

[12] ibid 6: '... in the west's obsession with death and mortality, our natality has been largely ignored. Yet it is in birth, in natality, that newness enters the world; and it is in the fact of new life that every other form of freedom and creativity is grounded'; Grace M Jantzen, *Foundations of Violence* (Routledge 2004).

[13] Arendt (n 11) 6.

[14] Gina Heathcote, *The Law on the Use of Force: A Feminist Analysis* (Routledge 2012).

the history of structurally and ideologically legitimated violence so central to the making and sustaining of racial formation in the triangular space that is the after-effect of trans-atlantic enslavement, would render the figure—let alone her embodied presence—'black woman' an oxymoron if not an impossibility.[15]

Lewis's understanding of the conditions of feminist authority to speak in Britain, and acknowledgement of the silencing contained within feminist approaches informs my final engagement with feminist dialogues attentive to those silences. In an attempt to listen with responsibility, I do not structure this chapter in line with previous chapters: instead the content engages a series of feminist dialogues in re-sponse to four questions and is not intended to provide closure. That is, the chapter asks a series of awkward questions as a prelude to future feminist dialogues on inter-national law, acknowledging that the answers are not mine to give or to formulate, and may require my silence, and my cultivating of space for others to speak over me. Following Otomo, thus 'paying attention to the form and tropes of language is one alternative way . . . of responding' which I regard as a relevant and necessary response to the range of texts drawn on throughout the book.[16] While Otomo uses poetry and prose, I have played, subtly to be sure, with the form of this chapter, as well as rethinking the sources considered as informing feminist dialogues on international law, to start (end) with those that exist in my home/s and which challenge me to re-flect on how I position my voice in relation to key texts.

My first question asks about the preoccupation with law and legal structures in feminist dialogues.[17] I incorporate Moira Buffini's play *Welcome to Thebes*, to question the assumed and embedded expectations of feminist dialogues on inter-national law.[18] My second question asks what is condoned and left unspoken in the requirement that international law 'saves women' and/or 'includes women', as a response to feminist dialogues. I problematise the convergence of the women, peace, and security agenda with the counterterrorism agenda and consider the pos-sibility of feminist disengagement from the women, peace, and security agenda.[19] I consider the 1915 Peace Resolutions as a different feminist placeholder to con-temporary gender and conflict approaches, before contrasting writing on nuclear disarmament with the women, peace, and security agenda and Hamzić's rendering of the violence of law as inescapable.[20] My third question turns to transnational

---

[15] Lewis, 'Questions of Presence' (n 1) 8–9.

[16] Yoriko Otomo, *Unconditional Life: The Postwar International Law Settlement* (Oxford 2016) 19, 161.

[17] Joan W Scott, *The Fantasy of Feminist History* (Duke University Press 2011); Maria Aristodemou, 'A Constant Craving for Fresh Brains and a Taste for Decaffeinated Neighbours' (2014) 25(1) European Journal of International Law 35.

[18] Moira Buffini, *Welcome to Thebes* (Faber & Faber 2010).

[19] Fionnuala Ní Aoláin, 'The "War on Terror" and Extremism: Assessing the Relevance of the Women, Peace and Security Agenda' (2016) 92 International Affairs 275.

[20] See further: Lela Costin, 'Feminism, Pacifism, Internationalism and the 1915 International Congress of Women' (1982) 5(3-4) Women's Studies International Forum 301; Felicity Hill, 'Reaching Critical Will' in Irmgard Heilberger and Barbara Lochbihler (eds), *Listen to Women for a Change* (WILPF 2010) 26 <http://www.barbara-lochbihler.de/fileadmin/user_upload/pdf/2011f/GEU_Bookproject_E_5_bm.pdf> last accessed 31 May 2018; Hamzić (n 8).

feminist projects outside of legal spaces as learning structures for future feminist dialogues on international law. I highlight responses to violence by feminist scholars that work outside of the law to challenge the turn to carceral and punitive models as a response to violence against women and sexual violence within global governance. I draw on Tamale's analysis of naked protest in Uganda, alongside analysis of Chinese feminist networks that mobilise digital modalities, to challenge gendered knowledge structures within feminist approaches that engage international law.[21] My final question asks how to listen to voices not visible/heard, and to render visible the naivety of my own desire for dialogues without recognition of the colonial and raced histories that give me voice and credence: histories I need not search for in the international as they exist to shape my everyday. As such, the chapter ends with the words of indigenous women from Australia, where I was born under the legacy of white settler privilege. I place indigenous Australian feminisms alongside/ in dialogue with the voice of Black British feminists whose struggles in Britain are not replicated in my own experience in the UK as a white migrant from a settler colony.

I argue that integral to the redevelopment of contemporary feminist approaches to international law is the insertion of feminist dialogues that explain the conditions of privilege in feminist spaces. As such, the study of authority within international law at once looks to how authority is gained and supported through gender law reform and looks to the conditions of the (assumed) authority to speak. Consequently, I make a space in dialogues on international law through listening to the understanding of knowledge, subjectivity, law and gender, race, and governance from feminist voices not usually heard in response to, or asked about, the contours of international law reform. I do not identify these as simple or even complete answers, rather as starting points for future feminist and mainstream dialogues. I struggled throughout the writing of this chapter with the question of how to make the act of listening present in a piece of writing. I argue that a crucial aspect of feminist dialogues is for women or feminists occupying spaces of privilege to make and to take the time to listen and hear at whose cost that privilege is gained. This chapter therefore asks at what, and at whose, cost feminist voices are invited to speak within the spaces of global governance. Underlying the chapter is the knowledge that feminist legal projects must work 'within' accepted legal paradigms/narratives, as well as from a position 'outside' mainstream perceptions of law/international law.

I shift between texts addressing the international and texts drawn from the homes in which I find myself—contemporary Britain and Australia—to render visible local feminist voices that articulate the ignorance of my privilege and the foundations from which my privilege is permitted to exist: the colonial stories and violence that

[21] Sylvia Tamale, 'Nudity, Protest and the Law in Uganda' (Inaugural Professorial Lecture, Makerere University, 28 October 2016) <http://www.searcwl.ac.zw/downloads/Tamale_Inaugural_Lecture.pdf> last accessed 31 May 2018; Cheryl M Hendricks and Desiree Lewis, 'Epistemic Ruptures in South African Standpoint Knowledge-Making: Academic Feminism and #FeesMustFall' (2016) 4(1) Gender Questions 18; Jia Tan, 'Digital Masquerading: Feminist Media Activism in China' (2017) 13(2) Crime, Media, Culture 171; Wang Zheng, 'Detention of the Feminist Five in China' (2015) 41(2) Feminist Studies 476.

I do not have to endure to experience myself as a speaking subject. I argue that listening to the raced and colonial histories in our homes is a crucial first step for feminist dialogues, or any dialogues, on international law. Consequently, it is not possible for me to speak on international law, on law, without making space for Black British feminisms to be heard and without making space to listen to indigenous Australian voices that identify me as a colonial subject. Likewise, the normative contributions of lesbian, trans, and gender queer feminists who are often entreated to account for their sexuality before speaking inform my approach. This renders necessary a need to recentre feminist dialogues that examine the discourses of heteronormativity that have made gender law reform within global governance possible. I argue that this requires a conscious acknowledgment that 'international law narrowly shapes acceptable female identities and operates to control and suppress female sexuality' and the plural subjectivities that enter feminist dialogues once this is recognised, listened to, and prioritised within feminist epistemologies are critically important to future dialogues on gender law reform within global governance.[22] In this way a feminist dialogue acknowledges 'everyday encounters with diversity can only be understood in the context of global and local inequalities, as well as the translocational subject positions of the people who take part in them'.[23] The chapter concludes that to enter feminist dialogues on international law there must be quiet and listening with the goal of undoing the violent imperial histories that continue to enact on non-white bodies, queer bodies, non-normatively abled persons, and in territories outside of the West. Without this work gender law reform within global governance will remain not-feminist.

2. Law as Authority

I want to begin this section with an extract from the closing section in Berman's article, 'In the Wake of Empire'; an odd choice after text specifically addressing the need to bring non-legal feminist voices into international legal feminist dialogues. Berman's work, alongside Anghie, Nesiah, and Kapur, addresses the colonial legacies that construct and inform international law and thus are important elements of the dialogues I am addressing and listening to in this chapter.[24] Berman draws in desire as a necessary component of understanding the political domination that characterises the imperial legacy of international law:

[22] Loveday Hodson, 'Queering the Terrain: Lesbian Identity and Rights in International Law' (2017) 7(1) feminists@law 1.

[23] Agata Lisiak, 'Other Mothers: Encountering In/visible Femininities in Migration and Urban Contexts' (2017) 117 Feminist Review 41.

[24] Vasuki Nesiah, 'Resistance in the Age of Empire: Occupied Discourse Pending Investigation' (2006) 27(5) Third World Quarterly 903; Anthony Anghie, 'Western Discourses on Sovereignty' in Julie Evans, Ann Genovese, Alexander Reilly, and Patrick Wolfe (eds), *Sovereignty: Frontiers of Possibility* (University of Hawai'i Press 2013) 19; Ratna Kapur, *Erotic Justice: Law and the New Politics of Postcolonialism* (Routledge 2005).

Just as you think that eliminating a particular kind of political domination will cleanse law of imperial taint, so you think that controlling a particular kind of sexual desire will cleanse pragmatism of colonial fantasies. You underestimate the polymorphousness of imperial desire ... let's not imagine that 'getting down to pragmatic law reform' means that desire can be set aside: desire is irreducible. Don't deny your desire, tell me of its quality.[25]

This short piece of writing, and the long article it is drawn from, has always struck me as one of the most important pieces of international law text, likely read by and familiar to most scholars in the field. Berman's searing transportation of empire into international law's present continues to ask readers of their desire and complicity in international legal histories as they are lived now. Likewise, Nesiah challenges the continued production of empire within international law and counsels for attention to international legal histories, as unfolding and requiring recognition that a 'different political imagination is grounding our vocabularies of resistance, we also need a different conception of time and history'.[26] In this section I want to explore the notion of desire, colonial fantasies, and law reform in the dialogues that form feminist writing on international law. I draw on the work of Scott, who interrogates the fantasy of feminist history, to ask about the fantasy of feminist law and authority granted to (international) law when it is the site of feminist agitation for change.[27] I use this section to question the turn to law as site of authority and solution for feminist endeavours. Following Scott, I want to ask what happens to gender law reform within international law when a feminist methodology acknowledges that:

Gender is, in other words, not the assignment of roles to physically different bodies, but the attribution of meaning to something that always alludes definition ... The vertigo that ensures ... deprives her of the certainty of her categories of analysis and leaves her searching only for the right questions to ask.[28]

While in the following section I explore the violence that feminist legal theory is potentially complicit in when appealing to law's authority, in this section, I am interested in the desire—and fantasies—exposed by the turn to law for solutions. The placement of woman as subject that occurs within the turn to law's authority reasserts woman as the category of analysis, potentially reifying sex difference at the same time.

To paraphrase Berman, above, imperial desire has a polymorphous quality.[29] The histories of gender law reform draw out the polymorphous nature of international law, from British women's interference in the lives of women living under the Palestinian Mandate to the production of the DRC as the 'rape capital of the world'.[30] The co-optation of feminist knowledge into imperial law—accepted,

[25] Nathaniel Berman, 'The Grotius Lecture Series: In the Wake of Empire' (1999) 14(6) American University International Law Review 1515, 1551.

[26] Nesiah, 'Resistance' (n 24) 922.   [27] Scott (n 17).   [28] ibid 6.

[29] Berman (n 25).

[30] Ellen Fleischmann, *The Nation and its 'New' Women: The Palestinian Women's Movement 1920–1949* (University of California Press 2003) 64–65; on the construction of the DRC as the 'rape capital' of the world, see Ngwarsungu Chiwengo, 'When Wounds and Corpses Fail to Speak: Narratives of Violence and Rape in Congo' (2008) 28(1) Comparative Studies of South Asia, Africa and the Middle East 78.

digested, forgotten—is not, for the most part, at the forefront of feminist dialogues on international law. Following Nesiah, however, the challenge is not to simply place this knowledge within the text, dialogue, and discussion but to listen to what is being said: there is something at the core, within dominant and mainstream feminist epistemologies, that attaches and adheres to the structures of knowledge of empire, imperialism, and colonialism. Recalling chapter 1, Nesiah writes of a 're-orientating of our critical energies from merely taking sides in a debate, to questioning the material and ideological lens that interpolates the debate'.[31] This, it seems, is larger than feminist approaches within international law can hear or accommodate and seems to ask for a turning away from law to listen elsewhere. This, I argue, is because of the complicity of law, international law, in the production of empire through deep-set desires that form the very contours which permit speaking subjects to act and be heard within international legal spaces.

Feminist legal projects, however, have—while attempting to diminish law's patriarchal power—turned back to law to give authority and voice to their desires for a transformative law. The result, as I have examined in chapters 2 and 3, in particular, has been a liberal-radical-cultural feminist set of gender law reforms and the production of liberal-radical female subjects dually constructed as victim and agent: vulnerable to sexual violence or available to prop up existing power structures via participation. Likewise, the reiteration of gender as woman and the production of gender to mean women within law recalls a cultural feminist approach that attends to women's difference from men in a manner that risks continued essentialism rather than the undoing of gendered subjects. Women, as either victims or agents, are permitted into the domain of international law as speaking subjects only to the extent that they envisage an international law that does not examine its own legacies of gender, of empire, of racisms, of homophobia and transphobia, of ableism, of material depravity and excesses. I have, for the most part, counselled a reimagining of feminist knowledge to inform the foundations of international law via the welcoming of plural and split subjects into legal frameworks. The alternative counsel offered in this chapter is to take feminist knowledge elsewhere and away from international law due to the complicity of gender law reform in the reproduction of empire. This would not be a failure to speak—or develop dialogues on international law—rather an acknowledgement that feminist dialogues on international law are circumscribed by the desire to maintain the structures of international law as part of feminist futures.

I am reminded of Moira Buffini's theatre piece *Welcome to Thebes*, set in '[a] city named Thebes, somewhere in the twenty-first century'.[32] The play follows the post-conflict period in the fictional (yet strangely familiar) city of Thebes where the new President, Eurydice, has secured peace and welcomes to Thebes, Theseus, the President of the neighbouring state and regional hegemon, Athens. The play follows the dialogues of the two Presidents, of the new (all female) cabinet of Thebes, child soldiers, and Antigone, Eurydice's niece. The arrogance of Theseus is juxtaposed

---

[31] Vasuki Nesiah, 'The Ground Beneath her Feet: "Third World" Feminisms' (2003) 4(3) Journal of International Women's Studies 30, 30.

[32] Buffini (n 18) 1.

with Eurydice's attempts to rebuild a city not dependent on the greed of neighbouring states. The following dialogue demonstrates the tension between Eurydice and Theseus—invested with gendered meanings, civilising motifs, and the material effects of economic inequalities reproduced as Other:

Theseus   What happens when a whole state
             When a place descends into—fuck
             It's like you bred some different kind of war out here

Eurydice   All war is savage, Theseus, whether it's fought
             close quarters with machetes or from afar with missiles
             and computer guided bombs. Are you more civilised
             because you can't hear people scream?

Theseus   Your war was bestial

Eurydice   Our war was very human[33]

Later in the play, Eurydice converses with the Theban Minister of Finance, Euphroysne, about strategy when it looks like Theseus will withdraw Athens's support for Thebes, after Eurydice rejected his flirtations with her. Eurydice underscores the model of governance she envisages with a project of peace which Euphrosyne argues must be defended with violence:

Eurydice   It must not come to that
             Our mission must remain a peaceful one
             Or what have we become?

Euphrosyne   Our government is unique in all the world
             It is worth fighting for

Eurydice   Our government will be unique if we can maintain power
             without resort to violence[34]

However, the male characters—Theseus and various military leaders—insist on reading Eurydice as woman first. Tydeus, leader of the opposition in Thebes, tells Theseus:

Tydeus   Eurydice will never hold it back
             The very female nature is chaotic
             They can't structure or impose
             They won't inspire respect[35]

The gendered language of war and peace, of greed and military manoeuvres, inflect Buffini's play. The play opens with the story of Meagara who tells the story of her rape by soldiers and subsequent becoming a solider herself, proclaiming herself no longer in need of law. As Meagara speaks to her fellow soldiers they come across the body of Polynice, the former military leader, now dead. The conversation that follows suggests that who they were fighting for was never clear.

---

[33] ibid 57.   [34] ibid 92.   [35] ibid 102.

Buffini's play cleverly threads these different motifs, of gender, violence, state-hood, transnational relations, transitional justice, and power into a play that also explores desire. Drawing on both Berman and Buffini's work and thinking through the contributions of feminist approaches to international law, the circumscribed spaces of gender law reform, and gender's entrenched relations with other vectors of power raises questions about the expectations contained in the turn to law. I explore this further in the next section.

3. Convergences?

In Buffini's play *Welcome to Thebes*, Eurydice is the new *female* President of the war-torn city of Thebes. Theseus is the *male* President of neighbouring power, Athens. However, it can be argued, perhaps should be argued, that the gender of these char-acters matters little—it is not Eurydice's femaleness that distinguishes her approach from Theseus's accusations of a bestial war. Likewise, it is not Theseus's maleness that makes his greed, proclivity for violence, his sexism and racism so objectionable, as the character of Theseus illustrates the intersection of patriarchy, capitalism, and greed. While Buffini usefully deploys motifs of gender to exaggerate the character-isation, what is interesting—and powerful—about Eurydice is not her gender but her feminist commitment to anti-militarism and non-violent political strategy.

The distinction between feminist knowledge and women's knowledge is impli-cated in the distinction I have drawn throughout this book between feminist meth-odologies and gender law reform. I have argued that this distinction is crucially important as a mechanism to acknowledge the gender structures and knowledge that already operate within international legal structures; without this, gender law reform seems destined to continue to underpin existing legal relations rather than transform them. Equally, the distinction between feminist knowledge and women's knowledge is important to dislodge the self-appointed positioning of specific women's lives as informing the contours of feminist messages and methodologies but must remain mindful of the real violence inflicted on gendered bodies, globally. Feminist legal strategies that ignore this distinction construct a feminist subject that incorporates their own world view, creating 'representations without interrogating them, or recognising their importance in shaping the subject position middle-class white woman'.[36] Implicit in such a world view is the white, Western feminist's re-lation to 'Other' women—where differences 'are managed by allowing "Others" voices and space within already established forums'.[37] The consequence is a need to 'connect subjectivity to the relations of the ruling'; with recognition that this in-cludes ruling (or dominant) feminist accounts on law.[38]

This section takes seriously the potential of feminist legal scholars disengaging from gender law reform within global governance because of the complicity that co-optation produces, not only in the structures of international law but equally in the histories of violence and displacement that are integral to international legal

---

[36] Moreton-Robinson (n 9) xxiv.   [37] ibid xviii.   [38] ibid xxi.

histories, past and present. In the final sections of this chapter I attempt to engage the silence required to hear difference within feminist dialogues on international law.

To imagine disengagement from law reform this section engages discussion of the eighth women, peace, and security resolution. The eight women, peace, and security resolutions issued by the UN Security Council have represented one of the most important sites of gender law reform within global governance since the year 2000.[39] In chapter 2 I examined the impact of the women, peace, and security framework on gender training within NATO. In chapter 3 I described the features of the women, peace, and security framework and how it provides a good example of which feminist projects become co-opted into gender law reform—pushing important feminist dialogues to the peripheries of feminist knowledge on global governance and fragmenting the representation and spaces of gender law reform. In chapter 5 I analysed the work of the Peacebuilding Commission (PBC), demonstrating the fragmented response to the women, peace, and security framework in the PBC's work. In this section I pick up these threads to provide an analysis of the authority of the Security Council to authorise violence (the use of force under article 42 of the UN Charter) and the role the veto power of the permanent members of the Security Council plays in the perpetuation of violence as a technique of global governance. Framing my engagement is the understanding that all law, not just that of the Security Council, 'cannot be other-than-violence'.[40] This is a knowledge contained and known in the history of law as empire.

Drawing on the work of Ní Aoláin, I examine the convergence of the women, peace, and security agenda from the UN Security Council with the countering terrorism agenda, while also noting the alignment of the targeted sanctions regime to justify the targeted strikes conducted by the US since 2007, in states unwilling or unable to implement antiterrorism measures, and the impact of arms sales by the permanent members of the Security Council on peace and security.[41] The importance of the awkward juxtaposition of women/feminism in feminist dialogues becomes apparent in this section. I reference the 1915 Peace Resolutions—as a forgotten international legal text drafted by women and, more importantly, expressing a feminist commitment to peace—alongside the background feminist work that lead to the 2017 Nobel Prize being awarded to ICAN (The International Campaign to Abolish Nuclear Weapons).[42] The tension between women as subject and feminism as method thus becomes central to a framing of feminist dialogues on international law. I therefore problematise women as the subject of feminism prior to arguing that the deployment of women, as feminist subject, reproduces the imperial, military mindset of Theseus.[43] Furthermore, in the words of Moreton-Robinson, '[a]ll women live with the history of their subjectivity but are not necessarily conscious

---

[39] Heathcote, *The Law on the Use of Force* (n 14) ch 2.   [40] Hamzić (n 8) 84.

[41] Ní Aoláin (n 19).

[42] Resolutions Adopted by the International Congress of Women, The Hague, Holland: 28 April–1 May 1915; Felicity Hill, 'I Can—Can You?' (2007) 100 Chain Reaction 40.

[43] Scott (n 17); Denise Riley, *'Am I that Name?': Feminism and the Category of Women in History* (Palgrave 1988).

of its impact on their behaviour and attitudes'.[44] A feminist dialogue must, therefore, be developed through recognising Eurydice as feminist, rather than as female, while also recognising the assumptions present in the voices of feminist scholars who adopt the capacity of starting the speaking, rather than the listening.

Across the UN era, the Security Council has, through its practice, developed its remit to incorporate humanitarian crises as threats to international peace and security, developed peacekeeping as a core element of its work, and created a functional model of peace enforcement to respond to some threats to international peace and security. At the same time, significant acts of inter- and intra-state violence have remained outside of the Council's sphere of action. I will analyse in this section one site of violence pushed to the peripheries of the collective security structure: targeted strikes against terrorist actors.

Targeted strikes against terrorist actors have not been explicitly addressed by the Security Council although the Council has an extensive regime of targeted sanctions that member states, particularly the US, rely on to justify targeted strikes. By 2018 the use of unmanned drones to conduct targeted strikes occurred across a range of conflicts, in particular Pakistan, Afghanistan, Yemen, and Somalia.[45] Feminist writing on the use of targeted strikes by the US has focused on the necro-politics, the embodied effects of drone attacks, and the need for renewed feminist engagement with the law of armed conflict.[46] Less commentary has appeared to address the legitimation of the collective security apparatus via the women, peace, and security framework in the era of targeted sanctions and targeted strikes against terrorist actors.[47] In contrast to the silence of the Security Council on the use of unarmed drones to conduct targeted strikes, the overwhelming support from member states at the launch of Security Council resolution 2242 on women, peace, and security should be noted.[48] The Arria format (open) meeting of the Security Council saw a record number of states presenting statements at the debate and coincided with the alignment of the Council's counterterrorism agenda with the women, peace, and security agenda. In resolution 2242 paragraphs 11 to 13 draw together the two sites of security work and:

Calls for the greater integration by Member States and the United Nations of their agendas on women, peace and security, counter-terrorism and countering violent extremism which

---

[44] Moreton-Robinson (n 9) 183.

[45] Jessica Prukis and Jack Searle, 'Obama's Covert Drone War in Numbers: Ten Times More Strikes than Bush' (*The Bureau of Investigative Journalism*, 17 January 2017) <https://www.thebureauinvestigates.com/stories/2017-01-17/obamas-covert-drone-war-in-numbers-ten-times-more-strikes-than-bush> last accessed 31 May 2018; Alejandro Chehtman, 'The *ad bellum* Challenge of Drones: Recalibrating Permissible Use of Force' (2017) 28(1) European Journal of International Law 173.

[46] Lisa Parks, 'Drones, Vertical Mediation and the Targeted Class' (2016) 42(1) Feminist Studies 227; Lauren Wilcox, 'Drones, Swarms and Becoming-Insect: Feminist Utopias and Posthuman Politics' (2017) 116 Feminist Review 25; Lauren Wilcox, 'Embodying Algorithmic War: Gender, Race and the Posthuman in Drone Warfare' (2017) 48(1) Security Dialogue 11; Judith Gardam, 'War, Law, Terror, Nothing New for Women' (2010) 32 Australian Feminist Law Journal 61.

[47] Dianne Otto, 'The Security Council's Alliance of Gender Legitimacy: The Symbolic Capital of Resolution 1325' in Hilary Charlesworth and Jean-Marc Coicaud (eds), *Fault Lines of International Legitimacy* (Cambridge University Press 2010) 239.

[48] Security Council Resolution 2122 (18 October 2013) UN Doc S/RES/2122; Security Council Resolution 2242 (13 October 2015) UN Doc S/RES/2242.

can be conducive to terrorism, requests the Counter-Terrorism Committee (CTC) and the Counter-Terrorism Committee Executive Directorate (CTED) to integrate gender as a cross-cutting issue throughout the activities within their respective mandates ...[49]

As a consequence of this provision in Resolution 2242, the Counter-Terrorism Committee (CTC) now includes a focus area titled 'The Role of Women in Countering Terrorism and Violent Extremism'. Incorporating the expertise of UN Women, this focus area maintains a dialogue on women's role as perpetrators of terrorist acts, victims of terrorism, and supporters of counterterrorism efforts. This draws on UN Women's Global Programme for Preventing Violent Extremism which develops country specific programmes and forums. Despite the call for the CTC to 'integrate gender as a cross-cutting issue' the CTC's additional focus areas—border management, human rights, information and communications technologies, law enforcement, and terrorism financing—are all absent of any gender work, although both the Security Council and the CTC include some references to women and gender within the reports and resolutions on foreign terrorist fighters.[50] This structure reiterates the design of gender strategies described in chapters 2 and 3: calling on the expertise of UN Women, appointed as gender experts, becomes the technique for integrating gender, while this work remains fragmented from the larger work of the institutional body. At the same time these are projects focused on women as actors, victims, and allies rather than sites for the deployment of feminist praxis. Through this work, the expertise of UN Women continues to expand across the specialised regimes within global governance yet within those specialised regimes, such as the counterterrorism agenda and the work of the CTC, gender expertise remains a separate sphere of reference, indeed a specialised regime of its own centred on the lives of women.

I am interested in the CTC and its policy and practice as a space where feminism might say no. Hamzić posits a similar argument in response to the Security Council's attention to LGBT individuals from Syria and Iraq who have suffered from the violence of ISIS, as a mechanism for developing the authority of the Security Council as an arena for good contrasted to the 'evil' of ISIS/terrorists.[51] Rather than advocating for the further expansion of gender to integrate into the work of the CTC, following Khalili, I am wondering about how

... the confluence of gendering and counterinsurgency practice works to create particular imperial hierarchies in which one's gender does not tell us anything about one's location in the hierarchies, and where different masculinities and femininities can coexist simultaneously if inflected through the lens of racialisation and class.[52]

---

[49] UNSC Res 2242 (2015) para 11.

[50] UN Security Council Resolution 2396 (23 December 2017) UN Doc S/RES/2396 paras 31, 38, 40.

[51] Hamzić (n 8) 90.

[52] Laleh Khalili, 'Gendered Practices of Counterinsurgency' (2010) 37 Review of International Studies 1471, 1476.

Khalili's approach challenges the isolated articulation of gender absent analysis of additional power structures, to better understand where gender is used to underscore and legitimate existing power relations. Khalili writes of 'the seam of encounter where genders are inflected through racial, class, or imperial hierarchies', warning of the risks associated with feminist scholars and actors attempting to insert and add gender law reform on to counterterrorism work. Khalili's work, moreover, calls for the identification of gender as a tool to engage the racial, class, and imperial hierarchies that deploy gender and sexuality to do their work.[53] For Khalili the 'colonial feminism of today deploys the language of humanitarian rescue'.[54] This reiterates Nesiah's study of humanitarianism and chimes with the necessity of gender as a process, a methodology that, in the words of Scott, 'alludes definition'.[55] The settling of gender's definition, in contrast, entrenches the gender binary of m and f, while distracting attention from the techniques through which gender is inflected through the raced, classed, ableist, heteronormative, and imperial dimensions of law.

The Security Council's bringing together of the counterterrorism and countering violent extremism agendas with the women, peace, and security framework, via paragraphs 11–13 of Security Council resolution 2242, must be read alongside writing like that of Khalili to remember that the women, peace, and security framework, thus far, has consistently deployed feminist approaches that are best described as US liberal feminist, radical feminist, and cultural feminist approaches. Each of these approaches has a limited theory of race, class, colonialism/imperialism, and ableism, and the articulation of sexuality within them remains largely derived from heteronormative lives.[56]

The Security Council's incapacity to respond to violations of international law, such as the use of force by the US on the territory of foreign states ostensibly to halt terrorism, must be rendered present in the discussion of integrating gender into the work of the CTC. However, making visible ongoing violence by the US renders the continued turn to the Security Council by feminist and gender actors difficult—as this requires condemnation (which would of course make the amenability of feminist projects to the Security Council's work impossible) or acceptance of the status quo of the privileges given to the permanent members of the Security Council via the veto power. Likewise, the history of human rights abuses by powerful states in the torture and detention of suspected terrorist actors must be rendered present in the articulation of gender perspectives on counterterrorism. Racial profiling, the gendering and un-gendering of civilians in decisions to deploy lethal force, and the cavalier expansion of the doctrine of self-defence, must be features of gender perspectives on counterterrorism.[57] The link between targeted sanctions—which include sanctions against perpetrators of sexual violence in armed conflict after Security Council resolution 1960—and targeted strikes as a mechanism to halt the

---

[53] ibid 1484.   [54] ibid 1488.

[55] Scott (n 17) 6; Vasuki Nesiah, 'From Berlin to Bonn to Baghdad: A Space for Infinite Justice' (2004) 17 Harvard Human Rights Journal 75.

[56] Janet Halley, 'Take a Break from Feminism?' in Karen Knop (ed), *Gender and Human Rights* (Oxford University Press 2004) 78.

[57] Wilcox, 'Drones, Swarms and Becoming-Insect' (n 46).

actions of suspected terrorist actors should raise further concerns about the very possibility of an alignment of the women, peace, and security framework and the Security Council's countering terrorism and violent extremism work.[58]

Kirby and Shepherd write of the 'futures past' of the Security Council's women, peace, and security framework and identify the feminist peace projects from over a century ago that sit behind the women, peace, and security resolutions, certainly the creation of Security Council resolution 1325.[59] Kirby and Shepherd thus call for a recognition that the Women's International League for Peace and Freedom (WILPF)

> never held that a gender perspective meant attention only to a set of specific 'women's issues', such as the victimization of women and girls in conflict, although that was a major part of its concern. On the contrary, several generations of activists set themselves against not only gender violence, but also militarism, white supremacy, global capitalism and the state system itself. The contemporary WILPF platform retains such policy prescriptions as 'total world-wide disarmament'.[60]

The authority of the Security Council to authorise military force, the reality of the Security Council in turning a blind eye to the illegal use of military force—and human rights abuses in the name of security—by its permanent members and their allies, and the legitimacy the Security Council gains through writing in gender law reform, challenges the reception and enlargement of WILPF's goals with respect to disarmament and antimilitarism. Security Council resolution 2370 on financing terrorism, addressing the flow of weapons and small arms to terrorists, for example, contains no gender language and is disconnected from the women, peace, and security agenda.[61] Ultimately, the authority gained by some feminist actors in the use of the Security Council for the production of gender law reforms is necessarily co-opted into the power of the Security Council to authorise force.

In contrast, key actors in WILPF have, elsewhere, away from the Security Council, and as a challenge to the military activities of the permanent members of the Security Council, mobilised international energy to create the Treaty on the Non-Proliferation of Nuclear Weapons, through the work of ICAN. This extends the legacy of WILPF into the twenty-first century and recalls the distinction between female and feminist praxis discussed above. Former WILPF Secretary-General, Felicity Ruby, writes of the complicity of the permanent members of the Security Council in the sale of arms and notes the references to anti-militarisation that were left out of the final draft of the Security Council resolution that became known as 1325.[62] Long time WILPF member, Rebecca Johnson writes on the importance of nuclear non-proliferation and the need to

---

[58] Security Council Resolution 1960 (16 December 2010) UN Doc S/RES/1960.

[59] Paul Kirby and Laura J Shepherd, 'The Futures Past of the Women, Peace and Security Agenda' (2016) 92(2) International Affairs 373.

[60] ibid 391.

[61] Security Council Resolution 2370 (2 August 2017) UN Doc S/RES/2370.

[62] Felicity Ruby, 'Security Council Resolution 1325: A Tool for Conflict Prevention?' in Gina Heathcote and Dianne Otto (eds), *Rethinking Peacekeeping, Gender Equality and Collective Security* (Palgrave 2014).

challenge and dismantle patriarchal assumptions and practices on personal as well as political levels. Never easy, this means taking on friends and colleagues as well as exposing the hypocrisy of governments that point fingers at non-state terrorists and declare an unending 'war on terrorism', while expanding military alliances like NATO and arming themselves with more bombs, guns, missiles, drones and all kinds of weapons.[63]

The 1915 Peace Resolutions likewise recognised that women's rights were an embedded component of the peace project that was being imagined during World War I and which was subsequently insufficiently realised through the creation of the League of Nations.[64] Feminist peace projects ask different types of questions and benefit from invoking gender as a process, unsettled, alluding definition, pursuing feminist methodologies as a means to ask more questions; to listen with greater care; to question the turn to law as a mechanism for peace when the same structures of law construct the conditions for the maintenance of war.

Tudor examines the conditions of political communities that shift from the reification of a gender binary to argue for 'a conceptualisation of entangled power relations that does not rely on fixed, pre-established categories, but defines subjectivity through risk in political struggle'.[65] The current configuration of gender law reform—as space of authority with regard to global governance—has been unable to address the gender binary or, more accurately, has entrenched a binary account of gender in global governance and thus failed to unsettle the pre-established categories of gender. The alignment on women, peace, and security with the countering terrorism and violent extremism agenda, furthermore, beyond a narrow reproduction of the gender binary provides a normalising of law's authority. Thus, naming gender law reform, such as the women, peace, and security resolutions, as spaces of designating gender as a tool to normalise specific bodies which are sexed, gender, heteronormative, and able-bodied draws out a disquiet with regard to gender law reform that attracts and grants authority to specific feminist traditions, centred on the subject of woman, at considerable cost. Alongside the legitimating of a specific gender regime and the normalising of the violence of both states and the collective security apparatus are the entrenched and unquestioned heteronormative relations preformed in the scripting of women and men as the gendered bodies placed in harm's way and/or at risk of recruitment by terrorist networks. The entwined racist, gendered, ableist, cis-gendered, and heteronormative categorisations have not, as yet, been challenged via gender law reform on countering terrorism and arguably are reified by the turn to the Security Council as an authoritative space for gender law reform.

[63] Rebecca Johnson, 'World Courts for Women: Against War, For Peace' (*Open Democracy*, 25 January 2016) <https://www.opendemocracy.net/5050/rebecca-johnson/courts-of-women-resisting-violence-and-war> last accessed 31 May 2018.

[64] Freya Baetens, 'International Congress of Women (1915)' in Rüdiger Wolfrum (ed), *Max Planck Encyclopedia of Public International Law* (Oxford University Press 2010).

[65] Alyosxa Tudor, 'Dimensions of Transnationalism' (2018) 117 Feminist Review 20.

4. Not Law?

In this section, mindful of the undercurrents contained in the turn by feminist actors to the Security Council, and thinking through Khalili's identification of the seam of the encounter between gender and imperialism that must be held present in feminist knowledge, I muse on spaces of disengagement, of turning away from the authority of law to think through feminist praxis differently. I pay attention to non-legal feminist action as a component of feminist dialogues on international law, exploring how protest and micro-level interventions might shift approaches to gender law reform towards dialogues on feminist methodologies, inside and outside of legal structures. This section questions gender law reform as the central dialogue from feminist scholars working on international law and considers how global governance might be approached through alternative, non-legal methodologies that embrace new media and protest. This approach asks which voices, practices, and histories monopolise the histories and formations of feminism and what is regarded as feminist knowledge.

I introduce three sets of knowledge in this section. First, I present Tamale's analysis of naked protest in Uganda as representative of a knowledge practice that engages resistance, gender, and power that 'entails a conceptualization of the body as an instrument of control as well as a source of disruption'.[66] I use Tamale's analysis as a link to the study of bodies and to centre non-Western knowledge practices as integral to feminist approaches to international law. Second, I draw in Nesiah's accounts of political imagination, feminisms and counterterrorism, and the need to historicise feminist 'achievements' within global spaces.[67] The third set of knowledge identifies the Youth Feminist Action School and technofeminist developments amongst feminist networks in China to interrupt the text with an account of feminist media activism in China.[68] Tan links contemporary feminist digital activism in China to the history of gender law reform in global governance and challenges the preoccupation with Western feminist knowledge practices that have fairly effectively dominated feminist approaches to international law. The section sees an echo across feminist knowledge practices from East Africa to China. While both Uganda and China, as sovereign states, encompass diverse communities that cannot be generalised, when Othered in feminist scholarship both become particularised and removed from visibility in terms of thinking through and understanding knowledge production. I place both in this section as sites of feminist traditions and interrogations of global governance that have been offered insufficient voice and recognition in feminist dialogues on international law.

---

[66] Tamale (n 21).
[67] Nesiah, 'Resistance' (n 24); Vasuki Nesiah, 'Feminism as Counter-Terrorism: The Seduction of Power' in Margaret L Satterthwaite and Jayne C Huckerby (eds), *Gender, National Security and Counter-Terrorism: Human Rights Perspectives* (Routledge 2013) 127; Vasuki Nesiah, 'Priorities of Feminist Legal Research: A Sketch, A Draft Agenda, A Hint of An Outline ...' (2011) 1 feminists@law <http://journals.kent.ac.uk/index.php/feministsatlaw/article/view/20/83> last accessed 31 May 2018.
[68] Tan (n 21).

Tamale writes:

When women strip in protest, at best they rewrite and overwrite the dominant sexual script associated with their nude bodies. At worst they render it illegible. It is an insult to undermine their mobilizing potential and their ability to rally against oppression. Naked protesting women are stretching the personal to relate it to the political in a dramatic fashion. Society must therefore 'read' their naked bodies as powerful icons of defiance and not as the objects of sexual display.[69]

Tamale's study of naked protest in Uganda examines her own initial sense of feeling 'shocked and horrified; embarrassed and ashamed' at the protest at Makerere University by Stella Nyanzi before examining the history of reading and protesting women's bodies in Uganda. In drawing in legal texts, the regulation of pornography, and studies of power Tamale argues:

Female naked protests represent a resistance and subversion of the dominant scripts engraved on women's bodies—scripts of subordination, passivity, sexuality, subservience, vulnerability, etc. Hence through the process of naked protests, women engage in a re-scripting and reconfiguration of their bodies. African women have employed this strategy against the wielders of power for many generations.[70]

Tamale's account draws together the complexity and diversity of African women's knowledge: a tool for reading the international with the legacy of gender and imperialism in the colonial encounter. At once 'read' through British laws and also understood through Ugandan custom, rendered meaningful in religious discourses and thought through in terms of gendered knowledge of age, power, and resistance, Tamale's account asks as many questions of feminist approaches to international law as it does of the Ugandan state's use of anti-pornography legislation to regulate feminist protest. A transnational feminist approach might link Tamale's reading of naked protest in Africa with the gendered insults constructed in Thailand against Yingluck Shinawatra's presidency that were directed at her body and femininity, and voiced through a language of disgust ('Yingluck Shinawatra's opponents so frequently alluded to her sexuality and her maternity to undermine her'), or with the shaming of Muslim commentator, Yassmin Abdel-Magied in Australia.[71] Gendered encounters embedded in race, religion, class, power and told through stories of the female body, rendered repulsive, always readable, always gendered, disruptive, resistant, sit underneath the gender law reform in global governance, present and yet particularised, silenced for the disruptive power and histories of knowledge that they hold.

Nesiah examines similar convergences of power, bodies, and representation that always require a looking outside of law to understand the conditions and silencing through which the law speaks. Nesiah calls for feminist scholars to 'be intellectually

[69] Tamale (n 21) 26.   [70] ibid 31.
[71] Rachel Harrison, 'Dystopia as Liberation: Disturbing Femininities in Contemporary Thailand' (2017) 116 Feminist Review 64; Yassmin Abdel-Magied, 'A Little Too Close to the Sun: Advocacy in the Modern Age' (2017) 56 Griffith Review 18.

robust and subversive of received truth claims' which she then links to a need to shift away from

defining feminist research agendas by celebrating and fortifying particular 'achievements', [so that] historicizing those achievements and their conditions of possibility should itself be the agenda. The agendas of twenty years ago cannot be the agenda of today; different historical circumstances call for different approaches. In other words, creative intellectual renewal and political relevance both demand that we develop a critical political imagination that constantly has its own assumptions in its crosshairs.[72]

Nesiah's recognition of the contested and diverse spaces of gender and feminist theorising outside of international legal feminisms requires an examination of formations of subjectivity within feminist thinking and within law. A feminist appraisal of authority within international law might commence, therefore, with the unspoken knowledge practices that sit behind dominant formations of feminism within global governance. Likewise, Nesiah's analysis of institutional convergences between feminist agendas and counterterrorism strategies opens up the space to ask 'whose feminism?' in such a way that knowledge production and subject formation within feminist approaches are brought to the fore.[73] This approach requires a loosening on the strictures of feminist legal theories that centre both law and a feminist subject defined through specific knowledge, histories, and encounters. The naked protest in Uganda, its engagement with colonial and precolonial legal histories, and its challenge to the neoliberal patterns of law experienced on gendered and racialised bodies is a space of feminist knowledge: intersectional, resistant, transnational.

Returning to Ahmed's analysis of transnational feminist encounters, there is a need to recognise that '[i]f transnational feminism involves crossing national borders, then we need to consider how it may do so in a way that does not simply reaffirm the border-crossings that are already taking place'.[74] While Ahmed analyses the flows of transnational labour, she also argues that 'the differences between us necessitate the dialogue'.[75] This is a dialogue that I have argued is yet to occur within gender law reform in global governance. For example, the Beijing Conference, so often engaged as an example of simultaneous transnational feminist potential and white Unitedstatesean feminist dominance, is rendered differently if the origins of feminist subjects and feminist knowledge are relocated. Zheng writes of the role of the Beijing Conference as a tool for the Chinese government to re-enter the global community:

After the brutal suppression of the students' movement in 1989 in Tiananmen Square and the international condemnation that followed, the Chinese government proposed to host the Fourth UN Conference on Women as a way to return to the international community.[76]

---

[72] Nesiah, 'Priorities' (n 67).   [73] Nesiah, 'Feminism as Counter-Terrorism' (n 67).
[74] Sara Ahmed, *Strange Encounters: Embodied Others in Postcoloniality* (Routledge 2000) 178.
[75] ibid 180.   [76] Zheng (n 21) 480.

Zheng complicates the meaning and effects of the Beijing Conference, first in acknowledging the consequent transformation of Chinese feminist agendas and, second, in demonstrating how the arrest and detention of the Feminist Five in March 2015, on the twenty-year anniversary of the Fourth UN Conference on Women, demonstrated a naivety of the Chinese state to the transnational aspect of local iterations of feminist knowledge:

> the timing of the arrest and detention of the Feminist Five reveals the national security system's sheer ignorance about—or contempt for—global feminist movements. They arrested the feminists right before International Women's Day (March 8) and the twentieth anniversary of the Fourth UN Conference on Women (March 9) where the United Nation's fifty-ninth Commission on the Status of Women was to assess global progress for women twenty years after the Beijing Declaration (Beijing+20).[77]

Furthermore, Zheng questions the role of the Chinese government and the United Nations for their failures to perceive feminist, including Chinese feminist, knowledge as relevant to security and governance encapsulated by the 'awkward silence' from the UN in response to the arrest and detention of the Feminist Five.[78] In terms of feminist dialogues, a space at the 'kitchen table' for Chinese feminist voices,[79] not as Other or stranger, but as actors giving meaning to histories and futures of feminist knowledge production is not yet realised within feminist approaches to global governance and international law.

In her study of the Feminist Five and Chinese knowledge production, Tan analyses the digital activism of the Youth Feminist Action School (YFAS) which 'creatively engages the media through the notion of "digital masquerading"' while promoting 'an all-inclusive feminism led by young, action-orientated feminists who leverage various platforms of communication to achieve their objectives'.[80] Tan draws out the idea of masquerading to examine the means through which gendered performance is both encapsulated and challenged in the various digital approaches to activism by the YFAS. On the one hand, relying on an understanding of the medium (for example, the constraint on the state in 'reading' (and thus removing) images in contrast to text) and, on the other hand, incorporating a sensibility to the risks of appearing to fall within non-Chinese histories of feminist knowledge, the YFAS are able to both perform the act of masquerading, 'remaking meanings by toying with the link between language and image' and stage 'controversial bodily performances for the media'.[81] Tan gives important examples of YFAS and the Feminist Five's use of digital manipulation and networks to speak in a space where they are otherwise silenced. At the same time, Tan reflects on the potential elitism of access to online media and the rife sexism and misogyny in digital spaces, contrasting this to YFAS as a space that can be linked to concrete political change and a new leverage of Chinese feminisms, outside of and yet in dialogue with the state. Nevertheless, Tan concludes

---

[77] ibid 481.   [78] ibid 482.

[79] Julie Mertus, 'The Kitchen Table' in Marguerite R Waller and Jennifer Rycenga (eds), *Frontline Feminisms: Women, War, and Resistance* (Routledge 2001).

[80] Tan (n 63) 173, 175.   [81] ibid 178.

with a reflection on voices not heard and not engaged in YFAS, alluding to different, intersectional exclusions and Othering. For the project at hand, Tan's analysis shifts the status quo of feminist knowledge—both in terms of form and in terms of histories. The productive use of feminist histories and engagements with the state, as well as the transnational networks—both online and in real life—demonstrate a site of knowledge that feminist approaches within global governance have discounted, or particularised.

The meaning and practices of naked protest in Uganda and the meaning and practices of digital activism amongst Chinese feminists both prod at law in different ways. They join global histories of feminist protest, only some of which have been able to inform the knowledge practices of dominant forms of feminist thinking that have been received within global governance. Following Wright, 'international law is not just the property of those who are already in positions of comfort and privilege. We need to be responsible in how we engage in the process of re-examining law on a global level'.[82] The unravelling, the silences, and the relearning what and how feminist methodologies arrive at law is an important aspect of the dialogues referred to throughout this book. The plural and split subjects within the text have histories of knowledge and histories of doing alongside contemporary practices that question the turn to law and the hoisting of specific feminist knowledge practices as the authority on law.

5. Listen

If the impress at the top of the palimpsest represents presence and absence of black women through deficiency, what forms of presence and being-ness might be revealed if, with precision and delicacy of hand, we bring to the fore the layers to be found in the depths? What other histories might be inscribed in the cross currents of triangular space in which black women reside and craft their presence and lived and ancestral connections?[83]

This book filters into its pages my own encounters with law and life. I have tried to show in this chapter that those encounters are invisible privilege markers that have given me voice and access at the cost of silencing others. This is a history of violence, gendered violence, raced violence, homophobic, able-bodied privileges, and anti-queer violence that constructs the spaces I call home; even if I have resisted and called out that violence it remains threaded into my privilege. To write feminist dialogues and to make feminist dialogues I have argued that conscious writing in of these violent histories is important to render the space for dialogue as a space that continues to open, to centre listening, and to ask for silence from and to interrupt dominant feminisms. This picks up and enlarges many of the themes and techniques

---

[82] Shelley Wright, 'The Horizon of Becoming: Culture, Gender and History after September 11' (2002) 71 Nordic Journal of International Law 215, 251.

[83] Lewis, 'Questions of Presence' (n 1) 13.

I have deployed across the book and which I describe as constituting feminist dialogues on international law.

I have found it necessary throughout the book to also, always, place feminist knowledge in dialogue with critical legal scholarship. This is in part to disrupt the ghettoising, feminist footnote effect in non-feminist scholarship, and to enrich and expand the range of topics feminist dialogues articulate as relevant to gender law reform.[84] As such, chapters 2 and 3 commenced a feminist dialogue on key contributions of critical legal scholarship—fragmentation and the study of expertise in the global order.

In chapter 2, through the focus on expertise I examined how the appointment of a gender expert has become a technique of global governance that undermines the effectiveness of gender law reform. I concluded the chapter with an introduction to intersectionality and the politics of listening as feminist methodologies. I argued that feminist action—whether in academic, activist, or policy settings—without an appreciation of intersectionality is destined for co-optation into existing governing structures. I define intersectionality as attention to the interlocking nature of power arrangements. Consequently, to write about gender and not write about race privilege, or sexuality, or ethnicity, or able-bodiedness, class, or religion as intersecting—not only in power relations but also in how knowledge is produced and understood—risks producing gender law reforms that do little to unsettle the status quo. As such, my quest for feminist dialogues on international law is about opening the space for different voices to be heard as foundational to feminist dialogues (not add-ons; foundational). I therefore also introduced Otto's articulation of the politics of listening as a necessary companion dialogue to intersectionality. As a response to the rise of gender expertise in the global order I concluded feminist methodologies that provoke feminist conversations on how knowledge is (re)produced through the work of gender expertise must be developed. I argued that to mobilise transnational feminist networks—that have histories of working against existing structures and which already speak alternative feminist knowledge practices—intersectionality provides a feminist methodology for alternative accounts to be listened to in such a way that dominant knowledge assumptions should be exposed and transformed.

The feminist dialogues introduced in chapter 2 in the analysis of gender expertise were used in chapter 3 to develop the idea of reimagining the construction of legal subjectivity to counter the effects of fragmentation. Through identifying critical legal scholarship that shifts from a fear of fragmentation in the global order toward a study of international law's refinement through the rise of diverse forums and regimes, I argued that this has the further of effect of fragmenting feminisms. I examined how fragmented feminisms occur both in the dispersal of gender law reform across a range of institutions and the narrow conception of feminist law reform accommodated within the global order. Through building on the feminist methodologies of intersectionality and the politics of listening in chapter 2, I developed plural subjectivities as a mechanism to challenge the production of the status

---

[84] Stacey Fox and Karen Hall, ' "Favourite Footnote"? Hilary Charlesworth on Feminism and International Law' (2006) 13(1) Limina: A Journal of Historical and Cultural Studies 1.

quo via gender law reform and to think about how difference might be retheorised within global governance.

I was inspired by the writing of Brah, Braidotti, and Kapur to conceive of an approach to legal subjectivity acknowledged as plural. Each theorises difference and the construction of knowledge through recognition of relational subjects whilst working to disrupt the inclusions and exclusions of knowledge structures. While Kapur's work speaks directly to international lawyers, Brah's and Braidotti's writing sits outside the discipline.[85] Bringing gender and feminist theorising from outside of law into dialogue with feminist scholarship on international law was a very conscious goal I had in the planning of the text. This was, in fact, inspired by my original introduction to the writing of Braidotti through Charlesworth and Chinkin's work, which drew on non-legal feminist writings to build early feminist analyses of international law.[86] Working within a British university with strong links to Black British feminist histories introduced me to Brah's work and, as is reflected throughout this chapter, my own history requires a dialogue with Black British and indigenous Australian writers to fully grasp and understand how my own privilege operates and is consolidated through state violence that silences women who do not look like me, speak like me, sound like me. Brah's articulation of the diasporic subject beautifully develops understanding of how communities enact privilege, how transnational encounters are lived within bodies, and speaks to how international law reproduces a male subject that is also raced. My focus on race over other vectors of difference, I hope, still permits—through the arrival of an appreciation of plural subjectivities—a continual expansion of understanding difference and centring difference as the key to speaking and, for some of us, for being silent and listening. If the fragmentation of international law into the plural structures of specialised regimes and legal adjudication is understood from a feminist perspective, I have argued, then a recognition of difference requires conversations with plural subjects to embed plural subjectivities that displace the myth of the unencumbered and isolated sovereign subject of international law.

The focus on theorising subjectivity as a site of knowledge production—defining and shaping law at its foundation—is further explored in chapter 4, which centred sovereignty and commenced a feminist dialogue for understanding state sovereignty. Beyond the plural subject, chapter 4 examines the possibility of centring the relational aspect of subjectivity and articulates split subjects as a means to describe state sovereignty. Creating the conditions for further dialogues on the compatibility and usefulness of split and plural subjects as feminist knowledge projects was my central goal, rather than articulating an overarching feminist theory. I argue that the split subject better describes how states interact and keeps the relational histories

---

[85] Rosi Braidotti, *Nomadic Subjects: Embodiment and Sexual Difference in Contemporary Feminist Theory* (2nd edn, Columbia 2011); Avtar Brah, 'Diaspora, Border and Transnational Identities' in *Cartographies of Diaspora: Contesting Identities (Gender, Racism, Ethnicity)* (Routledge 1996) 178; Ratna Kapur, *Erotic Justice: Law and the New Politics of Postcolonialism* (Glasshouse Press 2005).

[86] Hilary Charlesworth and Christine Chinkin, *The Boundaries of International Law: A Feminist Analysis* (Manchester 2000) 51–52.

of legal subjects in the present, despite the continued desire for legal subjects to be framed as isolated, or individual, units. I argued that a split subject, drawn from the moment of being born, recognises both relationality and separateness as a condition of being human, or in Wright's terminology, becoming human.[87] In examining the Responsibility to Protect and secession law, chapter 4 examined the usefulness of split subjects as a means to describe and account for global inequalities and legal change over time. The chapter, however, also stands as a cry to see the role of international law in the perpetuation of crisis in Syria—unfolding again and again as I write—that requires a larger shift than the responsibility to protect has been able to affect. I argue, rather than responding to crisis, there is a need to reimagine the foundations of international law, to hold difference, our relation to difference, and to develop strategies to work in concert rather than through coercion.[88]

Chapter 5 shifts from the analysis of sovereignty to an analysis of institutions. As gender law reform in institutions is reviewed at length in both chapters 2 and 3 via the discussions of expertise and fragmentation, chapter 5 focuses less on gender law reform in exchange for a feminist dialogue on international law which might understand the lawmaking powers and the constitutive frameworks of institutions. The chapter looked closely at three institutions—the Human Rights Council, the World Health Organisation, and the Peacebuilding Commission—weaving in a range of feminist approaches as a methodology for developing feminist dialogues on international institutions. In particular, I consider how the maternal is theorised in different feminist spaces and use this as a mechanism to question the assumption of universal patterns and experiences of childbirth in the work of the World Health Organisation, as well as a mechanism for configuring social reproduction differently. Drawing on Gedalof's account of mothering as interruption I explored the role of international institutions, such as the Human Rights Council, as working through a theory of interruption to disrupt the underlying tensions around representation. However, chapter 5 also analysed how a theory of interruption, or any account of the maternal, without attention to the politics of location and the political economy of violence, leaves feminist dialogues at risk of reproducing (rather than interrupting) histories of using privileged accounts to produce universals. As such, the study of the Peacebuilding Commission draws on the work of True and Shepherd to demonstrate how the narrow range of concerns that inform the approach of the PBC would benefit from reflection on how dialogue across feminist tensions is possible.[89]

In the account of the Peacebuilding Commission the capacity for institutions to be reimagined and rethought (interrupted) via new constitutive models that permit the General Assembly and the Security Council to act in concert is regarded as a series of hopeful acts.[90] The need for a political economy approach to peacebuilding, I argue—even in the novel institutional space of the PBC—requires dialogue with

---

[87] Wright (n 82).

[88] Valentine M Moghadam, 'Explaining Divergent Outcomes of the Arab Spring: The Significance of Gender and Women's Mobilisations' (2018) 6(4) Politics, Groups and Identities 666.

[89] Laura J Shepherd, *Gender, UN Peacebuilding and the Politics of Space: Locating Legitimacy* (Oxford University Press 2017).

[90] ibid 1.

indigenous feminisms, crip, and queer feminisms if these developments are to have lasting impact. As I have argued across the book this is not a prescriptive dialogue, rather one that centres the politics of listening and acknowledges the need for interruptions into its own assumptions. Chapter 5 demonstrates that none of these approaches constructs a feminist project in isolation and it is through placing different feminist accounts in dialogue that feminist futures within international law and global governance must be sought.

Despite focusing on engaging within the structures of international law throughout the text, this final chapter has asked what the conditions for that engagement require. I have focused on what this means in terms of the costs, in the sense of legitimating a system that continues to unleash and turn away from heinous violence, and in terms of the histories of violence that position me to call for feminist dialogues on international law. The latter means asking less what feminist dialogues on international law might be and instead interrogating the very conditions that give me access to feminist dialogues. My experience in Britain has required continual awareness, a conscious seeking out, of the Black British voices that are suppressed in political, legal, and cultural histories. One of my goals throughout the book as a whole has been to draw on Black British feminisms as a site of feminist knowledge that is distinctly not heard in international law. As a white migrant in London the shocking ease with which I could make the UK home stands as a marker of the racialised privilege that is rendered invisible in Britain. This led me to reflect on my birth home, Australia, as a product of white British histories and to read the writing of indigenous women. I found histories that are not told to white Australians and accounts of sovereignty, knowledge, and gender that are not mine to tell but must be listened to.

Charmaine Pwerle's image *My Grandmother's Country 7B* tells this story beautifully: interlocking, sweeping lines, colour, and movement shape and recall the paintings of Pwerle's mother and grandmother.[91] That this is her grandmother's country reminds me of the arrival of my foremothers in Australia, from England, Italy, France, and Finland. Unlike Black British feminist writing where stories of migration, belonging, and diaspora are central to disruptive knowledge about race and privilege in Britain, the history of Australian migration disrupts the telling of indigenous knowledges and resettles as mainstream accounts of belonging and citizenship, displacing indigenous histories and citizenship. For example, Pwerle's larger *oeuvre* contains large artworks themed around Awleye. Although I grew up in Australia, in second and third generation migrant families, I am not given the knowledge to decipher this word, or its meaning, or to read Pwerle's images. Unlike migrant experiences in Britain that are often expected to assimilate to the dominant British culture, in Australia cultural signifiers that travelled with white migrants as settler colonialism have ignored, destroyed, and displaced indigenous knowledge. I therefore have to learn that Awelye refers to women's ceremonies and body paint, which are deeply connected to the understanding of territory and sovereignty:

---

[91] Charmaine Pwerle (born 1975), *My Grandmother's Country (7B)* Acrylic on Linen.

The women paint each other's breasts and upper bodies with ochre markings, before dancing in a ceremony. The body designs are important and, painted on chest and shoulders, they relate to each particular woman's dreaming. The ochre pigment is ground into powder form and mixed with charcoal and ash before being applied with a flat padded stick or with fingers in raw linear and curving patterns. The circles in these designs represent the sites and movement where the ceremonies take place.[92]

This is not knowledge understood by white/migrant Australians as it is cast within contemporary Australian culture as the language and meanings of the Other. Pwerle's work therefore articulates both my alienation from indigenous Australia (which is normalised) and the alienation of indigenous women from voicing the contours of our shared histories. The necessity of silencing this history is interwoven into the violent colonial history that white settler Australia either has not told and/or actively renders invisible. Australia's colonial history, instead, is replayed in images of white men flying the British flag as the First Fleet arrives at Botany Bay in 1788 and with indigenous Australians as insignificant as the fauna in the image.[93] White and migrant Australia tells the story of the First Fleet until it is ingrained in the mythology of the nation, displacing again and again any knowledge of indigenous Australia before the First Fleet and after.

The displacement of indigenous knowledge, language, and histories in the articulation of Australian sovereignty was achieved through genocide, a history not spoken within white Australia, or rather what perhaps should be redescribed as migrant Australia. International law remains silent on the genocide of indigenous Australia. The final section of this book therefore, is an attempt to write in this history, reproducing a series of statements from indigenous women that speak to the themes of the book. I place no analysis or response—the feminist method is the space made and not the appropriation of indigenous voices: a politics of listening. The final comment is drawn from Lewis's piece—repeating a phrase from a quote used earlier in the chapter—perhaps listening is also a process of return, repeat, recall, remember. A feminist dialogue on international law must listen to the conditions through which it arrives at international law: that is its feminist future.

Indigenous sovereignty is often discussed within the textual confines of law, policy and history. It is rarely understood outside of these spaces, yet Indigenous people write from their sovereign positions as owners of the land . . . Our sovereignty is embodied and is tied to particular tracts of country, thus our bodies signify ownership and we preform sovereign acts in our everyday living. Writing by indigenous people is thus a sovereign act.[94]

We need to move beyond the conversation of the Aboriginal problem to a discourse on the problem of colonialism. The opportunity for these conversations has never been created; the conversations have been mostly *about* us—the 'other'—we are framed as the subject of

---

[92] Kate Owen, *Charmaine Pwerle*, Pwerle Gallery <http://www.pwerle.com.au/charmaine-pwerle/> last accessed May 2018.

[93] Algernon Talmage, *Sydney Cove, Jan 26th 1788t* (1937) oil sketch.

[94] Tracey Bunda, 'The Sovereign Aboriginal Woman' in Aileen Moreton-Robinson (ed), *Sovereign Subjects: Indigenous Sovereignty Matters* (Allen and Unwin 2007) 75.

the conversation, not even sitting as equals and a part of the conversation. For we have no power to determine the event.[95]

My research shows the degree to which white feminists' self-presentation belongs to the white centre ... and its enmeshed power relations ... white feminist academics, in expressing their views on race, gender and cultural difference, illuminated the contradictory and inconsistent nature of the representations of these differences. They have an engagement with the 'Other' within the boundaries of academic institutions and practices. The cultural differences of 'Others' are subordinated to these white academic values. White feminists do not change their pedagogy to include the 'Others'.[96]

The real challenge for white feminists is to theorise the relinquishment of power so that feminist practice can contribute to changing the racial order. Until this challenge is addressed, the subject position middle-class white woman will remain centred as the site of dominance.[97]

Sometimes the strategies of nonindigenous feminists can act as new forms of colonizing practices.[98]

one is not always at the centre and has no automatic entitlement to be so.[99]

---

[95] Irene Watson, 'Settled and Unsettled Spaces: Are We Free to Roam?' in Aileen Moreton-Robinson (ed), *Sovereign Subjects: Indigenous Sovereignty Matters* (Allen and Unwin 2007) 29–30.

[96] Moreton-Robinson (n 9) 183.   [97] ibid 186.

[98] Bronwyn L Fredericks, 'Reempowering Ourselves: Australian Aboriginal Women' (2010) 35(3) Signs 546.

[99] Lewis, 'Questions of Presence' (n 1) 15.

Bibliography

Abdel-Magied, Y, 'A Little Too Close to the Sun: Advocacy in the Modern Age' (2017) 56 Griffith Review 18.

Abdulmonem, M, 'Architectural and Urban Heritage in the Digital Age: Dilemmas of Authenticity, Originality and Reproduction' (2017) 11 International Journal of Architectural Research 5.

Ahmed, S, 'Close Encounters: Feminism and/in "the globe"' in S Ahmed, *Strange Encounters: Embodied Others in Post-Coloniality* (Routledge 2000).

Ahmed, S, *Strange Encounters: Embodied Others in Postcoloniality* (Routledge 2000).

Ahmed, S, 'You End Up Doing the Document Rather than Doing the Doing' (2007) Ethnic and Race Studies 590.

Akande, D, 'International Organisations' in M Evans (ed), *International Law* (Oxford University Press 2014) 248.

Alodaat, L, 'The Armed Conflict in Syria and its Disproportionate Impact on Women' (2014) *Focus Gender InfoBrief* <https://www.fes.de/gender/infobrief5//pdf_content/FES_IL5_FOCUS02.pdf > last accessed 31 May 2018.

Alodaat, L, 'No Women, No Peace in Syria' *The Huffington Post* (9 December 2016) <https://www.huffingtonpost.com/laila-alodaat/no-women-no-peace-in-syri_b_8762904.html> last accessed 31 May 2018.

Alodaat, L and Boukhary, S (eds), *Violations against Women in Syria and the Disproportionate Impact of the Conflict on Them: NGO Summary Report UPR of Syrian Arabic Republic* (WILPF November 2016).

Alsata, K and Kapilashrami, A, 'Understanding Women's Experience of Violence and the Political Economy of Gender in Conflict: The Case of Syria' (2016) 24(47) Reproductive Health Matters 5.

Alston, P, 'Reconceiving the UN Human Rights Regime: Challenges Confronting the New Human Rights Council' (2006) 7(1) Melbourne Journal of International Law 185.

Alzoubi, Z, 'Syrian Civil Society through Peace Talks in Geneva: Roles and Challenges' (2017) 29(1) New England Journal of Public Policy, art 11.<https://scholarworks.umb.edu/nejpp/vol29/iss1/ > accessed February 2018.

Andrijasevic, R, 'Sex on the Move: Gender, Subjectivity and Differential Inclusion' (2009) 29(1) Subjectivity 389.

Anghie, A, 'Finding the Peripheries: Sovereignty and Colonialism in Nineteenth Century International Law' (1999) 40(1) Harvard International Law Journal 1.

Anghie, A, 'Western Discourses on Sovereignty' in J Evans, A Genovese, A Reilly, and P Wolfe, *Sovereignty: Frontiers of Possibility* (University of Hawai'i Press 2013).

Anim-Addo, J, Scafe, S, and Gunaratnam, Y (eds), *Feminist Review Special Issue on Black British Feminism: Many Chants* (Palgrave 2014).

Arendt, H, *On Violence* (Harcourt 1970).

Arendt, H, *The Human Condition* (2nd edn, Chicago University Press 1998).

Aristodemou, M, 'A Constant Craving for Fresh Brains and a Taste for Decaffeinated Neighbours' (2014) 25(1) European Journal of International Law 35.

Aust, A, *Handbook of International Law* (2nd edn, Cambridge University Press 2007).

Baars, G, '#LesbiansAreHot: On Oil, Imperialism, and What it Means to Queer International Law' (2017) 7(1) feminists@law, <http://journals.kent.ac.uk/index.php/feministsatlaw/article/view/398> accessed February 2018.

Baetens, F, 'International Congress of Women (1915)' in R Wolfrum (ed), *Max Planck Encyclopedia of Public International Law* (Oxford University Press 2010).

Bailliet, CM (ed), *Non-state Actors, Soft Law and Protective Regimes: From the Margins* (Cambridge University Press 2012).

Baksh, R and Harcourt W (eds), *The Oxford Handbook of Transnational Feminist Movements* (Oxford University Press 2015).

Banda, F, 'Blazing a Trail: The African Protocol on Women's Rights comes into Force' (2006) 50(1) Journal of African Law 72.

Baraister, L, *Maternal Encounters: The Ethics of Interruption* (Routledge 2008).

Bastick, M, 'Gender, Militaries and Security Sector Reform' in R Woodward and C Duncanson (eds), *The Palgrave Handbook of Gender and the Military* (Palgrave 2017) 387.

Basu, S, 'Global South Write 1325 (Too)' (2016) 37(3) International Political Science Review 362.

Batchelor, T, 'Saudi Arabia Should Be Dropped from UN Human Rights Council, Say British Lawyers' *The Independent* (London, 1 February 2018) <http://www.independent.co.uk/news/world/middle-east/saudi-arabia-human-rights-council-un-yemen-lawyers-shrouded-in-secrecy-a8188511.html> accessed 28 February 2018.

Bengio, O, 'Game Changers: Kurdish Women in Peace and War' (2016) 70(1) Middle Eastern Journal 30.

Bell, C and O'Rourke, C, 'Peace Agreements or Pieces of Paper? The Impact of UNSC Resolution 1325 on Peace Processes and Their Agreements' (2010) 59(4) International and Comparative Law Quarterly 941.

Bellamy, AJ, 'When is a Ceasefire Not a Ceasefire? In Syria, Where Most of the Killing is Allowed' *International Global Observatory* (28 February 2018) https://theglobalobservatory.org/2018/02/ceasefire-syria-ghouta/ accessed 28 February 2018.

Bellamy, AJ and Reike, R, 'The Responsibility to Protect and International Law' (2010) 2(3) Global Responsibility to Protect 267.

Benvenisti, E and Downs, GW, 'The Empire's New Clothes: Political Economy and the Fragmentation of International Law' (2007) 60(2) Stanford Law Review 595.

Bergoffen, D, 'Toward a Politic of the Vulnerable Body' (2003) 18(1) Hypatia 116.

Berman, N, 'The Grotius Lecture Series: In the Wake of Empire' (1999) 14(6) American University International Law Review 1515.

Bernstein, E, 'Militarized Humanitarianism Meets Carceral Feminism: The Politics of Sex, Rights, and Freedom in Contemporary Antitrafficking Campaigns' (2010) 36(1) Signs 45.

Bianchi, A, *International Legal Theories: An Inquiry into Different Ways of Thinking* (Oxford University Press 2016).

Bone, KM, 'Trapped Behind the Glass: Crip Theory and Disability Identity' (2017) 32(9) Disability and Identity 1297.

Boyle, A and Chinkin, C, *The Making of International Law* (Oxford University Press 2007).

Brah, A, 'Diaspora, Border and Transnational Identities' in *Cartographies of Diaspora: Contesting Identities (Gender, Racism, Ethnicity series)* (Routledge 1996) 178.

Brah, A, *Cartographies of Diaspora: Contesting Identities (Gender, Racism, Ethnicity series)* (Routledge 1996).

Braidotti, R, *Nomadic Subjects: Embodiment and Sexual Difference in Contemporary Feminist Theory* (2nd edn, Columbia University Press 2011).

Broggiato, A, 'Marine Genetic Resources Beyond National Jurisdiction: Coordination and Harmonisation of Governance Regimes' (2011) 41(1) Environmental Law and Policy 35.

Broggiato, A, Arnaud-Haond, S, Chiarolla, C, and Greiber, T, 'Fair and Equitable Sharing of Benefits from the Utilization of Marine Genetic Resources in Areas Beyond National Jurisdiction: Bridging the Gaps between Science and Policy' (2014) 49(C) Marine Policy 176.

Brown, M, 'Palmyra's Arch of Triumph recreated in Trafalgar Square' *The Guardian* (London, 19 April 2016) <http://www.theguardian.com/culture/2016/apr/19/palmyras-triumphal-arch-recreated-in-trafalgar-square> accessed 28 February 2018.

Brown, TM, Cueto, M, and Fee, E, 'The World Health Organization and the Transition From "International" to "Global" Public Health' (2006) 96(1) American Journal of Public Health 62.

Buchanan, R and Johnson, R, 'The "Unforgiven" Sources of International Law: Nation-Building, Violence and Gender in the West(ern)' in D Buss and A Manji (eds), *International Law: Modern Feminist Approaches* (Hart 2005) 135.

Buffini, M, *Welcome to Thebes* (Faber & Faber 2010).

Bunda, T, 'The Sovereign Aboriginal Woman' in A Moreton-Robinson (ed), *Sovereign Subjects: Indigenous Sovereignty Matters* (Allen & Unwin 2007) 75.

Burch, S, 'A Virtual Oasis: Trafalgar Square's Arch of Palmyra' (2017) 11(3) International Journal of Architectural Research 58.

Buss, D, 'Racing Populations, Sexing Environments: The Challenge of Feminist Politics in International Law' (2000) 20(4) The Journal of The Society of Public Teachers in Law 463.

Buss, D, 'The Curious Visibility of Wartime Rape: Gender and Ethnicity in International Criminal Law' (2007) 25(1) Windsor Journal of Access to Justice 3.

Buss, D, 'Performing Legal Order: Some Feminist Thoughts on International Criminal Law (2011) 11 International Criminal Law Review: Special Issue on Women & International Criminal Law 409.

Buss, D, 'Measurement Imperatives and Gender Politics: An Introduction' (2015) 22(3) Social Politics: International Studies in Gender, State & Society 381.

Buss, D and Manji, A (eds), *International Law: Modern Feminist Approaches* (Hart 2005).

Buss, D, Lebert, J, Rutherford, B, Sharkey, D, and Aginam, O, *Sexual Violence in Conflict and Post-Conflict Societies: International Agendas and African Contexts* (Routledge 2014).

Butler, J, *Gender Trouble: Feminism and the Subversion of Identity* (Routledge 1990).

Campbell, M, 'CEDAW and Women's Intersecting Identities: A Pioneering Approach to Intersectional Identities' (2015) 11(2) Direito GV Law Review 479.

Carter, SE, Dietrich, LM, and Minor, OM, 'Mainstreaming Gender in WASH: Lessons Learned from OXFAM's Experience of Ebola' (2017) 25(2) Gender and Development 205.

Chaim, M, Eslava, L, Painter, GR, Parfitt, SR, and Peevers, C, 'History, Anthropology and the Archive of International Law' (2017) 5(1) London Review of International Law 3.

Chandler, D, '*The Responsibility to Protect*? Imposing the "Liberal Peace"' (2004) 11(1) International Peacekeeping 59.

Chappell, L, 'Nested Newness and Institutional Innovation: Expanding Gender Justice in the International Criminal Court' in ML Krook and F Mackay (eds), *Gender, Politics and Institutions: Towards a Feminist Institutionalism* (Palgrave 2011) 163.

Chappell, L, 'Authors Response: Addressing Gender Justice at the ICC: Legacies and Legitimacy' *EJIL Talk!* (22 December 2016) <http://www.ejiltalk.org/authors-response-the-politics-of-gender-justice-at-the-icc-legacies-and-legitimacy/#more-14704> accessed 28 February 2018.

Chappell, L, *The Politics of Gender Justice at the International Criminal Court: Legacies and Legitimacy* (Oxford University Press 2016).

Chappell, L and Durbach, A, 'Introduction: International Criminal Court: A Site of Gender Justice?' (2014) 16(4) International Feminist Journal of Politics 533.

Charlesworth, H, 'The Sex of the State in International Law' in N Naffine and R Owens (eds), *Sexing the Subject of Law* (Law Book Company 1997) 251.

Charlesworth, H, 'International Law: A Discipline of Crisis' (2002) 65(3) Modern Law Review 377.

Charlesworth, H, 'Feminist Reflections on the Responsibility to Protect' (2010) 2(3) Global Responsibility to Protect 232.

Charlesworth, H, 'Talking to Ourselves? Feminist Scholarship in International Law' in S Kouvo and R Pearson (eds), *Feminist Perspectives on Contemporary International Law: Between Resistance and Compliance* (Hart 2011) 17.

Charlesworth, H and Chinkin, C, *The Boundaries of International Law: A Feminist Analysis* (Manchester 2000).

Charlesworth, H and Wood, M, 'Women and Human Rights in the Rebuilding of East Timor' (2002) 71 Nordic Journal of International Law 325.

Charlesworth, H, Chinkin, C, and Wright, S, 'Feminist Approaches to International Law' (1991) 85(4) American Journal of International Law 613.

Charlesworth, H, Heathcote, G, and Jones, E, 'Feminist Scholarship on International Law in the 1990s and today' in S Kouvo (ed), 'Special Issue on Feminist Perspectives on International Law in Times of Transition' (2018) 26(1) Feminist Legal Studies (forthcoming).

Chavkin, W and Maher, JM (eds), *The Globalisation of Motherhood: Deconstructions and Reconstructions of Biology and Care* (Routledge 2010).

Cheeseman, N, Onditi, F, and D'Alessandro, C, 'Introduction to the Special Issue: Women, Leadership and Peace' (2017) 7(1) African Conflict and Peacebuilding Review 1.

Chehtman, A, 'The *ad bellum* Challenge of Drones: Recalibrating Permissible Use of Force' (2017) 28(1) European Journal of International Law 173.

Chimni, BS, *International Law and World Order: A Critique of Contemporary Approaches* (2nd edn, Cambridge University Press 2017).

Chinkin, C, 'The Legality of NATO's Action in the Former Yugoslavia (FRY) under International Law' (2000) 49(4) International and Comparative Law Quarterly 910.

Chinkin, C and Baetens, F (eds), *Sovereignty, Statehood and State Responsibility: Essays in Honour of James Crawford* (Cambridge University Press 2015).

Chinkin, C, Wright, S, and Charlesworth, H, 'Feminist Approaches to International Law: Reflections from Another Century' in D Buss and A Manji (eds), *International Law: Modern Feminist Approaches* (Hart 2005).

Chinkin, C, Heathcote, G, Jones, E, and Jones, H, 'Bozkurt Case (aka the Lotus Case) France v Turkey: Two Ships that Go Bump in the Night' in L Hodson and JT Lavers (eds), *Feminist International Judgement Project* (Hart 2019).

Chiwengo, N, 'When Wounds and Corpses Fail to Speak: Narratives of Violence and Rape in Congo' (2008) 28(1) Comparative Studies of South Asia, Africa and the Middle East 78.

Clisby, S and Enderstein, AM, 'Caught Between the Orientalist–Occidentalist Polemic: Gender Mainstreaming as Feminist Transformation or Neocolonialism Subversion?' (2017) 19(2) International Feminist Journal of Politics 231.

Cohn, C, 'Women and Wars: Toward a Conceptual Framework' in C Cohn (ed), *Women and Wars: Contested Histories, Uncertain Futures* (Polity Press 2013).

Combahee River Collective, 'The Combahee River Collective Statement' in B Smith (ed), *Home Girls: A Black Feminist Anthology* (Kitchen Table: Women of Color Press 1983) 272–83.

Connell, RW, 'Change among the Gatekeepers: Men, Masculinities, and Gender Equality in the Global Arena' (2005) 30(3) Signs 1801.

Copelon, R, 'Recognizing the Egregious in the Everyday: Domestic Violence as Torture' (1993–1994) 25 Columbia Human Rights Law Review 291.

Cornwall, A and Rivas, AM, 'From "Gender Equality" to "Women's Empowerment" to Global Justice: Reclaiming a Transformative Agenda for Gender and Development' (2015) 36(2) Third World Quarterly 396.

Costin, LB, 'Feminism, Pacifism, Internationalism and the 1915 International Congress of Women' (1982) 5(3-4) Women's Studies International Forum 301.

Cover, R, 'Nomos and Narrative' (1983–84) 97 Harvard Law Review 4.

Craven, M, 'The Problem of State Succession and the Identity of States under International Law' (1998) 9 European Journal of International Law 142.

Craven, M, 'Unity, Diversity and the Fragmentation of International Law' in J Klabbers and T Tuori (eds) (2003) 14 Finnish Yearbook of International Law 3.

Crawford, J, *The Creation of States in International Law* (Oxford University Press 2006).

Crenshaw, K, 'Mapping the Margins: Intersectionality, Identity Politics and Violence against Women of Colour' (1991) 43(6) Stanford Law Review 1241.

Crenshaw, K, *Gender Related Aspects of Race Discrimination* (UN Division of the Advancement of Women 2000) UN Doc EGM/GRD/2000/EP1.

Cullet, P, *Differential Treatment in Environmental Law* (Routledge 2003).

Davis, KE, Fisher, A, Kingsbury B, and Merry, SE, *Governance by Indicators: Global Power through Quantification and Rankings* (Oxford University Press 2012).

Davies, M, 'Feminism and the Flat Law Theory' (2008) 16(3) Feminist Legal Studies 281.

Davies SE, Nwokora Z, Stamnes E, and Tuitt, S, *Responsibility to Protect and Women, Peace and Security: Aligning the Protection Agendas* (Brill 2013).

Drakopoulou, M, 'The Ethic of Care, Feminist Subjectivity and Feminist Legal Scholarship' (2000) 8(2) Feminist Legal Studies 199.

Engle, K, 'International Human Rights and Feminism: When Discourses Meet' (1992) 13 Michigan Journal of International Law 317.

Engle, K, 'International Human Rights and Feminisms: Where Discourses Keep Meeting' in D Buss and A Manji (eds), *International Law: Modern Feminist Approaches* (Hart 2005).

Engle, K, 'Celebrity Diplomacy and Global Citizenship' (2012) 3(1) Celebrity Studies 116.

Engle, K, 'Feminist Governance and International Law: From Liberal to Carceral Feminism' (2017) in Janet Halley, Prabha Kotiswaran, Rachel Rebouché, and Hila Shamir (eds), *Governance Feminism: Notes from the Field* (University of Minnesota Press 2018).

Ferguson, L, '"This is Our Gender Person": The Messy Business of Working as a Gender Expert in Gender and Development' (2015) 17 International Feminist Journal of Politics 380.

Fernandez, B, 'Queer Border Crossers: Pragmatic Complicities, Indiscretions and Subversions' in D Otto (ed), *Queering International Law: Possibilities, Alliances, Complicities, Risks* (Routledge 2018).

Ferree, MM and Tripp AM (eds), *Global Feminism: Transnational Women's Activism, Organizing, and Human Rights* (NYU Press 2006).

Fineman, M, 'The Vulnerable Subject: Anchoring Equality in the Human Condition' (2008) 20 Yale Journal of Law and Feminism 8.

Fleischmann, E, *The Nation and its 'New' Women: The Palestinian Women's Movement 1920–1949* (University of California Press 2003).

Fletcher, AJ, 'More Than Women and Men: A Framework for Intersectionality Research on Environmental Crisis' in C Frölich, G Gioli, R Cremades, and H Myrttinen (eds), *Water Security Across the Gender Divide* (Springer 2018).

Foucault, M, 'Technologies of the Self' in L Martin (ed), *Technologies of the Self: A Seminar with Michel Foucault* (Tavistock 1988).

Fox, S and Hall, K, '"Favourite Footnote"? Hilary Charlesworth on Feminism and International Law' (2006) 13(1) Limina: A Journal of Historical and Cultural Studies 1.

Fraser, A, 'Becoming Human: The Origins and Development of Women's Human Rights' (1999) 21 Human Rights Quarterly 853.

Fredericks, BL, 'Reempowering Ourselves: Australian Aboriginal Women' (2010) 35(3) Signs 546.

Freedman, J, Kivilcim Z, and Özgür Baclaioğlu, N, *A Gendered Approach to the Syrian Refugee Crisis* (Routledge 2017).

Freeman, MA, Chinkin, C, and Rudolf, B (eds), *The UN Convention on the Elimination of all Forms of Discrimination Against Women: A Commentary* (OUP 2012).

Freedman, R, *The United Nations Human Rights Council* (Routledge 2013).

Gardam, J, 'War, Law, Terror, Nothing New for Women' (2010) 32 Australian Feminist Law Journal 61.

Gardam, J and Stephens, D, 'Concluding Remarks: Establishing Common Ground between Feminism and the Military' in G Heathcote and D Otto (eds), *Rethinking Peacekeeping, Gender Equality and Collective Security* (Palgrave 2014).

Garland-Thomson, R, 'Integrating Disability: Transforming Feminist Theory' in KQ Hall (ed), *Feminist Disability Studies* (Indiana University Press 2011).

Gayle, D, 'Woman Assaulted by PC Who Lost His Job Found Dead in Holloway Prison' *The Guardian* (London, 3 February 2016).

Gedalof, I, 'Interruptions, Reproduction and the Genealogies of Staying Put in Diaspora Space' (2012) 100 Feminist Review 72.

Gill, A, 'Feminist Reflections on Researching So-called "Honour Killings"' (2013) 21 Feminist Legal Studies 241.

Gilligan, C, *In a Different Voice: Psychological Theory and Women's Development* (Harvard University Press 1982).

Goggin, G, Steele, L, and Cadwaller, JR, 'Normality and Disability: Intersections among Norms, Law, and Culture' (2017) 31 (3) Continuum 337.

Goldblatt, B, 'Intersectionality in International Anti-discrimination Law: Addressing Poverty in its Complexity' (2015) 21(1) Australian Journal of Human Rights 47.

Goodley, D, 'Dis/entangling Critical Disability Studies' in A Waldschmidt, H Berrensem, and M Ingversen (eds), *Culture-Theory-Disability* (Verlag 2017).

Gray, C, 'Bosnia and Herzegovina: Civil War or Interstate Conflict? Characterisation and Consequences' (1996) 67 British Yearbook of International Law 155.

Grewal, I and Kaplan, C, 'Introduction: Transnational Feminist Practices and Questions of Postmodernity' in I Grewal and C Kaplan (eds), *Scattered Hegemonies: Postmodernity and Transnational Feminist Practices* (University of Minnesota Press 2006).

Grunfeld, F and Huijeboom, A, *The Failure to Prevent Genocide in Rwanda: The Role of Bystanders* (Brill 2007).

Gunaratnam, Y, *Death and the Migrant: Borders, Bodies and Care* (Bloomsbury 2013).

Gunning, I, 'Arrogant Perceptions, World-Travelling and Multicultural Feminism: The Case of Female Genital Surgeries' (1992) 23 Columbia Human Rights Law Review 189.

Hagay-Frey, A, *Sex and Gender Crimes in the New International Law* (Brill 2011).

Hall, K and Fox, S, '"Favourite Footnote"? Hilary Charlesworth on Feminism and International Law' (2006) 13 Limina: A Journal of Historical and Cultural Studies 1.

Halley, J, 'Take a Break from Feminism?' in K Knop (ed), *Gender and Human Rights* (Oxford University Press 2004).

Halley, J, 'Rape at Rome: Feminist Inventions in the Criminalization of Sex-Related Violence in Positive International Criminal Law' (2009) 30 Michigan Journal of International Law 1.

Halley, J, Kotiswaran, P, Rebouché, R, and Shamir, H (eds), *Governance Feminism: Notes from the Field* (University of Minnesota Press 2018).

Halley, J, Kotiswaran, P, Shamir, H, and Thomas, C, 'From the International to the Local in Feminist Legal Responses to Rape, Prostitution/ Sex work and Sex Trafficking: Four Cases Studies in Contemporary Governance Feminism' (2006) 29 Harvard Journal of Law and Governance 335.

Hamzić, V, 'Unlearning Human Rights and False Grand Dichotomies: Indonesian Archipelagic Selves beyond Sexual/Gender Universality' (2014) 4 (1) Jindal Global Law Review 157.

Hamzić, V, 'International Law as Violence: Competing Absences of the Other' in D Otto (ed), *Queering International Law Possibilities, Alliances, Complicities, Risks* (Routledge 2018).

Haraway, D, *Staying with the Trouble: Making Kin in the Chthulucene* (Duke University Press 2016).

Harrison, R, 'Dystopia as Liberation: Disturbing Femininities in Contemporary Thailand' (2017) 116 Feminist Review 64.

Heathcote, G, 'Feminist Reflections on the "End" of the War on Terror' (2010) 11(2) Melbourne Journal of International Law 277.

Heathcote, G, *The Law on the Use of Force: A Feminist Analysis* (Routledge 2012).

Heathcote, G, 'Naming and Shaming: Human Rights Accountability in Security Council Resolution 1960 (2010) on Women, Peace and Security' (2012) 4(1) Journal of Human Rights Practice 82.

Heathcote, G, 'From "People with Projects" to "Encountering Expertise": A Feminist Reading of Kennedy's A World of Struggle' (2016) 4(3) London Review of International Law 467.

Heathcote, G, 'Fragmented Feminisms: Critical Feminist Thinking in the Post-Millennium Era' in A Reinisch, ME Footer, and C Binder (eds), *International Law and ... Select Proceedings of the European Society of International Law 2014* (Hart 2016).

Heathcote, G, 'Robust Peacekeeping, Gender and the Protection of Civilians' in J Farrell and H Charlesworth (eds), *Strengthening the Rule of Law through the Security Council* (Cambridge University Press 2016) 150.

Heathcote, G, 'LAWs, UFOs and UAVs: Feminist Encounters with the Law of Armed Conflict' in D Stephens and P Babie (eds), *Imagining Law: Essays in Conversation with Judith Gardam* (University of Adelaide Press 2017) 153.

Heathcote, G, 'I am an Immigrant' (2017) 5(2-3) Poem: International English Language Quarterly 241.

Heathcote, G, 'Women and Children and Elephants as Justification for Force' (2017) 4(1) Journal on the Use of Force and International Law 66.

Heathcote, G, 'Humanitarian Interventions and Gendered Dynamics' in FN Aoláin, N Cahn, D Haynes, and N Valji (eds), *The Oxford Handbook on Gender and Conflict* (Oxford University Press 2018).

Heathcote, G, 'War's Perpetuity: Disabled Bodies of War and the Exoskeleton of Equality' (2018) 44(2) Australian Feminist Law Journal (forthcoming).

Heathcote, G and Otto, D (eds), *Rethinking Peacekeeping, Gender Equality and Collective Security* (Palgrave 2014).

Hemmings, C, *Why Stories Matter: The Political Grammar of Feminist Theory* (Duke University Press 2011).

Henkin, L, 'The Myth of Sovereignty' in State Sovereignty: The Challenge of a Changing World: New Approaches and Thinking in International Law *Proceedings of the 21st Annual Conference of the Canadian Council on International Law* (Ottawa 1992).

Henry, M, 'Peacexploitation? Interrogating Labour Hierarchies and Global Sisterhood Among Indian and Uruguayan Female Peacekeepers' (2012) 9(1) Globalizations 15.

Higate, P and Henry, M, *Insecure Spaces: Peacekeeping, Power and Performance in Haiti, Kosovo and Liberia* (Zed Books 2009).

Higgins, R, *Problems and Processes: International Law and How We Use It* (Clarendon Press 1994).

Higgins, R, 'A Babel of Judicial Voices? Ruminations from the Bench' (2006) 55(4) International and Comparative Law Quarterly 791.

Hill, F, 'Reaching Critical Will' in I Heilberger and B Lochbihler (eds), 'Listen to Women for a Change' (WILPF 2010) 26 <http://www.barbara-lochbihler.de/fileadmin/user_upload/pdf/2011f/GEU_Bookproject_E_5_bm.pdf> accessed 28 February 2018.

Hill, F, 'I Can—Can You?' (2007) 100 Chain Reaction 40.

Hodson, L, 'Women's Rights and Periphery: CEDAW's Optional Protocol' (2014) 25(2) European Journal of International Law 561.

Hodson, L, 'Queering the Terrain: Lesbian Identity and Rights in International Law' (2017) 7(1) feminists@law 1.

Hooper, C, *Manly States: Masculinities, International Relations and Gender Politics* (Columbia University Press 2001).

Hopkins, S, 'UN Celebrity "It" Girls as Public Relations-ised Humanitarianism' (2018) 80(2) The International Communication Gazette 273 <https://doi.org/10.1177/1748048517727223> accessed 28 February 2018.

Hudson, NF and Goetz, AM, 'Too Much that Can't Be Said: Anne-Marie Goetz in Conversation with Natalie Florea Hudson' (2014) 16(2) International Feminist Journal of Politics 336.

Human Rights Watch, 'UN: Suspend Saudi Arabia from Human Rights Council "Gross and Systematic" Violations in Yemen Threaten Council's Credibility' (29 June 2016) https://www.hrw.org/news/2016/06/29/un-suspend-saudi-arabia-human-rights-council accessed February 2018.

Hunter, R, 'Contesting the Dominant Paradigm: Feminist Critiques of Legal Liberalism' in M Davies and VE Munro (eds), *The Ashgate Research Companion to Feminist Legal Theory* (Routledge 2013).

Hurd, I, *International Organisations: Politics, Law, Practice* (3rd edn, Cambridge University Press 2018).

Hurley, M, 'Gender Mainstreaming and Integration in the North Atlantic Treaty Organisation' in R Woodward and C Duncanson (eds), *The Palgrave Handbook of Gender and the Military* (Palgrave 2018).

International Development Research Centre, *Responsibility to Protect: Report of the International Commission on Intervention and State Sovereignty* (ICISS 2001) <http://responsibilitytoprotect.org/ICISS%20Report.pdf> accessed 28 February 2018.

Jacobsen, K, *A Frozen Conflict and a Humanitarian Program the Works: UNHCR's Confidence Building Measures in the Western Sahara* (Feinstein International Center 2017).

Jantzen, GM, *Foundations of Violence* (Routledge 2004).

Jeffreys, S, *Gender Hurts: A Feminist Analysis of the Politics of Transgenderism* (Routledge 2014).

Jennings, RY, 'The Role of the International Court of Justice' (1997) 68 British Yearbook of International Law 58.

Johns, F, 'Global Governance through the Pairing of List and Algorithm' (2016) 34(1) Environment and Planning D: Society and Space 126.

Johnson, ML and McRuer, R, 'Introduction: Cripistemologies and the Masturbating Girl' (2014) 8(3) Journal of Literary & Cultural Disability Studies 245.

Johnson, R, 'World Courts for Women: Against War, For Peace' *Open Democracy* (25 January 2016) <https://www.opendemocracy.net/5050/rebecca-johnson/courts-of-women-resisting-violence-and-war> accessed 28 February 2018.

Kabir, F, 'Toward a More Gender-Inclusive Climate Change Policy' in N Mahtab, T Hague, I Khan, MM Islam, and IB Wahid (eds), *Handbook of Research on Women's Issues and Rights in the Developing World* (IGI Global 2018).

Kandiyoti, D, 'Between the Hammer and the Anvil: Post conflict Reconstruction, Islam and Women's Rights' (2007) 28 Third World Quarterly 503.

Kanetake, M, 'Whose Zero Tolerance Counts? Reassessing a Zero Tolerance Policy against Sexual Exploitation and Abuse by Peacekeepers' (2010) 17 International Peacekeeping 200.

Kapur, R, *Erotic Justice: Law and the New Politics of Postcolonialism* (Glasshouse Press 2005).

Kapur, R, 'The (Im)Possibility of Queering International Human Rights Law' in D Otto (ed), *Queering International Law: Possibilities, Alliances, Complicities, Risks* (Routledge 2018).

Kennedy, D, 'Challenging Expert Rule: The Politics of Global Governance' (2005) 27 Sydney Law Review 5.

Kennedy, D, *A World of Struggle: How Power, Law and Expertise Shape Global Political Economy* (Princeton University Press 2016).

Kerri Mahon, E, 'Lucy Parsons: An American Revolutionary' (*Scandalous Women*, 5 February 2008) <http://scandalouswoman.blogspot.co.uk/2008/02/lucy-parsons-american-revolutionary.html > accessed 28 February 2018.

Khademi, K [Multidisciplinary Artist] <www.kubrakhademi.org> accessed 28 February 2018.

Khartabil, B, *#NewPalmira*, Wikimedia Commons (2005) <http://www.newpalmyra.org/> accessed 28 February 2018.

Kingsbury, B, 'The Concept of "Law" in Global Administrative Law' (2009) 20 European Journal of International Law 23.

Kirby, P and Shepherd, LJ, 'The Futures Past of the Women, Peace and Security Agenda' (2016) 92(2) International Affairs 373.

Klabbers, J, *An Introduction to International Organisations Law* (3rd edn, Cambridge University Press 2015).

Klabbers, J, 'International Institutions' in J Crawford and M Koskenniemi (eds), *The Cambridge Companion to international Law* (Cambridge University Press 2012).

Klugman, J, *Women, Peace and Security Index 2017/18* (Georgetown Institute for Women, Peace and Security 2017) <https://giwps.georgetown.edu/wp-content/uploads/2017/10/WPS-Index-Report-2017-18.pdf> accessed 28 February 2018.

Kmec, V, 'The Establishment of the Peacebuilding Commission: Reflecting Power Shifts in the United Nations' (2017) 24(2) International Peacekeeping 304.

Knop, K, 'Re/Statements: Feminism and State Sovereignty in International Law' (1993) 3 Transnational Law and Contemporary Problems 293.

Knop, K, 'Here and There: International Law in Domestic Courts' (2000) 32 New York University Journal of International Law and Politics 501.

Knop, K, *Diversity and Self-determination in International Law* (Cambridge University Press 2002).

Kohen, MG, *Secession: International Law Perspectives* (Cambridge University Press 2006).

Koskenniemi, M, *From Apology to Utopia: The Structure of Legal Argument: Reissue with a new Epilogue* (2nd edn, Cambridge University Press 2006).

Koskenniemi, M, 'The Fate of Public International Law: Between Techniques and Politics' (2007) 70 Modern Law Review 1.

Koskenniemi, M and Leino, P, 'Fragmentation of International Law: Postmodern Anxieties?' (2002) 15 Leiden Journal of International Law 553.

Kotiswaran, P, *Dangerous Sex, Invisible Labour: Sex Work and the Law in India* (Princeton University Press 2011).

Kouvo, S and Pearson, Z (eds), *Feminist Perspectives on Contemporary International Law: Between Resistance and Compliance?* (Hart 2011).

Kouvo, S, 'The United Nations and Gender Mainstreaming: Limits and Possibilities' in D Buss and A Manji (eds), *International Law: Modern Feminist Approaches* (Hart 2005).

Krever, T, 'Quantifying Law: Legal Indicator Projects and the Reproduction of Neoliberal Commonsense' (2013) 34 Third World Quarterly 131.

Krisch, N, *Beyond Constitutionalism: The Pluralist Structure of Postnational Law* (Oxford University Press 2010).

Kriss, S, 'Views My Own: Why Recreating the Palmyra Arch in London was Smug, Hypocritical and Tacky' (*Vice*, 25 April 2016) <http://www.vice.com/en_uk/read/palmyras-arch-trafalgar-square-dubai-new-york> accessed 28 February 2018.

Kristeva, J, 'Motherhood According to Giovanni Bellini' in LS Roudiez (ed), *Desire in Language* (Columbia University Press 1980) 237.

Kristeva, J, trans. Jardine, A, and Blake, H, 'Women's Time' (1981) 7 Signs: Journal of Women in Culture and Society 13.

Krook, ML and MacKay, F (eds), *Gender, Politics and Institutions: Towards a Feminist Institutionalism* (Palgrave 2011).

Lacey, N, *Unspeakable Subjects: Feminist Essays in Legal and Social Theory* (Hart 1998).

Lacey, N, 'Feminist Legal Theory and the Rights of Women' in K Knop (ed), *Gender and Human Rights* (Oxford University Press 2004).

Lamb, C, *Farewell Kabul: From Afghanistan to a More Dangerous World* (William Collins 2015).

Lauterpacht, H, *Private Law Sources and Analogies of International Law* (2nd edn, Law Book Exchange 2012[1927]).

Law, V, 'Against Carceral Feminism' (*Jacobin*, 17 October 2014) <https://www.jacobinmag.com/2014/10/against-carceral-feminism/> accessed February 2018.

Letendre, L, 'Women Warriors: Why the Robotics Revolution Changes the Combat Equation' (2016) 6 PRISM 91.

Lewis, C, 'Systematic Silencing: Addressing Sexual Violence against Men and Boys in Armed Conflict and Its Aftermath' in G Heathcote and D Otto (eds), *Rethinking Peacekeeping, Gender Equality and Collective Security* (Palgrave 2014).

Lewis, D and Hendricks, CM, 'Epistemic Ruptures in South African Standpoint Knowledge-Making: Academic Feminism and #FeesMustFall' (2016) 4(1) Gender Questions 18.

Lewis, G, 'Presence through Violence' (2017) 117 Feminist Review 1.

Lisiak, A, 'Other Mothers: Encountering In/visible Femininities in Migration and Urban Contexts' (2017) 117 Feminist Review 41.

Long, R, 'Sexual Subjectivities within Neoliberalism: Can Queer and Crip Engagements Offer an Alternative Praxis?' (2018) 19(1) Journal of International Women's Studies 78.

MacGregor, S, *Routledge Handbook of Gender and Environment* (Routledge 2017).

MacGregor, S, 'Gender and Climate Change: From Impacts to Discourses' (2010) 6(2) Journal of the Indian Ocean Region 223.

Manji, A, 'The Beautiful Ones of Law and Development' in D Buss and A Manji (eds), *International Law: Modern Feminist Approaches* (Hart 2005).

Martineau, AC, 'The Rhetoric of Fragmentation: Fear and Faith in International Law' (2009) 22 Leiden Journal of International Law 1.

McCormick, J, Kirkham, R, and Hayes, V, 'Abstracting Women: Essentialism in Women's Health Research' (1998) 19(6) Health Care for Women International 495.

McDonagh, D and Deiana, MA, *Add Women and Hope? Assessing the Gender Impact of EU Common Security and Defence Policy Missions: A Policy Report* Paper No NA January 2017 (Dublin City University 2017) http://doras.dcu.ie/21744/1/Policy_Report_on_Add_Women_and_Hope_Feb_2017.pdf accessed February 2018.

McGlynn, C and Munro, V (eds), *Rethinking Rape Law: International and Comparative Perspectives* (Routledge 2010).

McRobbie, A, *The Aftermath of Feminism: Gender, Culture and Social Change* (Sage 2009).

McRuer, R, *Crip Theory: Cultural Signs of Queerness and Disability* (New York Univeristy Press, 2006).

Meinzen-Dick, R, Kovarik, C, and Quisumbing, AB, 'Gender and Sustainability' (2014) 39 Annual Review of Environmental Resources 29.

Meenakshi, P, 'My Gender is not Neutral, My Gender is Brown, and Hairy, and Lesbian'(*Gal-dem*, 25 December 2017) <http://www.gal-dem.com/my-gender-is-not-neutral-my-gender-is-brown-and-hairy-and-lesbian/> accessed 28 February 2018.

Merry, SE, 'Measuring the World: Indicators, Human Rights and Global Governance' (2011) 52(S3) Current Anthropology S83.

Mertus, J, 'The Kitchen Table' in M Waller and R Rycenga (eds), *Frontline Feminisms: Women, War, and Resistance* (Routledge 2000).

Mgbeoji, I, *Collective Insecurity: The Liberian Crisis, Unilateralism and the Global Order* (University of British Columbia Press 2004).

Mohanty, CT, 'Under Western Eyes: Feminist Scholarship and Colonial Discourse' (1988) 30 Feminist Review 61.

Moreton-Robinson, A, *Talkin' Up to the White Woman: Indigenous Women and Feminism* (University of Queensland Press 2000).

Moreton-Robinson, A, 'Writing Off Indigenous Sovereignty' in A Moreton-Robinson (ed), *Sovereign Subjects: Indigenous Sovereignty Matters* (Allen & Unwin 2007).

Morgera, E and Ntona, M, 'Linking Small-Scale Fisheries to International Obligations on Marine Technology Transfer' (2017) Marine Policy <https://doi.org/10.1016/j.marpol.2017.07.021> accessed 28 February 2018.

Mundkur A and Shepherd, L, 'How (Not) to Make WPS Count' (*LSE WPS Blog*, 23 January 2018) <http://blogs.lse.ac.uk/wps/2018/01/23/how-not-to-make-wps-count/> accessed 28 February 2018.

Murray, C,# and O'Donoghue, A, 'A Path Already Travelled in Domestic Orders? From Fragmentation to Constitutionalism in the Global Legal Order' (2017) 13 International Journal of Law in Context 225.

Murthy CSR, 'New Phase in UN Reforms: Establishment of the Peacebuilding Commission and Human Rights Council' (2007) 44 International Studies 39.

Naffine, N, 'The Body Bag' in N Naffine and R Owens (eds), *Sexing the Subject of Law* (Law Book Company 1997).

Naffine, N and Owens, R (eds), *Sexing the Subject of Law* (Law Book Company 1997).

Nash, J, 'Rethinking Intersectionality' (2008) 89 Feminist Review 1.

NATO/EAPC, Action Plan for the Implementation of NATO/EAPC Policy on Women, Peace and Security (2016) 5 <http://www.nato.int/nato_static_fl2014/assets/pdf/pdft_2016_07/160718-wps-action-plan.pdf> accessed 28 February 2018.

NATO, 'NATO Act Promotes Gender Perspective Training' (NATO Allied, Command, Transformation 2013-2018) <http://www.act.nato.int/nato-act-promotes-global-gender-perspective-training > accessed 28 February 2018.

Nesiah, V, 'The Ground Beneath Her Feet: "Third World" Feminisms' (2003) 4(3) Journal of International Women's Studies 30.

Nesiah, V, 'From Berlin to Bonn to Baghdad: A Space for Infinite Justice' (2004) 17 Harvard Human Rights Journal 75.

Nesiah, V, 'Resistance in the Age of Empire: Occupied Discourse Pending Investigation' (2006) 27(5) Third World Quarterly 903.

Nesiah, V, 'From Berlin to Bonn: Militarization and Multilateral Decision-Making' in H Charlesworth and JM Coicaud (eds), *The Fault Lines of International Legitimacy* (Cambridge University Press 2010).

Nesiah, V, 'Feminism as Counter-Terrorism: The Seduction of Power' in ML Satterthwaite and JC Huckerby (eds), *Gender, National Security and Counter-Terrorism: Human Rights Perspectives* (Routledge 2013).

Nesiah, V, 'Priorities of Feminist Legal Research: A Sketch, a Draft Agenda, a Hint of an Outline...' (2011) 1 feminists@law http://journals.kent.ac.uk/index.php/feministsatlaw/article/view/20/83 accessed February 2018.

Ní Aoláin, F, 'The "War on Terror" and Extremism: Assessing the Relevance of the Women, Peace and Security Agenda' (2016) 92 International Affairs 275.

Ní Aoláin, F, Haynes D, and Cahn, N, *On the Frontlines: Gender, War and the Post Conflict Process* (Oxford University Press 2011).

Nowrojee, B, ' "Your Justice is Too Slow": Will the ICTR Fail Rwanda's Rape Victims?' (2005) Occasional Paper #10, UN Research for Institute for Social Development (UNRISD).

O'Gorman, E, *Independent Thematic Review on Gender for the UN Peacebuilding Support Office (PBSO): Final Report* (UN Peacebuilding Support Office, March 2014).

O'Rourke, C and Swaine, A, 'CEDAW and the Security Council: Enhancing Women's Rights in Conflict' (2018) 67 International and Comparative Law Quarterly 167.

Ojeda-Garcia, R, Fernández-Molina, I, and Veguilla, V (eds), *Global, Regional and Local Dimensions of Western Sahara's Protracted Decolonization: When a Conflict Gets Old* (Palgrave 2017).

Okolosie, L, 'Beyond "Talking" and "Owning" Intersectionality' (2014) 108 Feminist Review 90.

Olakpe, O, 'State Sovereignty and Migrations: Straddling Human Rights and Security in a Globalised World' (PhD Thesis, SOAS University of London, forthcoming 2019).

Oosterveld, V, 'Evaluating the Special Court for Sierra Leone's Gender Jurisprudence' in CC Jalloh (ed), *The Sierra Leone Special Court and its Legacy: The Impact for Africa and International Criminal Law* (Cambridge University Press 2013).

Orford, A, 'Muscular Humanitarianism: Reading the Narratives of the New Interventionism' (1999) 10 European Journal of International Law 679.

Orford, A, *Reading Humanitarian Intervention: Human Rights and the Use of Force in International Law* (Cambridge University Press 2003).

Orford, A, *International Authority and the Responsibility to Protect* (Cambridge University Press 2011).

Otomo, Y, 'Of Mimicry and Madness: Speculations on the State' (2008) 28 Australian Feminist Law Journal 53.

Otomo, Y, 'Searching for Virtue in International Law' in S Kouvo and Z Pearson (eds), *Feminist Perspectives on Contemporary International Law: Between Resistance and Compliance?* (Hart 2011).

Otomo, Y, *Unconditional Life: The Postwar International Law Settlement* (Oxford University Press 2016).

Otto, D, 'Holding Up Half the Sky: A Critical Analysis of the Fourth World Conference on Women' (1996) 6 Australian Feminist Law Journal 7.

Otto, D, 'A Sign of "Weakness"? Disrupting Gender Certainties in the Implementation of Security Council Resolution 1325' (2006) 13 Michigan Journal of Gender and the Law 113.

Otto, D, 'The Exile of Inclusion: Reflections on Gender Issues in International Law over the Last Decade' (2009) 10 Melbourne Journal of International Law 11.

Otto, D, 'Power and Danger: Feminist Engagement with International Law through the UN Security Council' (2010) 32 Australian Feminist Law Journal 97.

Otto, D, 'The Security Council's Alliance of Gender Legitimacy: The Symbolic Capital of Resolution 1325' in H Charlesworth and JM Coicaud (eds), *Fault Lines of International Legitimacy* (Cambridge University Press 2010).

Otto, D, 'Beyond Legal Justice: Some Personal Reflections on People's Tribunals, Listening and Responsibility' (2017) 5(2) London Review of International Law 225.

Otto, D, 'Introduction: Embracing Queer Curiosity' in D Otto (ed), *Queering International Law: Possibilities, Alliances, Complicities, Risks* (Routledge 2018).

Otto, D (ed), *Queering International Law: Possibilities, Alliances, Complicities, Risks* (Routledge 2018).

Otto, D, 'Women, Peace and Security: A Critical Analysis of the Security Council's Vision' in FN Aoláin, N Cahn, DF Haynes, and N Valji (eds), *The Oxford Handbook on Gender and Conflict* (Oxford University Press 2018).

Owen, K, *Charmaine Pwerle*, Pwerle Gallery <http://www.pwerle.com.au/charmaine-pwerle/ accessed May 2018.

Oyèwùmí, O, *What Gender is Motherhood: Changing Yorùbá Ideals of Power, Procreation and Identity in the Age of Modernity* (Palgrave 2015).

Paige, TP, 'The Maintenance of International Peace and Security Heteronormativity' in D Otto (ed), *Queering International Law: Possibilities, Alliances, Complicities, Risks* (Routledge 2018).

Parks, L, 'Drones, Vertical Mediation and the Targeted Class' (2016) 42(1) Feminist Studies 227.

Parashar, S, Tickner, JA, and True, J, *Revisiting Gendered States: Feminist Imaginings of the State in International Relations* (Oxford University Press 2018).

Parfitt, R, 'Book Review of Brad R Roth Sovereign Equality and Moral Disagreement: Premises of a Pluralist International Legal Order' (2012) 23 European Journal of International Law 1175.

Paterson, VS (ed), *Gendered States: Feminist Revisions of International Relations Theory* (Lynne Reiner 1992).

Peacebuilding Fund, 'Gender and Youth Peacebuilding Initiative' <https://www.pbfgypi.org/> accessed June 2018.

Pederson, S, 'Metaphors of the Schoolroom: Women Working the Mandate System of the League of Nations' (2008) 66 History Workshop Journal 188.

Pedwell, C, *Affective Relations* (Palgrave 2017).

Perry-Kessaris, A, 'Prepare Your Indicators: Economic Imperialism on the Shores of Law and Development' (2011) 7 International Journal of Law in Context 401.

Perry-Kessaris, A, 'The Re-co-construction of legitimacy of/through the Doing Business Indicators' (2018) 13 International Journal of Law in Context 498.

Pesta, A, 'Leymah Gbowee: Nobel Winner Gbowee: Where are Angry American Women?' (*Daily Beast*, 3 September 2009) <https://www.thedailybeast.com/nobel-winner-gbowee-where-are-the-angry-american-women> accessed 28 February 2018.

Peters, A, 'The Refinement of International Law: From Fragmentation to Regime Interaction and Politicisation' (2017) 15 International Journal of Constitutional Law 671.

Powell, C, 'Gender Indicators as Global Governance: Not Your Father's World Bank' (2016) 17 Georgetown Journal of Gender and Law 777.

Powell, C, 'How Women Could Save the World if Only We Would Let Them: Gender Essentialism and Inclusive Security' (2017) 28 Yale Journal of Law and Feminism 271.

Pratt, N and Richter-Devroe, S, 'Special Issue Critically Examining UNSCR 1325' (2011) 13(4) International Feminist Journal of Politics 489.

Probyn, E, *Eating the Ocean* (Duke University Press 2016).

Prukis, J and Searle, J, 'Obama's Covert Drone War in Numbers: Ten Times More Strikes than Bush' (*The Bureau of Investigative Journalism*, 17 January 2017) <https://www.thebureauinvestigates.com/stories/2017-01-17/obamas-covert-drone-war-in-numbers-ten-times-more-strikes-than-bush last accessed February 2018> accessed 28 February 2018.

Prügl, E, 'Neoliberalising Feminism' (2015) 20 New Political Economy 614.

Ramcharan, BG, *The UN Human Rights Council* (Routledge 2011).

Rendall, J, *The Origins of Modern Feminism: Women in Britain, France and the United States 1780–1860* (Palgrave 1985).

Riles, A, 'View from the International Plane: Perspective and Scale in the Architecture of Colonial International Law' (1995) 6 Law and Critique 39.

Riley, D, *'Am I that Name?': Feminism and the Category of 'Women' in History* (Palgrave 1988).

Romany, C, 'Women as Aliens: A Feminist Critique of the Public/Private Distinction in International Human Rights Law' (1993) 6 Harvard Human Rights Journal 87.

Rottenberg, C, 'The Rise of Neoliberal Feminism' (2014) 28 Cultural Studies 418.

Ruby, F, 'Security Council 1325: A Tool for Conflict Resolution?' in G Heathcote and D Otto (eds), *Rethinking Peacekeeping, Gender Equality and Collective Security* (Palgrave 2014) 173.

Ruddick, S, *Maternal Thinking: Towards a Politics of Peace* (Beacon Press 1995).

Sakar, NN, 'The Impact of Intimate Partner Violence on Women's Reproductive Health and Pregnancy Outcomes' (2008) 28(3) Journal of Obstetrics and Gynaecology 266.

Scott, JW, *The Fantasy of Feminist History* (Duke University Press 2011).

Security Council Report, 'Syria Possible Vote on Humanitarian Draft Resolution and Meeting on Eastern Ghouta' (*What's In Blue*, 21 February 2018) <http://www.whatsinblue.org/2018/02/syria-possible-vote-on-humanitarian-draft-resolution-and-meeting-on-eastern-ghouta.php > accessed 28 February 2018.

Sellers, PV, '(Re)considering Gender Justice' in FN Aoláin, N Cahn, D Haynes, and N Valji (eds), *The Oxford Handbook on Gender and Conflict* (Oxford University Press 2018).

Seuffert, N, 'Queering International Law's Stories of Origins: Hospitality and Homophobia' in Dianne Otto (ed), *Queering International Law: Possibilities, Alliances, Complicities, Risks* (Routledge 2018).

Shepherd, LJ, *Gender, UN Peacebuilding and the Politics of Space: Locating Legitimacy* (Oxford University Press 2017).

Shepherd, LJ, 'The Women, Peace and Security Agenda at the United Nations' in A Burke and R Parker (eds), *Global Insecurity: Futures of Global Chaos and Governance* (Springer 2017).

Shepherd, LJ and Sjoberg, L, 'Trans-Bodies in/of War(s): Cisprivilege and Contemporary Security Strategy' (2012) 101 Feminist Review 5.

Showalter, E, 'Hysteria, Feminism and Gender' in S Gilman, H King, R Porter, GS Rosseau, and E Showalter, *Hysteria Beyond Freud* (California Press 1993).

Simpson, G, *Great Powers and Outlaw States* (Oxford University Press 2004).

Sultana, F, 'Gender and Water in a Changing Climate: Challenges and Opportunities' in C Frölich, G Gioli, R Cremades, and H Myrttinen (eds), *Water Security Across the Gender Divide* (Springer 2018).

Talmage, A, *Sydney Cove, Jan 26th 1788* oil sketch (1937).

Tamale, S, 'Nudity, Protest and the Law in Uganda' (Inaugural Professorial Lecture, Makerere University, 28 October 2016) <http://www.searcwl.ac.zw/downloads/Tamale_Inaugural_Lecture.pdf> accessed 28 February 2018.

Tamini, TT, 'Violence against Women in Palestine and Mediocre Accountability' (2017) 5 UK Law Student Review 75.

Tan, J, 'Digital Masquerading: Feminist Media Activism in China' (2017) 13(2) Crime, Media, Culture 171.

Teubner, G and Korth, P, 'Two Kinds of Legal Pluralism: Collision of Transnational Regimes in the Double Fragmentation of World Society' in M Young (ed), *Regime Interaction in International Law: Facing Fragmentation* (Cambridge University Press 2012).

Tisdall, S, 'Amid Syria's Horror a New Force Emerges: The Women of Idlib' *The Guardian* (London, 26 May 2018) <https://www.theguardian.com/world/2018/may/26/syria-idlib-women-children-society> accessed May 2018.

Tourme-Jouannet, E, 'The International Law of Recognition' (2013) 24 European Journal of International Law 667.

Tryggestad, TL, 'The UN Peacebuilding Commission and Gender: A Case of Norm Reinforcement' (2010) 17(2) International Peacekeeping 159.

Tripp, AM, 'The Evolution of Transnational Feminisms: Consensus, Conflict and New Dynamics' in MM Ferree and AM Tripp (eds), *Global Feminism: Transnational Women's Activism, Organizing, and Human Rights* (New York University Press 2006).

Tripp, AM and Badri, B (eds), *Women's Activism in Africa: Struggles for Rights and Representation* (Zed Books 2017).

Tripp, AM and Badri, B, 'African Influences and Global Women's Activism: An Overview' in AM Tripp and B Badri (eds), *Women's Activism in Africa: Struggles for Rights and Representation* (Zed Books 2017).

True, J, *The Political Economy of Violence against Women* (Oxford University Press 2012).

True, J, 'The Political Economy of Gender in UN Peacekeeping' in G Heathcote and D Otto (eds), *Rethinking Peacekeeping, Gender Equality and Collective Security* (Palgrave 2014).

Tudor, A, 'Dimensions of Transnationalism' (2018) 117 Feminist Review 20.

Tuff, B, 'Woman in Armour Protesting against Sexual Harassment in Kabul Pelted with Rocks' *The Independent* (London, 8 March 2015) <http://www.independent.co.uk/news/world/asia/woman-in-armour-protesting-against-sexual-harassment-in-kabul-pelted-with-rocks-10093830.html> accessed 28 February 2018.

Twining, W, 'Normative and Legal Pluralism: A Global Perspective' (2009) 20 Duke Journal of Comparative and International Law 473.

UK Prime Minister's Office, 'Chemical Weapons by Syria Regime: UK Government Legal Position' (Government Digital Service 29 August 2013) <https://www.gov.uk/government/uploads/system/uploads/attachment_data/file/235098/Chemical-weapon-use-by-Syrian-regime-UK-government-legal-position.pdf> accessed 28 February 2018.

UN [DAW, OHCR, UNIFEM], Report of Expert Group Meeting (Zagreb 2000) <http://www.un.org/womenwatch/daw/csw/genrac/report.htm> accessed 28 February 2018.

UN Development Programme, *Resource Guide on Gender and Climate Change* (UNDP 2009) <http://www.un.org/womenwatch/downloads/Resource_Guide_English_FINAL.pdf> accessed 28 February 2018.

Watson, E, 'Gender Equality is Your Issue Too' (*UN Women*, 20 September 2014) http://www.unwomen.org/en/news/stories/2014/9/emma-watson-gender-equality-is-your-issue-too accessed 28 February 2018.

UN-NGLS 'African Women's Decade (2010-2020), United Nations Non-Governmental Liaison Service (15 October 2010) <https://www.unngls.org/index.php/un-ngls_news_archives/2010/749-african-women%E2%80%99s-decade-2010-2020-officially-launched-on-international-day-of-rural-women> accessed February 2018.

UNWomen, 'SDG5: Achieve Gender Equality and Empower all Women and Girls' <http://www.unwomen.org/en/news/in-focus/women-and-the-sdgs/sdg-5-gender-equality> accessed 28 February 2018.

Watson, I, 'Settled and Unsettled Spaces: Are We Free to Roam?' in A Moreton-Robinson (ed), *Sovereign Subjects: Indigenous Sovereignty Matters* (Allen & Unwin 2007).

Weiler, J, 'Differentiated Statehood? "Pre-States"? Palestine@the UN' (2012) 24(1) European Journal of International Law 1.

Weizman, E, 'Saydnaya: Inside a Syrian Torture Prison' (Amnesty International, 2016) <https://saydnaya.amnesty.org/> accessed 28 February 2018.

World Health Organisation, 'MDG5: Improve Maternal Health' (WHO 2015) <http://www.who.int/topics/millennium_development_goals/maternal_health/en/> accessed February 2018.

World Health Organisation, *Maternal Mortality: Fact Sheet* (WHO 2016) <http://www.who.int/mediacentre/factsheets/fs348/en/> accessed 28 February 2018.

World Health Organisation, *WHO Recommendations: Intrapartum Care for a Positive Childbirth Experience* (WHO 2018) <http://www.who.int/reproductivehealth/publications/intrapartum-care-guidelines/en/> accessed February 2018.

Wiegman, R, *Object Lessons* (Duke University Press 2012).

Wilcox, L, 'Drones, Swarms and Becoming-Insect: Feminist Utopias and Posthuman Politics' (2017) 116 Feminist Review 25.

Wilkerson, A, 'Disability, Sex Radicalism and Political Agency' in KQ Hall (ed), *Feminist Disability Studies* (Indiana University Press 2011).

Williams, PJ, *The Alchemy of Race and Rights* (Harvard University Press 1991).

Williams, PR and Pecci, FJ, 'Earned Sovereignty: Bridging the Gap between Sovereignty and Self-Determination' (2004) 40 *Stanford Journal of International Law* 347.

Wright, S, 'The Horizon of Becoming: Culture, Gender and History after September 11' (2002) 71 Nordic Journal of International Law 215.

Yadav, P, *Social Transformation in Post-Conflict Nepal: A Gender Perspective* (Routledge 2016).

Yancopoulos, O, 'Does the United Nations Have a Real Feminist in the Next Secretary-General, António Guterres?' (*Ethics and International Affairs*, 25 October 2016) <https://www.ethicsandinternationalaffairs.org/2016/united-nations-real-feminist-next-secretary-general-antonio-guterres/> accessed 28 February 2018.

Young, M (ed), *Regime Interaction in International Law: Facing Fragmentation* (Cambridge University Press 2012).

Yuval-Davis, N, 'What is Transversal Politics?' (1999) 12 Soundings 94.

Yuval-Davis, N, 'Human/Women's Rights and Feminist Transversal Politics' in M Marx Ferree and AM Tripp (eds), *Transnational Feminisms: Women's Global Activism and Human Rights* (New York University Press 2006).

Yuval-Davis, N, 'Power, Intersectionality and the Politics of Belonging' in W Harcourt (ed), The Palgrave Handbook of Gender and Development (Palgrave 2016).

Zheng, W, 'Detention of the Feminist Five in China' (2015) 41(2) Feminist Studies 476.

Index